Korean Women Philosophers and the Ideal of a Female Sage

T0347604

OXFORD NEW HISTORIES OF PHILOSOPHY

Series Editors
Christia Mercer, Melvin Rogers, and Eileen O'Neill (1953–2017)

Advisory Board
Lawrie Balfour, Jacqueline Broad, Marguerite Deslauriers, Karen Detlefsen,
Don Garrett, Robert Gooding-Williams, Andrew Janiak, Marcy Lascano,
Lisa Shapiro, Tommie Shelby

Oxford New Histories of Philosophy provides essential resources for those aiming to
diversify the content of their philosophy courses, revisit traditional narratives about
the history of philosophy, or better understand the richness of philosophy's past.
Examining previously neglected or understudied philosophical figures, movements,
and traditions, the series includes both innovative new scholarship and
new primary sources.

Korean Women Philosophers and the Ideal of a Female Sage

Essential Writings of Im Yunjidang and Gang Jeongildang

A Translation and Study by

PHILIP J. IVANHOE AND HWA YEONG WANG

OXFORD
UNIVERSITY PRESS

OXFORD
UNIVERSITY PRESS

Oxford University Press is a department of the University of Oxford. It furthers the University's objective of excellence in research, scholarship, and education by publishing worldwide. Oxford is a registered trade mark of Oxford University Press in the UK and certain other countries.

Published in the United States of America by Oxford University Press
198 Madison Avenue, New York, NY 10016, United States of America.

© Oxford University Press 2023

All rights reserved. No part of this publication may be reproduced, stored in a retrieval system, or transmitted, in any form or by any means, without the prior permission in writing of Oxford University Press, or as expressly permitted by law, by license, or under terms agreed with the appropriate reproduction rights organization. Inquiries concerning reproduction outside the scope of the above should be sent to the Rights Department, Oxford University Press, at the address above.

You must not circulate this work in any other form
and you must impose this same condition on any acquirer.

Library of Congress Cataloging-in-Publication Data
Names: Ivanhoe, Philip J., 1954– author. | Wang, Hwa Yeong, author.
Title: Korean women philosophers and the ideal of a female sage : essential writings of
Im Yunjidang and Gang Jeongildang / Philip J. Ivanhoe and Hwa Yeong Wang.
Description: New York, NY, United States of America : Oxford University Press, [2023] |
Series: Oxford new histories philosophy series |
Includes bibliographical references and index.
Identifiers: LCCN 2022029895 (print) | LCCN 2022029896 (ebook) |
ISBN 9780197508695 (paperback) | ISBN 9780197508688 (hardback) |
ISBN 9780197508718 (epub)
Subjects: LCSH: Women philosophers—Korea. | Im, Yunjidang, 1721–1793. |
Kang, Chŏngiltang, 1772–1832.
Classification: LCC B5252 .I93 2023 (print) | LCC B5252 (ebook) |
DDC 181/.119—dc23/eng/20220830
LC record available at https://lccn.loc.gov/2022029895
LC ebook record available at https://lccn.loc.gov/2022029896

DOI: 10.1093/oso/9780197508688.001.0001

Paperback printed by Marquis Book Printing, Canada
Hardback printed by Bridgeport National Bindery, Inc., United States of America

Dedicated to two lineages of extraordinary women

江孫氏 *(祖母)* — 張夢蘭 *(母親)*
and
鄭福禮 *(外祖母)* — 裴順子 *(母親)*

Contents

Series Editors' Foreword

Oxford New Histories of Philosophy (ONHP) speaks to a new climate in philosophy.

There is a growing awareness that philosophy's past is richer and more diverse than previously understood. It has become clear that canonical figures are best studied in a broad context. More exciting still is the recognition that our philosophical heritage contains long-forgotten innovative ideas, movements, and thinkers. Sometimes these thinkers warrant serious study in their own right; sometimes their importance resides in the conversations they helped reframe or problems they devised; often their philosophical proposals force us to rethink long-held assumptions about a period or genre; and frequently they cast well-known philosophical discussions in a fresh light.

There is also a mounting sense among philosophers that our discipline benefits from a diversity of perspectives and a commitment to inclusiveness. In a time when questions about justice, inequality, dignity, education, discrimination, and climate (to name a few) are especially vivid, it is appropriate to mine historical texts for insights that can shift conversations and reframe solutions. Given that philosophy's very long history contains astute discussions of a vast array of topics, the time is right to cast a broad historical net.

Lastly, there is increasing interest among philosophy instructors in speaking to the diversity and concerns of their students. Although historical discussions and texts can serve as a powerful means of doing so, finding the necessary time and tools to excavate long-buried historical materials is challenging.

ONHP is designed to address all these needs. It will contain new editions and translations of significant historical texts. These primary materials will make available, often for the first time, ideas and works by women, people of color, and movements in philosophy's past that were groundbreaking in their day, but left out of traditional accounts. Informative introductions will help instructors and students navigate the new material. Alongside its primary texts, ONHP will also publish monographs and collections of essays that offer philosophically subtle analyses of understudied topics, movements, and figures. In combining primary materials and astute philosophical analyses, ONHP will make it easier for philosophers, historians, and instructors to include in their courses and research exciting new materials drawn from philosophy's past.

ONHP's range will be wide, both historically and culturally. The series plans to include, for example, the writings of African American philosophers, twentieth-century Mexican philosophers, early modern and late medieval women, Islamic and Jewish authors, and non-western thinkers. It will excavate and analyze problems and ideas that were prominent in their day but forgotten by later historians. And it will serve as a significant aid to philosophers in teaching and researching this material.

As we expand the range of philosophical voices, it is important to acknowledge one voice responsible for this series. Eileen O'Neill was a series editor until her death, December 1, 2017. She was instrumental in motivating and conceptualizing ONHP. Her brilliant scholarship, advocacy, and generosity made all the difference to the efforts that this series is meant to represent. She will be deeply missed, as a scholar and a friend.

We are proud to contribute to philosophy's present and to a richer understanding of its past.

Christia Mercer and Melvin Rogers
Series Editors

Conventions

People's ages are given according to the East Asian convention, which regards a person to be one year old at birth.

The names of historical and most modern East Asian people are given according to the East Asian convention, with family name first. The only exceptions to this are cases in which a modern person her- or himself uses an alternative format.

For the names of local places, we offer translations of place names to give readers a sense of the meanings. At times, these are quite speculative as we lack the background information needed to make more reliable translations.

Korean names and terms appear in the Romanization used by the Korean government. The only exceptions to this are these:

1. When Romanizing the family name 이, 김, 강, we will use *Yi*, *Gim*, and *Gang* respectively.
2. For family names in which contemporary people who have published in English employ an alternative Romanization, for example, Hai-soon Lee instead of Yi Hyesun, we follow the author's practice.
3. Other types of traditional names (e.g., pen names) are Romanized as if they were first names, for example, 德來 into Deokrae instead of Deongnae.

We use what are regarded as standard translations for the English titles of the Confucian classics and didactic books.

For terms of art, we provide Korean Romanization, Chinese Romanization, and Chinese characters in brackets, at the first occurrence. Afterward, only Korean Romanization is used.

Translations of Korean official titles follow those in the *Korean History Thesaurus* and the *Glossary of Korean Studies* (*Hangukhak Yeongmun Yongeo Yongnye Sajeon* 韓國學 英文 用語 用例 辭典, http://digerati.aks.ac.kr:94/ Home) maintained by the National Institute of Korean History and the Academy of Korean Studies respectively. When a variety of translations are given, we follow the one used in the English version of the *Veritable Records of Joseon Dynasty* (*Joseon Wangjo Sillok* 朝鮮王朝實錄). We have capitalized official government titles: for example, Secretary of State.

In cases when Korean Romanization is ambiguous among possible Chinese characters, for example, "Jin dynasty" could refer to either the (C. Qin) 秦 dynasty (221–206 BCE) or the (C. Jin) 晉 dynasty (265–420 CE), we provide additional information in order to make clear the proper reference. Once this is done within a given selection and the reference is clear, it is not repeated within that selection.

When citing texts, we follow the common citation style of "chapter.passage." The *Joseon Wangjo Sillok* and *The Daily Records of Royal Secretariat of Joseon Dynasty* (*Seungjeongwon ilgi* 承政院日記) are cited as follows: volume. passage [reign year(Roman year)/month/date#entry]. Thus, for example, *Seungjeongwon ilgi* 11.16b [10(1669)/01/04#24]. We consulted versions of the texts found in The Chinese Text Project (www.ctext.org), *Library of the Four Treasuries* (*Sago jeonseo*; C. *Siku quanshu* 四庫全書) Online, and Database of the Korean Classics (韓國古典綜合 DB, http://db.itkc.or.kr) as sources for the texts represented in this work.

Traditional East Asian texts include what in modern Western publications would be parenthetical comments or notes. In the original, these appear in smaller font Chinese characters. In our translation, all material that originally was in smaller case characters appears in the same sized font as surrounding text but within pointy brackets <>.

We provide a bibliography that includes all works cited in and consulted for this volume.

Acknowledgments

This work was supported by the English Translation of 100 Korean Classics program through the Ministry of Education of the Republic of Korea and the Korean Studies Promotion Service of the Academy of Korean Studies (AKS-2019-KCL-1230002).

We also thank Peter Ohlin, Executive Editor at Oxford University Press USA, for his initial interest in this project and to Professors Christia Mercer and Melvin Rogers, the series editors of Oxford New Histories of Philosophy, for their help and support throughout the process of developing and preparing our manuscript.

We thank Mr. Jaehyun Seo, who served as a graduate student research assistant during the first year of our project and provided substantial help in translation and supporting research as well as the compilation of the bibliography. Mr. Sim Juhyun and Ms. Nikolett Koroesi read, commented on, and discussed parts of the work in a graduate student seminar focused on the writings of Im and Gang that was held in the Spring Semester of 2020 at Sungkyunkwan University, which helped us refine our translation and presentation.

We thank Suhyun Ahn, Melanie Dorson, Lucia Kim, Professors So-yi Chung, Youngmin Kim, Jungwon Kim, Sook-in Lee, Justin Tiwald, and Robin R. Wang, who read through selected parts of the translation and introduction and offered important and valuable corrections, comments, and suggestions.

A Note on the Cover Illustration

The image that appears on the cover of this work is part of a painting entitled *Woman Reading* (책 읽는 여인) by the Joseon dynasty (1392–1910 CE) painter Yun Deokhui 尹德熙 (1685–1766 CE), whose courtesy name (*ja* 字) was Gyeongbaek 敬伯 and whose pen names (*ho* 號) were Nakseo 駱西, Yeonpo 蓮圃, and Yeonong 蓮翁. He was a son of the great painter Yun Duseo 尹斗緒 (1685–1766 CE), who is renowned for his *Self-Portrait* and who also produced a work on the theme of a woman reading, painted in the Chinese style. With *Woman Reading*, Yun Deok-hui interprets the same theme in a Korean style. He was highly skilled in both painting and calligraphy. He was particularly renowned for painting horses and immortals. The calligraphy and red seals are all his. The calligraphy that appears in the upper left-hand side of the complete painting is his signature, 蓮翁. The three red seals are his names: left top the courtesy name 敬伯, left lower personal name 德熙, and right his pen name 蓮翁. The image is used with the kind permission of the Seoul National University Museum (Republic of Korea).

Introduction

1. General Character of the Work

This volume contains annotated translations with brief introductions of the writings of two Korean women Confucian philosophers: Im Yunjidang 任允摯堂 (1721–1793 CE) and Gang Jeongildang 姜靜一堂 (1772–1832 CE). These women and their works are remarkable in a number of ways that we shall touch upon briefly here and highlight throughout the rest of this volume. They are perhaps most well known for arguing that on the basis of core, orthodox, neo-Confucian assumptions, women are fully capable of attaining the highest levels of moral and spiritual achievement to become "female sages" (*yeoseong*; C. *nüsheng* 女聖).[1] As remarkable and revolutionary as this particular claim is, it is but one reason they and their work are important. Their essays, letters, poems, and other writings are elegant examples of traditional literary Chinese composition. As works of literature, their texts are of great value.[2] Moreover, their writings constitute a rare and revealing resource for historians: the themes they explore offer great insight into what life was like for gentry (*yangban*; C. *liangban* 兩班) women in the latter part of the Joseon 朝鮮 dynasty (eighteenth and early nineteenth centuries) and in particular how such women were able to navigate the considerable impediments that denied women the opportunity to study and develop their philosophical abilities and literary talents. The letters these women exchanged with relatives and friends reveal a dimension of personal life and moral cultivation that is remarkable for its depth, insight, and power. The short personal missives (*cheokdok*; C. *chidu* 尺牘)[3] that Gang

---

[1] For short introductions to these aspects of Im and Gang's writings, which offer alternative interpretations of their sense and significance, see H. Gim 2004, Y. Kim 2011, and S. Kim 2014 and 2017.

[2] For general studies of women's literature in Korea, see Bak 2002 and H. Yi 2005. The latter contains a chapter on the work of Gang.

[3] "In contrast to the *seo* (C. *shu*) 書 genre of formal letters, which were expected to be passed around within the scholarly community, these letters served primarily as personal communication" (Haboush 2009, 186).

Korean Women Philosophers and the Ideal of a Female Sage. Philip J. Ivanhoe and Hwa Yeong Wang,
Oxford University Press. © Oxford University Press 2023. DOI: 10.1093/oso/9780197508688.003.0001

Jeongildang wrote to her husband are a unique resource for understanding how husbands and wives worked together to realize Confucian moral ideals. They vividly illustrate how only those who know us intimately, over time, and across circumstances are able to offer certain kinds of criticisms, advice, and encouragement, and how the trust and love one feels for such people play a critical role in the ultimate effectiveness of the counsel they provide. In addition, the fact that Gang Jeongildang was inspired by the life and work of Im Yunjidang, and explicitly acknowledged and extended her philosophical insights in her own writings, adds an additional, unique dimension to their work. Not only are these two the first Confucian women[4] to explicitly argue for the natural moral equality of women and men on the basis of core Confucian principles, when taken together, they and their work constitute the first and only explicit lineage of Confucian women philosophers, a female transmission of the Way (*yeo dotong*; C. *nü daotong* 女道統).[5]

While Im Yunjidang and Gang Jeongildang share a profound commitment to the natural moral equality of women and display stunning abilities as both thinkers and writers, their lives and works nevertheless are different and quite distinctive. Yunjidang developed more sophisticated philosophical positions and presented her ideas in numerous interpretive and critical essays and commentaries on select classical texts. In her "Biography of the Wife of Mr. Song Neungsang," she describes a woman who offers advice directly to her husband concerning moral assessment and cultivation, and in her "Admonition on Diligence in Learning: A Response to the Parting Poem of My Eldest Nephew" she offers similar advice to one of her relatives. For the most part, however, her writings address more abstract philosophical topics and offer general advice not tailored to a particular individual. This is but one difference between her and Jeongildang, who regularly appears in the roles of philosophical conversation partner, confidant, and spiritual coach for her

---

[4] There are important representative women throughout the tradition, many of whom produced exquisite writings of their own, but none presented developed philosophical arguments in support of natural moral equality. Important figures such as Yi Ji (C. Li Zhi) 李贄 (1527–1602 CE) in China made such arguments, but he was a man arguing on behalf of women and nothing he wrote portrays the day-to-day struggles, achievements, and aspirations of women, much less from their perspective and in their own voice. For women in the Confucian tradition, see Li 2000 and Ko, Haboush, and Piggott 2003. For Yi Ji, see Lee 2012.

[5] The notion of the transmission of the Way (Tillman 2004) became particularly important to later Confucians who traced the idea back to Maengja (C. Mengzi) 孟子; while neither Im nor Gang used this term, it is not implausible to see them in this light and perhaps even to believe they entertained something like this idea. As we shall show, both looked back to exemplary women of the golden age of the Ju (C. Zhou) 周 dynasty as their models and invoked them not only as personal guides but also as exemplars in their philosophical arguments.

husband, offering insight and counsel from the uniquely intimate perspective of a wife.

Jeongildang's writings contain a range of genres, but she most often expressed her thoughts through short personal missives and poems, partly perhaps because she saw herself as carrying forward the work and ideas first laid out by Yunjidang but also partly, perhaps, because her life afforded her less leisure for study, reflection, and writing. Jeongildang explores a broad range of philosophical themes in her works, but most often does so in the course of describing some aspect of her everyday life; her philosophy is more intimately related to and more tightly interwoven with her daily activities and challenges. She and her husband were financially hard-pressed throughout their lives; her writings are haunted by their poverty, while at the same time illuminated by her uncompromising strength, integrity, and commitment. Her poems and missives express her day-to-day experience as a woman working to cultivate herself morally and guide her husband's moral and career development while supporting herself and her husband through her needlework and the scrupulous management of their household. Traditional conceptions of and aspirations for success are not as prominent in her writings as they are in the work of Yunjidang. The circumstances of their respective lives led them to focus on different concerns; they offer very different insights, express the same virtues in different ways, and different virtues played a greater or lesser role in each woman's life.

As a consequence of the gender bias that both women worked so hard to overcome, neither lived to see her work published during her lifetime. Im Yunjidang's collected works were published by her brother and brother-in-law under the title *The Extant Writings of Yunjidang* (*Yunjidang yugo* 允摯堂遺稿), first appearing in 1796. This volume includes several pieces she wrote on behalf of her husband, some completing work he had left undone when he preceded her, passing away at the age of twenty-five. Even though Gang Jeongildang had achieved a significant reputation within her lifetime for her poetry, calligraphy, and writings on Confucian philosophy, her literary works were not published until 1836, after she had passed away at the age of sixty-one years old. They were published by her widower in a collection entitled *The Extant Writings of Jeongildang* (*Jeongildang yugo* 靜一堂遺稿). These editions are the basis for the translations found in this volume.[6]

---

[6] Specifically, we used the Kyujanggak edition of Yunjidang's work, published in 1796, and the 1836 edition of Gang's work. For these texts, see Database of the Korean Classics (Hanguk Gojeon

2. The Life and Works of Im Yunjidang and Gang Jeongildang

Im Yunjidang's ancestral home was Pungcheon 豊川. She is known by her pen name (*ho*; C. *hao* 號), Yunjidang 允摯堂, which was given to her by her brother, the famous Confucian scholar Nokmun 鹿門 Im Seongju 任聖周 (1711–1788 CE). The general meaning of her pen name is "devoted, sincere, and responsible"; its core sense is taken from a line written by Ju Hui (C. Zhu Xi) 朱熹 (1130–1200 CE): "completely devoted to Tae Sa (C. Tai Si) 太姒 and Tae Im (C. Tai Ren) 太任."[7] She was born in the city of Wonju 原州 in Gangwon Province (Gangwon-do 江原道), the daughter of Noeun 老隱 Im Jeok 任適 (1685–1728 CE), who served as Assistant Prefect (*Pan-gwan*; C. *Panguan* 判官) in the city of Hamheung 咸興; her mother was the daughter of Mr. Yun Bu 尹扶, whose family's ancestral home was Papyeong 坡平 and who attained the rank of Section Chief (*Jeongnang* 正郎) in the Ministry of Taxation (Hojo 戶曹). In all, she had five brothers and one sister: Im Myeongju 任命周 (1705–1757 CE), courtesy name Baeksin 伯新; Nokmun Im Seongju, mentioned above; Im Gyeongju 任敬周 (1718–1745 CE), courtesy name Jikjung 直中, pen name Cheongcheonja 青川子; Im Byeongju 任秉周 (1724–1756 CE), courtesy name Sukmun 叔文;[8] Im Jeongju 任靖周 (1727–1796 CE), courtesy name Chigong 稚恭, pen name Unho 雲湖; and an older sister, whom we know only as a wife of Won Gyeongyeo 元景輿 (n.d.).

In 1725, her father, at the age of forty-one, was appointed Assistant Prefect of Hamheung and moved his entire family to this city, located in what is now North Korea. However, he was accused of misconduct[9] in the requisition and

---

Jonghap 韓國古典綜合 DB). We translate all works within these editions written by Im or Gang but not works included in them that were written by others about these women or their works.

[7] Tae Sa (c. twelfth–eleventh century BCE) was the exemplary wife of King Mun (C. Wen) 文王 (1152–1056 BCE). Among her esteemed ancestors was U the Great, founder of the Ha (C. Xia) 夏 dynasty. She gave birth to ten sons, including King Mu (C. Wu) 武 (?–1043 BCE), founder of the Ju dynasty, and his younger brother, the Duke of Ju (C. Zhou) 周公. Tae Im was the wife of Gyeryeok (C. Jili) 季歷, a leader of the state of Ju during the Sang (C. Shang) 商 dynasty (c. 1600 BCE–c. 1046 BCE). His son King Mun and grandson King Mu defeated the Sang to establish the Ju dynasty. Tae Im, along with the mythical Gang Won (C. Jiang Yuan) 姜嫄, was credited with being responsible for the rise and success of the Ju. See the discussion of Yunjidang's pen name by her brother Im Jeongju in "Extant Affairs" (Yusa 遺事) in *The Extant Writings of Yunjidang*, Appendix (*burok*; C. *fulu* 附錄) 6a.

[8] Byeongju was adopted out to his younger uncle, Im Hyeong 任逈 (1698–1742 CE), the fourth son of his grandfather. Im Seongju wrote an epitaph for him. See the *Collected Works of Nokmun* (*Nokmun jip* 鹿門集) 23.41a.

[9] Her father's accusation may well have been a result of the factional politics of the time. Im Yunjidang's father belonged to the Old Doctrine (Noron 老論) faction, which, along with the

management of slaves within his bureau, which led to him being impeached. Although the king dismissed the impeachment proceedings against him, Im abandoned his post in 1727 and returned to Hanyang 漢陽 (Seoul). He had planned to try his hand at farming but died during an epidemic the following year. In 1729, when Yunjidang was nine years old, her family moved to a mountain village called Okhwadae 玉華臺 in Cheongju 清州, in accordance with her father's will. Her intellectual talents were recognized early on by her second brother, Im Seongju, a highly respected scholar and the most distinguished intellectual among her siblings, who, as a result, taught her the *Classic of Filial Piety*,[10] the *Biographies of Exemplary Women*,[11] the *Elementary Learning*,[12] and the *Four Books*,[13] as well as other works of philosophy and history. She discussed such works often with her brothers, and regularly received their recognition and praise for her careful and rigorous readings and trenchant insights.

In 1737, her family moved to Yeoju 驪州, a city in Gyeonggi Province (Gyeonggi-do 京畿道), in which the ancestral mountain (*seonsan*; C. *xianshan* 先山) of her father's lineage is located. In 1739, at nineteen years of age, she married Sin Gwang-yu 申光裕 (1722–1747 CE) of Wonju;

Young Doctrine (Soron 少論) faction represented a schism among the earlier Westerners (Seoin 西人), a faction that dominated Korea in the seventeenth century. Largely as a result of a rift between Song Siyeol 宋時烈 (1607–1689 CE) (see footnote 31), one of the most powerful and influential Westerners, and his student Yun Jeung 尹拯 (1629–1714 CE), the Westerners divided into the Young Doctrine faction, which opposed Song Siyeol, and the Old Doctrine faction, which supported him. In 1727, the Young Doctrine faction wrested power from the Old Doctrine. The accusation against Yunjidang's father occurred in the same year as this power change. Details of this event can be found in the *Veritable Records of King Yeongjo* (*Yeongjo sillok* 英祖實錄) 11.46a [3(1727)/6/12#3] and *The Daily Records of Royal Secretariat of Joseon Dynasty* (*Seungjeongwon ilgi* 承政院日記) 64.2a–b [3(1727)/6/12#17]. Cf. G. Gim 2019, 58–59.

[10] The *Classic of Filial Piety* (Hyogyeong; C. *Xiaojing* 孝經) is a text espousing the virtue of filial piety that is cast as a conversation between Gongja (C. Kongzi) 孔子 and his disciple, Jeungja (C. Zengzi) 曾子. It may date from the fourth century BCE, though it is more likely a product of the early Han (C. Han) 漢 dynasty (221–206 BCE). For a translation, see Makra 1961.

[11] The *Biographies of Exemplary Women* (Yeollyeojeon; C. *Lienüzhuan* 列女傳) is a work by the Han dynasty scholar Yu Hyang (C. Liu Xiang) 劉向 (77–6 BCE) that contains 125 biographical accounts of exemplary women taken from early Chinese histories. For a translation, see Kinney 2014.

[12] The *Elementary Learning* (Sohak; C. *Xiaoxue* 小學) was compiled in 1187 by Yu Cheongji (C. Liu Qingzhi) 劉清之 (1134–1190 CE), also known as Yu Jajing (C. Liu Zicheng) 劉子澄, a disciple of Ju Hui, at his master's command. It outlines the process of moving from the cultivation of the self to bringing peace to all-under-heaven described in the *Great Learning* (Daehak; C. *Daxue* 大學). It was adopted as a centerpiece of official scholarship by the Joseon dynasty.

[13] The *Four Books* (Saseo; C. *Sishu* 四書) are a collection of classic texts that Ju Hui promoted as the basic curriculum of Confucianism and adopted in the Myeong (C. Ming) 明 dynasty (1368–1644 CE) and Cheong (C. Qing) 清 (1644–1912 CE) dynasties as the basis for the civil service examination. They are the *Great Learning, Doctrine of the Mean* (Jungyong; C. *Zhongyong* 中庸), *Analects* (Noneo; C. *Lunyü* 論語), and *Mencius* (Maengja; C. *Mengzi* 孟子).

his ancestral home was Pyeongsan 平山. They had a daughter together, but she died in early childhood in 1747. In the same year, when Yunjidang was twenty-six years old, she also lost her husband, after only eight years of marriage. After being widowed, she remained with her in-laws and won renown for the exemplary way she served her two mothers-in-law (her husband's biological mother and foster mother). She lived in this home into old age, along with two of her husband's younger brothers, who esteemed her and treated her as if she were their mother.

Her younger brother-in-law, Sin Gwang-u 申光祐 (1726–1798 CE), was a highly successful official in Office of the Censor General (Saganwon 司 諫院). When she was more than forty years old, in order to ensure that a male descendant would continue her husband's family sacrifices, Yunjidang adopted his son, Sin Jaejun 申在竣 (1760–1787 CE). In 1757, her eldest brother, Im Myeongju, passed away; she composed a eulogy in Classical Chinese for him, a translation of which is included in the present volume, that greatly impressed all those who read it. In April 1765, she completed colophons on two extant works—one on the *Collected Commentaries on the "Book of Poetry"* (*Sigyeong jipjeon*; C. *Shijing jizhuan* 詩經集傳) and another on the *Songs of Cho* (*Chosa*; C. *Chuci* 楚辭)—that had been left behind by her husband; these too appear in this translation under the section entitled "Colophons."

In the spring of 1782, when she was sixty-one years old, her brother Im Seongju moved the family to Mountain Lake (Sanho 山湖) in Wonju. There is good evidence that in 1785, at the age of sixty-four, she organized her various writings into the form they later would take in her posthumously published collection and gave a copy of this manuscript to her son. Unfortunately, Sin Jaejun died unexpectedly in 1787 at the age of twenty-eight, six years earlier than Yunjidang. In 1788, the death of her second brother, Im Seongju, who had served as her mentor and close friend, caused her great sorrow and pain. Only her youngest brother, Im Jeongju, outlived her, and it fell to him to write a remembrance of his sister that appears in *The Extant Writings of Yunjidang*.[14] She died in 1793, at the age of seventy-three, on the fourteenth day of May, in the family home in Wonju. Her grave is in Flourishing Fungus Valley (*Mujigok* 茂芝谷) village in the Jeongjian 正之安 District of Wonju.[15]

---

[14] See the postscript (*bal*; C. *ba* 跋) by Im Jeongju in *The Extant Writings of Yunjidang*, Appendix 7b–8a.

[15] The current name of the place of her tomb is Mujang 茂長 village, in the Hojeo 好楮 district of Wonju.

Three years after her death, her younger brother Im Jeongju and brother-in-law Sin Gwang-u arranged for the publication of Yunjidang's literary works.

While in many respects Im Yunjidang led the regular life of a Joseon dynasty (1392–1910 CE) gentry (*yangban*) woman, the early passing of her parents, husband, and children—both natural and adopted—along with her close relationship to her brothers, afforded her considerably more freedom and leisure time than many. This should not be taken as implying that pursuing these opportunities and in particular her passion for study was easy; a number of sources testify to how she worked diligently to fulfill her family duties by day while assiduously pursuing her studies by night. Long before the notion came into prominence among modern Western feminists, she was shouldering a version of the double duty or the second shift.[16] As her younger brother-in-law wrote, "Sometimes, when I saw the flickering light of her lamp through my window I knew that the scholar was secretly engaged in the purposeful activity (*gongbu*; C. *gongfu* 功夫) of inquiry and study."[17] Her extant works include a number of scholarly expositions and discourses, as well as other genres of writing, amounting to a total of thirty-five separate titles. As noted above, these were published posthumously and entitled *The Extant Writings of Yunjidang*. She was one of only a few women to be published during the Joseon dynasty, along with Gang Jeongildang, whose life and work we will discuss later in this Introduction, and other remarkable women such as Seo Yeongsuhap 徐令壽閣 (1753–1823 CE)[18] and Yi Bingheogak 李憑虛閣 (1759–1824 CE).[19]

The original text of *The Extant Writings of Yunjidang* consists of two parts: upper (*sang*; C. *shang* 上) and lower (*ha*; C. *xia* 下). Yunjidang wrote what are now the first six selections of the upper part (i.e., the two biographies and the first six discourses) in her youth, in the time before she was married.

---

[16] The double burden, double shift, or double duty most often refers to the workload of people who earn money but are also responsible for significant amounts of unpaid domestic labor. For this idea see Hochschild 1989. In Im's case, it refers to her work at learning and self-cultivation while shouldering extensive responsibilities and work in the domestic realm. In the case of Gang Jeongildang, these senses are combined; she supported her family through her needlework, fulfilled the formidable duties of a married woman, and pursued her education, largely on her own initiative. See the section on Gang in this volume.

[17] See the postscript by Sin Gwang-u in *The Extant Writings of Yunjidang*, Appendix 6b.

[18] Seo Yeongsuhap was a mathematician and a poet. Hundreds of her poems are preserved in an anthology, included as an appendix to her husband's memoir.

[19] Yi Bingheogak was a gentry woman who wrote a book called *An Encyclopedia for the Inner Quarters* (*Gyuhap chongseo* 閨閣叢書), which is both a compendium of homemaking tasks in general and in particular an important cookbook of the period. It includes detailed descriptions of essential items for late Joseon dynasty homemakers and is a priceless resource for research into food culture going back more than two hundred years. For a translation, see Pettid and Cha 2021.

The remaining selections were written in the middle and later periods of her life, after her marriage to Sin Gwang-yu. The upper part contains two biographies (*jeon*; C. *zhuan* 傳), eleven discourses (*non*; C. *lun* 論) on historical figures, two colophons (*balmun*; C. *bawen* 跋文), and six scholarly expositions (*seol*; C. *shuo* 說). The lower part contains four admonitions (*jam*; C. *jian* 箴), which represent a kind of verse aimed at self-cultivation,[20] three inscriptions (*myeong*; C. *ming* 銘), one encomium (*chan*; C. *can* 讚), and three funeral orations (*jemun*; C. *jiwen* 祭文); there is also an author's prologue (*in*; C. *yin* 引) and two works commenting on the meaning of the Confucian classics (*gyeongui*; C. *jingyi* 經義).[21]

The six expository essays offer some of the most developed and systematic discussions of her understanding of core issues in neo-Confucian philosophy. These essays are entitled "Exposition on Pattern-Principle (*i*; C. *li* 理) and *Gi-Material* (C. *qi* 氣),[22] Heart-Mind and Nature (*Igi simseong seol* 理氣心性說)," "Exposition on the Human Heart-Mind and Heart-Mind of the Way, Four Sprouts and Seven Emotions (*Insim dosim sadan chiljeong seol* 人心道心四端七情說)," "Exposition on the Rites and Music (*Yeak seol* 禮樂說)," "Exposition on *Overcoming the Self and Returning to Rites Is Humaneness*[23] (*Geukgi bongnye wiin seol* 克己復禮爲仁說)," "Exposition on *Whether Good Order or Chaos [in a State] Depends on Getting the Right People* (*Chiran jae deugin seol* 治亂在得人說)," and "Exposition on *My Way Has One Thread Running through It* (*Odo ilgwan seol* 吾道一貫說)." In the course of these works, she presents her views on the nature and significance of Pattern-Principle and *Gi-Material*, on the Heart-Mind and nature, on the Four Sprouts and Seven Emotions, on the similarities and differences between human beings and other creatures, on the nature and origins of good and bad, and on the proper forms and practices of governance. Her

[20] "Self-cultivation" is our translation of the Chinese characters 修養, which concerns practices aimed at the cultivation or improvement of the self. While one must be personally committed and engaged with this work, it by no means is primarily, much less exclusively, an activity that is automatic or carried out without the help and support of other people, resources, or social context.

[21] *The Extant Writings of Yunjidang* also includes additional works about Yunjidang but not authored by her. These are not included in this volume.

[22] *Gi-Material* is commonly translated "psychophysical matter," "vital energy," or "vital matter"; in neo-Confucian philosophy, it is one of the fundamental constituents of the phenomenal world. We leave it Romanized in its Korean pronunciation since there really is no adequate English translation.

[23] "Humaneness" is our translation for the Chinese character 仁, which often is translated as "benevolence" and at times "complete virtue," etc. While these alternatives capture important aspects of the meaning of the character, we believe humaneness, meaning a general disposition to treat other people, creatures, and things in a caring and cultured way that expresses the character of the ideal Confucian agent, is best.

two works concerning the meaning of the Confucian classics are selective commentaries on the *Great Learning* and the *Doctrine of the Mean*, which contain brief explanations of important sections and sentences from these texts as well as her opinions and reflections on their overall meaning and significance.

Gang Jeongildang was a member of a clan whose ancestral home was Jinju 晉州; her childhood name was Jideok 至德; her pen name was Jeongildang 靜一堂.[24] The Jinju Gang clan were a gentry lineage, but before she was born the family had fallen on hard times, as none of its members had passed the civil service examination (*gwageo*; C. *keju* 科舉) and secured a position in the coveted bureaucracy for several generations. As a child, Jeongildang learned needlework from her mother, a skill that she and her future husband would come to rely upon to support them financially and sustain their lives. At the age of twenty, she was married to Tanjae 坦齋 Yun Gwangyeon 尹光演 (1778–1838 CE), whose ancestral home was Papyeong, but she was not able to move in with her husband for three years because his family was too poor to support her. After moving in, she began to learn the Confucian classics alongside her husband at first, ostensibly, in order to help him study for the first level of the civil service examinations. As attested in one of the poems included in the translations below, she began her own study of the Confucian tradition in earnest only about ten years later, around the age of thirty. As noted above, in order to enable her husband to concentrate on his preparation for the examinations, Jeongildang supported the family through plying her needlework and succeeded in maintaining the family's precarious existence, displaying great frugality and proving herself a highly skilled, creative, and strictly disciplined family manager.[25]

Despite his best efforts, Yun Gwangyeon failed, repeatedly, to pass the civil service examination, which were notoriously difficult in his age. Throughout his successive attempts, Jeongildang supported him, materially, psychologically, and intellectually. As is clear from this translation of her works, and in particular from the personal missives she exchanged with her husband, she often offered her husband regular advice about his own moral self-cultivation,

---

[24] Jideok 至德 means "highest virtue" and is a term found throughout early Confucian writings, for example in both the *Analects* and the *Doctrine of the Mean*. Jeongildang 靜一堂 means "hall of stillness and unity," two qualities essential for moral and spiritual attainment in a number of East Asian traditions. Her pen name was given to her by her husband, who thought it reflected core qualities of her moral character.

[25] Thus, as mentioned in note 16 above, she shouldered a distinctive version of what modern feminists refer to as the double burden, double shift, or double duty.

chiding him for and correcting his shortcomings while advising, guiding, and encouraging him in the development of virtue. She also supported and offered advice to him about the classics and the examinations, at times studying alongside him, at times working on her own and reporting to him about her progress, and at times expressing her frustration with not being able, like him, to devote herself completely to her own moral and intellectual development.

Her practical moral advice and theoretical reflections always arose from and were expressed in terms of the challenges she encountered in the course of her everyday life. In the face of their grinding poverty, she was scrupulous about not compromising herself or her husband morally when inappropriate material gain or reputational advantage was offered to them; examples of her struggling with how best to navigate through such practical moral challenges can be found throughout her writings. Despite the numerous challenges she had to overcome, she maintained an irrepressible optimism that through frugality, temperance, diligence, and study they would succeed, if not in the examinations and the competition for official position and social standing, then in the higher calling of moral self-cultivation. Eventually, following the advice of his wife, her husband abandoned his aspiration to pass the examinations and secure an official post and instead opened a local academy (*seodang*; C. *shutang* 書堂) to teach the Chinese classics to young men in their local area. As seen in some of the translations included here, Jeongildang regularly advised her husband not only about general policies concerning how to manage this enterprise but also on the relative quality and worthiness of individual students and how he should behave as master.

Gang Jeongildang gave birth to five sons and four daughters; tragically, every one of them died before she or he could learn to speak. There is no explicit account within her extant corpus describing the accumulated effects this had on her,[26] but these wrenching experiences offer further evidence not only of the immense difficulties she faced in the course of her life but also of her indomitable spirit and resolute will to meet and overcome every challenge, and by doing so strengthen and improve both herself and her family. In 1836, several years after her death in 1832, at the age of sixty-one, her husband arranged for the publication of a collection of her writings under the name *The Extant Writings of Jeongildang*, consisting of thirty-eight poems

---

[26] She does reveal her feelings about the loss of her last child, a daughter named Gyesuk 季淑, in the epitaph she wrote for her, which is discussed and included among the translations below.

(*si*; C. *shi* 詩), seven letters (*seo*; C. *shu* 書), fifty-nine brief personal missives to her husband, three commemorations (*gi*; C. *ji* 記), two forewords and postscripts (*jebal*; C. *tiba* 題跋), three epitaphs (*myojimyeong*; C. *muzhiming* 墓誌銘), three short biographies (*haengjang*; C. *xingzhuang* 行狀), three funeral orations, five inscriptions, and two miscellaneous writings (*japjeo*; C. *zazhu* 雜著)—"Reflections on the Predilections of [My Ancestors]" (*Sagirok*; C. *Sishilu* 思嗜錄) and "Exposition on an Inkstone" (*Yeonseol*; C. *Yanshuo* 硯說)—and a final section, called "Lost Works" (*Seubyu*; C. *Shiyi* 拾遺), which includes one poem and seventeen personal missives. Her writings roughly total 150 pieces.[27]

3. The Philosophical Views of Im Yunjidang and Gang Jeongildang

The writings of Im Yunjidang and Gang Jeongildang have yet to receive the attention and appreciation they richly deserve. This is at least in part owing to the fact that as women they were not able to join in many of the scholarly activities available to men in their time. For example, neither Yunjidang nor Jeongildang was able to participate in the major debates that define the mainstream of Korean Confucianism, such as the Four-Seven[28] or Horak 湖洛[29] debates. But of course, this in no way reflects on their abilities as philosophers; they did not have the chance to participate in such scholarly exchanges or any of the other standard forums or opportunities to express and develop their ideas simply because they were women.

Perhaps for similar reasons, one does not find among their extant writings certain traditional philosophical forms of writings, such as the complete, systematic commentaries one finds by many more orthodox and authoritative neo-Confucian authors. Instead, one finds a greater percentage of more personal reflection and poetry. At times, the form of orthodox philosophical writings worked to exclude them from the traditional canon.[30]

---

[27] While the precise textual history of her work is not clear, we do know that some of her writings have been lost. For example, after recovering from a serious illness in 1832, she discovered that two of her most substantial writings, "Answers to Questions" (*Dammunpyeon* 答問篇) and "A Record of Words and Actions" (*Eonhaengnok* 言行錄), had been lost. See *The Extant Writings of Jeongildang*, Appendix 7b.

[28] On the Four-Seven Debate, see Kalton et al. 1994, Chung 1995, Ivanhoe 2015, and H. Kim 2016.

[29] On the Horak Debate, see R. T. Kim 2016 and Choi 2019.

[30] The exclusion of women philosophers' writings from the history of philosophy does not only apply to Confucian or Asian philosophy. Women philosophers have been excluded from the Western

Of course, some widely acclaimed neo-Confucians such as Yuk Sangsan (C. Lu Xiangshan) 陸象山 (1139–1192 CE) and Wang Yangmyeong (C. Wang Yangming) 王陽明 (1472–1529 CE) did not write commentaries either, and both wrote many more personal reflections and philosophical poetry as well. Indeed, both Yuk and Wang insisted that the only effective way to teach is to focus on each person's personal life and offer individually crafted advice, just as a doctor prescribes medicine for each and every patient. The point is that differences in the genres most represented in a given thinker's corpus of writings not only do not imply a lack of deep and sophisticated philosophical reflection, but also can reveal important information about the social or political circumstances in which they wrote or offer important clues as to their particular philosophical approach and distinctive value. The examples of Yuk and Wang support this claim; both are regarded as iconoclasts who stand outside the orthodox tradition, and especially so in Korea.

This volume contains both of Yunjidang's biographies, which concern the lives, character, and moral achievements of women. This immediately brings into focus two of the most distinctive features of Yunjidang's philosophy: her concern with the ethical and spiritual status of women and her role as a woman philosopher. The first biography focuses on the life of Lady Han, a contemporary with whom Yunjidang manifestly identified and sympathized. They shared a deep intellectual connection in that Lady Han's husband, Song Neungsang 宋能相 (1709–1758 CE), was a direct descendant and follower of Song Siyeol 宋時烈 (1607–1689 CE),[31] who led the lineage of learning that Yunjidang and her brothers claimed as their own. Yunjidang describes a revealing, insightful, and philosophically interesting event in Lady Han's life by "reporting" a conversation between Lady Han and her husband that purportedly took place after an informal gathering at their home. During their visit, her husband's cousins had expressed great admiration for Yulgok's 栗谷[32] (1536–1584 CE) virtue, fame, and high status and their aspiration to

---

tradition as well, and women philosophers have often relied upon nonstandard genres. For example, Catherine Macaulay wrote in the epistolary style and Mary Wollstonecraft wrote fiction (Gardner 2018, especially chs. 2 and 4).

[31] Song Siyeol, also known by his pen name Uam 尤庵, was a prominent Joseon stateman, scholar, and philosopher. He played a central role in what is known as the Rites Controversy (*Yesong* 禮訟), which concerned the proper period of time the queen consort had to wear mourning attire after the death of her stepson, King Hyojong 孝宗 (r. 1649–1659 CE). Song was executed by the royal court for writing an inflammatory letter to King Sukjong 肅宗 (r. 1674–1720 CE).

[32] Yulgok is the pen name of Yi I 李珥, one of the two most prominent Confucian scholars of the Joseon dynasty, the other being his older contemporary Yi Hwang 李滉 (1501–1570 CE), whose pen name was Toegye 退溪.

emulate his achievements. After they left, Lady Han asked her husband what he thought of their remarks and he immediately and enthusiastically endorsed them. When she smiled, he asked the reason why and she explained that what made Yulgok great was his moral virtue. Had his cousins focused on this, it would have shown that they understood and sincerely admired virtue. Instead, they talked about his great fame and high status as well as his virtue, and this shows they were not primarily interested in nor did they most highly value morality. Her husband accepted her analysis and admonition, and thereafter, we are told, made even greater efforts to improve himself.

In this part of our first biography, we see a marvelous example of a Joseon dynasty wife serving as moral teacher and guide for her husband, a theme found throughout the writings of Yunjidang and even more prevalent in the works of Gang Jeongildang. The biography goes on to describe the challenges Lady Han faced in developing her own impressive intellectual talents in the face of the inhospitable, patriarchal atmosphere of Joseon society and how she succeeded in doing so while also patiently, masterfully, and cheerfully fulfilling her many roles as a married woman in a large and influential family. Yunjidang brings the biography to a close by embellishing it with a poem of praise in honor of Lady Han, thereby demonstrating her own remarkable skill as a poet.

The second biography is not of someone familiar or contemporary but concerns two women whose exploits were often discussed in Yunjidang's time: [mother] Choe 崔 and [daughter] Hong 洪, the wife and daughter respectively of a soldier who had been killed. The central theme is how these two women fulfilled their respective obligations of chastity and filial piety by plotting and carrying out revenge against the man who murdered their husband and father. As is true in the other biography she wrote, discussed above, Yunjidang employs the literary device of having these women speak for themselves; they describe their intentions and motivations in their own voices (G. Gim 2019, 96). They appear in their own biography as full moral agents who assess, judge, sentence, and punish a man they regard as having murdered their husband and father. Moreover, they further demonstrate their exceptional moral character by turning themselves in after completing their revenge and are pardoned on the basis of their remarkable virtue, sincerity, and honesty. Yunjidang makes a point of saying that their achievement was something "most men would prove incapable of doing."

Im Yunjidang did write the kinds of discourses and expositions that are characteristic of neo-Confucian philosophers and well represented among mainstream thinkers. These offer evidence that support her explicit arguments about the natural intellectual and moral abilities of women. Her discourses and expositions are remarkably sophisticated, elegant, and interesting and reveal important features about the social context in which she and Jeongildang wrote as well as some of the unique philosophical dimensions of their writings that are, to the best of our knowledge, unrecognized and as yet unappreciated in our time. In several of her discourses, as is the common practice, Yunjidang takes up, analyzes, and comments on some well-known figures or events. Given that she only composed eleven discourses, her choice of topics is itself a good gauge of what she thought most warranted careful and comprehensive treatment. Her "Discourse on What Anja (C. Yanzi) Took Joy In" (*Non Anja sorak* 論顔子所樂) is a beautifully written philosophical reflection on the source of Anja's joy, a common theme among orthodox neo-Confucian philosophers,[33] and something that must have had a particular and poignant significance for her. Yunjidang offers an elegant and original analysis, starting with the claim that the ultimate source of Anja's joy was heaven—as revealed in the *better angels of our nature*, or as neo-Confucians tend to express it: the goodness of our original nature—and specifically Anja's natural love of learning. She offers a memorable expression of how different such joy is from that sought and savored by most people, saying, "His joy is as different from theirs as heaven is from earth or insects are from snow geese."[34] She then explains that Anja's joy insulated him from the despair that often accompanies material want and claims, as other commentators had before her, that had Anja not suffered an early death he would have attained sagehood and thereby surpassed even Maengja[35] (C. Mengzi) 孟子. She moves from this assertion to an argument aimed at showing that sagehood is indeed something within the reach of all people, hinting at what she makes explicit in some of her other writings: that this clearly includes women. She closes the essay insisting that sagehood does not come easily; it is instead an achievement that requires a great deal of perseverance and hard work.

---

[33] Jeong I (C. Cheng Yi) 程頤 (1033–1107 CE) of the Song (C. Song) 宋 dynasty (960–1279 CE) began the tradition of writing essays on the topic of what Anja loved to learn. He composed his essay in response to a question posed to him by his teacher Ju Doni (C. Zhou Dunyi) 周敦頤 (1017–1073 CE). Since then, many neo-Confucian thinkers, including famous figures from the Joseon dynasty, such as Gobong 高峰 Gi Daeseung 奇大升 (1527–1572 CE) and Yulgok Yi I, wrote essays on the same theme.

[34] See "Discourse on What Anja Took Joy in," discourse 4 in this volume.

[35] Latinized as "Mencius" in most Western sources.

While incorporating and developing a number of themes that are characteristic of orthodox neo-Confucianism, Yunjidang does so in ways that represent her distinctive perspective as a woman. Unlike male scholars, in the society of her time, she had to struggle mightily to pursue her *love of learning*—something she was denied regular access to and had to pursue surreptitiously, in addition to her duties as a daughter, wife, and daughter-in-law simply because she was a woman. Learning was not just a commitment she had to make—as Gongja[36] (C. Kongzi) 孔子[37] did when he was fifteen—but a social transgression and lifelong struggle that she calmly yet doggedly pursued; one finds references to this struggle throughout her writings and, like the line above, testimonials to her tenacity by her brothers who steadfastly supported and encouraged her. This is why one often must read her work with an eye toward uncovering not only its overt content but also what it reveals about the different challenges she met and overcame as she followed her love of learning.

Another of her discourses shows even more clearly how her position as a woman in late Joseon dynasty Korea led her to explore and reveal new and interesting aspects of Confucian philosophy. In her "Discourse on Misaeng Go (C. Weisheng Gao) Begging Vinegar" (*Non Misaeng Go geolhae* 論微生 高乞醯) she takes up a passage from the *Analects*[38] that is not often the focus of sustained philosophical analysis and shows that in fact it is a rich resource for explicating the ways in which people can come to compromise their character in the day-to-day activities of everyday life—the realm where she spent almost all of her time.[39] Borrowing or "begging" vinegar is not something an average male philosopher did in Gongja's time or in Joseon dynasty Korea, nor is it something most male philosophers do in contemporary America or Korea. The philosophical focus of Yunjidang's attention is how Misaeng Go compromised moral principle in an effort to curry favor with another: begging vinegar from his neighbor with the sole aim of giving it to another person

---

[36] Latinized as "Confucius" in most Western sources.

[37] See *Analects* 2.4.

[38] *Analects* 5.24.

[39] This passage, being from the *Analects*, of course is commented upon and in interesting ways by a wide range of Confucians, including Ju Hui in China and disciples of Song Siyeol (see note 31 above) in Korea who touch on some of the same points, though none treats the passage with the care and comprehensiveness of Yunjidang. For example, see Ju Hui's (C. Zhu Xi) 朱熹 *Classified Sayings Master Ju* (*Juja eoryu*; C. *Zhuzi yulei* 朱子語類) 29.29a–32a and Gwon Sangha's 權尚夏 (1641–1721 CE) "Response to Min Seong-yu" (*Dap Min Seong-yu* 答閔聖猷) in *The Collected Works of Hansujae* (*Hansujae jip* 寒水齋集), 7.32b–33a. Thanks to Hanna Kim for pointing out and discussing some of these earlier precedents.

in order to bolster his own status and reputation. She relates this to core orthodox Confucian themes such as the need to be watchful over oneself—to avoid such compromises of character—and the need to be flexible in one's deliberations—to "weigh" (*gwon*; C. *quan* 權) alternatives in order to know when it might be appropriate to suspend, bend, or emend norms and policies in order to realize more important moral aims. At one point, a questioner presses her by asking, "If someone's father or brother[40] is ill and he comes and reports the hardship he is suffering and begs for medicine that one lacks but one's neighbor has, then should one still not ask one's neighbor to give him the medicine out of concern that it would harm one's uprightness?" Many contemporary philosophers and psychologists will immediately think of Kohlberg's (1973) famous hypothetical case about whether a man named Heinz should steal an expensive drug that he cannot afford to buy in order to treat his desperately ill wife and the different styles of moral reasoning he describes—contrasting the approaches of "Jake" and "Amy," who are taken to represent male and female "types" of moral reasoning respectively. Of course, for many, this recollection will also bring to mind the trenchant criticism of his analysis advanced by Gilligan (2016) and the contribution this has made to the development of care ethics, which at least began as a distinctively feminine approach to morality (Noddings 2003).

Another discourse offers an excellent example of how Yunjidang often objects as much to the style of someone's behavior as to the particular action that they take. In her "Discourse on On Gyo[41] Tearing the Hem of His Garment" (*Non On Gyo jeolgeo* 論溫嶠絶裾), she discusses the well-known case of On Gyo, who is renowned for the loyalty and dedication he showed to his ruler. When appointed to undertake a dangerous mission as the king's envoy to a distant and hostile state, On Gyo did not hesitate. When his aged mother beseeched him to stay, he did not falter or delay and, in his haste to depart, tore the hem of his garment, which she had grabbed onto, hoping to make him stay. Yunjidang questions his behavior and character, which shows her tremendous intellectual independence and courage. She argues that On Gyo actually behaved rather badly. First, she notes that On Gyo was not formally a minister of the king who ordered him to undertake this mission and

---

[40] The translation follows the original text, though the implied reference is broader: "parents and siblings."

[41] On Gyo (288–329 CE), whose courtesy name was Taejin (C. Taizhen 太真, known formally as Duke Chungmu (C. Zhongwu) of Sian (C. Shi'an) (*Sian Chungmu gong*; C. *Shian Zhongwu gong* 始安忠武公), was a renowned general and governor who lived during the Jin (C. Jin 晉 dynasty (265–420 CE).

so was not obligated to obey. Next, she asks whether the mission *really* was as pressing and critical as he claimed. She further questions if it was really the case that he alone was capable of undertaking this duty. If there were others whose family situation was not as precarious as his and whose mother did not need her son to stay with her, why could they not go instead? Finally, Yunjidang asks, if the mission really was so critical to the well-being of the ruler and state and her son really was the only man or the best qualified to undertake this responsibility, why did On Gyo not take the time to explain all of this to his mother but instead brusquely tore himself from her arms without deigning to address her concerns? Had he really needed to go and taken the time to explain the situation to his mother, Yunjidang contends, she would likely have seen the need and urged her son to do himself, his family, and his state proud. Reading this case and the questions Yunjidang raises, one cannot but recall Sartre's (1991) famous hypothetical scenario of a young man torn between staying to help his aged mother or leaving to fight with the Free French Forces opposing the Nazis during World War II. Yunjidang describes this kind of conflict of duties with much greater nuance and subtlety than Sartre demonstrated, showing that often there is a great deal of hidden complexity in such basic "existential" choices. Moreover, her analysis shows that one can approach such conflicts in ways that, while not avoiding hard choices, recognize and honor all the moral demands involved. Her analysis is nothing short of brilliant, but it is again clear that her concerns and approach are things that women and particularly mothers would be more likely to think of, focus upon, explore, analyze, and highlight and thus things that fall outside the standard ambit not only of Confucian but also of often modern philosophical discourse. Her writings open up and develop new and profound dimensions of familiar cases and problems in orthodox Confucian philosophy, and they do this in part because she comes to these cases and problems as a woman, living in a particular cultural and historical perspective.

The second exposition included among our translations explores the meaning and significance of four key terms of art, consisting of two sets of paired concepts, that were central to neo-Confucian moral philosophy: the Heart-Mind of the Way (*dosim*; C. *daoxin* 道心) and Human Heart-Mind (*insim*; C. *renxin* 人心), and the Four Sprouts and Seven Emotions (*sadan chiljeong*; C. *siduan qiqing* 四端七情). Both sets present modes, forms, or aspects of underlying unities that connect a pure and original moral realm with the morally mixed and more ambiguous everyday world. Yunjidang presents the exposition as a dialogue between herself and an unnamed interlocutor and interweaves her explanations with numerous quotations from the classics.

The Heart-Mind of the Way is the reservoir of heavenly Pattern-Principle within each human being that serves as a pure and perfect source of moral norms. This mode of the Heart-Mind lacks corporeal existence and comes into the world by being embedded in *Gi-Material*. In this latter form, the Human Heart-Mind is the phenomenal seat of human thought, feeling, and volition, but because it is embedded in the realm of *Gi-Material*, it inevitably is, to varying degrees, obscured and prone to error. Such obscuration in part is simply a function of being located in a particular physical form; this establishes a personal perspective, which inclines the Heart-Mind to be biased. Moreover, the *Gi-Material* which serves as host for the originally pure Heart-Mind is naturally mixed in quality and displays different degrees of balance, which makes it hard for the Heart-Mind to perceive its true nature and proper relationship to the rest of the world. Instead of recognizing, being moved by, and acting for the sake of the grand underlying unity that is the heavenly Pattern-Principle of its original nature, it tends to act on and for itself, which only deepens its alienation and sense of separation from the whole. This tendency toward self-centeredness,[42] reinforced by the feelings, thoughts, and actions that such a self regularly undertakes, presents the central moral challenge that moral self-cultivation aims to overcome.

This general tension between a pure and perfect original moral state and a mixed, more ambiguous self that is inclined to pursue its own self-centered desires against the underlying harmonious unity of the world and at the expense of the common good, is replayed in the contrast between the Four Sprouts and Seven Emotions. The Four Sprouts find their locus classicus in the *Mencius*, where they describe the nascent, immature expressions of reactive attitudes that underlie and incline us to develop the four core Confucian virtues of humaneness (*in*; C. *ren* 仁), righteousness (*ui*; C. *yi* 義), rites (*ye*; C. *li* 禮), and wisdom (*ji*; C. *zhi* 智). Among orthodox neo-Confucians

---

[42] "Self-centeredness" is our translation of *sa* (C. *si*) 私. It refers to the tendency to give preference to oneself and one's needs and desires in ways that violate what is morally "correct," which is how one would act if one were perfectly in accord with one's nature and the mandate of heaven. Those who are able to overcome self-centeredness realize their nature and the mandate and become "one" (*ilche*; C. *yiti*) 一體 with heaven, earth, and all things. As noted, "one" is our translation of 一體, which literally means "one body" and points to neo-Confucian metaphysical beliefs about the underlying unity of the universe. In order to help readers track the use of this concept, we consistently render it as "one" (or "oneness") throughout this work.

such as Yunjidang, who largely follow the commentary by Ju Hui, the Four Sprouts were conceived not so much as sprouts but as clues or indications of and pointers toward the original and underlying purity of heavenly Pattern-Principle. The Seven Emotions, enumerated in a number of contemporary texts, describe the everyday human repertoire of affective responses, and one of Yunjidang's central tasks in this exposition is explaining the relationship between the Four Sprouts and Seven Emotions. This was a perennial challenge and served as the focus of one of the most intense, long-running, and sophisticated debates within Korean Confucianism: the Four-Seven Debate. At the core of this debate was a set of related questions concerning how a pure and perfect moral realm can provide normative grounds and motivation for people living and acting in the world we know and share, how this underlying moral nature or Heart-Mind can be reconciled with and find expression in the everyday needs, feelings, and desires of human beings, how we can cultivate ourselves to fully instantiate this original, authentic nature, and how doing so properly locates and orients us to the people, creatures, and things around us.

The fourth exposition takes as its theme a famous line found in the opening section of Book 12 of the *Analects*. In response to a question about the nature of humaneness put to him by An Yeon (C. Yan Yuan) 顔淵, also known as Anja (C. Yanzi) 顔子, his most talented and advanced student, Gongja replied, "Overcoming the self and returning to the rites is humaneness."[43] In one important sense, the challenge of how to interpret this line, which has a remarkable and varied history in the commentarial tradition, is connected with the set of issues discussed in regard to the previous exposition. For in saying we must overcome or conquer the self in order to attain the highest and primary virtue of humaneness, Gongja's teaching appears to be calling on us, at least to some extent, to reject and turn away from the adulterated everyday world—the realm of the Human Heart-Mind and the Seven Emotions—and retreat into a pure, more ascetic form of life—described by the Heart-Mind of the Way and the Four Sprouts. In general terms, it poses the problem of how to relate neo-Confucian ideas about a pure and perfect original nature with a description of what it is like to be a human being pursuing the kinds of quotidian lives that most find appealing. As in the previous exposition, Yunjidang presents her explanation in the form of a dialogue between herself

---

[43] *Analects* 12.1.

and an anonymous interlocutor and regularly invokes ideas and examples from the classics.

She crafts her explanation by returning to and drawing upon other parts of the *Analects* that discuss An Yeon's character and his efforts at moral self-cultivation and augmenting these with ideas, references, and examples from other classics as well. In particular, she focuses on An Yeon's unwavering commitment to learn and practice the Way in an ongoing effort to purge himself of self-centered desires and return to his original nature, which is humaneness. In doing so, she connects the interpretation of this line with An Yeon's well-known *love of learning*, a theme that, as we have seen, was philosophically and personally salient and poignant for her. This, in turn, provided her with an opportunity to explore, in response to a "question" posed by her imaginary interlocutor, the issue of whether everyone is capable of successfully cultivating the self and attaining the ideal of sagehood. Yunjidang begins by noting that while An Yeon was fortunate in having been born with a particularly refined and balanced physical nature, he manifested remarkable perseverance and persistence in his quest for moral self-improvement. Tragically, he died young and, as many others have claimed, this was the only thing that held him back from becoming a sage; one of greatest lessons to learn from his example is the need to work incessantly and assiduously without regard to hardships or impediments to achieve the goal of becoming a sage. Like other great moral exemplars of the past, An Yeon serves as an effective and poignant reminder that *we all* share the same pure nature and are capable of achieving moral perfection. In the conclusion of her exposition, she brings these related points together and to bear on her own case and through her own case the case of all women: "Though I am a woman, still, the nature I originally received contained no distinction between male and female. Though I have not been able to learn what An Yeon learned, I earnestly share his commitment to become a sage."

The final selection we shall discuss consists of three brief inscriptions written by Yunjidang. In each, she takes as her theme physical objects: a mirror, a short sword, and a ruler and scale, which she then describes as embodying and symbolizing some moral virtue, attribute, or activity. In the second of her three inscriptions, she explains how she and we all must wield a keen-edged spiritual sword to cut down the obstacles that stand in the way of making moral progress. She makes clear that self-centered desires pose the most pervasive and persistent impediments to spiritual progress and urges us to eradicate them whenever and wherever they arise by launching a relentless, uncompromising, decisive, and thoroughgoing assault upon them. We must emulate earlier moral paragons, such as An Yeon, who wielded their spiritual swords with unwavering moral courage, cleared away every trace of self-centeredness, and established, through an awesome and vigilant campaign of moral improvement, a character that dissuaded any contrary inclination from ever daring to show itself. She concludes the inscription with a lovely piece of poetry extolling the virtues, efficacy, and results of the spiritual weapon she wields.

As noted earlier, Gang Jeongildang was directly inspired by the life and work of Im Yunjidang; she explicitly acknowledged the extent to which her predecessor motivated and informed her own study, thinking, and self-cultivation; it is clear that she adopted and extended several of Yunjidang's philosophical insights in developing her philosophical views, while also evolving unique and powerful ideas and forms of expression of her own. It is important to understand and appreciate the extent to which both her personal life and intellectual development gave rise to a distinct and valuable expression even of shared ideas and values. Nevertheless, the relationship between Im and Gang adds an additional, unique dimension to their work and lives.[44]

Like Yunjidang, Gang Jeongildang pursued her education and self-cultivation as a kind of guerrilla activity, carried out behind the scenes and almost always in the face of formidable challenges and resistance. In addition to the barriers that severely inhibited her education, movement, and expression—obstacles that all women faced in the highly patriarchal environment of late Joseon society—in her case, economic hardship added an additional profound burden that shaped both the form her writings took and the themes that dominated her reflections. For one thing, as noted above, she did not begin her formal study of the Confucian tradition until rather late in life and did not have the benefit of a dedicated teacher or mentor. Her husband did of course help her, but their relationship was clearly more a partnership and one in which she provided the economic support for both. In these and other ways, her situation differed importantly and in interesting ways from that of her contemporary and inspiration, Im Yunjidang. We have no extant discourses or explanations

---

[44] For further discussion of this issue, see note 5 above.

by Jeongildang;[45] her most extensive and interesting writings are her poems and the personal missives she wrote to her husband. The discussion of her philosophy presented below is based on a small sample of her writings; we offer it as an introduction to her larger oeuvre, which can best be explored by reading the translations contained in this volume.

Jeongildang's writings reflect how deeply she was embedded in and attentive to the everyday challenges of practical social life. Her work reveals, often in poignant and incisive ways, the practical dimensions not only of her life but of her philosophy as well. She forged her insights in a crucible of difficulty that regularly bordered on desperation and most often expressed them in short and highly focused writings produced in the brief and irregular periods of time she could carve out to think and write. Jeongildang constantly toiled to support her family and in particular her husband's ultimately unsuccessful attempts to pass the civil service examinations through her needlework and scrupulous family management. These concerns come through clearly in her poetry in which, at times, we can clearly hear the plaintive undertone of her own frustrated aspirations.

Some of her poetry is focused primarily on her own pursuit of learning and self-cultivation. For example, in the poem "Beginning to Study," we learn of the relatively late start she had in setting out along the Confucian Way and that she embarked upon and traveled this long and difficult journey without a dedicated teacher or mentor.

> At thirty, I begin my studies,
> Not knowing which direction to turn.

We further learn from this short poem how she scrupulously maintained her focus, shunning even the slightest complacency, and remained steadfastly dedicated to her ultimate ideal: "aspiring to be like the ancients."

Throughout her years of study, she was keenly aware of her late start and the quick passage of time, as is evident in her poem "Moved to Chant on New Year's Eve," which opens with the lines,

> I have wasted precious time doing nothing,
> Tomorrow, I shall be fifty-one years old!

---

[45] As noted earlier, we do know that certain specific works of hers, which were more traditional in genre, were lost, but we do not have a clear idea of the full extent of these losses. See note 27 above.

But, as always, she refuses to give in to frustration or despair and concludes the verse, instead, with an expression of dedication and resolve,

> What good to sigh with sadness halfway through the night?
> Better to cultivate oneself throughout the remaining days.

Her awareness of the need to make every minute count appears in the advice she offers to others as well and especially to the young. In another verse, "Encouraging the Youth," she counsels,

> Do not squander the vitality of youth.
> . . . .
> You should aspire to be a sage or worthy!

In works such as "Three Stanzas Written in Tanwon,"[46] we glimpse moments of genuine joy and a sense of achievement in the pursuit of learning:

> Living in the forest, drinking in the valley,
> Holding my books, enjoying myself.
> Reflecting on my prior efforts at self-cultivation,
> I come close to discerning something profound.

But even in such moments, she seems slightly daunted by the challenges she faced and returns to the theme of her advancing age.

> I am weak and find it difficult to drive on,
> Pausing my ascent, I sigh.
> Encountering these late years of life,
> What can I do about my sadness and distress?

Other of her poems take up and elaborate upon more traditional philosophical themes, elegantly working in quotations or allusions to classical texts. For example, "Human Nature Is Good" expresses not only the orthodox neo-Confucian belief in the innate goodness of human beings

---

[46] *Tanwon* is the name of Jeongildang's family residence. For a discussion of the meaning of its name, see note 19, page 177.

but also the need to work hard to bring out and manifest its full form and thereby become a sage,

> Human nature originally is wholly good,
> Developing it fully, one becomes a sage.

"Reading the *Doctrine of the Mean*" urges readers to maintain the meditative attitudes of awareness and vigilance in order to attain the ideals of inner peace and balance,

> If in the beginning one can be watchful and cautious,
> In the end one can achieve equilibrium and harmony.

Her "Hymn to Sincerity and Reverence" highlights the central importance of these two virtuous dispositions and makes clear the critical role they play in fully realizing the Confucian Way.

> If not sincere, how can you have it?
> If not reverent, how can you preserve it?
> Only with both of these
> Can you enter the gate of the Way.

Finally, some of her poetic works offer direct admonitions and encouragement to her husband. We have included two such poems. "For My Husband [1]" begins with a humble description of how she learned needlework as a young girl: the declaration of her "lack of talent and virtue," which opens the poem, is neither a description of poor natural ability or effort but stark testimony to the lack of opportunity women faced and the social resistance they endured to educate and cultivate themselves as Confucian scholars. Unforeseen and unanticipated, her skill in needlework, which in some sense became part of her own spiritual practice, enabled not only her own but her husband's study and cultivation. The verse closes with the ironic reminder that her labor freed her husband to concentrate on these loftier endeavors; of course, at the same time, it adds to her own already heavy domestic burdens, serving as a further impediment to her own pursuit of the Way.

> To my shame, I lack talent and virtue,
> But I learned needlework as a child.
> Authentic work requires exerting oneself;
> Do not be concerned about clothes and food.

"For My Husband [2]" acknowledges and celebrates her husband's on-going and persistent efforts to attain the Way, while at the same time bluntly posing the question of how much progress he has made. It clearly is urging him to exert greater effort but also implies a sense of disappointment or growing skepticism about the results.

> Since the day you began to follow Ganjae,[47]
> You have sought the Way and nothing else!
> Now it has been thirty years,
> How have you progressed in your studies?

The sixth letter that appears in Jeongildang's complete works is a message of condolence addressed to her uncle Jungsil, written soon after his wife passed away. Through it, we get a sense of some of the ways Jeongildang's precarious financial situation presented further impediments not only to her personal happiness but also to her pursuit of moral cultivation. In this instance, being hard-pressed prevented her from being with and offering direct consolation to her bereaved uncle and her nephew, his son, which caused her distress and gave her a sense of having failed in her duties toward them. In the letter, she also mentions her own poor health and the loss of one of her children, which only adds to the impression of how difficult it was for her to do all she would have liked to do to comfort her relatives in their hour of need; at the same time, that she could find and take the time and make the effort to compose such a heartfelt, sensitive, and moving letter is profound testimony to the depth and sincerity of her feelings and the strength of her character.

The seventh letter in her collected works was written to her husband in the winter of 1830. It opens with her good wishes and a brief description of some of the trials and tribulations that she had been facing at home, including her poor health and the need to see to the demands of guests who visited during his absence. In passing, she notes how these various challenges interrupt and unsettle her "inner harmony," thus posing an obstacle to achieving the desired state of "equilibrium and harmony" mentioned in her poem "Reading the *Doctrine of the Mean*," mentioned above. She then turns to a discussion of some lines from the *Analects* 12.1 that she had received from him in an earlier letter, which include Gongja's advice to An Yeon about how to achieve humaneness. The master told his young disciple not to look at, listen to, speak,

---

[47] It is not clear who this is.

or act in any way that is not in accord with the rites. Jeongildang celebrates this teaching and relates how one of her uncles often wrote these lines out as an exercise to focus his Heart-Mind and motivate his efforts to cultivate himself morally. She also, charmingly, suggests that they carve these lines into a plaque and hang it above their library for "good luck." Jeongildang goes on to offer a concise and trenchant analysis of what this teaching means, seeing it as a call to root out self-centered desires by regulating all one's conduct by the norms and standards manifested in the rites. One can, thereby, ensure that one's Heart-Mind is fully in accord with the heavenly Pattern-Principle that is our original nature. She concludes by urging her husband to put forth every effort to practice this teaching.

Jeongildang's personal missives to her husband are of immense interest and value; they cover a wide range of topics and circumstances that we cannot analyze thoroughly or comprehensively here. In this brief introduction, we focus on four types of problems that represent some of the characteristic philosophical issues and themes covered by this genre of her writings: the management of domestic affairs, administrative and pedagogical issues related to their academy, direct personal advice about her husband's moral behavior and character, and the question of women's capacity to engage in moral cultivation as well as the added challenges they faced as a result of the patriarchal nature of late Joseon society.

Several of the personal missives concern moral challenges that Jeongildang reported to her husband about how she managed different problems encountered in the carrying out of domestic affairs. For example, in the first missive, we see Jeongildang explaining to her husband how an old woman had come to their door and offered him "a peck of rice and a catty of meat" in gratitude for assistance he had offered her earlier, when she was accosted by vagabonds while traveling outside the town. After a brief conversation, Gang concluded that, given the optics of the proposed donation, she could not accept the gift without appearing to compromise moral principle. As she explained, "Though she offered her gift with the sincere intention [of expressing her gratitude], had I accepted it, I would have been suspected of selling your favor, and so I handled it in this way. I don't know what you think about this." In selection 10, Jeongildang notes that her husband allowed a guest to leave prematurely because of their poverty and her ill health. She reassures him that they still have "a few measures of rice in our storage jars, and my illness is slightly better than it was yesterday" and admonishes him for letting such concerns move him to violate the "rites governing the reception of a guest," cautioning him that in the future "you must not be the slightest re-miss in this regard." Our final example of this type of theme or issue is found in selection 36, in which Jeongildang describes her deliberations about a gift of firewood offered by one of her husband's students. Though both families were desperately poor she refused the gift not because it was beneath her but because "it was not his parent's idea . . . but something he came up with on his own." She makes clear that the value of the gift did not enter into her deliberations about the appropriateness of accepting it; had he offered a much more valuable gift approved by his parents and given in friendship, "it would have been inappropriate for me to refuse."

Like many of her works, these missives reveal how Joseon dynasty women such as Jeongildang wrestled with the application of Confucian values in the complex, subtle, and often ambiguous situations of everyday life and show the extent to which she shared and discussed such challenges with her husband. They make clear that both she and her husband took such matters very seriously, not only as practical problems that needed to be solved but also as opportunities to develop moral understanding and character. Such discussions, and especially those between husband and wife, reveal a hidden, highly significant, but largely unexplored dimension of the practice of Confucian self-cultivation.[48]

A second type of theme or issue found in Jeongildang's personal missives concerns administrative and pedagogical matters related to their private academy. In selection 16, she singles out for discussion several students, highlights their different strong points, suggests how her husband could suc-cessfully develop their talents, and urges him to accept them as students. In her concluding remark, she suggests that two of the examples she discusses offer precedents for deciding what to do in regard to other aspiring students. She does something similar in selection 18, urging her husband to make every effort to meet with and counsel two young men who have repeatedly but thus far unsuccessfully sought to meet and learn from him. In selection 22, she describes an earnest and resolute student who lives in an isolated rural village and "has no teachers or friends living nearby." Nevertheless, Jeongildang sees in him someone who is devoted to and truly loves the path of learning. After looking at his letters to her husband, she says, "A sense of

---

[48] While it was an important characteristic of Gang (and Im Yunjidang as well), it is unclear to what extent the level of communication she shared with her husband is unusual or representative of Joseon women. This is an issue that warrants additional study. Thanks to Professor Youngmin Kim for raising this point.

real learning permeates all that he has written." She urges her husband to make a special effort to connect with this young man and enable him to advance his education and development.

Section 23 finds Jeongildang urging her husband to be more "kind and loving" to their adoptive son, for "father and son are one." She uses his particular case to make the general point that "a teacher should regard his disciple as if he were his son." In selection 39, she mildly criticizes her husband for not going to pay his respects to his teacher, out of concern over their lack of money and her poor health. She again uses the occasion to draw a larger lesson about the proper conduct of a teacher, saying, "Visiting one's teacher to inquire about his welfare is not different from going to ask about the welfare of one's parents." She insists that her husband not allow their poverty and her ill health to interfere with the proper expression of filial reverence for his teacher. She resolutely declares, "Though my illness is severe, it is not necessarily fatal," and even if she were to die while he was off paying his respects, she would, like Gongja upon hearing that the Way was being practiced, die contented and happy.

The third type of problem discussed in her personal missives concerns personal advice to her husband about his moral behavior and character. In several of these communications, she offers direct, focused, and at times quite pointed criticisms of him. For example, in selection 4, she notes that she once heard him angrily reprimand someone and criticizes him, saying, "This is not the middle way. If you seek to correct this person in this way—without first being correct yourself—how can this be regarded as acceptable?" She offers a similar criticism, but in a more general way, in selections 9 and 43, which seems to imply that her husband tended to be quick-tempered and harsh in reprimanding others; she advises him that, in fact, such traits harm him and not the person who is the unfortunate object of his irritation and impatience. In selection 8, she urges him to be moderate in drinking wine, suggesting that he nurtured another unsavory inclination. Selection 14 presents an elegant appeal to focus on being virtuous for its own sake and not be concerned with whether one's virtue is recognized by others: "I want you, my husband, to work at real virtue. Do not be ashamed beneath heaven; do not be mortified upon the earth; do not be distressed whether people know or do not know." In our final example of this type of theme or issue, selection 40, we find Jeongildang cautioning her husband about his tendency to favor her at the expense of virtue. She insists that one must not show partiality to one's wife if it interferes with the service one owes to one's parents, lord, or teacher and proclaims that even if such improper partiality were to result in her "being rich, noble, peaceful, and at ease" she would "rather die from poverty and hunger."

The fourth and final type of problem we consider concerns the question of women's capacity to engage in moral cultivation and the particular challenges they faced as a result of the patriarchal nature of late Joseon society. Jeongildang was inspired by Yunjidang's declaration that women were equally endowed as men with all that is needed to become a sage. In selection 55, she quotes Yunjidang saying, "Though I am a woman, still, the nature I originally received contained no distinction between male and female." This was a dramatic claim to make at the time, but it was also clearly and fully consistent with the fundamental neo-Confucian view that each and every person, creature, and thing in the world is endowed with the Great Ultimate (*Taegeuk*; C. *Taiji* 太極), which is the sum of all the heavenly Pattern-Principles of the universe. Equally clear and fully consistent with fundamental neo-Confucian views is the implication that all one needed to do was to put forth enough effort of the right kind in order to fully realize one's nature and become a sage; this is precisely what Jeongildang makes clear in her missive: "If one is able to apply oneself then one can reach the level of a sage."[49] She concludes this selection by directly asking her husband what he thinks about these claims.

In selection 59, Jeongildang expresses her frustration at being restricted to traditional women's roles and having to carry the added burdens—as we have argued above, a triple burden—of providing for her family and being responsible for all domestic work, while at the same time doggedly pursuing her intellectual and moral pursuits. Her remarks make clear that she is poignantly aware of the injustice of suffering such restrictions and having to carry these additional burdens, while silently "longing to join those who have cultivated themselves in earlier times." She contrasts her own disadvantaged position with that of her husband, who "as a man . . . [is] free to establish a commitment and seek the Way, follow teachers and choose friends, and diligently improve yourself." Drawing upon their contrasting positions, she urges him not to waste the opportunity he has and to "make becoming a sage or worthy your highest imperative!"

---

[49] Neither Yunjidang nor Jeongildang ever explicitly challenged the idea that women and men have different social roles that require from each different and unequal "right effort," but, as we shall see, they did criticize ways in which women's efforts at moral self-improvement were severely restricted and hamstrung.

For the most part, the types of discussions and advice we see in Jeongildang's personal missives are not in themselves surprising. One finds examples of teachers engaging in such conversations and offering their disciples such advice throughout the Confucian tradition, but many will find it surprising and revealing to see such extensive, straightforward, honest, and at times pointed exchanges between a Joseon dynasty wife and her husband. This shows first and foremost the extent to which Jeongildang and her spouse not only thought of one another as equal partners in life and in pursuit of the moral Way but also how regularly they served as ethical and spiritual critics, advisers, and coaches to one another.[50] One of the most revealing and important aspects of such exchanges is the recognition that two spouses know each other in ways few people do or can, because of both the challenges and intimacy they share—and in the case of Jeongildang the challenges often were quite formidable, pressing, and enduring—and the extended period of time they spend together. Not only does this offer spouses a remarkable epistemological privilege, it also offers them the opportunity to hone their ability to give advice and ensures that the recipient of such advice will be inclined to trust that it is given with loving intent and often with a desire to facilitate their pursuit of a shared goal, in this case the quest for moral improvement. While all will acknowledge that the Confucian tradition sees the family as central to the good life and the locus of much of the most important work of moral improvement, research on Confucian self-cultivation has rarely focused attention on the ways in which husbands and wives work together, often in the pursuit of shared projects, to promote their mutual moral improvement. These personal missives between Jeongildang and her husband open a rarely encountered door into a neglected yet vital corner of the Confucian ethical world, one that holds deep and powerful lessons for those interested in how to move themselves and others toward the good. It offers yet another example of the distinctive and original ways in which her writings are of profound and critical value while, at the same time, perhaps also helping us understand why her work is so poorly understood or appreciated by modern scholars of the Confucian tradition.

Next, we introduce two of the three commemorations written by Jeongildang: one about the studio of a retired senior scholar she knew and one about her own home. The second commemoration that appears in

---

[50] Readers of Jeongildang's other writings will know that she regularly offered encouragement as well as criticism and correction to other family members as well.

her collected works is dedicated to Late to Awaken Studio (Manseongjae 晚醒齋), the retreat of the retired scholar Hong Jongseon 洪宗善. The name of his studio, Late to Awaken, is taken from a passage in the *Mencius* that describes those who are destined to awaken early (i.e., attain moral enlightenment before others) and their obligation to awaken and role in awakening others (i.e., those who are "late to awaken"). Hong Jongseon humbly named his studio Late to Awaken, and thereby offers Jeongildang a golden opportunity not only to discuss neo-Confucian views about self-cultivation, which she does by focusing on the role of reverence (*gyeong*; C. *jing* 敬), but also to extol the many virtues of the master of this studio. In the course of her commemoration, she also manifests an admirable humility herself by repeatedly questioning whether she is really qualified to discuss such lofty and sublime ideas.

The third and final commemoration is of her home, Tanwon,[51] which appears in a number of her poems, either as topic or simply a site of composition, and is mentioned in other of her writings as well. It obviously offered her a cherished sanctuary from the many pressing problems that hemmed in her life; at the same time, it served to symbolize a number of moral and aesthetic ideals that she held dear. In the course of her commemoration, she presents a history and description of the home and its surrounding garden and comments on how it both reflects and encourages several virtuous traits that were characteristic of its owner—her husband. She supports the account and claims she makes by drawing from the classics and embellishing her commemoration with a well-crafted verse. This short and charming composition takes shape around and concludes with a central theme: "How can this compare to wandering in a garden and always having an even and easy place?"

We conclude our brief introduction to Jeongildang's philosophy by discussing one of two funeral epitaphs that she wrote. We have chosen the epitaph she composed for one of her daughters, whose name was Gyesuk 季淑. This is an especially interesting piece, because most works of this kind are written by a father, who speaks for himself and his wife, but this epitaph is written by a wife (Jeongildang) on behalf of and for her husband. On the one hand, it speaks for both of them, but, on the other hand, the actual author's emotions and experiences are vividly on display. As mentioned in this work and noted in section 2 of this introduction, Jeongildang gave birth

[51] See note 46 above.

to nine children all of whom perished before they were able to speak; Gyesuk was the last to be born. This epitaph is one of the few sources that offer us a glimpse into how these wrenching losses affected her and her husband, and as one might expect, it overflows with tenderness, love, anguish, regret, and sorrow. With palpable joy, it describes a good-natured and highly intelligent child who, "at the age of three to four months . . . was able to recognize her mother's and father's faces," but laments that she passed away so early that her father and mother "never heard . . . [her] call them 'mother' or 'father.'" It also describes in excruciating detail Jeongildang's inability to produce enough milk to suckle her daughter, how difficult it was to find wet nurses to augment her meager supply of milk, and how they tried desperately to supplement this with rice gruel when milk was unavailable. The epitaph continues telling the story of their daughter's short life, describing her downward spiral into illness that so soon led to her premature death. When Gyesuk died, her bereaved mother was so weak that she could not travel all the way to their family graveyard, and so Gyesuk was put to rest in a grave beneath a hill near their village, which her parents hoped people in later times would not "plow over and ruin." While the epitaph stoically attempts to proclaim that all life "must come to an end" and, citing the *Mencius*, that "there is nothing that is not according to fate," its author admits that she cannot set aside her grief or let go of her emotions.

THE EXTANT WRITINGS OF YUNJIDANG

任允摯堂

Im Yunjidang
1721–1793

The image above is a portrait of Im Yunjidang created by Ok Munseong 玉文星 in 2017; it is based on facial characteristics of modern descendants of the Pungcheon Im family. There is no extant, contemporary image or description of Im Yunjidang, as is the case for most women from the Joseon. Photo courtesy of History Museum of Wonju (Republic of Korea).

Biographies (傳)

1. Biography of the Wife of Mr. Song <Neungsang>

The first biography is about Lady Han, whose husband was in the scholarly lineage of Song Siyeol, one of the most distinguished philosophers of the late Joseon dynasty; Yunjidang and her brothers regarded him as their intellectual progenitor. Yunjidang makes clear that Lady Han scrupulously fulfilled her familial duties but also developed her intellectual abilities, overcoming the formidable challenges impeding such an education in her time. The biography contains a memorable account of Lady Han's gently but decisively instructing her husband about the true aim of learning—moral self-cultivation—and warning him to avoid being tempted to pursue fame and high social status.

The daughter of Han Gyejin 韓啟震,[1] who was Fourth Inspector (*Jipyeong* 持平) [in the Office of the Inspector-General (Saheonbu 司憲府)], married Mr. Song [Neungsang].[2] She lost her mother when she was young and showed absolute sincerity in her grief and suffering. When she married [and was preparing to leave for her new home], she happened to be looking through some cases and trunks and came upon a piece of calligraphy written by her mother; she was immediately overcome with sorrow and cried until the tears soaked the clothes she was wearing.

Once, when her husband's cousins were describing their highest aspirations to him, they said, "We admire Yulgok's moral virtue as well

---

[1] Han Gyejin (1689–? CE). His ancestral home was Cheongju 清州; his given name was Gyemyeong 季明. He was a younger brother of Han Wonjin 韓元震 (1682–1751 CE), pen name Namdang 南塘, and studied under Gwon Sangha 權尚夏 (1641–1721 CE), pen names Suam 遂菴 and Hansujae 寒水齋, who is known as the foremost disciple of Song Siyeol. Han attained the rank of Third Minister (*Chamui* 參議) in the Ministry of Taxation (Hojo 戶曹). Han Gyejin was also a friend of Im Seongju.

[2] Song Neungsang 宋能相 (1709–1758 CE) was a late Joseon dynasty philosopher and a direct descendent of Song Siyeol. His ancestral home was Eunjin 恩津; his courtesy name (*ja*; C. *zi* 字) was Saryong 士龍, and his pen names were Unpyeong 雲坪 and Donghaeja 東海子. Song Neungsang knew and exchanged views with Yunjidang's brother Im Seongju; both were members of the Old Doctrine faction.

Korean Women Philosophers and the Ideal of a Female Sage. Philip J. Ivanhoe and Hwa Yeong Wang, Oxford University Press. © Oxford University Press 2023. DOI: 10.1093/oso/9780197508688.003.0002

as his great fame and high status." Her husband agreed with what they said, but once all of them had left, Han asked her husband, "What did you think of what your cousins said?" Her husband replied, "It was good." Han quietly smiled and her husband asked, "Why are you smiling?" She replied, "I think about it in the following way. Moral virtue is what made Yulgok the man he was. Had he been poor and lowly and lived in a mean and narrow lane deep in the mountains, would that have diminished his virtue in any way? Though he enjoyed great fame and high status, what did this add to his virtue? Now, had your cousins only talked about his moral virtue, then they would [have shown that they] sincerely admire virtue. But they talked about his great fame and high status together with his virtue; this is not to admire virtue. The true state of their minds is that they admire high status. You think this good, but isn't it impermissible?" After listening to her comments, her husband deferred to her view. Subsequently, he committed himself to his own moral cultivation with the aim of becoming a true Confucian.

Han served her parents-in-law and completely fulfilled the duties of being a good wife. Her mother-in-law often would personally reel silk from cocoons; her sons' wives asked her to let them do this for her, but she declined. Thereupon, the wives left; each returning to her own room; only Han did not presume to do so, but instead kept the fire going and continued to serve her mother-in-law; agile and alert, reverential and respectful, she was never remiss or negligent. She covered up the difficulty of her labors and wanted to help her mother-in-law with the cooking in order to make things easier. Han not only carried out such duties, but also had great literary talent. Her father believed in the popular practices and ideas of his day and so did not provide her with a formal education. Nevertheless, she often devoted herself to the study of the classics and histories and so gained a comprehensive understanding of their great principles. Unfortunately, her life was destined to be short, and she died. Is this not lamentable!

The encomium says,

> [Lady] Han was the wife of Mr. Song;
> She was a woman of great virtue and achievement.
> She was filial to her parents;
> And greatly advanced in understanding.
> She led her husband to follow the Way;
> And encouraged him in his studies.

The ancients called such a woman a "heroic wife";[3]
Does this not refer to her?
She was not granted a full span of life;
But I never saw her stop short.[4]
Why is one given life? Why is it taken away?
It is difficult to have faith in[5] Pattern-Principle.

2. Biography of Two Women: Choe and Hong

The second biography is about two women whose exploits were often discussed during Yunjidang's time.[6] The central theme is how this mother and daughter fulfilled their respective obligations of chastity and filial piety by plotting and carrying out righteous revenge against the man who murdered their husband and father. They further demonstrated their exceptional moral character by turning themselves in after completing their revenge but were pardoned on the basis of their moral excellence. Yunjidang makes a point of saying that their act was something "most men would prove incapable of doing."

[Mother] Choe 崔 and [daughter] Hong 洪 refer to the wife and daughter of a soldier named Hong 洪 from the Samga District (Samga-hyeon 三嘉縣) [in Gyeongsang Province (Gyeongsang-do) 慶尙道]. This soldier was killed and these two women wanted to take revenge against the man responsible for killing him. They said to one another, "The only way in which human beings

---

[3] A heroic wife is literally a "female knight or scholar" (*yeosa*; C. *nüshi* 女士). See the *Book of Poetry*, Mao #247. In the corpus of Korean neo-Confucian funeral orations and epitaphs, *yeosa* often was used to praise a woman's intelligence and virtuous deeds, describing them as comparable to what the best male Confucian scholars (*sa*; C. *shi* 士) might achieve. Jeong Hyeon (C. Zheng Xuan) 鄭玄 (127–200 CE) and Gong Yeongdal (C. Kong Yingda) 孔穎達 (574–648 CE), in their commentaries on this passage, explain a *yeosa* as a woman who performs scholarly actions (士行), who therefore is able to produce a worthy and wise (賢智) son. See Gong Yeongdal's *Commentaries and Explanations on the Mo Tradition of Poetry* (*Mosi juso*; C. *Maoshi zhushu* 毛詩注疏) 24.49b–50b.

[4] Cf. *Analects* 9.21, "The Master said of Anja, 'Alas! I saw his constant progress; I never saw him stop short.'" Like Lady Han, Anja, who is also known as An Yeon, died young; he was the favorite disciple of Gongja.

[5] Cf. the "Common Possession of Pure Virtue" (*Ham yu il deok*; C. *Xian you yi de* 咸有一德), section of the *Book of History* (*Sangseo*; C. *Shangshu* 尙書), which says in part, "Oh! It is difficult to have faith in Heaven; its mandate is not constant!" (嗚呼! 天難諶, 命靡常)

[6] Gim Gyeongmi (2019, 95–96) points out that the story of Choe and Hong was well known and discussed in several other Korean works and speculates that Yunjidang may have heard of it from her brothers. Gim further notes that Yunjidang elaborated the tale by including the conversation between the two women in which they decided to take revenge, offering the important insight that by letting the two women speak for themselves, Yunjidang presents them as full moral agents who were perfectly at ease, not only to criticize but to punish a man they regarded as morally reprehensible.

differ from birds and beasts is in having the virtues of chastity and filial piety. That a wife takes revenge for [the killing of] her husband is [part of] chastity. That a child takes revenge for [the killing of] her father is [part of] filial piety. Now, unfortunately, my husband and your father suffered harm at the hands of another. If we do not take revenge simply because we covet our own lives, then how could we bear to face him in the world below? Moreover, [if we fail to act,] how can we take our stand in this world?"

From that moment onward, they held their daggers at their sides and kept their eyes on the family [of the man] against whom they sought to take revenge. After several years had passed, they saw an opportunity [to act] and stabbed him to death. [Afterward,] they entered the district [court] and reported what they had done. The Provincial Governor (*Taesu* 太守) listened to their account and the royal court decided the case, pardoning them for the crime of murder and exempting their family from further liability.

Noble people say that what these two women did was resolute, filial, and, moreover, courageous. Most men would prove incapable of doing what they achieved. The *Book of Poetry* (*Sigyeong*; C. *Shijing* 詩經) says, "Members of our family accept their fate and never alter their course."[7] Does this not apply to the case of these two women?

---

[7] See the *Book of Poetry*, Mao #68.

Discourses (論)

1. Discourse on Ye Yang

The first discourse is about Ye Yang, a famous assassin in the early days of the Warring States period (c. 475–403 BCE). He was widely admired as an exemplar of loyalty and righteousness because he repeatedly attempted to exact vengeance against the man responsible for the death of his lord. Yunjidang argues against this view and concludes that Ye Yang was in fact "a rather pedestrian man."

The whole world claims that Ye Yang (C. Yu Rang) 豫讓 (fl. 450 BCE)[1] was a righteous scholar (*uisa*; C. *yishi* 義士), but in my view he was not truly a righteous scholar. A filial child, even though his father is not kind to him, still serves his father with filial piety. A loyal minister, even though his lord does not treat him in a ritually correct manner, still serves his lord with loyalty. Now, Ye Yang had served both the Beom (C. Fan) 范 and Junghang (C. Zhonghang) 中行 clans.[2] When Ji Baek (C. Zhi Bo) 智伯[3] wiped them out, instead of taking revenge on Ji Baek, he served him as a minister. This was because the Junghang clan had treated Ye Yang with no more courtesy than they treated anyone else. And yet, when Viscount Yang of Jo (Jo Yangja; C. Zhao Xiangzi 趙襄子) (r. 458–425 BCE) killed Ji Baek,[4] Ye Yang sought revenge against him repeatedly.[5] This was because Ji Baek had treated Ye Yang

---

[1] Ye Yang was originally a minister before he set on the path of vengeance. He lived in the state of Jin (C. Jin) 晉 around 450 BCE.

[2] These were two of six influential ministerial clans of the Jin State, the other four being Ji (C. Zhi) 智, Jo (C. Zhao) 趙, Wi (C. Wei) 魏, and Han (C. Han) 韓.

[3] He was a member of the Ji clan mentioned in the previous note and is also known as Ji Yo (C. Zhi Yao) 智瑤 (d. 453 BCE).

[4] The Ji, Wi, and Han clans mentioned above turned against Ji Yo and his clan because Ji Yo was too greedy and tried to take advantage at their expense. Allied together, they killed Ji Yo in 453 BCE. Jo Yangja's personal animosity toward Ji Yo was so great that after killing him, he used his skull as a drinking cup.

[5] Ye Yang made two attempts on Jo Yangja's life. He was discovered after the first, but Jo was so moved by his loyalty that he released him. When discovered again and about to be killed by Viscount Jo's guards, Ye Yang asked for the Viscount's robe and stabbed it three times in a ritual display of his intent to assassinate him. Ye Yang then took his own life.

Korean Women Philosophers and the Ideal of a Female Sage. Philip J. Ivanhoe and Hwa Yeong Wang, Oxford University Press. © Oxford University Press 2023. DOI: 10.1093/oso/9780197508688.003.0003

with the courtesy due a scholar of the state. And so, Ye Yang was simply acting in light of the ritually correct treatment he received; he was not seeking revenge out of loyalty. Had Ji Baek treated Ye Yang the way the Junghang clan had, Ye Yang would have turned to serve Jo Yangja. This is what made Ye Yang who he was; it was just his special luck [to have been treated well by Ji Baek]. Moreover, since Ye Yang was treated as a scholar of the state, [his lord] should have listened to everything he said. So, when Ji Baek sought to expand his territory at the expense of Han and Wi,[6] why didn't Ye Yang correct this wrong behavior even at the risk of his own life, getting Ji Baek to see that it was wrong and unrighteous? When Ji Baek attacked [the other clans] at the Battle of Jinyang (C. Jinyang) 晉陽,[7] why didn't Ye Yang oppose him, even at the risk of his own life, in order to prevent his lord from meeting his own death? What does it matter that he merely clasped a dagger and planned to take his revenge?[8] Oh! Ye Yang was unable to serve and influence the Junghang clan and unable to correct and save Ji Baek; in the end, they both died. At the most, he can be regarded as a rather pedestrian person; on what basis can he be considered loyal and righteous?

2. Discourse on Bo Gwa

The second discourse concerns Bo Gwa,[9] another figure from the Warring States period, who is often admired for being able to navigate the vicissitudes of his difficult age by pursuing clever strategies for survival. Yunjidang argues he was in fact profoundly self-interested, which led him to be "disloyal and unfilial." She compares him unfavorably even to Ye Yang, the subject of the first discourse.

If a minister is too fond of himself, he cannot be completely loyal. If a member of the ruling clan is too fond of himself, he cannot maintain his ancestral sacrifices (i.e., his family line). Bo Gwa changing clans is an

---

[6] Ji Baek sought to expand his territory at the expense of the other three families, which, as we have noted, aligned against and destroyed both Ji Baek and his clan.

[7] This battle was fought between the four remaining ministerial clans of the state of Jin in 434 BCE. It led to the division of the state into the three states of Jo, Wi, and Han, and marked the beginning of the Warring States.

[8] In his first attempt to assassinate Jo Yangja, Ye Yang changed his name and became a servant in the Jin palace. He hid in a lavatory, concealing a dagger, and waited for his chance but was discovered before he could act.

[9] Bo Gwa (C. Fu Guo) 輔果 is better known by his original name, Ji Gwa (C. Zhi Guo) 知果. He lived in the state of Jin 晉.

example of this. Ji Seonja (C. Zhi Xuanzi) 智宣子[10] intended to establish [his favorite son] Ji Baek (C. Zhi Bo) 智伯[11] as his heir and did not heed Ji Gwa's (C. Zhi Guo) 知果 remonstrances against this proposal. Ji Gwa then changed his surname [to Bo (C. Fu) 輔], remained out of sight, and avoided catastrophe.[12] How could he be so good at working for himself and so bad at working for his state? Is this really the righteousness appropriate for a minister of a ruling clan?

Oh! If only Ji Gwa had even the slightest understanding of the importance of the ancestral sacrifices and the principle of suffering and celebrating together with family, he would have assisted the designated heir and done his utmost to correct and save him. If, in the end, there was nothing he could do [to help], he would have followed him even in death. If he had been like Historian Eo,[13] who remonstrated even in death, then even though Ji Baek was stubborn, how could Ji Gwa have known that he would not be able, through sincerity, to move him to correct his errors, and thereby avoid the annihilation of the Ji clan? Even if Ji Gwa had died [in the attempt to accomplish this], wouldn't it have been better than to go on living [as he did]? As an alternative, if Ji Seonja failed to follow his advice,[14] Ji Gwa should have gathered up the sacrificial vessels [of the Ji clan] and fled, as did the Viscount of Mi (Mi Ja; C. Wei Zi 微子) of the Eun (C. Yin) 殷 dynasty (ca. 1600–1050 BCE).[15] This too would have been better than changing his surname and thereby cutting himself off from his clan in order simply to go on living. But Ji Gwa turned his back on his lord and forgot his ancestors. So petty, he was too fond of himself; all he cared about was avoiding catastrophe. How profoundly disloyal and unfilial was he! Ye Yang was a minister to a hegemonic clan, but still he did not forsake his responsibilities as a scholar of the state;

---

[10] He became the head of the Ji clan in 493 BCE.

[11] As noted in the previous discourse, he was also known as Ji Yo (C. Zhi Yao) 智瑤. See note 3 above.

[12] After his advice was ignored and Ji Baek was designated as heir, he drew the ire of Jo, Wi, and Han, who then aligned against and destroyed the power of the Ji clan, killing many of them, including Ji Baek. (See the previous discourse.) Foreseeing catastrophe, Ji Gwa abandoned the Ji clan prior to this conflict and took the surname Bo. As a result, he was able to avoid the fate of the rest of this clan.

[13] Historian Eo (C. Yü) 史魚 was a historian of the Spring and Autumn period whose lord repeatedly ignored his advice. When Historian Eo died, he instructed his son to put his corpse beneath his lord's window so he would be moved to reconsider Historian Eo's counsel. Gongja said of him, "Truly straight was Historian Eo. When good government prevailed in his state, he was like an arrow. When bad government prevailed, he was like an arrow." See *Analects* 15.7.

[14] Earlier, when Ji Seonja had intended to establish Ji Yo as his heir, Ji Gwa remonstrated with him, recommending Ji So (C. Zhi Xiao) 智宵 instead, but his advice was ignored.

[15] Mi Ja (C. Wei Zi) 微子, whose personal name was Gye (C. Qi) 啓, was an older half-brother of the bad last king of the Eun dynasty, for which an alternative name is Sang 商.

he sacrificed his own life in an effort to take revenge for his lord. Ji Gwa was a minister to a noble ruling family and acted quite in the opposite manner. Oh! What was in his Heart-Mind?

3. Discourse on Misaeng Go Begging Vinegar

The third discourse concerns a well-known figure, Misaeng Go,[16] mentioned in the Analects, *who is criticized by Gongja for begging vinegar from a neighbor. Gongja's original complaint focuses on Misaeng Go's aim, which turned out to be not helping the person in need but surreptitiously securing the vinegar in order to curry favor with the one who had come to him for help. Yunjidang extends and develops the analysis of this case, considering several additional aspects and hypothetical variations. In the process, she brings to light a number of important moral concerns that while general in nature and related to the problem of moral signaling are particularly salient for relational theories of morality, such as Confucianism.*

[Yunjidang said,] "The Pattern-Principle underlying the creation and transformation of heaven and earth is exceptionally upright.[17] Human beings receive this upright Pattern-Principle at birth and it is without anything crooked or corrupt. Any slight corruption they might incur results in the destruction of the Pattern-Principle received at birth. And so, noble people must be watchful [over their endowment of Pattern-Principle]![18] They are reverent in order to straighten the inner life and righteous in order to square the outer life[19]—all in order to preserve this upright Pattern-Principle. "Although the corruption Misaeng Go incurred in begging vinegar from his neighbor in order to curry favor with another is slight, the injury done to [his] uprightness was great."[20] It is fitting that he did not escape the censure of the sage [i.e., Gongja]. As for those who are upright, they have or lack certain things and take or give certain things; in all respects, though, they remain attentive to what is righteous. If they pretend to lack something that they

---

[16] The theme of this discourse concerns *Analects* 5.24.

[17] Literally, the character translated here as "upright" means "straight" (*jik*; C. *zhi*) 直. Cf. *Analects* 13.18.

[18] Cf. chapter 1 of the *Doctrine of the Mean*, which cautions, "The noble person is watchful over himself when alone."

[19] See section 11 under the hexagram *Gon* (C. *Kun*) 坤 in the *Book of Changes* (*Yeokgyeong*; C. *Yijing* 易經). *Gon* is the second hexagram in the *Book of Changes* and represents earth.

[20] This is a quotation from Jeong I cited by Ju Hui in his commentary on *Analects* 5.23. See Ju Hui, *Collected Commentaries on the "Analects" (Noneo jipju*; C. *Lunyu jizhu* 論語集注) 5.36a.

have, if they pretend to have something that they lack, if they should not take something but take it, or if they should not give something but give it—in all such cases they fail to be upright. How could Go be considered upright!"

Someone asked, "There are situations that are difficult to handle. Consider, for example, if those close to you have a compelling need for something, rely on you to give it to them, and are sincerely reporting their situation. Since one understands that they are going without and their entreaties grow increasingly strong, what is one to do? From what I infer, Go must have had compelling reasons like this. I doubt whether [giving them what they lack in such circumstances] would injure the genuine and generous Way of the noble person. Isn't what you say excessive?"

[I] replied, "Be that as it may, noble people are absolutely straightforward and trustworthy in preserving their Heart-Minds and managing affairs and do not allow the slightest compromise. And so, Gongja would not grant the request of An Ro (C. Yan Lu) 顏路 to sell his carriage in order to buy an outer shell for his son's coffin.[21] In general, one goes against a sincere Heart-Mind and the upright Way when it is not appropriate to give something and one compromises and gives it [anyway]—how could this be so only in the case of An Ro's self-centered [request]? If one "twists one's intentions in order to follow along with things,"[22] one falls into the category of compromise and a lack of uprightness. Though the noble person is genuine and generous, I have never heard of one following such a way."

Someone said, "Be that as it may, if someone's father or brother is ill and he comes and reports the hardship he is suffering and begs for medicine that one lacks but one's neighbor has, then should one still not ask one's neighbor to give him the medicine out of concern that it would harm one's uprightness?"

[I] replied, "No, it would not. Human life is a weighty matter, weightier than the repugnance one feels toward begging from one's neighbor. When there is a weighty matter in play, in response, the repugnance becomes lighter. When Maengja said one should reach out to save one's drowning sister-in-law and that this is a matter of weighing the alternatives,[23] he offered a good example of this kind of case. On the other hand, vinegar is a trivial thing of no

---

[21] See *Analects* 11.8, "When An Yeon died, An Ro begged the carriage of the Master to sell and get an outer shell for his son's coffin."

[22] This is part of Ju Hui's commentary on *Analects* 5.23. See Ju Hui, *Collected Commentaries on the "Analects"* 5.36a.

[23] In *Mencius* 4A17, Maengja argues that one should override the general standing prohibition against men and women touching one another in exceptional cases such as the one presented to him, in which one's sister-in-law is at risk of drowning.

consequence, while begging is an action that by nature we are not inclined to do. How can Go alone not feel this way? Nevertheless, Go forced himself to perform an action most do not want to do in order to secure something of no consequence on behalf of another. The Heart-Mind that motivated his action surely lies in a desire 'to poach the merit of others in order to curry favor.'[24] This is like stealing something from a person's home in order to give it to another. What could entail a greater violation of uprightness than this! If you simply consider this one act, you can understand what kind of man he was. And so, this is why the master repudiated him in such a harsh manner.

When considering whether to beg something from one's neighbor, a noble person must decide the matter by weighing what is heavy and light. If one begs [from one's neighbor] in order to give [to another] and the need involves something substantial—then uprightness is found in doing just this.[25] One cannot simply stick to a single, inflexible rule. Nevertheless, to call Go upright, would this not be odd and perverse? On another day, the master said, 'Human beings are born to be upright. If they lose their uprightness, they will be lucky to escape with their lives.'[26] Those like Misaeng Go would indeed be lucky if they escape with their lives—wouldn't they?"

4. Discourse on What Anja Took Joy in

The fourth discourse again picks up an idea first raised in the Analects *but in this case made famous by Jeong I in his essay on the same theme.[27] Gongja commended Anja, his favorite disciple, for being able to take joy in learning despite his poverty. Yunjidang explores this theme, claiming that the source of Anja's joy was the heaven he discovered within himself. She goes on to explore a number of issues concerning Anja's joy, presented through the form of a dialogue in this discourse. Among these are how he managed to not let his poverty undermine his ability to provide for his parents (for if he failed to provide for them, how could he savor his own joy), how his joy differed from that of Gongja, and whether sagehood and the joy that comes with it are things one can acquire through learning.*

---

[24] This is part of Ju Hui's commentary on *Analects* 5.23. See Ju Hui, *Collected Commentaries on the "Analects"* 5.36a.

[25] Cf. *Analects* 13.18 in which Gongja describes a son who conceals his father's wrongdoing and claims "uprightness is found in doing just this."

[26] *Analects* 6.19.

[27] For a translation, see Tiwald and Van Norden 2014, 152–154.

Someone asked me, "The master said Anja was someone who did not allow his joy to be affected [by hardship].[28] What was it that Anja took joy in?"

I replied, "He took joy in heaven. What is heaven? Heaven is Pattern-Principle. Heaven inherently is within my nature; this is what Anja took joy in. Maengja said, 'The myriad things all are complete within me. To reflect on myself and find that I am sincere—there is no greater joy than this!'[29] Most people have this joy but lose it. Sages possess this joy as their nature[30] and fully develop it. Students [of the Way] understand this joy and seek for it. Nevertheless, joy comes only after learning; without learning, one cannot attain such joy. Among the things that Anja said was, 'What kind of person was Sun (C. Shun) 舜?[31] What kind of person am I? One who exerts oneself [as Sun did] will be like Sun.'[32] The master also said that [Anja] was the kind of person who, 'if he came into possession of one good thing, would clasp it to his breast and not lose it.'[33] This was how earnestly he loved learning. And so, from the fact that he could go 'for three months without having anything contrary to [the standard of] humaneness [in his Heart-Mind]'[34] and 'even when he wanted to give up [learning] he could not'[35] we can understand his joy. He fell short of the joy of sages only ever so slightly. He looked upon the joy of average people as not going beyond concerns about honor and disgrace, gain and loss; why stop at saying [only] that his joy is as different from theirs as heaven is from earth or insects are from snow geese?"

[The questioner further] said, "This is so, but the master said that Anja 'often was in want.'[36] So how could An Ro [his father] have avoided having only bean soup to eat and water to drink?[37] Ordinary people must feel the need to provide for their parents. Could someone as worthy as Anja not worry about not being able to provide for his parents and still be content in his own joy?"

---

[28] *Analects* 6.11.

[29] *Mencius* 7A4.

[30] *Mencius* 7A30 says that "Yo and Sun took it as their nature; Tang (C. Tang) 湯 and Mu (C. Wu) 武 (reigned c. 1046–1043 BCE) embodied it; the Five Hegemons borrowed and made a show of it. Borrowing it for a long time without returning it—how can we know that they did not in fact possess it?" The "it" in question is thought to be humaneness or humaneness and rightness.

[31] Sun was a legendary sage ruler; he is said to have lived sometime between 2294 and 2184 BCE.

[32] *Mencius* 3A1.

[33] *Doctrine of the Mean*, chapter 8.

[34] *Analects* 6.7.

[35] *Analects* 9.11.

[36] *Analects* 11.19.

[37] In the "Dangung" (C. Tangong) 檀弓 chapter (lower part) of the *Book of Rites* (*Yegi*; C. *Liji* 禮記) we find, "Gongja said, 'Only being able to supply one's parents bean soup to eat and water to drink, if one makes them happy, this can be called being filial.'"

I replied, "This is not the case. How could you not have heard about Jeungja (C. Zengzi) 曾子, who was so poor that 'when he straightened his hat, the chin strap would break; when he fastened his collar, his elbows would poke through his jacket'[38] and yet who always provided his parents with wine and meat while working to nurture his resolve?[39] Though Anja was poor, how do you know that he did not work at nurturing his parents as assiduously as Jeungja worked to strengthen his resolve but instead simply ended up with [his father] having only bean soup to eat and water to drink? Moreover, though he worried about being unable to provide for his parents, the object of his worry was [in accord with] heavenly Pattern-Principle; this is to take joy in heaven.[40] How can this be described [simply] as worrying, and how can you suspect that he would allow this to affect his joy? I believe that, for Anja, being in want was his joy in heaven. How could this be? Because in his joy of heaven he forgot his poverty. And so, he was unaware of his poverty and did not consciously seek to avoid it. When he came to be in want, he regarded his being in want as his joy in heaven; is this not fitting? This is why Gongja profoundly admired and commended him. The joy of Gongja and Anja was equally heavenly, but Gongja 'could find joy in eating coarse grain, having only water to drink, and using his bended arm for a pillow,'[41] while Anja, 'having but a single bamboo dish of rice, a single ladle of water to drink, and living in a mean and narrow lane, did not allow his joy to be affected.'[42] The difference between them concerned [finding joy] in [the midst of poverty] versus not allowing [poverty to affect one's joy], making an effort and not making an effort, maintaining [one's joy][43] and transforming [one's joy].

---

[38] Jeungja was another of Gongja's disciples. For the story cited here, see the "Kings Who Have Wished to Resign the Throne" (*Yangwang*; C. *Rangwang* 讓王) chapter of the *Jangja* (C. *Zhuangzi*) 莊子.

[39] The *Jangja* passage previously cited goes on to say that "he who nourishes his resolve forgets about his physical form."

[40] That is to say, his primary concern was making his parents happy and in this he found joy. How he could achieve this might still be a source of worry, but the worry was about the best practical means to this end and not about the ultimate aim of his life.

[41] *Analects* 16.9, where Gongja says that those born with knowledge are the highest type, and those who attain knowledge through learning come next.

[42] *Analects* 6.11.

[43] *Analects* 15.13 describes the need not only to reach the Way through understanding but also to *maintain* what one achieves through humaneness. *Mencius* 2A2 describes different types of courage and says that *maintaining* a state of fearlessness is superior to macho forms of courage and yet inferior to moral courage. So, working to maintain a state, even a good state, still falls short of transforming oneself to fully embody a virtue. Anja had to work to maintain his joy against the challenge posed by deprivation; Gongja found joy simply in pursuing the Way. This is quite close to the distinction that Aristotle drew between the continent and the fully virtuous.

It is not that there are two different types of joy. Had Anja lived into old age[44] in a short time, he would have been transformed and [his joy] would have been the same as that of the sage [Gongja]. How, then, could he have been considered merely a secondary sage! This is why Gongja loved him so profoundly and mourned for him excessively."[45]

[The questioner further] said, "Sages are born with knowledge;[46] this is not something one can attain through learning. And yet, you say that had Anja lived into old age he would not [merely] be regarded as a secondary sage. If this is so, is sagehood something one can attain through learning? I am confused about this."

I replied, " 'Sages and I are the same in kind.'[47] Ordinary people and sages all receive the Pattern-Principle of the Great Ultimate as their nature. It is only because of differences in the degree to which they are ensnared by their endowments of *Gi-Material* and benighted by their desires for things that there are different levels of understanding and ignorance, worthiness and unworthiness. Nevertheless, in terms of the original nature with which they are endowed, they are all the same. And so, those who have awakened understand that the nature they received [at birth] is the same as that of Yo (C. Yao) 堯[48] and Sun. If you seek for it, you will attain it[49]—like someone on the road seeking shelter or someone eating seeking to be full[50]—in order to reach the level of a sage. As for the name 'sage,' it simply denotes someone who is 'great and transforms others.'[51] Maengja said, 'Everyone can become a Yo or a Sun.'[52] If even ordinary people can become a Yo or a Sun, how much more possible is this for someone like Anja, who had the ability of a secondary sage? Nevertheless, if you want to become a sage you should first seek for what Anja took joy in. If you want to seek for what Anja took joy in, you should first learn Anja's love of learning. How can you love learning? By attending to the four prohibitions.[53] [If you want to attend to] the four

---

[44] Anja died prematurely, at the age of thirty-three. See *Analects* 11.10.

[45] See *Analects* 11.10, which describes how deeply Gongja was aggrieved by the early death of Anja.

[46] See *Analects* 16.9. The knowledge here is moral knowledge of the Way.

[47] *Mencius* 6A7.

[48] Yo was a legendary sage ruler; his traditional dates of rule are c. 2356–2255 BCE.

[49] This is a clear reference and close parallel to *Mencius* 7A3.

[50] This line is from a comment by Ho Anguk (C. Hu Anguo) 胡安國 (1074–1138 CE) that is quoted by Ju Hui in his commentary on *Analects* 9.11. See Ju Hui's *Collected Commentaries on the "Analects"* 5.3b-4a.

[51] *Mencius* 7B25.

[52] *Mencius* 6B22.

[53] *Analects* 12.1. The four prohibitions are to not look, listen, speak, or act in any way that is contrary to the rites.

prohibitions, you should begin by [studying] broadly and restraining [your-self in accordance with the rites]."[54]

5. Discourse on Jaro

The fifth discourse addresses several issues that perplexed Yunjidang about the actions of Gongja's disciple Jaro. She notes that while Jaro was quick to criticize Gongja for meeting with a person of questionable reputation, Jaro himself served the state of Wi, which was widely regarded as morally corrupt. Among other things, two successive rulers of the state grossly violated filial piety, behaving "as though they had no fathers." Not only did Jaro not recognize this, but he also failed to understand Gongja's criticism of their behavior, nor apparently did he heed the good advice of his fellow disciples. Yunjidang concludes, "Jaro, de-spite having a great sage as his teacher, and so many worthies as his friends, still violated what was right in his decisions and died an unnatural death."

I have always personally been perplexed by things that Jaro (C. Zilu) 子路 did. Even after reflecting on these carefully, I do not understand why he did as he did. Gongja said, "Do not enter a state that is in danger; do not reside in a state that is in chaos. When all under Heaven has the Way, show yourself; when it lacks the Way, remain hidden."[55] How could someone as worthy as Jaro not understand this principle?[56]

Moreover, Jaro was not pleased that the master visited Namja (C. Nanzi) 南子 (d. ca. 480 BCE).[57] The reason he was not pleased is that it is contrary to righteousness to visit a bad person. While this does not acknowledge that the Way of the sage "lacks any course that is always acceptable or any course that is always forbidden,"[58] still, the principle is correct. Nevertheless, Jaro served the state of Wi. While a bad person (i.e., Namja) served as the mother of the

---

[54] *Analects* 6.27.

[55] *Analects* 8.13.

[56] As is clear by what is described further on, Jaro's most dramatic mistake was serving the ruler of Wi, a state that was morally disordered. This eventually led to Jaro's early death, something that Gongja had predicted.

[57] *Analects* 6.28. Namja was the wife of Duke Ryeong (C. Ling) of Wi (C. Wei) 衛靈公 and wielded considerable influence upon state affairs. She created tension between her husband and son, Goeoe (C. Kuaikui) 蒯聵 (see note 59 below), when she told her husband that Goeoe wanted to kill her. After the death of her husband, she had an incestuous relationship with her brother Song Jo (C. Song Chao) 宋朝, which greatly distressed Goeoe.

[58] *Analects* 18.8.

state, Jaro was one of its ministers, without feeling that this was contrary to righteousness; this contradicts the displeasure he expressed [toward Gongja] earlier. Why? How could someone as worthy as Jaro do something like this? This is the first thing I do not understand [about Jaro's behavior].

Moreover, Goeoe[59] wanted to kill his mother and was driven out of the state by his father; [Goeoe's son] Cheop (C. Zhe) 輒 became the ruler [of Wi], in order to block his father [from ascending the throne]. Both [Goeoe and Cheop] behaved as though they had no father.[60] What could cause greater harm to human relationships and throw into confusion the norms governing them than this! "When someone personally is guilty of doing wrong, a noble person will not associate with him."[61] Jaro had heard this principle proclaimed by the master, and so expressed doubt about the master's desire to accept the invitation of Pil Hil (C. Bi Xi) 佛肸.[62] But now, to the contrary, he abandoned himself to a state where the ruler is without a father, and in the end he died amid its chaos.[63] This is the second thing I do not understand [about Jaro's behavior].

Moreover, Jaro once asked the master, "The ruler of Wi is waiting for you to administer his government. [What will be your first order of business?]"[64] The ruler of Wi, [at the time], was [Goeoe's son] Cheop. The master responded [to Jaro] by discussing the rectification of names. [Jaro] doubted this, saying, "You are wide of the mark." When one considers his response, one can see how profoundly misguided it is, for one as worthy as Jaro, to start off not recognizing that the ruler of Wi was someone who behaved as though he had no father. This is the third thing I do not understand [about Jaro's behavior].

---

[59] Goeoe was the son of Namja and Duke Ryeong of Wi; Goeoe's son succeeded the Duke and became Duke Chul (C. Chu) of Wi 衛出公 but was eventually removed from office. Goeoe ascended the throne as Duke Jang (C. Zhuang) 莊公 (r. 480–478 CE). After assuming office, he had Namja executed.

[60] Cf. *Mencius* 3B14, where Maengja decries how Mukja (C. Mozi) 墨子 is someone who acts as though he was without a father.

[61] *Analects* 17.7.

[62] Jaro explained that since Pil Hil was in active rebellion against his ruler, it would be improper to accept his invitation. See *Analects* 17.7.

[63] In 480 BC, Jaro was serving as a retainer of Gong Hoe (C. Kong Kui) 孔悝, head of the powerful Gong clan in the state of Wi. Goeoe, who was the maternal uncle of Gong Hoe, plotted a coup to depose his own son, Duke Chul, and forced Gong to assist him. He succeeded in ousting his son and ascended the throne. Hearing of this while away, Jaro rushed back to rescue his lord. He entered the city to confront Goeoe but was killed by Goeoe's men. According to the *Book of Rites*, after Jaro was killed, his body was chopped into pieces and pickled. See the "Dangung" chapter (upper part) of the *Book of Rites*.

[64] *Analects* 13.3.

In light of all this, how can we explain Jaro's decision to serve the state of Wi? If his aim was to implement the Way, then the Way of Yo and Sun is nothing more than filial piety and brotherly respect. Is it possible that all under heaven would prefer to have someone who causes great harm to human relationships and throws into confusion the norms governing them implement the Way in their state?

I often have seen the people of the world show their ignorance about "when to undertake duties and when to remain hidden"[65] and instead drown in the desire for profit, indulge themselves in rank and salary, and end up losing their own lives and destroying their families. This moves me to sigh and say, "There is nothing people desire more than life and nothing they hate more than death; how can they exchange their lives for wealth and high status?"[66] Moreover, if one is not able to protect one's own life, how will one be able to use wealth and high status? When I contemplate the behavior of Jaro, I am moved to sigh and say, "The *Book of Poetry* says, 'Intelligent and wise is he, protecting his own person.'"[67]

For someone as worthy as Jaro to serve a ruler who behaved as if he was without a father is to support oneself with an unrighteous salary. Moreover, if like him, one in the end meets with calamity, how can the remonstrances of others be effective? I have heard that Jaro was courageous in the performance of what is right,[68] but when what one hears is not attested by behavior, one fears it is only hearsay. "Whenever someone told him that he had overstepped the bounds of what is right, Jaro was pleased."[69] Is it not the way of true friends to remonstrate and encourage each other to be good? And he had worthy friends such as the disciples An Hoe (C. Yan Hui) 顏回, Jeung Sam (C. Zeng Shen) 曾參, Jae Yeo (C. Zai Yu) 宰予, Min Son (C. Min Sun) 閔損, Jayu (C. Ziyou) 子游, and Jaha (C. Zixia) 子夏. Being in the company of such people, he had those who could "faithfully advise and skillfully lead him"[70] concerning "when to undertake duties and when to remain hidden." Nevertheless, he did as he did—how is this possible? Perhaps Jaro was well advised and still regarded his not knowing as knowing[71] because he believed

---

[65] *Analects* 7.11.

[66] Cf. *Mencius* 6A10.

[67] *Book of Poetry*, Mao #260.

[68] Jaro was renowned for being dauntless and eager to take on heroic tasks. See *Analects* 4.8, 4.26, 7.11, etc.

[69] *Mencius* 2A8.

[70] *Analects* 12.23. This is part of Gongja's response to the question of Jagong (C. Zigong) 子貢 about the nature of friendship.

[71] Cf. *Analects* 2.17.

he was right and simply would not listen! Eeee! One as worthy as Jaro, despite having a great sage as his teacher, and so many worthies as his friends, still violated what was right in his decisions and died an unnatural death. To be like this and moreover never wake up and realize his error but pettily to regard "not letting his cap fall to the ground" as the right way to die[72]—this leads me to even greater confusion. In the end, I am unable to understand [Jaro's behavior]. Perhaps it was because he had an excess of courage but a deficiency of wisdom; so, lacking good judgment, he came to such an end? The master once said, "One like Yu[73] (Jaro) will not die a natural death."[74] Now, this is how things turned out. Is it not sad?

6. Discourse on Ga Ui

Discourse 6 focuses on the Han dynasty scholar-official Ga Ui, a person of impressive talents who also enjoyed the rare good fortune not only of being born in a flourishing age but also being recognized and entrusted with position and power by a worthy lord. Still, Yunjidang argues, Ga Ui failed to deploy his talents effectively and take advantage of all his good fortune; the reason for this was a set of tragic character flaws: he was overly ambitious, impatient, and anxious. These traits eventually eroded the ruler's confidence in him and sowed suspicion and distrust, so that, "in the end, he was unable to develop his abilities and 'died without realizing his aims.'"

Scholar Ga (Ga Saeng; C. Jia Sheng 賈生)[75] spent his youth as a student in Nak Yang (C. Luo Yang) 洛陽.[76] [He lived] in the age of Emperor Mun

[72] When Jaro returned to Wi to defend his lord, he was confronted by Goeoe's soldiers, who attacked him with their spears, cutting the strings of his cap. Jaro's dying words were, "A noble person does not let his cap fall to the ground when he dies." Having said this, he tied the strings again and died. See the *Chronicle of Jwa* (*Jwa Jeon*; C. *Zou Zhuan* 左傳), Fifteenth Year of Duke Ae (C. Ai) 哀公.

[73] Referring to Jaro by his proper name, Jung Yu (C. Zhong You) 仲由 (542–480 BCE).

[74] *Analects* 11.13.

[75] Ga Ui (C. Jia Yi 賈誼) (c. 200–169 BCE), who is also known as Scholar Ga (Ga Saeng; C. Jia Sheng 賈生), as in the discourse below, was a Chinese writer, poet, and politician of the Western Han dynasty and one of the most respected early practitioners of the rhapsody (*bu*; C. *fu* 賦) style of poetry. He is famous for his essay "Discourse on the Faults of the Jin" (*Gwa Jin ron*; C. *Guo Qin lun* 過秦論) in which he criticizes the policies of the dynasty and analyzes the reasons for its collapse, and for the two rhapsodies "On the Owl" (*Bok Jo bu*; C. *Fu Niao fu* 鵩鳥賦) and "Lament for Qu Yuan" (*Jo Gul Won bu*; C. *Diao Qu Yuan fu* 吊屈原賦).

[76] Nak Yang is a city located in the confluence of the Nak and Yellow Rivers in western Hanam (C. Henan) 河南 province.

(C. Wen) 文帝,[77] when everything under heaven was orderly and peaceful and the people took delight in their work; one could say he was born in a flourishing age. Scholar Ga had the ability of Wang Jwa (C. Wang Zuo) 王佐[78] and happened to meet a virtuous ruler, so one can say he was able to serve a worthy ruler. Since he happened to be born in a flourishing age, served a worthy ruler, and also possessed ability, one can say he had the good fortune of living in a period of good order. Since ancient times, it has proven difficult to bring good order [to the world] because even when there were competent rulers, they lacked ministers who could support them, and even when there were talented ministers, they lacked lords they could support. Now, Scholar Ga possessed ability and served a [good] lord; he ought to have developed and extended all that had come his way, but he was unable to do so. Why is this? Was it perhaps because he was too impatient about implementing reforms and his advice was too extreme, which led Emperor Han to suspect he was frivolous and therefore chose not to make use of him? If this were not the case, why then would Emperor Han have been close to him in the beginning but grew distant from him in the end?[79]

Emperor Han was delighted when he first met Scholar Ga and made him a "professor" (baksa; C. boshi 博士) [of the classics]. At the time, Ga Ui was only a little more than twenty years old, but within a year he was promoted, vaulting to the position of Grand Master of the Palace (Taejung Daebu; C. Taizhong Dafu 太中大夫). One could say that he did not follow the standard career path in employment. Scholar Ga requested that the starting day of the calendar be revised, that the color of officials' garments be changed, that the names of offices be fixed, that rites and music be reinvigorated, that Han institutions be set up, and Jin (C. Qin) 秦 (221–206 BCE) laws be amended. The Emperor humbly declined, saying he could not at the time implement [these requests], but he did not reject them outright. Ga Ui then argued that agriculture should be the most fundamental [activity

---

[77] Emperor Mun of the Han 漢文帝 was the fifth emperor of the Han dynasty and had the reputation of consulting with and trusting his ministers. In 165 BCE he introduced the civil service examination as a way to select government officials (220–157 BCE; r. 180–157 BCE).

[78] Wang Jwa (C. Wang Zuo) 王佐 (1126–1191 CE) was an able statesman of the Song dynasty renowned for his loyalty; even after losing an arm in service to his lord, he steadfastly went on to offer him wise counsel.

[79] In the very early stages of his career, Ga Ui enjoyed great favor at court and rose swiftly, but his agitation for institutional reform generated a backlash among older officials, which eventually led to Ga being banished to Jangsa (C. Changsha) 長沙. Ga was brought back in 172 BCE and appointed Grand Tutor, but a riding accident led to the death of the Emperor's youngest son, who was his charge. Ga felt responsible for the accident and died, guilty and grief-stricken, about a year later.

in the state]. The Emperor was moved by his words and personally plowed the fields to lead the people under heaven [to follow his example]. One cannot say that [the Emperor] did not follow his advice. Nevertheless, this is where it ended; one does not hear of [the Emperor] making much further use of Ga Ui's counsel. Must there not be some reason for this?

When Emperor Go (C. Gao) 高祖 (256–195 BCE)[80] "built the foundation of his inheritance and handed down his rule,"[81] So Ha (C. Xiao He) 蕭何 (d. 193 BCE)[82] set up the laws and institutions of the Han (C. Han) 漢 dynasty (202 BCE–220 CE). The grand principles of these already were well established, and their minor features were perfected over the period of time when the Three Dynasties[83] ruled all under heaven; Emperor Mun was a ruler who preserved and perfected these. He only worked at developing genuine virtue and was not at all anxious about initiating reforms. This being so, his natural abilities were refined and outstanding, and his resolve and spirit were bold and high-minded. He was not content with a lower state of peace and prosperity and set his sights of achieving great accomplishments.

What a shame! Scholar Ga's ambition was too sharp, and he did not attend to his affairs in a gradual and steady manner. If one is without the ability to benefit the world, then that will be the end of it, but Ui had the ability. If one does not meet [the right] ruler, then that will be the end of it, but Ui met with a worthy ruler. Since he had the ability and also had [the right kind of] ruler, he should have shown the resolve to serve his ruler just as Go (C. Gao) 皋,[84] Gi (C. Kui) 夔,[85] Yi (C. Yi) 伊,[86] and Bu (C. Fu) 傅[87] displayed and looked to the cultured governance of Yo, Sun, and Tang (C. Tang) 湯 (ca. 1675–1646 BCE)[88] to inspire himself and his ruler. He should have presented forthright[89]

---

[80] Emperor Go was founder and first emperor of the Han dynasty; he reigned from 202 to 195 BCE.

[81] *Mencius* 1B21.

[82] So Ha (C. Xiao He) 蕭何 (d. 193 BCE) was an official who ably served Emperor Go throughout his life, helping him come to power and to defend and develop his reign. After the founding of the dynasty, he became Chancellor and held the office until his death.

[83] The Three Dynasties were the Ha (C. Xia) 夏 (2070–1600 BCE), Eun (C. Yin) 殷 (1600–1046 BCE), and Ju (C. Zhou) 周 (1046–256 BCE).

[84] Go Yo (C. Gao Yao) 皋陶 was Minister of Law under the sage-emperor Sun and a senior adviser to U (C. Yu) the Great 帝禹.

[85] Gi (C. Kui) 夔 was Minister of Music for the sage-emperor Sun.

[86] Yi Yun (C. Yi Yin) 伊尹 was a high minister who helped King Tang of the Eun dynasty defeat King Geol (C. Jie) 桀, the last and wicked ruler of the preceding Ha (C. Xia) 夏 dynasty, and subsequently served the newly established Eun administration.

[87] Bu Yeol (C. Fu Yue) 傅說, also known as Hu Jak (C. Hou Que) 侯雀, was originally a laborer, skilled at making defensive walls. King Mu Jeong (C. Wu Ding) 武丁 (r. 1324–1265 BCE) of the Eun dynasty was impressed by his reputation and devised a way to bring him to court to serve as his minister. He later served as Premier and gained the reputation of being an exemplary official.

[88] King Tang 湯 (c. 1675–1646 BCE), who defeated King Geol, founded the Eun dynasty.

[89] Reading 嘉 as 昌 in the original.

advice and excellent policies to him every day; what should be followed would have been followed; what needed to be revised would have been revised. He should have calmly and gently "opened his heart to enlighten [his ruler]"[90] and "introduced his important lessons [as his ruler's] intelligence allowed";[91] he should have gradually worked to accomplish his aims, polishing his efforts over months and years. Had he done this, how could [a ruler] as worthy as Emperor Mun of Han possibly have failed to make use of him in the end? Ga Ui did not understand this and simply fretted anxiously over changing and revising the laws and institutions, which elicited suspicion and opposition from his ruler. So, in the end, he was unable to develop his abilities and "died without realizing his aims,"[92] with the consequence that for ten thousand generations those under heaven will not recall his past achievements and pass them down to later generations. Is this not sad! Is this not regrettable! Alas! Ability cannot be borrowed from another age, but Ga Ui could have been the Yi Yun or Bu Yeol of his time. And yet, that his worthy lord, in the end, did not make use of his ability must be the work of heaven. What could Ga Ui do about heaven?

7. Discourse on Yi Reung

Discourse 7 concerns the controversial general Yi Reung of the Han dynasty. When defeated by the Hyungno nomads, Yi Reung defected to their side. Some speculate that he did this only to bide his time and wait for a chance to strike down the leader of Hyungno. The Han emperor, taking the advice of ministers who slandered Yi Reung, executed his mother; Yi Reung then wholeheartedly allied himself with the Hyungno. Yunjidang stridently argues against any mitigation of Hyungno's behavior, insisting he was a traitor to both ruler and state. She rejects the idea that he or any defeated general could "bide his time" and one day prove himself loyal, likening his obligation to the strict fidelity a wife must maintain toward her husband.

---

[90] Referring to a line from the "Charge to Yeol" section (*Yeolmyeong*; C. *Yueming* 說命) (upper part) of the *Book of History*.

[91] Quoting a line from the comments on the hexagram *Gam* (C. *Kan*) 坎 in the *Book of Changes*.

[92] Quoting a line from a rhapsody by the poet Gang Am (C. Jiang Yan) 江淹 (444–505 CE) "On Regret" (*Han Bu*; C. *Hen Fu* 恨賦).

[Yunjidang said,] "Whenever I read the *History of the Han Dynasty* (*Hanseo*; C. *Hanshu* 漢書), when I get to the part about Yi Reung (C. Li Ling) 李陵 (d. 74 BCE),[93] I never fail to close the book."

Someone replied, "Yi Reung's surrendering to the Hyungno (C. Xiongnu) 匈奴[94] was not really a dereliction of duty. He lacked the strength to overcome them and his situation had become hopeless, and so he had no choice but to pretend to surrender for the time being so he could plan, at a later date, to avenge the Han dynasty. Were it not for the actions of Yi Seo (C. Li Xu) 李緒,[95] Emperor Mu would not have killed Yi Reung's mother, and had Emperor Mu not killed his mother, Yi Reung surely would have taken the head of the *Seonu* (C. *Chanyu*) 單于,[96] thereby avenging the Han and being forgiven for his crime (of surrendering). Yi Reung's turning against the Han was not his fault; Emperor Mu goaded him into doing so. This is why I say it was not a real dereliction of duty."

[Yunjidang] said, "Such is not the case. Since he already had been derelict in his duty, what is the point of making the distinction between what is real and false [in regard to his surrender]? 'A loyal minister does not serve two lords; an upright woman does not vacillate between two husbands.'[97] A woman who abandons her husband and follows another man, even if she returns [to her husband] the following day, is [still] a wife who has been derelict in her duty. A minister who abandons his lord and serves another state, accepts from it a position and lives off a salary they pay him, even if he returns [to his lord] the following day, flush with success, is still a minister who has been derelict in his duty. Maengja said, 'Life is something I truly desire; righteousness is something I truly desire. If I am forced to choose between them,

---

[93] Yi Reung, courtesy name Sogyeong (C. Shaoqing) 少卿, was a general during the Han dynasty who served Emperor Mu of the Han.

[94] The Hyungno was a confederacy of nomadic people who inhabited the Eurasian Steppe from the third century BCE to the late first century CE.

[95] A year after Yi Reung's defeat and defection, seeing that he too was partly to blame for the fiasco, Emperor Mu sent Gongson O (C. Gongsun Ao) 公孫敖 to rescue Yi Reung. Gongson failed in this mission but captured a Hyungno soldier, who reported that "Yi Sogyeong was training Hyungno troops for the *Seonu*." (For the meaning of *Seonu*, see following note.) Concluding that Yi Reung was indeed a traitor, Emperor Mu had Yi Reung's entire family executed. It was later revealed that Yi Reung was innocent and that Yi Seo 李緒, another high-profile Han defector, was the one who was training Hyungno forces. The confusion arose because Yi Seo happened to share the same courtesy name with Yi Reung: i.e., Sogyeong (C. Shaoqing).

[96] *Seonu* (C. *Chanyu*) 單于 is the abbreviated form of *Taengni Godo Seonu* (C. *Chengli Gutu Chanyu*) 撐犁孤塗單于, which is the title used by the supreme ruler of the Hyungo during the Jin (C. Qin) 秦 (221–206 BCE) and Han (206 BCE–220 CE) dynasties.

[97] Quoting the "Biography of Jeon Dan" (*Jeon Dan Yeoljeon*; C. *Tian Dan Liezhuan* 田單列傳). See the *Records of the Historian* (*Sagi*; C. *Shiji* 史記) 82.5a.

I will give up life and choose righteousness.'[98] Yi Reung was a minister of the Emperor of the magnificent Central Kingdom. On the day of his military defeat, he could not face death and instead kneeled in submission and let himself be imprisoned, willingly becoming the servant of our savage and barbarous enemies. He was abundantly satisfied with himself; he was at peace and felt not the slightest shame. Surely not even dogs or pigs would eat his leftovers. Alas! 'To compromise one cubit in order to make eight cubits straight'[99] is not a path the noble person will follow. To rely on Yi Reung to one day succeed in avenging the Han would be the greatest compromise of all! How could mere trivial achievements ever atone for the dereliction of such an important duty? To serve a lord as minister but to desire to kill him is to be of two minds; this is something not even Master Ye[100] would do.[101] So don't people like Yi Reung offend against Master Ye?"

Someone further asked, "Although at first Yi Reung was derelict in his duty, what do you think about later on? Could he make amends for his transgression?"

[Yunjidang] said, "Given the path that Yi Reung followed, whether at the beginning or the end, there was only death. When his forces were defeated and there was nothing he could do [to reverse the outcome], had he fought with all his strength to the death, like Han Yeonnyeon (C. Han Yannian) 韓延年 (d. 99 BCE),[102] he would not have failed to be a loyal minister. Since he proved incapable of doing this, had he, when hearing that his mother had been killed, sent a memorial to Emperor Mu, saying,

> When I received your orders to strike the enemy, I dared not fail to exert all my strength in doing so. But the few cannot stand against the many, and so I brought disgrace to my lord's command. There is no greater disloyalty than this. I could not face and report this to you, my liege. Instead, I aimed to bear the disgrace for the time being and plan for another day. Though this[103] was my initial intention, the disgrace I have brought to myself and to you my lord is a crime that warrants ten

---

[98] *Mencius* 6A10.

[99] *Mencius* 3B6.

[100] Master Ye refers to the famous assassin Ye Yang 豫讓; see discourse 1.

[101] The idea is that if Yi Reung swore allegiance to the *Seonu* but all along did so in order to assassinate him, this is a degree of deceit and duplicity that not even the assassin Ye Yang would deem acceptable.

[102] Han Yeonnyeon (C. Han Yannian) was Yi Reung's second-in-command who died fighting the Hyungno.

[103] Reading 非 as 其 in the original.

thousand deaths by execution. Nevertheless, I had hoped to enjoy the overwhelming kindness of my liege's humanity, that you would grant me a few more months' time so that I could wring the neck of the *Seonu* right in the celestial court. In this way I might have repaid my liege one ten-thousandth of [what I owed] and brought some solace to the heart of my aged mother. Now, my liege has heeded mistaken information that was conveyed to him and on this basis killed my mother. I am the cause of the death of my mother. Since I disgraced my lord's command and brought shame to my country, I am a disloyal minister. My indescribable offense has now also resulted in my mother's death, making me an unfilial son. To be both disloyal and unfilial is to be the greatest criminal under heaven in ten thousand generations. How can I remain in the world for even a single day more? And so I will kill myself in order to repay my lord and parents.

Had Yi Reung fallen upon his sword and died when the Emperor's envoy arrived, he could have redeemed one ten-thousandth of his prior transgression. But not only was Yi Reung not able to do this, when the envoy the Emperor had sent sought out Yi Reung, he responded to him angrily, saying, 'How can I trust the Han when they have executed my family?' He then became the son-in-law[104] of the *Seonu*, indulged in honors and benefits, and enjoyed wealth and high station. He did not show the slightest care or concern, grief or pain. Oh! Yi Reung's lack of humaneness and disloyalty all reached such a degree as this! Moreover, Yi Reung was not satisfied with only himself becoming a traitorous minister, on behalf of the *Seonu*, he also tried to persuade So Mu (C. Su Wu) 蘇武 (140–60 BCE)[105] to join him. This is just what the lines from the *Book of Poetry* refer to when they say, 'When one stands face to face with another, [one can see him through and through.]'[106] When So Mu refused to listen to him and swore that he would resist unto death, Yi Reung thereupon sighed and said, 'Ah! Such a righteous scholar!

---

[104] The *Seonu* showed Yi Reung considerable favor, giving him his daughter's hand in marriage and conferring upon him the title King Ugyo (C. Youxiao) 右校王, a position of the same rank as the *Seonu*'s chief adviser.

[105] So Mu 蘇武 was a Han ambassador held by the Hyungno. Yi Reung was dispatched twice by the *Seonu* to persuade him to capitulate, as Yi and So had worked together in the past and were good friends. However, So Mu rejected his appeals and instead spoke powerfully and elegantly about how much he valued the honor and responsibility the motherland had given him, telling Yi Reung that for him it is either honor or death. So Mu endured harsh treatment through most of his long captivity while remaining faithful to his mission and homeland.

[106] *Book of Poetry*, Mao #199.

The crimes that I and Wi Yul (C. Wei Lu) 衛律[107] committed reach all the way up to heaven!' He then began to sob and took his leave. Alas! The unvarying standard (byeongyi; C. bingyi 秉彝)[108] is rooted in the Heart-Mind and can never be effaced. Isn't this why [he felt and acted] this way? Yi Reung had lost sight of his original Heart-Mind, but when he saw the genuine virtue and loyalty of So Mu, without even realizing it, he sighed and began to sob. His tears were not put on for others to see; his innermost Heart-Mind broke through and was revealed in the expression on his face.[109] And so, it is said, 'One cannot deceive heaven.'[110] Alas! That whereby human beings differ from birds, beasts, and barbarians is that they have the Three Bonds[111] and Five Human Relationships.[112] In the case of Yi Reung, these relationship and bonds had been destroyed and cut off without a trace. [He was] a human being who had descended to the level of birds and beasts; [a resident of] the Central Kingdom who had become a barbarian. Is this not indeed painful? Is this not indeed sad?"

8. Discourse on On Gyo Tearing the Hem of His Garment

The eighth discourse is about On Gyo,[113] a minister widely renowned for his loyalty and filial piety. Yunjidang argues he was in fact neither filial nor loyal but rather self-centered and covetous of fame. On Gyo has been praised for being so devoted to his lord that when assigned a dangerous mission he immediately broke free from his mother's desperate attempt to hold him back, "tearing the hem of his garment." Yunjidang argues that On Gyo acted on orders

---

[107] Wi Yul was another contemporary defector from the Han dynasty who was favored by the *Seonu*.

[108] The "unvarying standard" refers to the inherent moral disposition of the Heart-Mind. It is first found in the *Book of Poetry*, Mao #260, and cited, with minor textual variation, in *Mencius* 6A6, which employs the variant 秉夷.

[109] The language here is highly reminiscent of *Mencius* 2A6, where Maengja argues that the alarm and concern one spontaneously feels for a child in imminent danger is not put on for others to see in an attempt to bolster one's reputation, etc.

[110] The idea is that one cannot act against one's heaven-endowed nature and avoid feeling ill at ease when one faces what one has done.

[111] The Three Bonds (*sam gang*; C. *san gang* 三綱) are the bond between ruler and subject, parent and child, and husband and wife.

[112] The Five Relationships (*o ryun*; C. *wu lun* 五倫) are the relationship between ruler and minister, the relationship between father and son, the relationship between elder and younger brother, the relationship between husband and wife, and the relationship between friends. The first of the five relationships, between ruler and minister, is defined by loyalty.

[113] The story of On Gyo first appears in the "Blameworthiness and Remorse" (*Uhoe*; C. *Youhui* 尤悔) chapter of *A New Account of the Tales of the World* (*Seseol sineo*; C. *Shishuo xinyu* 世說新語).

*from someone who was not at the time his lord, and so he could have declined
without violating duty. She also argues that it is implausible to believe that On
Gyo was the only person qualified to complete this mission. Furthermore, even
granting that the mission was essential to the survival of the state and On Gyo
was the only one qualified to complete the task, he still should have explained
all of this to his mother and sought her blessing instead of brusquely tearing
himself from her arms. Had he done so, she likely would have sent him to do his
duty, but had she told him to remain, he should have turned down the assignment, for filial piety is the most basic of human relationships and essential for
other virtues, such as loyalty.*

The *Analects* says, "Master Yu[114] said, 'Filial piety and brotherly respect—are
they not the roots of humaneness!'"[115] An ancient text also proclaims, "If you
seek for loyal ministers, look at the gate of filial sons."[116] There has never been
anyone who failed to be filial to their parents and yet proved loyal to their
lord. On Gyo[117] of the Jin (C. Jin) 晉 dynasty (265–420 CE) originally had a
reputation for being earnestly filial throughout his county and village. When
the Western Jin dynasty collapsed (317 CE), the world was thrown into
chaos and confusion, barbarians gathered like clouds on the horizon, and
people like Yu Gon (C. Liu Kun) 劉琨,[118] Dan Pilje (C. Duan Pidi) 段匹磾
(d. 321 CE),[119] and others swore blood oaths with one another and dispatched
representatives and submitted petitions in an attempt to influence the Prince
of Nang Ya (C. Lang Ya) 琅琊 [to assume the throne].[120] Yu Gon said to

[114] Yu Yak (C. You Ruo) 有若 was a disciple of Gongja. He was a native of No (C. Lu) 魯. His courtesy name was Jayak (C. Ziruo) 子若.

[115] *Analects* 1.2.

[116] This line appears in the sixteenth biography (*Yeoljeon je sibyuk*; C. *Liezhuan di shiliu* 列傳
第十六) of the *History of the Later Han* (*Hu Han Seo*; C. *Hou Han Shu* 後漢書), chapter (*gwon*;
C. *juan* 卷) 26.

[117] On Gyo, whose courtesy name was Taejin (C. Taizhen) 太真, known formally as Duke
Chungmu (C. Zhongwu) of Sian (C. Shi'an) (*Sian Chungmu gong*; C. *Shian Zhongwu gong* 始安忠武
公), was a renowned general and governor who lived during the Jin dynasty.

[118] Yu Gon was a Jin general who for years fought but ultimately lost Byeong (C. Bing) Province 并
州 (what is now modern central and northern Sanseo (C. Shanxi) 山西 Province to the Han Jo (C.
Han Zhao) 漢趙 (304–329 CE), a Southern Hyungno state and adversary of the Jin.

[119] Dan Pilje was the governor of Yu (C. You) Province 幽州 (what is now modern Bukgyeong (C.
Beijing) 北京, Cheonjin (C. Tianjin) 天津, and northern Habuk (C. Hebei) 河北.

[120] When Sama Eop (C. Sima Ye) 司馬鄴 or 司馬業, who became Emperor Min of Jin 晉愍
帝 (300–318 CE), the last Western Jin monarch, was captured by the Han, former officials like Yu
Gon, Dan Pilje, and others plotted together to re-establish the Jin dynasty to their own advantage.
Dan killed Yu in 318 CE when he came to believe Yu posed a threat to his own designs on power.
The Prince of Nang Ya is Sama Ye, who became Emperor Won (C. Yuan) of Jin 晉元帝. When the
Hyungno captured Jang An (C. Chang An) 長安 in 316 CE, the capital of Jin, the Emperor, Sama Ye,
was forced to abdicate the throne. Sama Ye had escaped from Jang An to Geon-gang (C. Jiankang)
建康, present-day Namgyeong (C. Nanjing) 南京, and declared himself the new Emperor of Jin.

Taejin (i.e., On Gyo), "I am accomplishing great things in the area north of the Yellow River; you should spread word of this south of the Yellow River and urge him [Sama Ye (C. Sima Rui) 司馬睿 (276–322 CE; r. 317–322 CE)] [to claim the throne]."[121] Taejin accepted this mission and made preparations to depart. As he was about to leave, his mother, Madam Choe (C. Cui) 崔, took hold of his lapel, but Taejin pulled away abruptly, tearing the hem of his garment, and departed. His mother's taking hold of his lapel was the highest expression of a mother's love for her child. Not considering the moral imperative to save the world in her time, she thought only that he might fall into danger and perish. Her son tore the hem of his garment because he worried that his mother would not let go and he would be unable to successfully complete his work and gain renown throughout the world. Alas! The relationship between parent and child is the first of the Five Relationships, and mutual love between them is heavenly Pattern-Principle. Completing one's work is the basis for gaining fame and benefit, but the desire for success is self-centered.[122] To allow the self-centered [desire] to complete one's work to harm the greatest affection to be found among the Five Relationships—even someone lacking in humaneness would be unlikely to do such a thing. How much less someone like Taejin, who enjoyed the reputation of being filial? How could he bear to do this?

Oh! For those who serve as ministers, on occasions when they must carry out their lord's commands in circumstances of danger and chaos, it is right that they are not swayed by personal affection. Nevertheless, they should keep in mind their parents' anxiousness and distress, remember that they are in their parents' thoughts, and should find it difficult whenever they must bow and take leave of them. [Moreover,] what Taejin did was not a case of carrying out his lord's commands; rather, this was the command of Yu Gon. So why did Taejin not accede to his mother's request and arrange for someone else to carry out [this mission]?"

Someone said, "Yu Gon had to send Taejin; isn't this clearly the case? If he had sent someone else and that person had miscarried the affair, then the revival of the Jin could not be assured. This is also the reason Taejin could not refuse the mission."

Yunjidang replied, "That is not so. There has never been an age with as much overflowing talent as was available in their time. How could there be

---

[121] In other words, Yu Gon commissioned On Gyo to make his way to Geon-gang to present Sama Ye, the Prince of Nang Ya, with his petition to assume the imperial title, which subsequently he did.

[122] On the concept of self-centeredness, see note 42, p. 18.

no one other than Taejin to take up this assignment? Moreover, at the time, Taejin and Emperor Won were not yet established in the relationship of ruler and minister, and so had he acceded to his mother's request and not gone, what harm would that have done to his loyalty? Oh! When he tore the hem of his garment and left, what did this do to his mother's heart? The *Book of Poetry* says, 'Oh father!—you gave me life; Oh mother!—you nourished me. . . . The kindness I wish to repay is as limitless as the heavens.'[123] If Taejin was as earnestly filial as was said of him in his time, how could he have endured behaving as he did? This is why I say, when we consider this affair, we know that he was not really sincerely filial; we also know that he was not really loyal to his lord."

Someone said, "Originally Taejin had the reputation of being fervently loyal and magnanimous because when his state had been destroyed and his lord disgraced and he was overcome with sincere sadness and indignation, he worked together with Yu Gon and others of like mind to establish Emperor Won and plan for the revival of the state. The survival or destruction of the Jin depended on their actions. Though you say that, at the time, Taejin and Emperor Won were not yet established in the relationship of ruler and minister, how, on that day, could any minister of Jin bear to sit idly by and watch as the temples and ancestral altars [of the Jin] were cut off and the territory of the Central Kingdom lost [to barbarians] without thinking of some way to revive the state? It is true that Taejin was unable to realize both perfect loyalty and filial piety; why though do you criticize him so severely?"

Yunjidang replied, "That too is not so. Had his mother been fortunate enough to enjoy a thorough understanding of the situation, as Jin Yeong's (C. Chen Ying) 陳嬰 (d. 183 BCE) mother[124] was, she would have urged him to be careful but still sent him on his mission. Then, from the very start, he would have been able to realize both loyalty and filial piety. Now, since this was not the case, as a son, he should have assumed a pleasing countenance and pleasant expression, explained [to his mother] in detail the extreme situation the state was in and what duty demanded of him as a minister. He should have waited until he was able to resolve any remaining doubts she might have and ensure that she was at ease; then, he should have calmly

---

[123] *Book of Poetry*, Mao #202.

[124] Jin Yeong lived at the very end of the Jin (C. Qin) 秦 dynasty (221–206 BCE) and the beginning of the Han 漢 dynasty. As the Jin collapsed, a group of people who were leading the revolt came to him and urged him to declare himself king. His mother, though, advised him against this, arguing that since the overthrow of the Jin was not complete, to accept such a sudden rise in status would pose great peril. He followed his mother's advice and refused to accept the title of king.

bowed and taken his leave. In this way, within (i.e., toward his family) he would have realized filial piety to his parents and without (i.e., to his lord) he would have fulfilled his duty to be loyal to the state. What, in the end, are his renowned achievement and outstanding reputation worth, given that he earned them by tearing the hem of his garment, stabbing [the heart of his mother's] affection, and being able to endure forsaking his obligation to be a filial son? Maengja said, 'If the blind man (i.e., Emperor Sun's father) had killed someone, Sun would have fled secretly carrying his father on his back and settled by the shore of the sea, delighting in his life and forgetting all about the empire.'[125] If even the empire can be regarded [so lightly], how much easier should this be when it is merely self-centered achievement and advantage? Abandoning his parents and stabbing [the heart of his mother's] affection with an eye toward realizing mundane ends—is this really the way a filial son behaves? Can one who behaves this way avoid offending against the great [Emperor] Sun? If, as someone said, there was no one else who could have been sent on this mission, Taejin was the one person needed to ensure the revival of the Jin dynasty, he had no prospect of resolving his mother's doubts, he felt the difficulty of fulfilling both the duties of loyalty and filial piety, and [under these circumstances] he acted as he did, then Taejin's behavior might be forgiven. Now, since this was not the case, and still he behaved as he did, we must wonder how a son could bear to do such a thing and how it could be motivated by anything other than a self-centered desire for gain.

Oh! The supreme tender feelings of a loving mother will always focus on her son's safety in times of chaos; it is only fitting that such feelings will go to any extreme. If her son, after tearing the hem of his garment and departing, died amid the chaos and she was unable to see him again, what pain would this loving mother have felt to the end of her days! Even if he did not die while abroad, if when he returned, his aged mother, ill with anxiety and worry, had already passed away, even if Taejin were then to have wept until he was old and toothless, what good would it have done? Though he mourned until he was withered and wasted, how could this atone for his behavior? One who is filial is accommodating and compliant. Can one really call Taejin's tearing the hem of his garment and departing accommodating and compliant? Alas! Someone like Taejin is indeed lucky that the learned have not condemned him. I cannot believe he really had the reputation for

---

[125] *Mencius* 7A35.

being earnestly filial in his time. Alas! Filial piety is the source of the hundred good types of behavior. Since he lost the original source, even if he fully developed all the worthy capabilities under heaven, he still would not be worth talking about. Even if one completely exhausts oneself in working ardently for the imperial family, still, if one is not filial to one's parents, one cannot really be loyal to one's lord. What would such efforts amount to? If, when his mother took hold of his lapel, Taejin had immediately acceded to her will, politely declined Yu Gon's request, and to the end of his life taken care of her in a simple thatched hut, thereby being the perfection of a filial son, then, though he might not have been famous in his own time, how could he not have enjoyed glory for ten thousand generations thereafter?[126] In the past, Jegal Gongmyeong (C. Zhuge Kongming) 諸葛孔明[127] lived at the end of the Han dynasty. He plowed his own fields and did not seek to become famous. Later on, in response to three personal visits by Emperor Soyeol (C. Zhaolie) 昭烈皇帝,[128] he subsequently served him and succeeded in implementing his 'three-legged tripod' strategy,[129] which led to his immortal reputation. And so, if one cultivates virtue in oneself, then one's reputation naturally will become outstanding. If one lacks virtue and first thinks about establishing a name for oneself, though one might achieve some renown in a given age, one will not avoid being held up as the subject of critical discussions for ten thousand generations. Dong Jungseo (C. Dong Zhongshu) 董仲舒 (179–104 BCE)[130] said, 'Humane people correct their principles and do not plot to achieve gain; they make clear the Way and do not calculate their personal achievement.'[131] We can say that people like Taejin turn their back on the

---

[126] The idea being both that the only reputation worth having is to be a moral person and that good people do in fact often attain a kind of immortality for their good deeds.

[127] Better known as Jegal Ryang (C. Zhuge Liang) 諸葛亮 (181–234 CE), his courtesy name was Gongmyeong (C. Kongming) 孔明. He was a politician, military strategist, writer, engineer, and inventor who lived during the Three Kingdoms period 三國時代 (220–280 CE) in China. He is widely recognized as the most accomplished strategist of his era. He was the Prime Minister of Yu Bi (C. Liu Bei) 劉備 (see following note) and along with general Yi Eom (C. Li Yan) 李嚴 (d. 234 CE), whose courtesy name was Jeongbang (C. Zhengfang) 正方 and was also known as Yi Pyeong (C. Li Ping) 李平, was appointed by Yu Bi as regent to his son and successor Yu Seon (C. Liu Shan) 劉禪 (207–271 CE, r. 223–263 CE).

[128] Emperor Soyeol is the posthumous name of Yu Bi (C. Liu Bei) 劉備 (161–223 CE), whose courtesy name was Hyundeok (C. Xuande) 玄德. He founded the state of Chok Han (C. Shu Han) 蜀漢 (221–263 CE) during the Three Kingdoms period.

[129] In which he pitted different states against one another in ways that all contributed to the victory of the lord he served.

[130] Dong Jungseo was a Han dynasty Chinese scholar. He is traditionally associated with the promotion of Confucianism as the official ideology of the Chinese imperial state.

[131] These lines appear in Dong Jungseo's *Luxuriant Dew of the "Spring and Autumn Annals"* (*Chunchu beollo*; C. *Chunqiu fanlu* 春秋繁露) 17.14a.

proper standard of the Way and put working for gain as their highest priority. They themselves ruin the source of the hundred good types of behavior; is this not why they cannot avoid the censure of noble people?"

9. Discourse on Sama Ongong

The ninth discourse focuses on the famous Song (C. Song) 宋 *dynasty (960–1279 CE) scholar-official Sama Gwang (C. Sima Guang)* 司馬光 *(1019–1086 CE) and his historical masterpiece, the* Comprehensive Mirror on Government.[132] *Yunjidang objects to Sama Gwang's support, in this work, of the warlord and poet Jo Jo and his son as constituting the legitimate line of succession of the Han dynasty. Yunjidang insists Jo Jo intentionally worked to weaken and undermine the legitimate heir and usurp his throne. She rejects several of Sama's arguments and others put forth by an anonymous interlocutor and insists that his support and praise of Jo Jo's disloyalty and desire for power violate an eternal "constant governing heaven and earth and an unchanging principle from ancient times to the present." She concludes that Sama and his historical masterpiece are morally flawed and cannot compare to Gongja and his composition of the* Spring and Autumn Annals. *Gongja purportedly composed the latter work in a way that always makes clear who acted rightly and wrongly by employing a complex and at times subtle strategy of historical "praise and blame" (popyeom; C. baopian* 褒貶*).*[133]

Sama Ongong (C. Sima Wengong) 司馬溫公 was a worthy minister of the Song dynasty. [On the basis of his claim that] "Throughout the course of my life, I have never said anything improper to another,"[134] one can know just how worthy he was. What more is there to say on the matter? Nevertheless, some of his views are contrary to the greatest principle expressed in the *Spring and Autumn Annals*.[135] How could this have come about? Was it

---

[132] Ongong (C. Wengong) 溫公 was one of posthumous names of Sama Gwang, who was a Chinese historian, writer, and politician and author of the monumental historical work the *Comprehensive Mirror on Government* (*Jachi tonggam*; C. *Zizhi tongjian* 資治通鑑). Sama was a political conservative and fiercely opposed the comprehensive social, economic, administrative, and military reforms, collectively known as the "New Policies" (*Sinbeop*; C. *Xinfa* 新法) of Wang Anseok (C. Wang Anshi) 王安石 (1021–1086 CE). (See Yunjidang's "Discourse on Wang Anseok," discourse 10 in this volume.)

[133] For a discussion of this method of historical writing and the general theory and practice of Chinese and Japanese historiography, see the selections in Beasley and Pulleyblank 1961.

[134] Something Sama Gwang said of himself as quoted in his biography in the *History of the Song* (*Song Sa*; C. *Song Shi* 宋史) 336.17a.

[135] As is clear in what follows, Yunjidang sees this work as offering the clearest and most important principles governing the proper relationship between a minister and his ruler.

simply, as Emperor Sinjong (C. Shenzong) 神宗 (r. 1067–1085 CE) said, because he was abstruse and recondite,[136] or was it because he suffered from some blind spot and was not aware of his error? How could such a worthy man be like this? I have always personally been perplexed about this and have yet to explain it to my own satisfaction. And so, I here write down my views on [this matter] and offer them for discussion.

Heaven gave birth to the myriad things, but what makes human beings alone the most precious[137] is that they have the Three Bonds and Five Relationships. Among the Five Relationships, that between ruler and minister[138] is foremost. The principle governing [this relationship] is, in every way, decided, and one should not violate it in the slightest. This is a constant governing heaven and earth and an unchanging principle from ancient times to the present. And so, when Gongja wrote the *Spring and Autumn Annals* (*Chun Chu*; C. *Chun Qiu* 春秋), he was particularly careful about this [i.e., the principle governing the relationship between ruler and minister].[139] Jo Don (C. Zhao Dun) 趙盾 (d. circa 601 BCE)[140] was not punished for being a brigand, but the book [i.e., the *Spring and Autumn Annals*] proclaims, "Jo Don killed his lord."[141] When Jin Hang (C. Chen Heng) 陳恒 (d. 345 CE)[142] killed Duke Gang (C. Kang) 康, [Gongja] was compelled to carry out

<hr>

[136] Emperor Sinjong asked Yeo Gongjeo (C. Lü Gongzhu) 呂公著 (1018–1089 CE) whether Sama Gwang was abstruse and recondite. Yeo answered that even Gongja and Maengja were considered abstruse. See the *Desultory Records from the Studio of Corrigibility* (*Neung gae jae mallok*; C. *Neng gai zhai manlu* 能改齋漫錄) 13.16a–b. For the references to Gongja and Maengja, see *Analects* 13.3 and the *Records of the Historian* 74.1b.

[137] A very close paraphrase of lines found in a variety of early texts including the *Yeolja* (C. *Liezi*) 列子, *Garden of Persuasions* (*Seol Won*; C. *Shuo Yuan* 說苑), and *Confucius's Family Teachings* (*Gongja gaeo*; C. *Kongzi jiayu* 孔子家語) but used here to make a quite different point.

[138] This could also be translated "ruler and subject," and at times the second suggested translation is more in keeping with the argument that follows.

[139] This invokes a widely held belief that in composing the *Spring and Autumn Annals* Gongja did so in a way that subtlety encoded "praise and blame" judgments about the people and events covered by the text.

[140] Jo Don, posthumously known as Viscount Seon of Jo (Jo Seonja; C. Zhao Xuanzi 趙宣子), was a nobleman and minister of the state of Jin (C. Jin) 晉. In 607, Duke Ryeong of Jin (Jin Ryeonggong; C. Jin Linggong 晉靈公) attempted to assassinate Jo Don but failed. After learning of the duke's intention, Jo Don fled; his cousin Jo Cheon (C. Zhao Chuan) 趙穿 killed the duke in a peach orchard while Don was making his escape. Since Jo Don agreed with his cousin's intent and was the duke's subject and minister, Gongja's verdict was that he had "murdered his lord."

[141] See the *Spring and Autumn Annals*, Second Year of Duke Seon (C. Xuan) 宣公.

[142] Jin Hang, also known as Jeon Sang (C. Tian Chang) 田常, was a high minister of the state of Je (C. Qi) 齊 during the late Spring and Autumn period (770–fifth century BCE). In 481, Jeon Sang assassinated his erstwhile partner Gam Ji (C. Kan Zhi) 闞止 and Duke Gan (C. Jian) 簡公 (r. 484–482 CE) and enthroned the Duke's brother Prince O (C. Ao) 鰲, also known as Duke Pyeong (C. Ping) 平公 (r. 481–456 CE) and declared himself Counselor-in-Chief of Je. He was posthumously granted the title Viscount Jeon (Jeon Seongja; C. Tian Chengzi 田成子).

ablution and request that he be punished.[143] How could this principle [i.e., that governing the relationship between ruler and minister] not be regarded as supremely serious and important! Alas! There is nowhere between heaven and earth where one can flee and avoid the principle governing the relationship between ruler and minister. If one violates this principle, unless one's lord's crimes are as reprehensibly bad as those of Geol and Ju (C. Zhou) 紂,[144] or one is a minister who served heaven by saving the people, like King Tang or Mu,[145] one will not be able to avoid being branded as a rebel and traitor. How much less permissible is it [to violate this principle] in a case like that of Emperor Heon (C. Xian) 獻,[146] who in his youth inherited the morally bankrupt practices of Emperors Hwan (C. Huan) 桓 and Ryeong (C. Ling) 靈[147] and was manipulated by the traitor [Dong] Tak (C. Zhuo) 卓 (d. 182 CE).[148] While Emperor Heon did not have the talent and virtue to overcome [the growing internal] chaos, neither did he commit any wrong worth mentioning. But the cunning villainy of Jo Jo (C. Cao Cao) 曹操 (155–220 CE),[149] following and extending the sly treachery of [Dong] Tak, coerced and deceived [the Emperor] into allowing chaos and rebellion to take hold, his lord-and-father to be put in dire jeopardy, and the power of the Empress dowager to be usurped and her life taken.

---

[143] *Analects* 14.21 says, "Jin Seongja (C. Chen Chengzi) 陳成子 murdered Duke Gan 簡公 of Je. Gongja bathed, went to court, and informed the duke Ae (C. Ai) 哀, saying, 'Jin Hang has killed his sovereign. I beg that you will undertake to punish him.'"

[144] For King Geol, see note 86 above. Ju was the last and wicked king of the Eun dynasty.

[145] King Tang or "Tang the Successful" (Seong Tang; C. Cheng Tang 成湯) overthrew Geol, the last ruler of the Ha dynasty, and founded the Eun dynasty. King Mu overthrew Ju, the last ruler of the Eun dynasty, and founded the Ju dynasty; he is also known as King Mu of Ju (Ju Mu wang; C. Zhou Wu wang) 周武王. In both cases, they were subjects of the rulers they overthrew, but their rebellions were understood as serving heaven, not their own ambitions, and so they are regarded as pious liberators and not rebels.

[146] Emperor Heon (C. Xian) of Han 漢獻帝 (181–234 CE) was the fourteenth and last emperor of the Eastern Han dynasty (the restored Han dynasty; 25–220 CE). Throughout his reign, he served as the puppet for various warlords and in the end was forced by Jo Jo's (C. Cao Cao) 曹操 (c. 155–220 CE) son to abdicate, marking the formal end of the Han dynasty and the beginning of the Three Kingdoms period in China.

[147] Emperor Ryeong of Han 漢靈帝 (156–189 CE) was the twelfth emperor of the Eastern Han dynasty. He was chosen to be Emperor after the death of his predecessor, Emperor Hwan (C. Huan) of Han 漢桓帝 (132–168 CE) who had no heir of his own.

[148] The warlord Dong Tak deposed the previous emperor, Emperor So (C. Shao) of the Han 漢少帝 (176–190 CE), whose name was Yu Byeon (C. Liu Bian) 劉辯, and replaced him with his puppet, Emperor Heon. Dong Tak then murdered the former emperor along with his mother, Empress Dowager Ha (C. He) 何皇后 (d. 189 CE).

[149] Jo Jo was a Chinese warlord and the second to last chancellor of the Eastern Han dynasty. He is often portrayed as a cruel and merciless tyrant but has been praised by others as a brilliant ruler and military genius. He had great success as the Han chancellor, but his handling of Emperor Heon of the Han was heavily criticized and seen as the cause of a continuing and later escalating civil war. He was posthumously granted the title Grand Ancestor Emperor Mu of Wi (C. Wei) 魏太祖武皇帝.

[Jo Jo] did everything that a [true] minister could never dare or bear to do. In the end, after [facilitating the] usurping of the throne, he said to his son, "I have become [another] King Mun."[150] Alas! King Mun was a great sage. All under heaven who had cases to litigate went to King Mun and not to Emperor Ju; those who sang songs of praise, sang of King Mun and not Emperor Ju.[151] And so, while King Mun commanded [the allegiance of] two-thirds of all under heaven, *he still led the state that would rebel against the Sang*, in service to the Eun (Sang).[152] And so, Gongja commended him as someone of superlative virtue.[153] Now, [Jo] Jo used his cunning arts to threaten the Son of Heaven and steal his throne. The only thing he did not do is to force the king to abdicate and directly take his place. But for him to have the temerity to declare himself another King Mun is like the usurper Wang Mang (C. Wang Mang) 王莽 (ca. 45 BCE–23 CE)[154] comparing himself to the Duke of Ju! Oh! It makes one groan with pain! His darkly cunning and brutally venomous crimes reach all the way to heaven; he is ten times worse than [Wang] Mang or [Dong] Tak. For a thousand years to come, people's hatred of him will still lead them to want to dine on his flesh. Later historians are proper and correct to courageously and with clear eyes write at length and with special focus to rectify his crimes of rebellion and usurpation so that he is not counted as one among the legitimate line of emperors or kings, and so ten thousand generations of rebellious ministers and treacherous sons can gain some understanding of why the great principle governing the relationship between ruler and minister absolutely cannot be violated. But an exception [to this rule] is found in the opinions of Sama Gwang, who says, "When the ruler of

---

[150] While some view Emperor Heon as a puppet under Jo Jo's control, Jo adhered to a strict oath that he would not usurp the throne. When his own supporters urged him to do so he replied that should heaven bring about the King's abdication, he would "become another King Mun." His point was that he himself would not claim the throne but would instead prepare the way for his son to do so (as King Mun prepared the way for his son King Mu). This in fact is what happened; Jo Jo's second son, Jo Bi (C. Cao Pi) 曹丕 (c. 187–226 CE), forced Emperor Heon to abdicate and took over the throne in 220 CE.

[151] Cf. *Mencius* 5A5, 6.

[152] Emphasis added. The first and last phrases of this sentence are from *Analects* 8.20. The middle clause, "he still led the state that would rebel against the Sang," is part of Ju Hui's commentary on a poem about King Mun in the *Book of Poetry*. See his *Collected Comments on the "Book of Poetry"* (*Sigyeong jipjeon*; C. *Shijing jizhuan* 詩經集傳) 1.9a. In the original, the second Sang 商 appears as Eun, which is an alternative name of the same dynasty. The line celebrates the virtue of King Mun, who attracted the support of the people of the Sang but who, being a vassal of the dynasty, refused to openly rebel against the Sang, His son, King Mu, did so and established the succeeding Ju dynasty.

[153] This is said in the concluding line of *Analects* 8.20.

[154] Wang Mang, whose courtesy name was Geogun (C. Jujun) 巨君, was a Han dynasty official who seized the throne from the Yu (C. Liu) 劉 family and founded the Sin (C. Xin) 新 dynasty, ruling from 9 to 23 CE. Traditionally, he is regarded as a definitive example of a usurper.

Han had moved,[155] the Grand Ancestor (i.e., Jo Jo) welcomed and assisted him, working earnestly to remove obstacles and impediments and establish the dynasty. His fame and honor were enough to bind the people together." He also said, "Jo Jo[156] took all under heaven from a thief;[157] he did not take it from the house of Han,"[158] and "[Emperor] Mu of Wi[159] (i.e., Jo Jo) attained a great achievement for all under heaven."[160] I for one do not understand what Sama Gwang meant by "a great achievement." Had Jo Jo been purely and completely loyal and virtuous, upheld and welcomed the heaven-appointed king, cleared away all the thieves and robbers, saved the royal line in order to secure the ancestral temples and altars and settle all within the four seas, then of course one could say this of him (i.e., that he had "achieved a great achievement for all under heaven"). Now, Jo Jo applied his Heart-Mind and exerted every effort, was always hurrying about pursuing urgent matters, but he did so not on behalf of the imperial house. Rather it was all part of his hidden plot to usurp the throne; it was only gutter-level self-centeredness and nothing more! How can it possibly qualify as a "great achievement"? One can say the same thing about [his] gutter-level sons, grandsons, ministers, and people. How could Sama Gwang describe it as he did? Since he said what he did, what does this imply about people who behave as Jo Jo did? In the end, don't Sama Gwang's words imply that all those who, since ancient times, have pacified disorder and suppressed thieves in their states while usurping the power of their lords should be described as "[those who] took power from

---

[155] In 195, Emperor Heon managed to escape from Jang-an, where he had been under the control of former subordinates of the recently assassinated Dong Tak, and return to the ruins of Nak Yang 洛陽. Without resources or advice, the young emperor soon became stranded, but a year later, Jo Jo led his forces into Nak Yang, received Emperor Heon, and took him under his protection; he escorted him to Heo (C. Xu) 許, now called Heo Chang (C. Xu Chang) 許昌, where the new imperial capital was established.

[156] The text literally reads Wi (C. Wei) 魏 (220–266 CE), also known as Jo Wi (C. Cao Wei) 曹魏, which was one of the three major states that competed for supremacy over China in the Three Kingdoms period. It was established by Jo Bi in 220 CE, based upon the foundations laid by his father, Jo Jo, toward the end of the Eastern Han dynasty. The name "Wi" first became associated with Jo Jo when he was named the Duke of Wi 魏公 and later vassal King of Wi 魏王 by the Eastern Han ruler Emperor Heon. In 220, Jo Bi forced Emperor Heon to abdicate and took over the throne, establishing the state of Wi. However, Yu Bi 劉備 immediately contested Jo Bi's claim to the Han throne and declared himself Emperor of Chok Han 蜀漢. A year later, Son Gwon (C. Sun Quan) 孫權, who was nominally a vassal king under Wi, declared independence and eventually proclaimed himself Emperor of O (C. Wu) 吳 (222–280 CE), thereby establishing three competing states.

[157] That is to say, he took it from the usurper Dong Tak, who put Emperor Heon in power and then manipulated him.

[158] See the *Records of Surveying the Past* (*Gyegorok*; C. *Jiguqi* 稽古錄) 30.22a.

[159] Emperor Mu of Wi 魏武帝 is part of the posthumous name of Jo Jo.

[160] See the *Comprehensive Mirror on Government* 68.32a.

thieves" and not "rebels and traitors"? This is an issue over which I have felt profoundly perplexed.

Moreover, since Emperor Soyeol of the Han was a relative in the [legitimate] lineage of the house of Han and possessed both the natural disposition of a hero and was renowned throughout all under heaven for being trustworthy and righteous, surely he would have been able to rid the state of wicked thieves, realize the great work of illuminating and offering aid to all, and thereby lead the house of Han to flourish. [But] by means of a treacherous plot, [Jo Jo] first occupied a position of power, then surreptitiously siphoned away the authority of the Han, swallowing up half of all under heaven. The state of O (C. Wu) 吳, moreover, occupied all the land east of the Yangja (C. Yangtze) 揚子 River. And so, Emperor Soyeol was only able to maintain one-third of the tripod, in the area of Yangik (C. Liangyi) 梁益,[161] and before he could achieve half of his great work, unfortunately, he died in midcourse. This is something that for a thousand years shall cause great heroes and resolute scholars to wring their hands and sigh. How one applies the title "emperor" is a weighty and important issue, and a principle the *Spring and Autumn Annals* upholds with supreme seriousness and rigor. And yet, now, Sama Gwang grants that the state of Wi represents the legitimate line of succession and confers the title "emperor" upon Jo Jo; contrary to [this important principle], he regards the ruler of Chok Han as a usurping "king" and casts Yu Bi as representing an illegitimate line of succession. What can this mean?

Someone said, "In their time, different heroic figures were vying with each other within the four seas. While the three kingdoms [of Chok Han, Wi, and O] each represented one of the three legs of a tripod, the state of Wi controlled eight-tenths of all under heaven. There is a natural ranking between [those with] a greater [share] and [those with] a lesser [share]; if this is used to decide who is legitimate and who illegitimate, then the legitimate line of succession properly belongs to the one with the greater share. This is the basis upon which Sama Gwang continued to recognize the status quo of the history of the state of Jin[162] and could not but grant that the state of Wi [was the legitimate successor]."

---

[161] Meaning he held one-third of the land within the Three Kingdoms. Yangik is a combination of Yang Province 梁州 and Ik Province 益州 and is now part of contemporary Sacheon (C. Sichuan) 四川 Province.

[162] The Western Jin (C. Jin) 西晉 (266–316 CE), which initiated the Jin dynasty 晉朝 (266–420 CE), was established as a successor state to Jo Wi (C. Cao Wei) 曹魏 when Sama Yeom (C. Sima Yan) 司馬炎, whose courtesy name was Anse (C. Anshi) 安世, usurped the throne and declared himself to be Emperor Mu (C. Wu) of Jin 晉武帝.

Yunjidang replied, "This is not so. According to the principle observed by the *Spring and Autumn Annals*, even if the imperial house is small and weak, it must be honored; even if a usurping state is large and powerful, it must be regarded as illegitimate. What one honors and what one deems illegitimate are determined only from the perspective of principle. How can one make such an assessment based upon whether [a state] is large or small? If one were to follow such a line of reasoning, then Wang Mang[163] should be regarded as [the legitimate] Emperor of the Sin (C. Xin) 新 dynasty; how then can one not regard Wang Mang as Emperor and only single out Jo Jo as worthy of such? [According to such a line of reasoning,] Emperor Won (C. Yuan) 元帝 (276–323 CE)[164] did not inherit the legitimate line of succession in the state of Jin; how then can one grant [the title of emperor] to Won and only single out Soyeol as illegitimate? If, at that time, the state of Chok Han did not exist and Wi possessed all under heaven, then one could not regard them as usurpers and there would be no legitimate candidate to continue the line of succession. Now, though Ik Province[165] was tired and worn out, it was still the legitimate descendant of the house of Han. Although it was unable to unify all under heaven and rectify all of the people within the four seas, nevertheless it continued the legitimate succession of the rule of Emperor Heon and showed that the house of Han had not come to an end or been cut off. And so, if we do not grant them the proper and legitimate line of succession, then to whom should we grant this?

It is only appropriate and proper to trust completely the words of someone as worthy and wise as Jegal Gongmyeong; this is why Yu Bi went to pay his respects to him three times even though he was living in a simple straw cottage. When [Yu Bi] first claimed the throne and declared himself the Soyeol Emperor, the Soyeol lineage became the legitimate line of succession for the Han dynasty. Isn't it evident and exceedingly clear that the Yu Song (C. Liu Song) 劉宋 dynasty (420–479 CE)[166] no longer had any claim worth

---

[163] See note 154 above. Traditionally viewed as a usurper, which is the view that Yunjidang upholds, others have understood him as a visionary and selfless social reformer whose efforts unfortunately ended in chaos.

[164] Emperor Won (C. Yuan) of Jin (C. Jin) 晉元帝 (276–323 CE), whose personal name was Sama Ye (C. Sima Rui) 司馬睿 and courtesy name Gyeongmun (C. Jingwen) 景文, was an emperor of the Jin (226–420 CE) and the first of the Eastern Jin (317–420 CE).

[165] Ikju (C. Yizhou) 益州 was one of thirteen administrative regions established by Emperor Mu of Han dynasty. At its height it included parts of today's Sacheon, Junggyeong (C. Chongqing) 重慶, Unnam (C. Yunnan) 雲南, Gwiju (C. Guizhou) 貴州, most of Hanjung (C. Hanzhong) 漢中 and northern Myanmar, and a small part of Hobuk (C. Hubei) 湖北. Here it refers to the state of Chok Han.

[166] The Yu Song dynasty, also known as Former Song 前宋 or Southern Song 南宋, was the first of the four Southern Dynasties that succeeded the Eastern Jin 東晉 (317–420 CE). It was founded by Yu

discussing? And yet, Sama Gwang thereupon said, 'As for the relationship of the Soyeol lineage to the Han, since the time of King Jeong of Jungsan (Jungsan Jeong Wang; C. Zhongshan Jing Wang 中山靖王),[167] the relatives of this clan stretch over a long period of time; we cannot accurately recount how many generations have passed, and their names and the positions they held are difficult to distinguish clearly. And so, I dare not compare Emperor Gwangmu (C. Guangwu) 光武 (5 BCE–57 CE)[168] with Emperor Won of the Jin or trace all of the lineal descendants of So (C. Zhao) of Han 漢昭帝 (94–74 BCE).'[169] Yet, of what value would such [information] be? If we say Soyeol is not a legitimate progeny of the Han lineage, wouldn't [Jegal] Gongmyeong be deceiving us? If we say the relatives of his clan stretch over a long period of time and we cannot affirm all of the descendants of So of Han, then can we single out usurping thieves and affirm them as legitimate perpetuators of the lineage? He [Sama Gwang] refers to Soyeol (Yu Bi) as a 'King of Han' and then refers to him as 'Emperor [of Han].' [But] when Han attacked Wi, he described this as 'Jegal Ryang, the minister of the Han, [launched a foreign] invasion';[170] when Wi attacked Han, he referred to this as 'the Emperor attacked Han.'[171]

When I read the *Comprehensive Mirror on Government*, whenever I get to places like this in the text, I can't bear to look and don't want to look. Without being aware of what I am doing I turn away from the text and sigh. Oh! While people's opinions are not always the same, how can it be that someone as worthy as Sama Gwang could be so wrong! Alas! Had Ju Hui not written his *Outline and Detailed Account of the "Comprehensive Mirror on Government"*

Yu (C. Liu Yu) 劉裕 (363–422 CE), whose surname together with "Song" forms the common name for the dynasty.

[167] King Jeong of Jungsan (Jungsan Jeong Wang; C. Zhongshan Jing Wang 中山靖王) is the posthumous name of Yu Seung (C. Liu Sheng) 劉勝 (d. 113 BCE). His father was Emperor Gyeong (C. Jing) 景 (188–141 BCE), and he was the elder brother of Emperor Mu of Han.

[168] Emperor Gwangmu (C. Guangwu) of the Han 漢光武帝 (5 BCE–57 CE), born Yu Su (C. Liu Xiu) 劉秀, was an emperor of the Han dynasty. He restored the dynasty in 25 CE and thus founded the Later Han or Eastern Han. He ruled over parts of China at first but consolidated all of China by the time of his death. Yu Su was one of the many descendants of the Han imperial family. Following the usurpation of the Han throne by Wang Mang and the ensuing civil war during the disintegration of Wang's short-lived Sin dynasty, he emerged as one of several descendants of the fallen dynasty claiming the imperial throne.

[169] Emperor So (C. Zhao) of Han 漢昭帝 (94–74 BCE), born Yu Bulreung (C. Liu Fuling) 劉弗陵, was the Emperor of the Western Han dynasty from 87 to 74 BCE. Emperor So was the youngest son of Emperor Mu of Han. By the time he was born, Emperor Mu was already sixty-two. Prince Bulreung ascended the throne after the death of Emperor Mu in 87 BCE. He was only eight years old. See the *Comprehensive Mirror on Government* 69.16a–b.

[170] *Comprehensive Mirror on Government* 1b.

[171] Cf. *Comprehensive Mirror on Government* 78.5b. "昭欲大舉伐漢." So 昭 indicates Sama So (C. Sima Zhao) 司馬昭 (211–265 CE), Emperor Mun (C. Wen) of Jin 晉文帝.

(*Jachi tonggam gangmok*; C. *Zizhi tongjian gangmu* 資治通鑑綱目)[172] in order to make clear the meaning of the *Spring and Autumn Annals*, those in later ages who harbor wickedness [in their hearts] or look askance at the sacred position of the Emperor, would rely on this as a pretext and grow innumerable in number; who could control the calamity they would cause? Alas! The harm that comes from failing to investigate thoroughly always brings about this kind of result!"

10. Discourse on Wang Anseok

The subject of discourse 10 is another famous Song dynasty scholar-official, Wang Anseok. Wang was a renowned scholar who won the attention and support of Emperor Sinjong, who endorsed and implemented a series of reforms, known as the "New Policies," that Wang had proposed to enrich and strengthen the state. Despite his immense learning and the support of his ruler, Yunjidang claims he failed to achieve "a single good result." The reason, she suggests, is that he put the material welfare of the state above the practice of humaneness and righteousness. As a result, he in fact weakened the state, leading to its eventual defeat at the hands of a Jurchen-led army. Wang's obsession with his New Policies was fed by his failure to learn from the classics and consult and cooperate with his peers, which in turn led to his indulging in and stoking factionalism within the court. These various personal character flaws led Yunjidang to conclude that "his Heart-Mind and actions truly are those of a petty person."

There are two ways to govern the states of the world; one is called the Way of the True King, the other the Way of the Hegemon. What is meant by the Way of the True King? It is to carry out humaneness and righteousness with a solid and sincere Heart-Mind. This was [the way of] King Yo, Sun, Tang, and Mun. What is meant by the Way of the Hegemon? It means to make a pretense of humaneness and righteousness in order to get the people to submit. This was [the way followed by] Duke Hwan (C. Xuan) of Je (C. Qi) 齊桓 and Duke Mun (C. Wen) of Jin (C. Jin) 晉文. Maengja said, "The Five Hegemons offend against the three kings."[173] Nevertheless, such people [i.e., those who employ the Way of Hegemons] still know how fine humaneness and righteousness

---

[172] A reworked, condensed version of the *Comprehensive Mirror on Government*, written by Ju Hui.
[173] *Mencius* 6B27.

are, and if they "hold on to it for a long time without returning it"[174] they can "unify and rectify the whole kingdom."[175] If we look at people like Wi Ang (C. Wei Yang) 衞鞅 (390–338 BCE)[176] or Beom Jeo (C. Fan Ju) 范雎 (d. 225 BCE),[177] they did not understand what it is to accord with humaneness and righteousness but only how to realize [material] benefit. They only worked at enriching the state and strengthening the military. They promoted their ideas among the rulers of their day, poisoning and afflicting the people, and causing utter misery throughout all under heaven. Such people differ [from hegemons] and so Maengja [went on to] say, "The feudal lords today offend against the Five Hegemons."[178] Oh! [The desire for material] benefit truly is the pivot upon which chaos turns! And so noble people take humaneness and righteousness to be of benefit; they do not take benefit (i.e., material profit) to be of benefit.

Now, Wang Anseok (C. Wang Anshi) 王安石 (1021–1089 CE)[179] is famous throughout all under heaven as a Confucian scholar of the classics. The great scholar-officials throughout the world all say, "If Anseok did not come forth, how would things have been for the people?" From this one can know that he carried the hopes of his age. He also enjoyed the good fortune that Emperor Sinjong was committed to achieving something great. Having heard of Wang Anseok's fame, he raised him up and delegated to him the weighty affairs of all under heaven. One cannot say either that Wang Anseok's support from the ruler or his ability to implement his policies in governing the state were short-lived or less than absolute. [And so,] he should have approached the ruler and warned him to accord with the Way of the ruler, as exemplified by Yo and Sun, and exerted himself to follow the Way of the minister, as exemplified by [Hu] Jik (C. Hou Ji) 后稷[180] and Seol (C. Xie) 契.[181] Had he

[174] *Mencius* 7A30, which says that those who practice the Way of the Hegemon for long enough, who feign the Way of the True King and become habituated to it, can achieve many of the benefits of sagely rule and may even, perhaps, become virtuous.

[175] *Analects* 14.17 says, "Gwan Jung (C. Guan Zhong) 管仲 acted as Prime Minister to the Duke Hwan (C. Huan) 桓, made him hegemon over all the princes, and unified and rectified the whole kingdom." He achieved this end by less than ethical means and so does not represent the ideal of the Way of the True King.

[176] Wi Ang, also known as Sang Ang (C. Shang Yang) 商鞅, was a strategist employed by the Emperor of the Jin (C. Qin) 秦 dynasty.

[177] Beom Jeo, whose courtesy name was Suk (C. Shu) 叔, was a strategist from the state of Wi (C. Wei) 魏 (430–225 BCE) who lived during the Warring States period.

[178] *Mencius* 6B27.

[179] Wang Anseok, whose courtesy name was Gaebo (C. Jiefu) 介甫, was a Song dynasty economist, poet, and official. He served as chancellor and is famous for attempting to implement a radical and controversial set of social and economic reforms known as the New Policies (see note 191 below).

[180] Hu Jik was Emperor Sun's Minister of Agriculture.

[181] Seol was Emperor Yo's Minister of Commerce.

done so, he would have brought order and peace to all under heaven and enabled the myriad people to take joy in their work; so how would he ever have suffered a lack of needed material resources?

Yuja (C. Youzi) 有子[182] said, "When the hundred surnames have enough, how could the ruler alone fail to have enough? When the hundred surnames do not have enough, how could the ruler alone have enough?"[183] What excellent words! Only once those who work for all under heaven understand this principle[184] shall their kindness flow to those below and their governing be successful. Oh! How could Anseok aspire to anything that falls short of the standard set by Jik and Seol? And yet, if we look at what he did, he went well beyond what even the Five Hegemons did not do. He put what is primary and essential outside and what is secondary and derivative inside. He only cared about material goods and profit; he only thought about wealth and power. He ardently followed in the footsteps of Wi Ang and Beom Jeo and failed to focus on the hardships and distress of the people or worry about bringing peace to all under heaven. Subsequently, he caused the virtue[185] of the Song dynasty gradually to decay until one day it began to gallop into ever greater chaos and destruction from which none could save it. It ended in the northern attack[186] suffered by Emperors Hwijong (C. Huizong) 徽宗 (1082–1135; r. 1100– 1126 CE) and Heumjong (C. Qinzong) 欽宗 (1100–1161; r. 1126–1127 CE), which forced Emperor Gojong (C. Gaozong) to move south.[187] Alas! Who is to blame for this?"

---

[182] Yu Yak (C. You Ruo) 有若 (518–458 BCE), whose courtesy name is Ja Yu (C. Zi You) 子有, was a disciple of Gongja.

[183] *Analects* 12.9.

[184] Reading 意 as 義 in the original.

[185] The word translated here and elsewhere as virtue is *deok* (C. *de*) 德, which has the sense of moral excellence, power, vitality, and innate disposition.

[186] This refers to what is widely known as the "Jeonggang Incident" (*Jeonggang sabyeon*; C. *Jingkang shibian* 靖康事變) or the "Humiliation of Jeonggang" (*Jeonggang ji chi*; C. *Jingkang zhi chi* 靖康之恥), which occurred in 1127 when the Jurchen-led army of the Geum (C. Jin) 金 dynasty (1115–1234 CE) laid siege to and sacked Byeonnyang (C. Bianliang) 汴梁, present-day Gaebong (C. Kaifeng) 開封, which was then the capital of the Song dynasty. The Jin forces captured the Song ruler, Emperor Heumjong (see following note) along with his father, Hwijong (see following note) and many members of the imperial family as well as many officials of the Song imperial court.

[187] Emperor Hwijong (C. Huizong) of Song 宋徽宗 (1082–1135; r. 1100–1126 CE) was the eighth Song emperor. He abdicated in 1126, when the Jurchen-led Jin army attacked the Song and passed the throne to his eldest son, Jo Hwan (C. Zhao Huan) 趙桓, who assumed the title Emperor Heumjong (C. Qinzong) 欽宗 (1100–1161; r. 1126–1127 CE) (while Hwijong assumed the honorary title of "Retired Emperor" (*Taesang Hwang*; C. *Taishang Huang* 太上皇). The following year, the Song capital was conquered by Jin forces in an event historically known as the Jeonggang Incident (see previous note). Emperor Hwijong, along with Emperor Heumjong and the rest of their family, were taken captive by the Jurchens and brought back to the Jin capital in 1128. The Jurchen ruler, Emperor Taejong (C. Taizong) 太宗 (1075–1135; r. 1123–1135 CE) gave the former emperor Hwijong a title, Duke Hondeok (*Hon Deok Gong*; C. *Hun De Gong* 昏德公; literally "Besotted

Someone said, "Lord Hyeong (C. Jing) 荊 (Wang Anseok)[188] loved learning and immersed himself in [the affairs and works of] ancient times. And so, his vision was far-ranging and broad, but his personality was narrow and limited, and he was prone to being stubborn and inflexible. And so, consequently, he ended up harming his state and gained a reputation for being a petty person. [But] as for his intent, he was an honest and incorruptible scholar; simply to describe him as a petty person is unfair."

Yunjidang replied, "That is not so. Formerly, I used to think along the lines of what you say. Now, after reconsidering the record of his words and actions along with what the Grand Scribe (Tae Sa Gong; C. Tai Shi Gong 太史公)[189] has noted and reflecting on it carefully, I have concluded that his Heart-Mind and actions truly are those of a petty person. Why do I say this? The policies and actions of noble people are like the cool breeze that blows or the moon that rises after it rains; their Heart-Minds are like the bright sun high in the heavens. They do not deviate in even the slightest way from what is proper but are just, public-spirited, easygoing, and upright. They do not separate themselves from things; they 'take the Heart-Mind of heaven and earth as their own Heart-Mind.'[190] Now, Anseok, being an accomplished Confucian scholar of the classics, regularly looked upon the laws and government of the former kings with his own eyes and recited the instructions bequeathed by the sages and worthies with his own mouth; he met up with a ruler committed [to achieving something great], who gave him responsibility for the grand affairs throughout all under heaven, and he had command of the state for ten years. And yet, there is no record of him achieving a single good result; all he ever did was delight in those who agreed with him and loath those who did not. He delighted in and was close with those who approved of implementing the New Policies.[191] He loathed and rejected those who disapproved of implementing the New Policies. The result was

---

Duke"), to humiliate him. After his surviving son, Jo Gu (C. Zhao Gou) 趙構, declared himself Emperor Gojong (C. Gaozong) 高宗 (1107–1187; r. 1127–1129 CE), the dynasty's tenth emperor, the Jurchens used him, Heumjong, and other imperial family members to put pressure on Gojong and his court to surrender.

[188] Wang Anseok was often called Lord Hyeong (C. Jing) 荊公, "Thorny Lord."

[189] Tae Sa Gong (C. Tai Shi Gong) 太史公 indicates Sama Cheon (C. Sima Qian) 司馬遷, the author of the *Records of the Historian*, the first comprehensive history of China.

[190] The quote is a paraphrase of a line from the biography of Po Seon (C. Bao Xuan) 鮑宣 (d. 3 CE), courtesy name Jado (C. Zidu) 子都, a Han dynasty censor known for his integrity and courage. See the *History of the Former Han Dynasty* (*Jeon Han Seo*; *Qian Han Shu* 前漢書) 72.33a.

[191] The New Policies were a sweeping set of reforms devised and enacted by Wang Anseok, including policies concerning government organization, the economy, and the military, designed to enrich and strengthen the state.

that with each day he came closer and closer to becoming a petty person and grew farther and farther from being a noble person. This is what Guyang Su (C. Ouyang Xiu) 歐陽脩 (1007–1072 CE)[192] meant when, in his 'Discourse on Factionalism,'[193] he said, 'Cultivated people become friends with cultivated people; petty people become friends with petty people.'[194] What an exemplary maxim this is! Now, all those that Anseok promoted and employed were wicked, treacherous, slanderers, flatters, extortionists, and exploiters,[195] so how could Anseok avoid ending up becoming a petty person? A great minister employs people to serve his lord, but Anseok blocked and drove away those who did not hesitate to speak forthrightly [to the ruler]. 'A great minister serves his ruler with the Way; if something is inappropriate, he stops,'[196] but whenever Anseok's proposals were not accepted, he immediately went to his lord and pressured him [to agree]; when his lord expressed appreciation for his proposals, he would stop and not bring them up again. What he held in his Heart-Mind and how he managed the affairs [of state] were never wholly aligned. This is how he consistently behaved—is this really the manner of a Confucian scholar?

Moreover, a ruler should stand in awe of natural disasters and be anxious about what people say, but Anseok said, 'Natural disasters do not warrant awe; one should not worry about what people say.'[197] From ancient times down to the present, there has been no end to those who have earned the reputation for being petty people, but I have yet to hear of any who have said anything like this! There was only one reason Anseok said such things: it was simply because he feared that the New Policies would not be implemented. In the end, when the New Policies proved disastrous for the state, even Anseok must have recognized this. And yet he firmly maintained them without change; what was in his Heart-Mind?] Looking at it in this way, [it is clear

---

[192] Guyang Su, whose courtesy name was Yeongsuk (C. Yongshu) 永叔, was a Chinese scholar-official, essayist, historian, poet, calligrapher, and epigrapher of the Song dynasty.

[193] Guyang Su's essay "Discourse on Factionalism" (Bung Dang Ron; C. Peng Dang Lun 朋黨論) was aimed to overcome the worst effects of factional politics by appealing to the difference between cultivated and petty people and the values that unite them.

[194] See A Later Collection on the True Treasure Great Compendium of Detailed Explanations of Ancient Writings (Sangseol Gomun jinbo daejeon hujip; C. Xiangshuo Guwen zhenbao daquan houji 詳說古文眞寶大全後集) 7.4b–5a.

[195] Reading 剖剋 as 掊克 in the original.

[196] Analects 11.24.

[197] Wang Anseok was notorious for proposing what is widely known as the "Three Things That Do Not Warrant Awe" (Sam bu jok oe; C. San bu zu wei 三不足畏), which are recorded in his biography in the History of the Song. There he says, "[Sudden] natural changes are not worthy of awe; one's ancestral lineage is not a worthy model; one should not worry about what people say." See History of the Song 327.14a.

that] even though adopting [the New Policies] would lead to the collapse [of the state], he simply did not care. Alas! Had Wang Anseok controlled the state for an additional ten years, then the disgrace of the attack in the north would not have waited until the time of Emperors Hwijong and Heumjong; the need to move the capital south would have occurred during the time of Emperor Sinjing. This is why I say that the only reason the Song imperial line was fortunate enough not to be cut off was because Wang Anseok left the state after not too long and died!"

11. Discourse on Ak Bi Obeying the Order to Recall the Army

The eleventh and final discourse focuses on the actions of the Han dynasty General Ak Bi. Emperor Gojong had ordered Ak Bi to destroy the invading Jin army and he pursued this mission with zeal and commitment. After dealing the Jin forces a devastating blow, Ak was about to complete his victory when orders came to withdraw and return to the capital. Yunjidang argues against the view, advanced by an unnamed interlocutor, that he was right to immediately obey the order to withdraw, arguing that he should have garrisoned his troops and dispatched an urgent request for more time to complete his conquest of the invading forces. She notes that the command to withdraw was instigated by the wicked chancellor Jin Hoe and so did not directly represent the Emperor's view. Furthermore, it contradicted his original order, which was perfectly aligned with the strategic good of the state. Yunjidang notes that when a general is abroad, he enjoys greater independence of judgment; drawing upon a famous passage in the Mencius *for support, she argues that General Ak failed to rely upon his own discretion (gwon 權), something one must do in order to achieve "action that always is proper."*

Someone said, "Everyone thinks that Ak Mumok (C. Yue Wumu) 岳武穆 (1103–1142 CE)[198] [obeying the order] to recall the army was wrong. Nevertheless, Gongja hastened to obey his ruler's order; [upon receiving news that he was summoned] "he did not wait for the horses of his carriage

---

[198] Ak Bi (C. Yue Fei) 岳飛, whose courtesy name was Bunggeo (C. Pengju) 鵬舉 and posthumous name (*siho*; C. *sahu* 諡號) Mumok (C. Wumu) 武穆, was a Han Chinese general best known for leading Southern Song forces in the wars during the twelfth century between Southern Song and the Jurchen-ruled Jin dynasty to the north. He was put to death by the Southern Song government in 1142 after being falsely accused of dereliction of duty but is widely regarded in China as a patriot, folk hero, and the epitome of loyalty.

to be yoked but set off immediately."[199] How then could Ak Mumok, who, in one day, received twelve gold tablets [with the Emperor's orders written on them] not recall the army?"[200]

Yunjidang replied, "That is not correct. Gongja's not waiting for the horses of his carriage to be yoked is the ritual norm for serving one's ruler. Duke Ak's case differs from this; he was under orders to suppress the traitors. The Emperor gave Ak the order, 'I delegate to you responsibility for the restoration of the state.'[201] Duke Ak replied to his ruler, 'Now, since you desire to restore the state, you first must correct the foundation of the state in order to give peace to the Heart-Minds of the people. Then you must not remain for long in the place you now reside,[202] in order to show that you have not forgotten your intention to take revenge.'[203] Ruler and minister took a vow, calmly but resolutely encouraging one another to take revenge [upon the invading Jin army]. Duke Ak, with his enduring loyalty, spit in his hands [and slapped them together], dedicating himself to the task of avenging his state; such was his commitment that he swore to sacrifice his life without regret and no matter what! At this time, the people of Jin had violated the [peace] treaty [with the Song], which multiplied his army's fighting spirit a hundred-fold; there was no stopping them! His forces had dealt the barbarians a severe blow, and he was close to restoring the original borders [of the state]. His advance [across the territory] was like the rolling up of a mat. Though the orders of his ruler were a weighty matter, how could he retreat and return home after only going halfway and completely abandon the task ahead? It is eminently clear that it was not proper for him to withdraw."

[Someone] said, "That is true enough but it is not the whole truth. When, earlier, he embarked on his punitive expedition he was following his ruler's

---

[199] *Analects* 10.13.

[200] In 1141, Emperor Gojong, following the advice of his chancellor, Jin Hoe (C. Qin Hui) 秦檜 (1090–1155 CE), ordered Ak Bi to abandon his successful campaign against the Jin army and return to the capital. His orders were delivered on twelve gold tablets. Gojong did not want the Song army to defeat the Jurchens, as this might enable his half-brother, the last emperor of the Northern Song dynasty, Emperor Heumjong, who was living in exile, to be recalled, which would result in Gojong losing power. Emperor Gojong then imprisoned Ak Bi on trumped-up charges and had him and his son put to death.

[201] A close paraphrase of lines found in the *History of the Song*, chapter 365, year 10.

[202] Emperor Gojong had re-established the Song dynasty (historically known as the Southern Song) and was proclaimed Emperor Gojong in the city of Geon-gang, which at the time was a temporary residence for the remnants of the Song. Ak Bi was urging him not to remain there for too long in order to avoid giving the impression that he accepted the status quo and did not intend to retake the north.

[203] A close paraphrase of lines found in the *History of the Song*, chapter 365, year 10.

orders. On this day, his withdrawal of the army was also following his ruler's orders. In both cases he was equally following his ruler's orders. Now, on the day in question he received twelve [golden] tablets [conveying his ruler's orders] and yet did not return, so he clearly was guilty of failing to obey his orders. Given the path that Ak Mumok was on, what could he have done that would have enabled him to honor both of the orders [i.e., the earlier and later orders, that he had received]?"

[Yunjidang] replied, "That is the case. Duke Ak should have garrisoned his troops in Eonseong (C. Yancheng) 郾城[204] and dispatched an urgent memorial to the Emperor saying,

> I, your minister, received orders to suppress the traitors, and their complete annihilation is imminent. I request my liege to grant me a few more months' time; I swear that I will offer the ears of our enemies before the imperial ancestral shrine and take revenge against those with whom we cannot bear to live under the same sky. I shall wipe away the shame that for ten thousand generations would be difficult to efface. I will thoroughly cleanse the area south of the Mongolian Desert and restore the central plains. Afterward, I will return, bow my head before the great axe, and accept punishment for my crime of violating your orders; I, your minister, will smile when entering the underworld and die without regret. This opportunity [to annihilate the enemy] cannot be lost; such a chance will be difficult to realize again. And so, I cannot obey your imperial edict.

If he had done this, even though Emperor Gojong was confused at the time, he certainly would not have issued another decree. Even though [Chancellor] Jin Hoe was wicked, he would not have dared to open his mouth again. Afterward, [Ak Bi] could have led the Three Armies [of the Song] to thoroughly cleanse the central plains, return them to the two emperors [Emperor Gojong and his father, who was being held captive at the time], and turn himself in to the minister of punishment to answer for his earlier crime. His awe-inspiring loyalty and righteousness and the glory of his achievements would have moved heaven and earth and rivaled [the

---

[204] The site of a decisive engagement, known as the Battle of Eonseong (*Eonseong ji jeon*; C. *Yancheng zhi zhan*) 郾城之戰, which took place in 1140 near modern-day Ruha (C. Luohe) 漯河 in Hanam Province. Under Ak Bi's command the Chinese forces won a major victory against the Jurchen-led Jin army, despite being outnumbered.

brilliance of] the sun and the moon. Then, even though Emperor Gojong had lost sight of his original good Heart-Mind, the unvarying standard endowed by heaven cannot be eradicated and effaced. Above, he would have delighted in having his father, the Emperor, and his mother, the Empress, return alive; below, he would have enjoyed the good fortune of regaining the territory of his ancestral line. Without being fully aware of it, 'His hands would begin to dance and his feet would step in time.'[205] While the Emperor could not reward Ak Bi for his accomplishment, he would not think any crime had been committed! Alas! While discretion (*gwon*; C. *quan* 權) in responding to changing circumstances and handling affairs is something that must not be used lightly, it is also something that at times one cannot but employ. For example, Emperor Sun married without first informing his parents[206] and Maengja endorsed grabbing the hand of one's sister-in-law [to prevent her from drowning].[207] Had Sun first informed his parents [of his intention] he would not have been able to get married; had he not gotten married he would have been without posterity and become a violator of filial piety.[208] If one does not grab one's [drowning] sister-in-law's hand she will perish, and if one's sister-in-law dies one will become a killer of his sister-in-law. How does Ak Bi's obeying the imperial edict, withdrawing the army, and thereby failing to exact revenge [against the Jin] differ from these examples? The teaching about discretion refers to weighing and measuring things that are heavy and light;[209] this is [the way to achieve] what is called 'action that always is proper.'[210]

Oh! Duke Ak's wisdom did not reach the point of comprehending discretion; he did not realize that he had, to the contrary, fallen into the class of those who are disloyal to the state. Moreover, when a general is abroad, there are certain of his ruler's commands that he should not accept. Under normal circumstances, a ruler remains deep within the imperial palace, so he is not able to assess foreign military affairs in far-away regions. And so, Emperor Mun of the Han said to Ju Abu (C. Zhou Yafu)[211] 周亞夫 (d. 143 BCE), 'Affairs outside the imperial realm are under the control of you, my

---

[205] Lines used by Maengja to describe the spontaneous way we can begin to accord with moral principle. See *Mencius* 4A27.

[206] *Mencius* 4A26 and 6A2.

[207] *Mencius* 4A17.

[208] *Mencius* 4A26.

[209] *Mencius* 1A7.

[210] *Doctrine of the Mean*, chapter 25.

[211] Ju Abu was a famous Han dynasty general who was responsible for putting down a major rebellion; he was known for his honesty, integrity, and military discipline.

general.'[212] Gojong already had commissioned Ak Bi to suppress the traitors; because of the treachery of Jin Hoe, the Emperor later summoned him to return, but the summons really was made by Jin Hoe and not Gojong; so, was it proper for Ak Bi to immediately return without questioning the command? Had Gojong himself issued the summons, since [Ak] Mumok already had been given responsibility for [military operations] outside the imperial quarters, his duty to avenge the state would be weighty, while the offense of disobeying orders would in contrast be light; so it would definitely not have been proper to suddenly withdraw the army upon receiving the imperial edict, since this would have been to work against the strategic plans of the state. Alas! Ak Bi did not understand 'action that always is proper.'[213] On the one hand, he could not annihilate the traitors on behalf of the state and enjoy being loyal throughout the course of his life; on the other hand, he could not see the opportunity and take it, and be like Han Sechung (C. Han Shizhong) 韓世忠 (1089–1151 CE),[214] riding his donkey along the shores of West Lake. Instead, both father and son were executed and lost their heads at the hands of a wicked traitor. What a pity! This is why I make a special effort to discuss this case, as a warning to those in later generations who do not understand the propriety of discretion and might, to the contrary, fall into disloyalty."

---

[212] A line found in the biographies of Jang Seokji (C. Zhang Shizhi) 張釋之 and Pung Dang (C. Feng Tang) 馮唐, two outstanding scholars who served Emperor Mun of the Han. See *Records of the Historian*, Biographies (*Yeoljeon*; C. *Liezhuan* 列傳), chapter 42.

[213] *Doctrine of the Mean*, chapter 26.

[214] Han Sechung was a contemporary Chinese general who, like Ak Bi, dedicated his life to serving the Song dynasty. He performed many legendary feats; it is said that he had scars all over his body and, by the time he retired, there were only four fingers left on each of his hands. When Ak Bi was executed, he realized the extent of the corruption that plagued the Song court and retired from military service. After he retired, he often was seen riding a donkey along the shores of West Lake (Seoho; C. Xihu 西湖). He would take a bottle of wine, sit beside Ak Bi's grave, and sprinkle a bit of wine upon it. As he did so, he would address Ak Bi with soft and moving words.

Colophons (跋)

1. Addendum to Carrying Forward My Late Husband's Work on the *Book of Poetry*

Eee! This is a work by my late husband that he could not complete. Among the handwritten manuscripts left behind by my husband are works on the *Book of History* (*Sangseo* C. *Shangshu* 尚書), *Book of Poetry*, the *Songs of Cho*, and some miscellaneous writings. But his work on the *Book of Poetry* was only half complete, the characters were written in a variety of different styles, and the work was mixed in with some of his old papers. If he had had a son, then he could have carried forth his father's intention and completed this work. Now, since he did not have a son, completing this work posed a challenge. Since it was mixed in with his old writings, making sure it did not become scrap paper used to cover some jar[1] was also a challenge. I am poignantly aware that it is inappropriate for me, his surviving wife, to wield my brush and carry forward my husband's work. Nevertheless, this was all he left to us. Had I not completed this piece while my remaining breath was yet to expire, then the traces he had left behind would simply have faded into oblivion. I was secretly anguished about this, and yet whenever I thought of carrying forward these unfinished remnants, I could never find the time. In the summer of 1758, when I went back to visit my natal home, I dared to bring the manuscript along with me. Beginning in the late autumn,[2] I wrote whenever I could find the time, but it was not until April of the following year that I was able to complete the task. From the "Cry of the Ospreys" in the "Odes of Ju (C. Zhou) 周 and the South,"[3] to "The Conjunction [of the Sun and Moon] in the Tenth Month" within the "[Decade of] Gi Bo (C. Qi Fu) 祈

---

[1] Reading 瓶 as 瓿 in the original.
[2] Refers to the third month of autumn, and the ninth month of the lunar calendar.
[3] The "Odes of Ju and the South" (*Ju Nam*; C. *Zhou Nan* 周南) is the opening section of the "Airs of the States" (*Gukpung*; C. *Guofeng* 國風), which is the first chapter of the *Book of Poetry*. The "Cry of the Ospreys" is the first ode in this section.

Korean Women Philosophers and the Ideal of a Female Sage. Philip J. Ivanhoe and Hwa Yeong Wang, Oxford University Press. © Oxford University Press 2023. DOI: 10.1093/oso/9780197508688.003.0004

父" in the "Minor Hymns of the States" (*So A*; C. *Xiao Ya* 小雅),[4] everything up to the fourth sentence of the second stanza was written by my husband. Everything from the fifth sentence onward was written by me. Moreover, I wrote the chapter titles and Main Point [sections] of "Two [Odes of the] South in the Airs [of the States] (*Gukpung*; C. *Guofeng* 國風), the [Minor and Greater] Hymns (*A*; C. *Ya* 雅), and Eulogies (*Song*; C. *Song* 頌)."[5] [Once I had finished the work,] I endeavored to make it more presentable and then stored it away in a bamboo book box. Alas! Most people have sons and grandsons to esteem and value their extant works. Now, who will esteem and value [this work]? Is it not sad?

2. Addendum to Carrying Forward My Late Husband's Work on the *Songs of Cho*

Alas! This is another work my husband was writing but could not complete. My reasons for carrying forward this work are similar to what motivated me to carry forward his work on the *Book of Poetry*. My husband wrote everything from "Encountering Sorrow" up to "Nine Pieces." The first sixty-four sentences in the third piece (i.e., "Heavenly Questions" *Cheonmun*; C. *Tianwen* 天問) were written by my husband; I wrote the last two sentences (i.e., the last two sentences of the eighth stanza of "Heavenly Questions") and what follows to the end of "Wandering Afar."[6] [Once I had finished the work,] I endeavored to make it more presentable and then stored it away in a bamboo book box along with his work on the *Book of Poetry*. For the time being, I console the secret anguish in my heart [with this work]. In [this], the intercalary month of summer in 1759, Widow Im weeps as she writes.

---

[4] The "The Conjunction [of the Sun and Moon] in the Tenth Month" is the ninth ode in the "Decade of Gi Bo" (*Gi Bo ji sip*; C. *Qi Fu zhi shi* 祈父之什) section, which is the fourth part of the "Minor Hymns of the States," which, in turn, is the second chapter of the *Book of Poetry*.

[5] Dividing the *Book of Poetry* into four sections—the "Airs of the States," "Minor Hymns," "Greater Hymns" (*Dae A*; C. *Da Ya* 大雅), and "Eulogies"—became popular in the Song dynasty.

[6] "Encountering Sorrow" is the first poem and constitutes the first major section of the *Songs of Cho*; "Nine Pieces" is the fourth section and appears just before "Wandering Afar." So Yunjidang completed a work begun by her husband that covered the first four sections of the *Songs of Cho*, which contains a total of seventeen major sections.

Expositions (説)

1. Exposition on Pattern-Principle, *Gi-Material*, Heart-Mind, and Nature

The first exposition examines and explains the meaning and significance of four key terms of art, consisting of two sets of paired concepts, that were central to neo-Confucian moral philosophy. Pattern-Principle refers to the underlying metaphysical norms for all things that each and every thing possesses as its original or fundamental nature. Gi-Material is the psychophysical stuff that serves as the basis for the phenomenal world. When Pattern-Principle is embedded within the realm of Gi-Material, *it inevitably is less than fully manifest and is prone to error. Heart-Mind is the seat of consciousness, perception, thinking, feeling, and volition; the Heart-Mind not only contains but can become aware of all Pattern-Principle. Nature exists in two forms: the original nature, which is the complete endowment of Pattern-Principle and therefore pure and perfect, and* Gi-Material *nature, which is the original nature embedded in* Gi-Material.

What is heaven? Its physical form is awesome and majestic;[1] it thereby reaches the full extent of its greatness. Its Heart-Mind is to create and create;[2] it thereby reaches the full extent of its humaneness. What is earth? It is the mate of heaven, which enables it to complete the process of creation and transformation. What are human beings? They receive the mean between heaven and earth, are born in between them, are preeminent among the myriad creatures, and serve as a third power along with heaven and earth. How is it that heaven and earth are the greatest of things and yet human beings, with such small and tiny bodies, stand between them and form a triad with them? It is because they are able to embody the Way of heaven and earth and unite with their virtue.[3]

---

[1] Cf. *Analects* 8.18 and 19; *Mencius* 3A4.

[2] The idea that heaven expresses its humaneness through its unceasing activity of creation is a characteristic theme of Jeong I and Ju Hui.

[3] For the word "virtue," see note 185, page 74.

Someone asked, "I have heard that heaven and earth give birth to (i.e., create) the myriad things and in receiving life all the myriad things are constituted by the Pattern-Principle of the movement and rest and the unification and dispersal of yin and yang. And so, the myriad things share a single source. Though human beings and other creatures are very different in physical form and features, in terms of the Way, it is proper to make no distinction between them. Why then is it that human beings alone are able to embody the Way of heaven and earth and unite with their virtue, while no other creature can dare to undertake this? Furthermore, can we hear about the Way by which heaven and earth create and transform?"

I replied, "The Way of heaven is marvelous and unfathomable. This is why 'The master's teachings about human nature and the Way of heaven cannot be heard.'[4] If one has not completely comprehended Pattern-Principle, fully developed one's nature, and thereby understood heaven,[5] one is not prepared to discuss such things. Nevertheless, sages and worthies have left behind instructions on wood and bamboo (i.e., ancient books) that illuminate the [Way of heaven] for future students as brightly as the sun and stars, so how can they simply see this as marvelous and beyond comprehension, remain stuck in the realm of being unable to know, and not reflect on what will enable them to completely comprehend Pattern-Principle? Based upon this, may I now first talk about the Way of creation and transformation and next discuss the Heart-Mind and nature of human beings and other creatures in order to teach what can be known?

Master Yeomgye (C. Lianxi) 濂溪[6] spoke of 'what is without limit and yet the Great Ultimate.'[7] He also said, 'The truth of what is without limit marvelously combines with the essence of the two fundamental principles[8] and the Five Phases[9] and congeals.'[10] Ju Hui said, 'The Great Ultimate along with the two fundamental principles and the Five Phases originally mix together and become inseparable.'[11] In general, the Way of heaven and earth is none other than this: the *Gi-Material* of yin and yang and the Five Phases, along with

---

[4] *Analects* 5.13.

[5] See section 1 under the hexagram *Seol* (C. *Shuo*) 說 in the *Book of Changes*. Cf. *Mencius* 7.1.

[6] A pen name of Ju Doni.

[7] Ju Doni, *Diagram Explaining the Supreme Ultimate* (*Taegeukdo seol*; C. *Taijitu shuo* 太極圖說) in the *Collected Works of Ju Doni* (*Juwongong jip*: C. *Zhouyuangong ji* 周元公集) 1.1b.

[8] Ju Doni, *Diagram Explaining the Supreme Ultimate* 1.3b. See also the *Reflections on Things at Hand* (*Geunsarok*; C. *Jinsilu* 近思錄) 1.3b.

[9] The two fundamental principles are yin and yang.

[10] The Five Phases (*ohaeng*; C. *wuxing* 五行) are wood, fire, earth, metal, and water.

[11] Ju Hui's comment on the line in the *Reflections on Things at Hand* 1.3b.

the flawless Pattern-Principle of the Great Ultimate, are endowed to things and cause them all to nurture their lives. Pattern-Principle is the underlying essence[12] of *Gi-Material*; *Gi-Material* is the vessel of Pattern-Principle. They are one and yet two, two and yet one. Many people mistakenly believe that Ju Hui taught that 'first there is Pattern-Principle and only later is there *Gi-Material*'[13] and that the Great Ultimate is an ideal, self-sufficient[14] thing that transcends physical form and *Gi-Material*. This most definitely is not the case. If there were no *Gi-Material*, what would Pattern-Principle depend upon in order to complete the process of creation and transformation? The Great Ultimate is nothing more than the Pattern-Principle of yin and yang; it is not the case that beyond yin and yang there is some separately existing Pattern-Principle. Pattern-Principle is simply what we call yin and yang in this, their natural state. The Great Ultimate is simply what we call Pattern-Principle extended out to its ultimate extreme, beyond which nothing can be added. If we deny [the existence of] Pattern-Principle, from the start, *Gi-Material* will lack an origin; if we deny [the existence of] *Gi-Material*, how will Pattern-Principle come into being [as material phenomena]? It is only when [Pattern-Principle] is with *Gi-Material* that it becomes possible to grasp its meaning. [Pattern-Principle and *Gi-Material*] do not separate [from] or join together [with one another], do not divide or fuse, do not rend or mend, and so how can one talk about which comes before or after the other?"

[Someone] asked, "Ju Doni said that 'the Great Ultimate moves and produces yang, is still and produces yin.'[15] He also said, 'Yang changes and yin comes together, producing water, fire, wood, metal, and earth.'[16] Based on this, yang is produced only after the Great Ultimate moves, yin is produced only after [the Great Ultimate] is still, and the Five Phases are produced only after yang changes and yin comes together. So the sequence and order

---

[12] "Underlying essence" translates *che* (C. *ti*) 體, which means what a thing fundamentally is in itself. It is commonly translated as "substance." Underlying essence typically is paired with the complementary notion of "function" (*yong*; C. *yong* 用), which connotes the natural operation of any given thing. Roughly, the former refers to the essential nature of a thing and the latter to the unhindered operation or functioning of that nature. A lighted lamp (substance) emits lamp light (function); the basic nature of human beings (substance) is humaneness (function).

[13] Ju Hui, the *Questions and Answers on the "Four Books"* (*Saseo hongmun*; C. *Sishu huowen* 四書或問) 1.4b.

[14] "An ideal, self-sufficient thing" translates 一圓圈之物, which literally means "a circular thing." We take Yunjidang to have intended this phrase metaphorically to mean something independently perfect and self-sustaining.

[15] Ju Doni, *Diagram Explaining the Supreme Ultimate* 1.1b.

[16] Ju Doni, *Diagram Explaining the Supreme Ultimate* 1.2b.

of which comes earlier and which comes later is clear and beyond doubt. Doesn't this show that your view is mistaken?"

I replied, "Since ancient times, those who have talked about the Way in itself (i.e., its underlying essence) have all said the same kind of thing. Students should see how it applies in their actual lives; they will be fine if they do not allow the literal expression to harm the meaning of what is said.[17] In regard to the *Doctrine of the Mean*, Ju Hui explained the line 'What heaven decrees is called the nature' by saying, 'By means of the yin and yang and the Five Phases, heaven transforms, giving birth to the myriad creatures. It uses *Gi-Material* to complete the physical forms and endows each with Pattern-Principle.'[18] If you attend just to the literal expression, then he is saying that *Gi-Material* first completes the physical forms and only then is Pattern-Principle endowed to each thing. Is this acceptable? In general, *Gi-Material* has physical form and is easy to see, while Pattern-Principle works through nonaction and is hard to perceive. Ju Hui feared that people would only know of the existence of *Gi-Material* and not know of the existence of Pattern-Principle, would only know that the two fundamental principles and Five Phases freely operate in varying, unequal ways and not know that they all originate in a single Great Ultimate. And so, he wanted to point out, in this way, what was easy to grasp. Ju Doni's ideas also are like this. In general, this is because they formulated their teachings about *what is yet to be* (emphasis added), but they did not say that Pattern-Principle somehow exists on its own suspended in a vacuum and at times moves or is still, changes or comes together, thereby giving birth to the two material forces (yin and yang) and the Five Phases, and then begins the process of transformation and creation of the myriad things.

Movement is yang but the Pattern-Principle that produces movement is the Great Ultimate. This is why [Ju Doni] said 'the Great Ultimate moves and produces yang.'[19] Stillness is yin, but the Pattern-Principle that produces stillness is the Great Ultimate. This is why [Ju Doni] said, '[It] is still and produces yin.'[20] Moreover, its movement and stillness are always gradual. And so, when it starts to move, only the slightest yang begins to be produced. Once movement reaches its maximum extent, yang is abundant, but then

---

[17] Cf. *Mencius* 5A4.
[18] See chapter 1 of *The "Doctrine of the Mean" in Sections and Sentences* (*Jungyong janggu*; C. *Zhongyong zhangju* 中庸章句) 1b.
[19] Ju Doni, *Diagram Explaining the Supreme Ultimate* 1.1b.
[20] Ju Doni, *Diagram Explaining the Supreme Ultimate* 1.1b.

it begins to ebb and returns to stillness. When it starts to be still, only the slightest yin begins to be produced. Once stillness reaches its maximum extent, yin is abundant but then it ebbs and reverts to movement. It cycles like this without beginning or end. This is what is called 'alternately moving and still; each taking a turn as the base';[21] this is how it is. Moreover, in terms of the Five Phases, what is material is set upon the earth, while what is *Gi-Material* moves through the heavens. Teachings about 'alternately changing and coming together and thereby giving birth to the Five Phases'[22] also concern what is yet to be.[23] As for the sequence of creation, it is not that the yin and yang and the Five Phases are divided into two distinct affairs. This is why he says, 'The Five Phases are one with yin and yang. Yin and yang are one with the Great Ultimate. The Great Ultimate originally is without limit.'[24] Yin and yang are different positions; movement and stillness are different moments, but none of them ever is separate from the Great Ultimate. [Each of] the four seasons has a different [place in the] sequence [of a year]; [each of] the Five Phases is a different substance, but none of them ever is outside the Great Ultimate. The most refined and the most coarse, the roots and branch tips, the Five Phases and the two material forces (yin and yang) are neither this nor that, neither excessive or deficient, and yet the Great Ultimate is without physical form or sign about which one can talk. This is why it is called '[what is] without limit.' The movement and stillness of the Great Ultimate is the free operation of the Way of heaven, that which is referred to in [*the Great Appendix*'s claim that] 'the alternation of yin and yang is called the Way.'[25] To come together, separate, contract, and extend, this is the innate capacity of yin and yang. To create, mature, collect, and store away, this is the innate disposition of the nature of the Five Phases. The innate capacity and innate disposition of the nature are what make the Great Ultimate the Great Ultimate. And yet what is called the Great Ultimate is not something that can be said to be either separate from or mixed in with the yin, yang, and Five Phases. It is not that standing apart from the yin, yang, and Five Phases there separately exists a Great Ultimate that transcends them on high and gives birth to the yin, yang, and Five Phases. This is simply what is called the Way in itself. And so Jeongja (C. Chengzi) 程子 said, 'The Way is implements; implements are

---

[21] Ju Doni, *Diagram Explaining the Supreme Ultimate* 1.1b.

[22] A close paraphrase of Ju Doni's *Diagram Explaining the Supreme Ultimate* 1.2b.

[23] Reading 源 as 原 in the original.

[24] Ju Doni, *Diagram Explaining the Supreme Ultimate* 1.3a.

[25] Section 5 of the "Great Appendix" (*Gyesajeon*; C. *Xicizhuan* 繫辭傳) (upper part) to the *Book of Changes*.

the Way.'[26] He also said, 'Movement and stillness have no point of origin; yin and yang have no beginning. If not one who understands the Way, who is capable of understanding this?'[27] If Pattern-Principle and *Gi-Material* had some primordial [sequence of] earlier and later that one could talk about, then not only would movement and stillness, yin and yang have a point of origin and a beginning but also implements and the Way would be a single thing and not two. How then could the Masters Jeong have said what they did and how could Master Ju have said that 'originally they were mixed together and inseparable?'[28] It is clear why one cannot hold on to the words and become confused about the meaning! In the end, the Way of *Geon* (C. *Qian*) 乾[29] changes and transforms and freely operates without cease; its process of creation and transformation completes this Pattern-Principle. In heaven it becomes the Four Virtues of heaven, namely: originating (*won*; C. *yuan* 元), penetrating (*hyeong*; C. *heng* 亨), advantageous (*i*; C. *li* 利), and authentic (*jeong*; C. *zhen* 貞).[30] These [Four Virtues] complete the beginning and the end and inexhaustibly create and create life. They are endowed to [all] things, and human beings and things each is endowed with Pattern-Principle so that they become the nature of yin-yang and the Five Constants;[31] namely, humaneness (*in*; C. *ren* 仁), righteousness (*ui*; C. *yi* 義), rites (*ye*; C. *li* 禮), wisdom (*ji*; C. *zhi* 智), and trustworthiness (*sin*; C. *xin* 信). All things possess this nature, but because of [different] endowments of *Gi-Material* there are differences in regard to the level of partiality, correctness, penetration, and blockage. And so there are differences in the [manifested] natures of people and things. Those that receive [both] penetrating and correct [*Gi-Material*] become human beings. And so they display all Five Aspects of the nature and all the Myriad Good Acts.[32] Those that receive the blocked and partial [*Gi-Material*] become things, and so, they are not able to completely possess the

---

[26] Jeong Myeongdo's (C. Cheng Mingdao) 程明道 words in the *Great Compendium on Human Nature and Principle* (*Seongni daejeon seo*; C. *Xingli daquan shu* 性理大全書) 34.22a.

[27] Jeong Icheon's (C. Cheng Yichuan) 程伊川 words, cited in *the Classified Sayings of Master Ju*. The second sentence is a very close paraphrase.

[28] Ju Hui added one character 本 in his commentary to Ju Doni's "混融而無間" in the *Reflections on Things at Hand* 1.2b. See also Ju Doni, *Diagram Explaining the Supreme Ultimate* 1.4a.

[29] *Geon* (C. *Qian*) 乾 is the first hexagram in the *Book of Changes* and represents heaven.

[30] The opening line of the *Book of Changes* says that the hexagram *Geon* "is great and originating, penetrating, advantageous, and authentic."

[31] *Geonsun* (C. *jianshun* 健順) refers to yin and yang, while *osang* (C. *wuchang* 五常) refers to *ohaeng*. See *the Classified Sayings of Master Ju* 62.19b. The Five Constants are humaneness, righteousness, ritual, wisdom, and trustworthiness. See Ju Doni, *Diagram Explaining the Supreme Ultimate* 1.8b and the *Collected Works for the Two Jeongs* (*I Jeong munjip*; C. *Er Cheng wenji* 二程文集) 9.1b.

[32] The Five Aspects of the nature (*oseong*; C. *wuxing*) 五性 refers to the Five Constants; see prior note.

Five Constants or penetrate through to and synthesize the original nature in itself. Nevertheless, they all receive equal endowments of this Pattern-Principle from the one source, and so, everywhere one can see evidence that they all possess heaven's unvarying standard. For example, tigers and wolves acknowledge the relationship between father and son, ravens provide food to their mothers once they have grown into adults, bees and ants have lords and ministers, otters offer sacrifices, ospreys maintain a proper separation in regard to male and female. This is what is called the nature of heaven and earth and there is nothing within heaven and earth that is outside this nature."

It was further asked, "There are myriad inequalities among living things; there are those that are conscious and can move; there are those that lack consciousness and cannot move. Among those with consciousness, who receive an equal allotment of this nature, are some in which sprouts of this nature are visible.[33] Among those that lack consciousness, how can we know that they too have an equal endowment of this nature? Is it that from the moment of their birth, they simply lack the heavenly endowed nature or that they have the same nature but it is constrained because of their *Gi-Material*—that is to say, they have a complete endowment of the nature itself but are simply unable to realize its full function?"

I replied, "What you suggest is not the case. That things are unequal[34] is something originally decreed by heaven. Though each is influenced by its *Gi-Material* nature to have its own [particular] nature, each possesses the Great Ultimate.[35] This is their [original] nature; this is the nature of Pattern-Principle. How can one talk about the nature in any way other than this and say either that things originally lack the heavenly endowed nature or doubt that Pattern-Principle is constrained by *Gi-Material*? In general, all things that lack blood *Gi-Material* and consciousness, such as grass and trees,[36] suffer from partiality and being blocked because of their partial and blocked physical form and *Gi-Material*. And so the Pattern-Principle within such things, following their physical form and *Gi-Material*, is [manifested] as the Pattern-Principle of that one particular thing. Though this cannot be equated with the [original] nature decreed by heaven, nevertheless, their blossoming

---

[33] The language here is reminiscent of Maengja's teachings about the Four Sprouts. See *Mencius* 2A6.

[34] The idea that, naturally, things are unequal is an explicit teaching of Maengja. See *Mencius* 3A5.

[35] See Ju Hui, *The Collected Works of Hoeam* (*Hoeam jip*; C. *Huian ji* 晦庵集) 46.52b.

[36] For these views about the nature of grass and trees, see Ju Hui, *The Collected Works of Hoeam* 59.59a.

and withering and their flourishing and decline display the ability to follow a particular order and thereby each has its own natural Way. So how can they be said to lack this nature? Now, when the sun is at its highest point in the heavens, if it enters through an open window, a great volume of light pours in and illuminates [what is inside]. If the window is just cracked open, then only a small volume of light enters and illuminates [what is inside]. Nevertheless, in both cases [what enters and illuminates] is sunlight. How is the nature of human beings and things any different from this? When something changes without being moved, it is [the work of] heaven. When something is completed without anyone acting to do so, it is the decree.[37] What heaven does not intend but naturally is as it is—this is the Heart-Mind of heaven. What heaven does not decree but naturally is as it is—this is the decree of heaven. How could heaven intend to create things and then create them; how could heaven purposely command things and then command them? Things simply are this way naturally.[38] That grass and trees are not equal [to human beings], that flying and running creatures have different endowments—all of these are the natural results of heaven's decree. And so how could there be any thing that lacks the [original] nature. If there were any thing that lacked the [original] nature, the Way of creation and transformation would have expired long ago. In general, Pattern-Principle is without penetration, obstruction, partiality, or completeness, while *Gi-Material* cannot be without penetration, obstruction, partiality, or completeness. And so, in those who possess [*Gi-Material* that is] penetrating and complete, Pattern-Principle in itself is complete, and so their original nature manifests humaneness, righteousness, rites, and wisdom. In those who possess [*Gi-Material* that is] partial and blocked, they are fettered by *Gi-Material*; as a result, Pattern-Principle is partial, and so their original nature manifests only one of the Five Constants. Heaven in creating living things establishes for each a norm.[39] Since the physical form and *Gi-Material* [of different things] vary, then the norms for each type of thing will not be the same; this too is established by Pattern-Principle. So how can one say that they have a complete endowment [of the nature itself] but are simply unable to realize its full function? If we talk about Pattern-Principle at the beginning of things being born, then

---

[37] Cf. *Mencius* 5A6, "That which happens without anyone doing it is the work of heaven. That which occurs without anyone bringing it about is the work of the decree."

[38] The thought is that heaven acts spontaneously, without the need to reflect, choose, intend, will, or act.

[39] Cf. *Mencius* 6A6.

human beings and other things all come from a single, common source. And so, [Ju Doni] says, 'All things completely embody the Great Ultimate.'[40] If we consider how things are after they are combined with *Gi-Material* and are born, then each thing has its individual nature. And so, [Ju Doni] says, 'Each of the myriad things possesses the one Great Ultimate.'[41] This is talking about 'the correct nature that each thing receives'[42] as a matter of [heaven's] decree. I will try to talk about this [idea]. Now, I will use the examples of a white feather, white snow, and white jade to discuss it. To be white and light in weight are [qualities] resulting from the *Gi-Material* of a feather, but the nature of a feather is to be good at [catching] the wind. To be white and not firm in constitution are [qualities] resulting from the *Gi-Material* of snow, but the nature of snow is to be extremely cold. As for jade, its *Gi-Material* is pure and its material unadulterated; by nature, it is warm and lustrous—lovely indeed! Jade is the kind of thing that can be compared to a noble person. This is why 'A noble person always wears jade.'[43] The different natures [of feathers, snow, and jade] are all the result of variations in their *Gi-Material*, which naturally causes each to have a particular nature. To be fast and strong is the nature of horses. To plow and be docile is the nature of oxen. To bark and guard is the nature of dogs. To crow and announce the dawn is the nature of roosters. In all these cases, the cause of them possessing the natures they have can be traced to inequalities in their *Gi-Material*; each one receives something different. To be substantial, heavy, and immobile is the nature of mountains. To flow onward without ceasing is the nature of water. In the case of these two things, their *Gi-Material* is not at all alike, and so their natures are extremely different from one another. Beautiful indeed is the nature of water; it can be compared to the manner in which the Way of heaven flows onward. This is why when Gongja looked upon a flowing stream he exclaimed, 'It flows on like this—does it not, never stopping day or night!'[44] Now, if you want to set aside being substantial and heavy and discuss the nature of mountains or set aside flowing onward and discuss the nature of water, how would this be different from setting aside humaneness, righteousness, rites, and wisdom and

---

[40] See his *Diagram Explaining the Supreme Ultimate* 1.4b. The idea is that each and every thing completely possess the Great Ultimate as its original nature.

[41] See his *Diagram Explaining the Supreme Ultimate* 1.4b. The idea is that the particular nature of each and every thing expresses some aspect of the Great Ultimate.

[42] See Jang Jae's (C. Zhang Zai) 張載 (1020–1077 CE) *Complete Works of Master Jang* (*Jangja jeonseo*; C. *Zhangzi quanshu* 張子全書) 1.27a.

[43] The idea is that having a piece of jade close to one's body will inspire one to emulate its virtues. See chapter 13, "The Jade-Bead Pendants of the Royal Cap" (*Okjo*; C. *Yuzao* 玉藻) of the *Book of Rites*.

[44] *Analects* 9.17.

discussing the nature of human beings? The sourness of wood, pungent taste of metal, sweetness of earth, bitterness of fire, warmth of wolf's bane, and coolness of rhubarb[45] all offer further examples. If the fact that the qualities [described above] cannot be interchanged or taken away from these things doesn't show that the sourness, pungent taste, sweetness, bitterness, warmth, and coolness are their fundamental nature, then what does it show? If you say that humaneness, righteousness, rites, and wisdom are the shared nature of human beings and [nonhuman] things but things don't manifest the nature of humaneness, righteousness, [rites, and wisdom] simply because they are constrained by *Gi-Material* and not able to penetrate through, but this is not how they are in themselves (i.e., their essence or original substance), this is profoundly not the case. Here is where one must pay attention to the four-character teaching 'Pattern-Principle is one but its manifestations are many' (*i il bun su*; C. *li yi fen shu* 理一分殊)[46] in order to see clearly for oneself. The Pattern-Principle of the 'one Pattern-Principle' definitely is Pattern-Principle, but is the Pattern-Principle of the 'many manifestations' somehow *not* Pattern-Principle? The term 'many manifestations' should also be seen in terms of Pattern-Principle. Many people today see it in terms of *Gi-Material*, mistakenly believing that the 'one' is Pattern-Principle but the 'many' is *Gi-Material*. In the extreme, this leads to the view that things possess a complete endowment of Pattern-Principle in itself (*chejeon*; C. *tiquan* 體全) but [simply] are unable to fully penetrate (*yong budal*; C. *yong buda* 用不達).[47] This is wrong."

It was further asked, "Since I have heard your instructions about how the nature of human beings and things are not equal and yet all receive a complete endowment of the Great Ultimate, [I would like to ask about] Jang Jae's remark that 'the people are my siblings.'[48] In general it is said that human beings all receive the most penetrating and correct *Gi-Material* of heaven and earth. Since their [original] nature is the same and their physical form is not very different from one another, they are like my brothers, born of the

---

[45] The association of flavors with the Five Phases is part of the general correlative cosmology of this scheme (the fifth phase, water, is associated with the flavor saltiness); the warmth of wolf's bane and the coolness of rhubarb refer to the disposition of these plants to produce warmth and coolness respectively.

[46] This idea, a core teaching in the Jeong-Ju (C. Cheng-Zhu) 程朱 School, originated with Jeong I.

[47] The idea was discussed above and rejected, the point being that it is simply *the nature of creatures and things* that they can only manifest certain Pattern-Principles. By following their particular physical natures, they accord with Pattern-Principle.

[48] See the *Western Inscription* (*Seomyeong*; C. *Ximing* 西銘) by Jang Jae, which refers to the original source or state of *Gi-Material* in the *Complete Works of Master Jang* 1.5a.

same womb. If we look at this teaching, it seems fitting to say that the material endowment people receive is in no way different. And yet since ancient times there has been the difference between sages and fools. Why is this?"

I replied, "What is perfectly good and without wickedness is the [original] nature; it is rooted in the one Pattern-Principle and what all human beings have in common. What is unequal in quality in regard to things like being dull, bright, strong, or weak is talent; it is the result of *Gi-Material*, and human beings differ in this respect. In general, Pattern-Principle is without different grades of refinement or coarseness, but because *Gi-Material* differs in purity and turbidity there is the difference between sages and fools. If one's endowment of *Gi-Material* is pure and unadulterated one can make bright and sincere the great function of the nature in itself and one's virtue will match that of the Lord on High. This is what it is to be a sage. If one's endowment of *Gi-Material* is adulterated and turbid, one will be dull and unable to recognize that the highest good decreed by heaven is within oneself; one's Heart-Mind will be enslaved by things, and one will lose one's original nature. This is what it is to be a fool. Nevertheless, in terms of the great root of their nature, the sage and the fool are one. And so it is said, 'Everyone can become a Yo or a Sun.'[49] As for what makes Yo and Sun Yo and Sun, it is simply that their nature displays the highest good and their virtue displays the height of greatness. If people can understand that the highest good of Sun's nature is also within themselves and exert themselves to study it, if they can fill out what they have in common and change wherein they are different,[50] then there will be no difference in their *Gi-Material*'s purity or impurity, and all can attain the good and return to the original state of their nature. This is what is referred to as 'when they attain success, then they are one.' "[51]

It was further asked, "Setting aside a discussion of the difference between the greatest sages and most foolish, if we simply consider the differences between the majority of people in terms of their being bright or benighted, good or bad, some are several, one thousand, or even ten thousand times [better or worse]. What is the reason for this?"

I replied, "This too is only because of inequalities in *Gi-Material*. The origin of *Gi-Material* is primordial unity.[52] This primordial unity is the vast,

---

[49] *Mencius* 6B22.

[50] "What they have in common" is their purely good nature. "Wherein they are different" refers to the flaws and shortcomings that result from their impure and adulterated endowments of *Gi-Material*.

[51] See the *Doctrine of the Mean*, chapter 20.

[52] The term "primordial unity" or "calm unity" (*dam il*; C. *zhan yi* 湛一) is first found in the *Western Inscription* 2.35a and refers to the original source or state of *Gi-Material*.

flowing *Gi-Material*[53] of heaven and earth, which fills up the six directions [of the universe]. From the sages to the ordinary person on the street, there is none who does not receive an equal measure of this primordial unity; in this regard it is fitting to say that there is no difference among people. But when it comes to the purity or turbidity of the *Gi-Material* of the majority of people, there are naturally numerous differences in quality, and in accord with their particular endowments, they are, more superficially or deeply, to a greater or lesser extent, ensnared by external things. And so, in terms of their being bright or benighted, good or bad, some are several, one thousand, or even ten thousand times [better or worse]. Nevertheless, the particular mixture of purity and turbidity is found after *Gi-Material* has flowed over its course; it is not the original state of *Gi-Material*. This is why it is said, 'Sages and I are the same in kind.'[54] If one is able to make one thousand times the effort needed by another[55] and one's virtue is able to overcome the effects of one's *Gi-Material*, then the root of primordial unity will be restored to completeness within one and there will be no inequality."

It was asked, "People's talent and virtue are in every case a result of the elevated or lowly quality of their endowment [of *Gi-Material*]. Virtue is the root, whereas talent is the tip of the branch.[56] If one's natural, initial endowment [of *Gi-Material*] is indeed elevated, then one will have virtue, and without doubt one will also have talent. If one's natural, initial endowment [of *Gi-Material*] is indeed low, then since one lacks the root, how can one talk about having the tip of the branch? And yet from ancient times on down to the present, on occasion there have been those who lack virtue but whose talent is exceedingly fine. Why is this?"

I replied, "In such cases, the partiality of their *Gi-Material* obscures the root but is revealed in the tip of the branch. In general, what we call talent falls into three broad categories. There are those whose virtue is sincerely formed within and whose talent penetrates all. This was the beauty of the talent of the Duke of Ju (Ju Gong; C. Zhou Gong) 周公.[57] This is the great talent of

---

[53] See *Mencius* 2A2.

[54] *Mencius* 6A7.

[55] See the *Doctrine of the Mean*, chapter 22.

[56] In other words, the former is fundamental, prior to, and the foundation for the latter. The idea, roughly, is that if one has moral character (virtue) one will develop the practical skills (talent) necessary to serve society and succeed. But practical skills unguided by moral character, over the long run, often will not prove successful or sustain one.

[57] The Duke of Ju (eleventh century BCE) played a major role in consolidating the kingdom established by his elder brother King Mu. He was renowned for acting as a capable and loyal advisor to his young nephew, serving as regent to the young prince of Ju and prepared him to be a great ruler instead of usurping power for himself. He is also credited with writing both the *Book of Changes* and

sages, which penetrates to what is above and what is below. This is known as 'Those with virtue must have talent.'[58] There are those whose initial, natural endowment is outstanding and whose talent surpasses the norm, such as Jo Jageon (C. Cao Zijian) 曹子建,[59] who could compose a poem after walking only seven paces, or Yu Mokji (C. Liu Muzhi) 劉穆之,[60] who was shrewd in regard to the analysis and deciding [of state affairs]. Such are examples of *Gi-Material* obscuring the root but being revealed in the tip of the branch. This is known as 'Those who have talent do not necessarily possess virtue.'[61] Yet another category [of talent] is seen in people like Sang Sin (C. Shang Xin) 商辛,[62] whose talent and strength surpassed that of most people. Though [at first] he seemed not at all foolish, if we consider how he ended up, then he surely was a fool. Such people are what Gongja had in mind when he said, 'The most foolish cannot change.'[63] How can a single rule cover all the cases?"

It was further asked, "I have heard that 'the Heart-Mind is the citadel of the nature.'[64] When human beings or other things are born, in general, they all are endowed with this Heart-Mind and possess this nature. But I still don't understand what the Heart-Mind of birds, beasts, grass, and trees is like or how the nature that they possess is partial or blocked relative to one another. [I also don't understand] what the Heart-Mind of sages and regular people are like or how the nature that they possess is unequal relative to one another. I would like to know what makes these things so."

I replied, "Excellent questions! As for what is called the Heart-Mind, it is the spiritual intelligence of the primordial unity. The spiritual intelligence

the *Book of Poetry*. For Ju Hui's comment on the Duke of Ju, see *the Classified Sayings of Master Ju* 30.50b-54a.

[58] *The Classified Sayings of Master Ju* 44.31b. Cf. *Analects* 14.4.

[59] Reading 健 as 建 in the original. Jageon is an adult name of Jo Sik (C. Cao Zhi) 曹植 (192–232 CE) who was a prince and accomplished poet of the Three Kingdoms period. In the *Romance of the Three Kingdoms* (*Samgukji yeonui*; C. *Sanguozji yanyi* 三國志演義), a fourteenth-century work of historical fiction that depicts life in the Eastern Han dynasty and Three Kingdoms period (220–280 CE), he is challenged to write a poem after taking only seven steps, which he does, brilliantly.

[60] Yu Mokji (360–417 CE) was a capable administrator and writer who greatly assisted Emperor Mu (C. Wu) 武 (363–422 CE) of the Yu Song (C. Liu Song) 劉宋 dynasty (420–479 CE), who entrusted him with the great decisions and affairs of state.

[61] *The Classified Sayings of Master Ju* 44.31a.

[62] Je Sin (C. Di Xin) 帝辛 (1075–1046 BCE), last king of the Eun dynasty, most commonly referred to as King Ju, which is a pejorative posthumous name. In the early part of his reign he demonstrated remarkable abilities. He was extraordinarily intelligent and strong enough to hunt wild beasts with his bare hands. Later in his reign, he abandoned himself to drinking and womanizing and neglected the affairs of state. Later ages have regarded him as the epitome of a wicked and cruel ruler.

[63] *Analects* 17.3.

[64] See *the Classified Sayings of Master Ju* 60.2b.

of the primordial unity is the Heart-Mind of heaven and earth that gives
birth to things. Human beings and other things are born between the two
of them (i.e., heaven and earth) and equally receive this Heart-Mind that
gives birth to things as their own Heart-Mind. It is fitting that the Pattern-
Principle this Heart-Mind possesses is the same [for all of them]. It is only
because birds and beasts receive partial and blocked up *Gi-Material* and
their Heart-Minds reinforce these impediments, that they lack the ability
to complete the Heart-Mind of heaven and earth. And so, although those
with blood *Gi-Material* have some degree of consciousness, the nature that
they possess is unable to resist following what is partial and benighted. Grass
and trees are not endowed with blood *Gi-Material* and so lack it [i.e., this
Heart-Mind]. [In their case,] what we call the Heart-Mind is nothing more
than the structured pattern of veins within them, which, to some extent, can
be traced and through which the life *Gi-Material* flows and circulates. And
so, apart from their blossoming and withering and their flourishing and
decline, there is nowhere to look for evidence of the Heart-Mind, and the
nature with which they are endowed is blocked in multiple ways. The word
'partial' hardly suffices to describe their condition. As for the Heart-Mind of
human beings, they receive the Heart-Mind of heaven and earth that gives
birth to things. Although we say that they are one with the myriad things,
the correct and penetrating *Gi-Material* that they receive and the partial and
blocked up *Gi-Material* [received by things] determine the vast dissimilarity
between human beings and things. And so, if the primordial unity in itself is
free of obstruction or interference, their Heart-Minds will directly and perfectly penetrate; their sublime intelligence will thoroughly understand, and
the Pattern-Principle with which they are endowed will be fully luminous.
'The myriad things are complete [in me],'[65] and so there surely is no difference between sages and ordinary people; it is only because it is not possible
to wholly avoid having some of what is perverse and turbid getting mixed
in with what is correct and penetrating during the process of *Gi-Material*
forming into material. And so, the original state of the Heart-Mind itself
cannot but be obscured by *Gi-Material* and the nature that the Heart-Mind
possesses cannot but be fettered by this [*Gi-Material*]. Though there are
myriad inequalities between the wise and the foolish, the worthy and unworthy, nevertheless, the brightness of their [Heart-Mind's] original state is
ever-present. And so, if one is good at returning to it then the Heart-Mind of

[65] *Mencius* 7A1.

heaven and earth and the nature are within oneself. This is why it is said that 'noble people do not regard the *Gi-Material* nature as their nature.'[66] As for the Heart-Mind of sages, their endowment of *Gi-Material* is absolutely pure and without the slightest turbidity, absolutely unmixed and completely una-dulterated. And so, through lively transformation their spiritual brightness[67] becomes one with heaven, and a myriad of good traits are abundantly present within them. Nevertheless, this is just according with the Heart-Mind and the nature; how could it be the result of their receiving even a hair's breadth more than the endowment that is provided to the mass of humanity! This is why it is said that 'everyone can become a Yo or a Sun.'"[68]

It was asked, "Jeongja said that good and bad are all the nature.[69] As for na-ture, this is what heaven decrees for me[70] and what I use to become virtuous. That being so, then the sageliness of Yo, Sun, and Gongja is a matter of nature, and the wickedness of Geol, Ju, and Robber Cheok (C. Zhi) 盜跖[71] also is a matter of nature. They are no different in regard to implementing the nature. Good certainly is beautiful, but wickedness is something that cannot be com-pletely eliminated, and yet the *Book of Changes* says, 'Continuing goodness completes the nature,'[72] and Maengja said, 'Human nature is good.'[73] You too, master, have said [the nature] is perfectly good and without anything bad.[74] If all this is so, then is Jeongja's teaching that 'good and bad are all the na-ture'[75] incorrect? I am confused about this."

I replied, "Does not the *Book of Poetry* say, 'Heaven gave birth to the multitude of people, and for each thing it established a norm. The people's

[66] A close paraphrase of a line of Jang Jae in the *Complete Works of Master Jang* 2.36b. See also the *Collected Works of Hoeam* 61.15b. This is adapting a line by Maengja to the particular context of neo-Confucian discourse. What he said was, "The ways in which the mouth is disposed to delicious flavors, the eye to what is beautiful, the ear to pleasant sounds, the nose to appealing scents, and the four limbs to ease and rest is a matter of nature, but there is also an aspect of the decree in these things, and so the cultivated person does not call this the nature." See *Mencius* 7B24.

[67] Spiritual brightness (*sinmyeong*; C. *shenming* 神明), here, and often in neo-Confucian writings, refers to a kind of understanding that is so profound and thoroughgoing as to grant the possessor im-pressive powers of perceptiveness, judgement, and insight.

[68] *Mencius* 6B22.

[69] A close paraphrase of what Jeongja said in the *Extant Works of the Two Jeongs* (*I Jeong yuseo*; C. *Er Cheng yishu* 二程遺書) 1.16a–b.

[70] Closely paraphrasing the opening line of the *Doctrine of the Mean*.

[71] Robber Cheok of the *Spring and Autumn Period* was commonly used as a stock figure of an amoral brigand.

[72] Section 5 of the "Great Appendix" (upper part) to the *Book of Changes*.

[73] Cf. *Mencius* 6A2.

[74] See the line that begins "What is perfectly good and without wickedness . . . " earlier in this exposition.

[75] *The Classified Sayings of Master Ju* 95.24b. Ju's original says, "Good and bad are all heavenly Pattern-Principle."

unvarying standard is to love this constant virtue.'[76] 'Constant virtue' consists of humaneness, righteousness, rites, and wisdom, and [the people's] 'unvarying standard' means to hold it firmly as if clasping it securely. This is the good; it is provided at birth and is the root of the nature. Wickedness is something that exists only after physical forms have taken shape. It is appropriate to call this the 'Gi-Material nature' (gijil ji seong; C. qizhi zhi xing 氣質之性). It is profoundly wrong to call this the nature we have from the start and that is decreed by heaven. Within the nature there is only humaneness, righteousness, rites, and wisdom—these four; when has wickedness ever come from [the nature]? Nevertheless, there is nothing in the world outside the nature. Although originally everything [in the nature] is good, since it can get covered up by Gi-Material and drift into wickedness, it is appropriate to say that this is not the original state of the nature, but if one says that this is not the nature, then what gives rise to wickedness? This is why [Jeongja] said that good and bad are all the nature. This is not saying that within the nature there originally exist these two opposing things which subsequently are born.[77] In general, since heaven first gave birth to the people, human beings all have had this nature and all have had this physical form as well. Within they have a sublime intelligence, which serves as a guard tower, to support the nature and respond to the myriad affairs [it encounters]; its name is the Heart-Mind. This is what is referred to as [the Heart-Mind being] 'the citadel of the nature';[78] when it operates there are the feelings. There are two forms of the Heart-Mind: the Human Heart-Mind (insim; C. renxin 人心) and the Heart-Mind of the Way (dosim; C. daoxin 道心). There are seven forms of emotion: happiness, anger, grief, joy, love, hate, and desire.[79] Since there is the physical form, consisting of ears, eyes, mouth, nose, hands, feet, and four limbs, as well as exterior things, such as sounds, sights, scents, and tastes, there cannot but be contact between these. Once things have come before one and make contact with the bodily faculties, they cannot but move one on the inside and bring forth the Seven Emotions. It is precisely at this point that the names human [Heart-Mind] and [Heart-Mind of] the Way become established. But the Human Heart-Mind is self-centered and has a difficult time being public-spirited; the Heart-Mind of the Way is tenuous

---

[76] Book of Poetry, Mao #260. Quoted, with slight variation, in Mencius 6A6.
[77] See the Extant Works of the Two Jeongs 1.16a–b.
[78] See note 64 above.
[79] This list is one that appears with minor variation in a number of early texts, for example, the "Ceremonial Usages" (Yeun; C. Liyun 禮運) chapter of the Book of Rites.

and difficult to manifest clearly. And so expressions of the Heart-Mind of the Way are covered over by the Human Heart-Mind, and the correctness of the nature decreed [unto human beings] is obscured and no longer bright. Human beings are able to understand this; if they investigate it carefully, select what is most refined, and hold onto it securely, they must ensure that the Heart-Mind of the Way always stands as a lord in one's guard tower, while the Human Heart-Mind stands below the tower as one's minister. Whether [the Heart-Mind] is in a state of movement or of stillness, whether it is going out or coming in, as long as one obeys the orders of the Heart-Mind of the Way, then one can oppose self-centeredness, act with public-spiritedness, reveal what is subtle, and attain what is bright; one's Heart-Mind will be rectified and one's self will be cultivated.[80] If one responds to affairs in this way, they will attain what is fitting; if one engages with things, they will achieve their proper place. If one uses this to regulate the family, then every family will be well regulated. If one uses this to order the state, then every state will be well ordered. If one uses this to bring peace to all under heaven, then all under heaven will be peaceful.[81] In minor applications, use it to regulate every aspect of your conduct as well as your speech and silence, and they will always attain the proper measure. In major applications, use it to interact with the myriad things under heaven, and they all will be moved and transformed. This is what is called 'establishing a happy order throughout heaven and earth and nurturing the myriad things.'[82] This is the highest achievement of learning and something only sages are capable of attaining. This is what Tang and Mu returned to and what Yo, Sun, and Gongja took as their nature.[83] They followed the same principle and all serve as orthodox teachers for a hundred generations. If the Human Heart-Mind is the master and the Heart-Mind of the Way obeys its commands, then the heavenly lord [safeguarding the nature] will become weaker each day. None will be able to control [the proliferation of] thieves. It will then reach the point where the heavenly Pattern-Principle is squandered and annihilated and the remnant of one's spiritual guard tower will have fallen under the control of a throng of human desires. It can be likened to a situation in which the ruler of a state has become weak and feeble while thieving ministers have become powerful and ascendant. Is

---

[80] Paraphrasing chapter 2 of the *Great Learning*, which says, "Once the Heart-Mind has been rectified, the self will be cultivated."

[81] This and following three sentences are paraphrasing a sequence described in chapter 2 of the *Great Learning*.

[82] Chapter 1 of the *Doctrine of the Mean*.

[83] Cf. *Mencius* 7A30 and 7B33.

there anyone who can protect and preserve such a state? How is this case any different? This is how the dark and violent natures of Geol, Ju, and Robber Cheok came to be, and why they became the most despised villains in the past thousand years. Can they be discussed as in some way comparable to sages who take goodness as their nature? Maengja said, 'To rise with the crowing of the cock and earnestly apply oneself to doing good—such are the disciples of Sun. To rise with the crowing of the cock and earnestly apply oneself to profit—such are the disciples of [Robber] Cheok.'[84] As for the good, it is the public-spiritedness of heavenly Pattern-Principle. As for profit, it is the self-centeredness of human desire. In the beginning, the difference between these two (i.e., good and profit) is less than a hair's breadth, but in the end the space between them is immense—greater than the distance between heaven and earth. This is why it is said, 'By thinking, become a sage; by not thinking, become a savage.'[85] The difference between a sage and a savage is simply the choice between thinking and not thinking. Alas! This is something that is worthy of fear!"

It was asked, "Goja (C. Gaozi) 告子 said, 'Inborn is what is meant by nature.'[86] Jeongja also said, 'Inborn is what is meant by nature.'[87] How do these two agree, or is there something that makes them different?"

I replied, "Goja's view of the nature concerns *Gi-Material*. And so what he says refers to the *Gi-Material* with which one is born. Jeongja's view of the nature concerns Pattern-Principle. And so what he says refers to [the nature] that 'combines the sublime and *Gi-Material*.'[88] How can one know this is the case? Goja observed *Gi-Material* but didn't understand Pattern-Principle. And so he saw that human beings and other creatures have consciousness and are able to move about and, consequently, he said this is our nature. It was on this basis that he propounded this theory. But if you examine his idea, in general, it says that whatever one's Heart-Mind desires is what the nature has from the start; if one desires to eat one eats, if one desires sex one has sex; one's likes and dislikes, what one deems good and bad depends on what one's nature deems appropriate. The heavenly nature of Yo and Sun was originally good. And so, following what they took as the nature, they became sages. The heavenly nature of Geol and Ju was originally bad. And so, following what

---

[84] *Mencius* 7A25.

[85] Paraphrasing lines from the "Book of Ju" (*Ju Seo*; C. *Zhou Shu* 周書) section of the *Book of History*.

[86] *Mencius* 6A3.

[87] A saying of Jeong Ho. See *Extant Works of the Two Jeongs* 24.3a.

[88] See Jang Jae, *Complete Works of Master Jang* 2.6b. Cf. Ju Hui's commentary to *Mencius* 7A1.

they took as the nature, they became wicked people. [On such a view] the nature that heaven endows at birth does not allow for human activity; why must one talk only about humaneness and righteousness![89] [On such a view] humaneness and righteousness are exterior [to the nature]; they are not like the desires for food and sex which the nature has from the start. This is similar to the theories of Sunja (C. Xunzi) 荀子 and Yang Ung (C. Yang Xiong) 揚雄[90] and is not worth refuting.

As for what is referred to as the nature, it simply concerns the Pattern-Principle that the myriad things receive in order to live. This is why Jeongja often said, 'Nature is Pattern-Principle'[91]—using these three words to convey his teaching—he said, 'In regard to heaven it is called the decree; in regard to human beings it is called the nature.'[92] He also said, 'Human beings are born in stillness; what is prior to this does not allow explanation.'[93] 'Does not allow explanation' means that the state prior to human beings being born is not something to which the term 'the nature' should be applied. This is why he said, 'Inborn is what is meant by nature.' [Jeongja] was afraid that people would talk about the nature while suspended in a vacuum.[94] In general, Jeongja regarded Goja as someone who did not recognize that human beings have a pure and absolutely good nature and instead thought that their crudest qualities were their nature. And so he elucidated the meaning of the term 'nature' in this way. But the nature and *Gi-Material* fundamentally cannot be separated from one another. And so he also said, 'The nature is *Gi-Material*; *Gi-Material* is the nature.'[95] Although the language they used seems similar, their meanings are farther apart than Yeon (C. Yan) 燕 and Wol (C. Yue) 越."[96]

It was asked, "I already have received your instructions about why Pattern-Principle and *Gi-Material* cannot be separated from one another, but where does this Pattern-Principle reside prior to the birth of heaven and earth?"

---

[89] This is a reference to *Mencius* 1A1, a passage in which Maengja contrasts these themes with talk of profit.

[90] Sunja's view can be found throughout his work, but see in particular the chapter "Human Nature Is Bad" (Hutton 2016, 248–257). For Yang Ung's view, see his *Exemplary Sayings* (*Beobeon*; C. *Fayan* 法言) (Yang 1965, chapter 3, 10–11).

[91] A saying of Jeong I. See the *Extant Works of the Two Jeongs* 22A24a.

[92] See the *Extant Works of the Two Jeongs* 24.7a.

[93] See the *Extant Works of the Two Jeongs* 1.16b. The first phrase is in the "Records of Music" (*Akgi*; C. *Yueji* 樂記) in the *Book of Rites* and refers to the nature.

[94] I.e., he feared they would engage in unsubstantiated speculation about the nature.

[95] See the *Extant Works of the Two Jeongs* 1.16a.

[96] These are the most northern and most southern states respectively of the Warring States period.

I replied, "What words are these? Since you just said that Pattern-Principle and *Gi-Material* cannot be separated from one another, you already know the answer; yet still you harbor such doubts? This makes it seem that you have not yet understood. As for what is referred to as heaven and earth, these two also cannot be separated into independently existing things. Their physical bodies are composed of the *Gi-Material* of yin and yang; their governor is the Pattern-Principle of yin and yang. Had you said that this Pattern-Principle does not exist, then that would have been the end of it, but since you say that it exists, how can there be a time when there is no heaven or earth and yet there is this Pattern-Principle, suspended in a vacuum and relying on nothing? Had you just said that there is a single heaven and earth [i.e., only one world cycle], then I would have held my tongue and remained silent. But since you say that [heaven and earth] open and close without end, then heaven and human beings simply are one. When it comes to Pattern-Principle, there is no greater or lesser, if you put yourself in place of heaven and investigate the matter, you probably will confirm this.

What leads the Human Heart-Mind to be still or stimulated is the movement or stillness of yin and yang. What leads it to awaken or sleep is also the movement or stillness of yin and yang; this is the Pattern-Principle of the opening and closing of a single [cycle of] heaven and earth. The stillness, stimulation, waking, and sleeping of human beings proceed in an endless cycle and the nature resides in all of these. So how could the Pattern-Principle of heaven and earth be outside of this? When an earlier [cycle] of heaven and earth has been annihilated and the current [cycle] of heaven and earth has yet to open and unfold, the Great Ultimate is still and gives birth to yin, and so Pattern-Principle resides in yin. Once stillness has reached its extreme it reverts to movement; the current [cycle] of heaven and earth is about to begin; the Great Ultimate moves and gives birth to yang, and so Pattern-Principle resides in yang. Now yin, now yang, now opening, now closing yet these two remain unfathomable. And so it is said, 'The spiritual is without set form; the changes are without fixed embodiment.'[97] Prior to [the current cycle] of heaven and earth, I do not know how many times it has opened and closed; once [the current cycle of] heaven and earth passes away, it all becomes an undifferentiated mass, which then will open up again, and after opening up again, it will become an undifferentiated mass again—the process extending inexhaustibly and without end. How could there be a time

[97] Section 4 of the "Great Appendix" (upper part) to the *Book of Changes*.

when Pattern-Principle depends upon nothing? The only thing one has no way of knowing about is what is below the earth. Roughly speaking, heaven enfolds the earth and the earth lies within it; its physical form resembles a chicken egg. Above and below the earth there is the same heaven. Given this, the sun, moon, stars, and planets revolve along with the cycles of heaven; their illumination is densely packed across the sky; is this not just as we find them in this world? Mountains, rivers, grass, and trees, the myriad things and phenomena, are they not just as we find them in this world? If we infer from these, our understanding can penetrate what is above and below and attain a unified grasp of heaven and earth. The Way of yin, yang, and the Great Ultimate does not seem to allow for the separation of this and that. Doesn't the Western theory of the world as being composed of six dimensions[98] also, to some degree, appeal to the same Pattern-Principle? The ancients said, 'What is beyond the six directions should be preserved but not discussed.'[99] Today, the more people think about this the more confused they become. It would be better not to think about it—wouldn't it? Nevertheless, while the various teachings about this are chaotic and disordered, if one were to choose the wisest among them, wouldn't Master Ju's theory that below the earth everything is water[100] offer the best chance to decide this matter?"

2. Exposition on the Human Heart-Mind and Heart-Mind of the Way, Four Sprouts and Seven Emotions

The second exposition explores the meaning and significance of four key terms of art, consisting of two sets of paired concepts that were central to neo-Confucian moral philosophy. The Human Heart-Mind refers to the phenomenal seat of human thought, feeling, and volition. Because it exists within the realm of Gi-Material, it inevitably is prone to error. The Heart-Mind of the Way is the heavenly Pattern-Principle within each human being that serves

[98] The six dimensions (*yungneung*; C. *liuleng* 六稜) seem to refer to the theory of a cubic-shaped earth (*yungmyeon segye seol* 六面世界說) by Sin Yu 申愈 (1673–1706 CE), which was inspired by Western metaphysical ideas introduced by Matteo Ricci (1552–1610 CE). According to this theory the world consists of six regions defined by the planes of this cube. Although this theory was not widely discussed in Korea, it certainly had a big impact on scholars of the Old Doctrine School, even the great grandson of Song Siyeol, the faithful follower of Ju Hui. Song Neungsang was an advocate of this theory, and Im Yunjidang wrote a biography for his wife. Im Yunjidang must have been aware of this theory. See Gim 2019, 171–173.

[99] The six directions are east, west, north, south, up, and down. The translated line is a close paraphrase of lines from the "Equality of Things" (*Jemullon*; C. *Qiwulun* 齊物論) chapter of the *Jangja*.

[100] *See the Classified Sayings of Master Ju 2.26b–27a.*

as a pure and perfect moral norm. The Four Sprouts find their locus classicus in the Mencius, *where they describe the nascent manifestations of four core Confucian virtues. The Seven Emotions, enumerated in a number of contemporary texts, describe the everyday human repertoire of affective responses. Describing the relationship between the Four Sprouts and Seven Emotions was a perennial challenge and served as the focus of one of the most intense, long-running, and sophisticated debates within Korean Confucianism.*

Someone asked, "Emperor Sun told U (C. Yu) 禹,[101] 'The Human Heart-Mind is precarious; the Heart-Mind of the Way is subtle. Always be discriminating [in regard to the former] and always be unified [with the latter]. Hold fast to the mean [between the two].'[102] How is it that while there is only one Heart-Mind the text talks about the Human Heart-Mind and the Heart-Mind of the Way?"

[I] replied, "It does not say that in the Heart-Mind-in-itself there are two Heart-Minds, only that in what emerges from the Heart-Mind-in-itself there are two modes or forms [of Heart-Mind]. Human beings are born with the most refined *Gi-Material* of the Five Phases, and their natures are the most noble. Nevertheless, were it not for the Heart-Mind, the nature would have nothing to latch on to and Pattern-Principle would have no way to be what it is. And so, it is said, 'Human beings can enlarge the Way. The Way cannot enlarge human beings.'[103] 'Way' refers to the nature; 'human beings' refers to the Heart-Mind. Nevertheless, what do we mean by the Heart-Mind? It is none other than the Heart-Mind of heaven and earth that gives birth to things and the spiritual luminosity of the primordial unity. This spiritual luminosity of the primordial unity descends into human beings and becomes the essence of their amorphous intelligence. It carries the nature and serves as the governor of the person and the root of the myriad affairs. This is what is referred to as the Heart-Mind of the Way. Nevertheless, human beings all have a physical form, and so they cannot avoid having a Human Heart-Mind. The Human Heart-Mind is born of the self-centeredness[104] of the physical *Gi-Material*. The Heart-Mind of the Way originates in the correctness of

---

[101] U (C. Yu) the Great (c. 2200–2100 BCE) was a legendary sage-ruler most famous for his tireless and selfless devotion to flood control. He established the Ha (C. Xia) 夏, the first historical dynasty in China.

[102] See the "Counsels of the Great U" (*Dae U Mo*; C. *Da Yu Mo* 大禹謨) section of the *Book of History*.

[103] *Analects* 15.29.

[104] See note 42, p. 18.

the nature and the mandate. Even sages, since they have a body composed of blood and flesh, cannot avoid having a Human Heart-Mind. Even a bad person equally receives the Pattern-Principle of the Great Ultimate, and so cannot but have the Heart-Mind of the Way. Nevertheless, when we talk about bad people having the Heart-Mind of the Way, this does not refer to anything beyond the occasional manifestations of the unvarying standard and Four Sprouts. When we talk about sages having the Human Heart-Mind, though it depends on the physical form in order to be manifested, 'They can follow what their Heart-Mind desires without ever overstepping what is proper';[105] their Human Heart-Mind is the Heart-Mind of the Way. As for the Heart-Minds of most people, the majority are born of *Gi-Material* and only a few originate in the nature and the mandate. Their Heart-Minds of the Way are profoundly beclouded and have difficulty shining through, while their Human Heart-Minds easily run wild and are difficult to control. This is what is referred to by saying, 'The Human Heart-Mind is precarious; the Heart-Mind of the Way is subtle.' When the Heart-Mind is manifested it becomes emotion. If people are able to examine what their Heart-Minds are manifesting and investigate the subtle springs of good and bad, select what is good and firmly hold fast to it, know what is bad and resolutely eliminate it, 'constantly ensure that the Heart-Mind of the Way governs and the Human Heart-Mind obeys its commands, then what is precarious will be settled, what is subtle will be manifest, and in action and stillness, speech and deed one naturally will avoid the errors of overstepping or falling short [of the proper standard].'[106] This is what is meant by saying, 'Always be discriminating [in regard to the former] and always be unified [with the latter]. Hold fast to the mean [between the two].'"

Someone said, "If what are called the Four Sprouts are manifestations of this Heart-Mind, then they likewise are emotions; so why are they separately referred to as the Four Sprouts?"

[I] replied, "The Four Sprouts refer to the four aspects of the nature— humaneness, righteousness, rites, and wisdom—when these are stimulated into movement and directly come forth. The Seven Emotions is simply a collective name for what is manifested when the nature and the mandate are combined with physical form and *Gi-Material*. It is not saying that outside of

---

[105] *Analects* 2.4.
[106] The quoted section is a close paraphrase of Ju Hui's preface to his *"Doctrine of the Mean" in Sections and Sentences.*

the Seven Emotions the Four Sprouts exist separately. If you don't distort the meaning by being overly literal,[107] you will get it."

Someone asked, "In that case, what does it mean when people talk about the nature manifesting or the Heart-Mind manifesting?"

[I] replied, "That is not how it is.[108] The nature is the Pattern-Principle with which the Heart-Mind is endowed, while the Heart-Mind is a vessel in which the nature is lodged. They are two and yet one. And so the unfathomable changes and transformations of the spiritual luminosity of one's amorphous intelligence are the Heart-Mind, but what enables the unfathomable changes and transformations of the spiritual luminosity of one's amorphous intelligence is Pattern-Principle. Pattern-Principle is without action; the Heart-Mind engages in action. Pattern-Principle leaves no trace behind; the Heart-Mind leaves traces behind. If there were no Pattern-Principle there would be nothing to manifest; if there were no Heart-Mind there would be no way to manifest. How could a blended mixture of Pattern-Principle and *Gi-Material* manifest only nature or only the Heart-Mind? Although earlier worthies have put forth such theories,[109] I have never dared to believe them. I offer my tentative thoughts on this matter, awaiting someone with understanding."

3. Exposition on the Rites and Music

The third exposition concerns two core features of Confucian moral learning. The rites (ye; C. li 禮) are the set of social practices that on the one hand enable one to develop the virtues and on the other enable one to manifest such traits of character. The rites include everything from what today we would call social etiquette to grand religious ceremonies. Music (ak; C. yue 樂) refers to the classical forms of music supported by the sage-kings of old. This music consisted of both dance and musical accompaniment and was thought to exert a direct

---

[107] This is a reference to *Mencius* 5A4, which teaches that one "must not insist on a term so as to distort the meaning of a sentence" if one wants to understand the meaning of the *Book of Poetry*.

[108] As Yunjidang makes clear in what follows, she rejects any interpretation that strongly separates the nature and Heart-Mind. It becomes clear that she attributes such a view to the school associated with Yi Toegye, which was the rival of the school of Yi Yulgok to which she and her brothers belonged. Yunjidang was critical of Toegye's view that Pattern-Principle and *Gi-Material* are separable. For more details of the Four-Seven Debate in English, see Kalton et al. 1994 and H. Kim 2016, 49–68.

[109] Here the reference is to the views of Toegye and his school. See prior note.

and dramatic power to shape the character of those who experienced and were moved by it.

The *Doctrine of the Mean* says, "If one is not the son of Heaven, he should not discuss the rites." It also says, "Though one has the throne, if he lacks the requisite virtue, he should not presume to create rites or music."[110] Great indeed are the ways that rites and music contribute to the practice of righteousness! "The rites are the regulating and adorning of heavenly Pattern-Principle, the standard and norm for human beings,"[111] and that through which the Way of humanity is established. Music is what harmonizes this regulation, softens its strictness, and moves people each day to make progress toward the good without realizing that they are perfecting the Way of humanity. In general, rites are based on reverence; music is based on harmony. Rites are based on strictness; music is based on softness. When harmony and reverence are balanced, this is the source from which the Way proceeds. And so neither rites nor music can be used in a one-sided manner. If rites dominate, there will be an excess of strictness, which can easily result in [people] turning away. If music dominates, there will be an outpouring of harmony, which can easily result in [people] lacking restraint. This is why Yuja (C. Youzi) 有子 said, "In the practice of the rites, harmony is most valued. Within the Way of the former kings, this is what was considered most fine, and so in things small and great we act accordingly. Yet harmony is not to be implemented in every case. If one, understanding harmony, manifests it without regulating it with the rites, this cannot be carried out."[112] How apropos, this saying! In general, the rites draw in people's Heart-Minds and intentions and bind together their sinews and bones; these are things human beings find bitter. Music delights the ears and eyes and harmonizes intentions and *Gi-Material*;[113] these are things human beings enjoy. And so it is easy to move from reverence to harmony but difficult to move from harmony to reverence. This is why harmony is most valued in the practice of the rites and yet the rites are also the root of music.[114] Human beings differ from birds and beasts in being regulated by the rites. The former kings understood this and

---

[110] See the *Doctrine of the Mean*, chapter 28.

[111] Ju Hui's commentary on *Analects* 1.12. See the *Collected Commentaries on the "Analects"* 1.5b. Cf. note 114 below.

[112] *Analects* 1.12.

[113] *Mencius* 2A2 talks about how intentions can guide the *Gi-Material* and thereby lead to proper behavior.

[114] The point is that while the rites are connected to basic emotions, proper music is founded only on ordered and cultivated emotions, which requires the practice of the rites. For similar ideas, see section 28 of the "Record of Music" chapter of the *Book of Rites*.

so carefully examined Heavenly Pattern-Principle, investigated human affairs, and instituted regulation by the rites, so they could hand down their teachings to later generations under heaven. From [the ceremonies of] capping, marriage, mourning, and sacrifice, to district drinking festivals and archery contests, and the banquets held for hosting visitors and guests[115]—none is not regulated by the rites. In the three hundred [major] and three thousand [minor ceremonies], none is not part of the rites, and yet the ceremonies of capping, marriage, mourning, and sacrifice are the root of the rites. In later generations, most scholar official families don't recognize that the rites and righteousness are this important; instead, they say, "Born in the present age, we should follow the customs of the times. Why must you talk about the rites?" Those who delight in simplicity and dislike being restricted and constrained rush ahead like this in all they do; it is fitting that they gallop headlong into the realm of birds and beasts, without realizing what they are doing. Xuuu! It is enough to make one sigh! It has been a long time since the Way of true music was abandoned. Now, I cannot go into the details; nevertheless, to be devoid of anything lacking in reverence is the essence of the rites and to apply them in an orderly, calm, and relaxed way is the harmony of music. This will give one a general idea of how music contributes to the Way. The master said, "People who are not humane, what can they have to do with the rites? People who are not humane, what can they have to do with music?"[116] Jeongja said, "If one is not humane, one will lack orderliness and harmony."[117] Orderliness and harmony refer to the rites and music, while humaneness refers to virtue. "As for the rites and music, do they refer to nothing more than jade, silk, bells, and drums?"[118] Only someone with virtue can create the rites and music. If one lacks virtue, though one exchanges jades and silks, strikes the bells and beats the drums, still one cannot call these the rites or music. Reverence is the aggregation of virtue; if one is able to be reverent, one must have virtue. This is why I say, "Reverence is the pivot of the rites and harmony the unity of music." If one is able to be reverent and harmonious, the rites and music will be complete and one's virtuous nature perfected. Jagong (C. Zigong) 子貢 said, "Look at their rites and you will know their governance; listen to their music and you will know their

---

[115] Descriptions of them can be found in texts such as the *Book of Etiquette and Ritual* (*Uirye*; C. *Yili* 儀禮) and the *Book of Rites*.

[116] *Analects* 3.3.

[117] A paraphrase of the original, cited by Ju Hui as part of his commentary on *Analects* 3.3, in his *Collected Commentaries on the "Analects"* 2.1b.

[118] A close paraphrase of *Analects* 17.11. Jade, silk, bells, and drums refer to ritual equipment and musical instruments.

virtue."[119] Gongja said, "The So (C. Shao) 韶 [music] is perfectly beautiful and perfectly good."[120] Ju Hui explained this by saying, "By 'good' he means the substance of the sound."[121] Substance here refers to virtue. And so, to help the rites and music flourish, nothing is more important than honoring one's virtuous nature.

4. Exposition on *Overcoming the Self and Returning to the Rites Is Humaneness*

Our fourth exposition is focused on a famous line from the Analects,[122] *which has been interpreted in a variety of ways throughout the course of the Confucian tradition. The core issue concerns to what degree the self and, in particular, our everyday emotions need to be overcome—and in what sense—in order to accord with the rites and realize the moral way. On the one hand, one can incline toward a kind of ascetic ideal that jeopardizes the widely held belief in the goodness of human nature; on the other, one can allow greater accommodation of human emotions, which risks moral slackness and indulgence.*

The accumulated refined essence of heaven and earth gives birth to the myriad creatures; those that receive the most correct and penetrating part of this endowment become human beings. Fundamentally, their endowment is pure and without corruption; it is radiant and the highest good. Its purity is the Pattern-Principle of care and the complete virtue of my Heart-Mind. Its radiance is the Pattern-Principle of yielding and the ritual norm (*uichik*; C. *yize* 儀則) for human affairs. [Originally] all human beings have this uncorrupted [endowment] and all possess the highest good. Nevertheless, once their physical form has taken shape, outside things unavoidably make contact with it. Once outside things make contact with their physical form, people cannot avoid being moved within. When they are moved within, the Seven Emotions issue forth; these are called pleasure, anger, grief, joy, love, hate, and desire. Once the emotions are moved and gallop forth, if one does not know how to restrain them, they drift into chaos and one forgets the way back. If one carries out affairs guided by one's physical form and *Gi-Material*,

---

[119] *Mencius* 2A2.
[120] *Analects* 3.25.
[121] Ju Hui's comment on the above passage from his *Collected Commentaries on the "Analects"* 2.9a.
[122] The quoted line that provides the theme is from *Analects* 12.1.

one loses the essence that [originally] is the highest good, devoid of corruption. The physical form and *Gi-Material* refer to the self. The highest good refers to the rites. The difference between not being humane and being humane is nothing more than the distinction between the self and the rites. And so, for this reason, one who has awakened [morally] understands this and certainly will investigate critically, choose meticulously, and hold firmly to the distinction between them [i.e., self and the rites] with the aim of reaching the radiant highest good and returning to one's original essence. One's "original" [essence] refers to humaneness. I have heard that among the ancients, there was An Yeon who was the kind of man who loved to learn. He once asked the master about humaneness and the master said, "To overcome the self and return to the rites is humaneness."[123] Anja followed his teacher's instructions and fully exerted his talents to make clear and distinguish the line between heavenly Pattern-Principle and human desire and to single-mindedly preserve this distinction. If he understood something to be human desire, he would restrain and extinguish it, overcome and eliminate it. His only fear in this regard was that he would neglect this effort even momentarily. If he understood something to be heavenly Pattern-Principle, he would reverence, cherish, and "clasp it tightly to his breast."[124] His only fear in this regard was that he would be remiss in performing some minute aspect of the rites. Once he reached the point where he had accumulated a reservoir of authenticity and prolonged effort, he was completely cleansed of human desires and fully immersed and permeated by heavenly Pattern-Principle. [Even when he] wanted to abandon [his learning], he was unable to do so.[125] Once his Heart-Mind no longer was contrary to humaneness, he was 99 percent of the way toward being a sage. The only respect in which he fell short was that he still had to "make an effort to hit to mark."[126] Had he been granted more years of life,[127] his humaneness and sageness would have been beyond measure!

In general, ever since *Geon* and *Gon*[128] gave rise to the universe, from the ancients Bok Hui (C. Fu Xi) 伏羲[129] and Sin Nong (C. Shen Nong)

---

[123] *Analects* 12.1.

[124] *Doctrine of the Mean*, chapter 8.

[125] *Analects* 9.11, where An Yeon says this of himself, "[The master has] broadened me with culture and restrained me with the rites. Even when I feel a desire to abandon his learning, I cannot."

[126] *Doctrine of the Mean*, chapter 22, says that "One who is perfectly sincere hits the mark without making effort and grasps it without having to reflect."

[127] When he was only twenty-nine years old, An Yeon's hair turned white; he died a few years later, leading Gongja to exclaim, "Heaven has forsaken me! Heaven has forsaken me!" (*Analects* 11.9).

[128] The two fundamental forces in the universe, associated with heaven and earth respectively.

[129] Bok Hui is a mythological cultural hero who, along with his sister Yeowa (C. Nüwa 女媧), is credited with creating humanity and inventing hunting, fishing, and cooking.

神農[130] down to Kings Geol and Ju and Robber Cheok, all have had the same heaven-mandated nature, but then what do sages do that makes them sages? What do I do that makes me a common person? It is because I am constrained by *Gi-Material*, beclouded by desires for things, and thereby lose my originally [endowed] humaneness. If one were to say that the nature originally contains what is bad, that would be the end of it. But now, since that is not the case, the nature possessed by Yo, Sun, [the Duke of] Ju, Gongja, Anja, and Maengja is something I inherently have,[131] and so how could I alone be incapable of learning what Anja learned?

Someone asked, "Do you not overstate the case? In native capacity, Anja was close to those who are born knowing,[132] and so for him it was easy to overcome the self and easy for him to return to the rites. It was easy for him to be humane, because his *Gi-Material* was extremely clean and pure. Most people, who have turgid and adulterated *Gi-Material*, seek to change and become fine, but though they make one hundred times the effort he put forth, how could they succeed in transforming themselves? This is why there are none in later times who are able to return, as Anja did, to a state where their [Heart-Minds are] not contrary to humaneness and why they are unable, even with study, to reach such a state."

[I] replied, "That is not so. Though people's endowments of *Gi-Material* are not equal, if we trace back to the original essence of the primordial unity that they received, then the sages and common people are the same. It is only that as the flowing *Gi-Material* congeals and collects, the turgid, adulterated dregs thoroughly mix together and form common people. If such people really are able to exert one thousand times the effort of others in eliminating the admixture of dregs, then the original essence of the primordial unity will return and remain there within them and they can return to their original humaneness. Nevertheless, what is the first step one must take in making this effort? [I] say nothing is more important than to establish a commitment and earnestly practice.[133] If one is just able to establish a commitment and earnestly practice, one can adopt what Anja described as the Heart-Mind that thinks, 'What kind of man was Sun? What kind of man am I?,'[134] fully comprehend

---

[130] The "Divine Farmer" Sin Nong is a mythological Chinese deity in Chinese folk religion; more generally, he is venerated as a mythical sage ruler of prehistoric times.

[131] For the idea that we inherently have an innate good nature, see *Mencius* 6A6.

[132] Identified as those who come into the world with the greatest natural talent. See *Analects* 16.9.

[133] To establish a commitment (*ipji*; C. *lizhi* 立志) and earnestly practice (*dokhaeng*; C. *duxing* 篤行) are regular themes in classical Confucian texts. See, for example, *Mencius* 5B1 and chapter 20 of the *Doctrine of the Mean* respectively.

[134] *Mencius* 3A1.

the Pattern-Principle of the myriad things, investigate the subtle springs of good and bad, understand what is bad and overcome and eliminate it, understand what is good and firmly guard it, make earnest and unremitting effort, be cautious and fearful and not burdened by the slightest vestige of self-centered desire or ever be separated, even for a moment, from heavenly Pattern-Principle—whether in motion or at rest, in speech or in silence—and always follow the norm of heavenly Pattern-Principle—this is what is known as 'overcoming the self and returning to the rites is humaneness'; this is what is known as 'making bright one's bright virtue.'[135] Bright virtue is what one gets from heaven and is 'the great root of heaven and earth.'[136] Once the great root is established and the all-pervading Way is implemented, heaven and earth will take their proper places, the myriad things will be nourished, and one will 'flow in the same stream as heaven and earth.'[137] One who is like this is a sage, and this is also what made Anja a secondary sage. The reason there are no great worthies in later ages is only because people have not firmly established a commitment. Since the time of Jeong I and Jang Jae, we have had the theory of the *Gi-Material* nature. If people really are able to apply themselves to transform the partiality [of the *Gi-Material* nature], those who are weak can change and become strong, those who are foolish can change and become enlightened. Those who are turgid and adulterated can change and become clean and pure. If they are not able to change [the *Gi-Material* nature], then to the end they remain as they are. Whether one becomes humane or does not become humane depends only on oneself.[138] And so I say, nothing is more important than establishing a commitment and making genuine effort. This is why noble people do not refer to the *Gi-Material* nature as the nature.[139] Oh! When has heaven ever created human beings who are not humane? It is only because their Heart-Minds become enslaved by their physical form that they are satisfied doing violence to and throwing themselves away,[140] and then say, 'My *Gi-Material* is not fine! How can I dare to learn to become a sage or a worthy!' Fearful and foolish, they only follow along in this way[141] and only act in ways contrary to the rites. They happily descend to the

---

[135] See the opening chapter of the *Great Learning*.

[136] See the opening chapter of the *Doctrine of the Mean*.

[137] *Mencius* 7A13.

[138] *Mencius* 7A3.

[139] The idea is that noble people do not regard the lower parts of their nature as their true or destined nature. See *Mencius* 7B24.

[140] See *Mencius* 4A10 for people who do violence to and throw themselves away.

[141] Reading 循 as 徇 in the original.

lowest level and never realize how pathetic it is that they rot away along with the [fallen] grass and trees or how shameful it is that they are not far removed from the birds and beasts! Oh—is this not lamentable! Those who are like this are already so chronically beclouded that one cannot even talk with them about humaneness. Truly, as the master said, 'In the end, what can one do for them?'[142] Eeee! Though I am a woman, still, the nature I originally received contained no distinction between male and female. Though I have not been able to learn what An Yeon learned, I earnestly share his commitment to become a sage. And so, I have made a summary of what I have observed and written it down here to collect my thoughts."

5. Exposition on *Whether Good Order or Chaos [in a State] Depends on Getting the Right People*

Exposition 5 explores a characteristically Confucian theme regarding the basis of good government. Specifically, the theme is whether good order depends on having not only a wise and capable sovereign but also worthy ministers who can advise and assist him. Confucians insist that sustainable and successful government can only be achieved when morally cultivated individuals occupy positions of power and influence. In her treatment of this theme Yunjidang emphasizes that even the most talented and morally good ruler, a sage ruler, requires ministers of equal ability and character in order to achieve, sustain, and pass down a peaceful and prosperous reign.

As for whether good order or chaos [in a state] depends on getting the right people, since the time of Yo, Sun, and the Three Dynasties, even when a sage ruler [occupied the throne] above, there was also a need for a minister of outstanding talent supporting and assisting him below before there could be a well-ordered government. What is the reason for this? Even the most astute of hearing cannot listen to everyone; even the clearest of vision cannot look at everything. And so, an enlightened [ruler] and outstanding [minister][143] must find one another, those above and those below must help one another, and only then can they "share heaven's posts and order heaven's offices"[144]

---

[142] See *Analects* 9.24.

[143] The idea that enlightened ruler and outstanding minister must work together is expressed in the "Ik (C. Yi) 益 and Jik (C. Ji) 稷" section of the *Book of History*.

[144] *Mencius* 5B12.

and thereby bring peace to heaven's people; this is a natural Pattern-Principle. I would like to try to raise and discuss the general outlines of this principle.

Emperor Yo was a sage of the highest order and he had Sa Ak (C. Si Yue) 四岳[145] [as his minister]; he raised Sun up from the fields and had him assist in the great affairs of state; thereupon there was great good order. When Sun ruled all under heaven, he needed the help of Go (C. Gao) 皋,[146] Gi (C. Kui) 夔,[147] Jik (C. Ji) 稷,[148] Gye (C. Xie) 契,[149] and a total of some twenty-two ministers, and all under heaven again enjoyed great good order. [When Sun abdicated,] U of the Ha dynasty took over; he continued to use Sun's ministers to carry out his rule. His son Gye (C. Qi) 啓 also proved to be worthy and was able to keep his father's ministers and not alter his father's administration. He reverently continued the achievements of U's reign and also did not allow his legacy of good order [in government] to fall. When the virtue of the Ha declined and reached the age of [the tyrant] King Geol, a violent ruler occupied the throne above, worthy men [fled into] the wilds, and all under heaven fell into great chaos. Heaven then bestowed its mandate on Tang the Successful,[150] who was able to get Yi Yun (C. Yi Yin) 伊尹[151] from the wilds of Yu Sin (C. You Shen) 有莘.[152] He drove out Geol in order to save the people and afterward all under heaven again enjoyed good order. Following him, Go Jong (C. Gao Zong) 高宗[153] of the Sang was also able to get Bu Yeol [to assist him] and extended the reign of good order. When the virtue of the Eun (also known as the Sang dynasty) had declined and resulted in King Ju ascending the throne, worthy ministers were executed while villainous ones were employed. They worked hard at what was contrary to the Way and all under heaven again fell into great chaos.

---

[145] Sa Ak advised Yo on matters such as flood control and the king's succession, advancing Sun as the best candidate for the latter. See the "Canon of Yo" section of the *Book of History*.

[146] Go Yo (C. Gao Yao) 皋陶 served as Minister of Law under Emperor Sun and became a political senior adviser of Emperor U.

[147] Gi (C. Kui) 夔 was Sun's music master. See the "Record of Music" chapter of the *Book of Rites*.

[148] Jik (C. Ji) 稷 or Hu Jik (C. Hou Ji) 后稷 was Minister of Agriculture under Shun. See *Mencius* 3A4.

[149] Gye (C. Xie) 契 was Minister of Education under Sun. See *Mencius* 3A4.

[150] King Tang (c. 1675–1646 BCE) was the first king of the Sang dynasty. His name appears as Tae Eul (C. Tai Yi) 大乙 on oracle bone inscriptions.

[151] See following note.

[152] Yi Yun was Yu Sin's slave; when Yu Sin's daughter married King Tang, he became Tang's slave. Noticing his gifts as a cook, Tang made him his chef and Yi used this opportunity to discuss current affairs with the King. He helped Yi plan and carry out the defeat Geol of Ha and found the new dynasty.

[153] Go Jong is better known as King Mu Jeong, who reigned c. 1250–1192 BCE (traditional reign dates: 1324–1266 BCE). He is the earliest figure to be confirmed by historical records.

Kings Mun and Mu received the mandate of heaven and also got Grand Master Sang Bo (C. Shang Fu) 尚父.[154] [They] then annihilated King Ju and brought peace to all under heaven, so that all under heaven again enjoyed a period of great good order. King Mu said, "I have ten able ministers."[155] *Nan sin* (C. *Luan chen*) 亂臣 [in this context] means orderly or able ministers. In general, the Duke of Ju, Duke So (C. Shao) 召,[156] Duke Tae (C. Tai) 太,[157] Duke Pil (C. Bi) 畢,[158] and others were his great worthy and sage ministers. Oh! In the ancient past, sage emperors and enlightened kings ruled all under heaven and individual states. And yet, even such great, sage rulers needed to get worthies to assist them, and only then were they able to extend order throughout the world, as we have seen. In later ages, when mediocre rulers and inferior ministers governed states, to expect them to achieve such order is very difficult. How much more so when violent rulers and obsequious ministers govern states; is it possible for them to avoid disorder? As for the way in which the great sages Yo, Sun, and U were able to pass down their reign from one to another, this required nothing more than the method of keeping their Heart-Minds discriminating and unified.[159] The worthy and capable ministers who supported and assisted them also all ordered themselves through this method and employed it to report to their lords. And so the means by which sage rulers and worthy ministers mutually reinforced one another and extended good order—how could it depend on anything other than this! This is what Yi Yun meant in saying, "We both (i.e., I and King Tang) possess pure virtue."[160] Oh! Since the Ju dynasty decayed, none in the world has managed to understand this principle. They do not understand what [the expression] "We both possess pure virtue" is all about. They one-sidedly rely upon their own point of view; they like it when people are obsequious toward them. When they speak, no

---

[154] See the "Decade of King Mun" (*Mun wang ji gye*; *Wen wang zhi shi* 文王之什) sections of the *Book of Poetry*, Mao #236.

[155] *Analects* 8.20. See also the "Great Declaration II" (*Tae seo jung*; C. *Tai shi zhong* 泰誓中), section of the *Book of History*.

[156] The Duke of So was known as a loyal minister and the progenitor of the clan name So 召.

[157] The Duke of Tae (Taegong; C. Taigong 太公) is also known as Grand Duke Mang (Taegong Mang; C. Taigong Wang 太公望), Gang Taegong (C. Jiang Taigong 姜太公), and Yeo Sang (C. Lu Shang 呂尚). As a Chinese ancient noble, he bore an ancestral name, Gang, as well as a clan name, Yeo. His given name was Sang (C. Shang) 尚. He is celebrated as a masterful strategist and famous for helping to overthrow the Sang dynasty.

[158] Go, Duke of Pil 畢公高, was a son of King Mun of Ju and went on to serve the Ju as a loyal minister.

[159] See note 102 above.

[160] See the "Common Possession of Pure Virtue" chapter of the *Book of History*.

one offers a contrary view. It only makes sense that with each day there is less good order and more chaos. Xuuu—this makes one sigh!

6. Exposition on *My Way Has One Thread Running through It*

Exposition 6 is focused on another famous line from the Analects,[161] *which has been interpreted in a variety of ways throughout the course of the Confucian tradition. In the early stages of the tradition, commentators most often sought to explain how the various practical teachings of Gongja all hang together to form a consistent and coherent system. Neo-Confucian thinkers tended to interpret it in terms of how their ontological and metaphysical theories provided a foundation that unified and correlated each and every norm and standard described in the more practical aspects of Gongja's philosophy. The latter strategy is followed in this exposition.*

Someone asked me, "Heaven is high and earth is low—this [relationship] is fixed in the hexagrams *Geon* and *Gon*—and together they create, nurture, and complete the myriad things. For everything born between heaven and earth, each has its particular nature and governing norm. In the course of this process, sages come forth; they understand what heaven decrees as the proper standard and what conduct is correct for people and creatures, and they fashion methods and regulations in order to instruct them, so that each can follow its nature and norm. Human beings have the Way of humans; creatures have the Way of creatures, and this is true not only of human beings and creatures. In regard to human beings, the major regulations concern the Five Relationships[162] and Hundred Forms of Proper Conduct; the minor regulations concern the nine apertures[163] and hundred bodily parts, each of which has its particular norm. It is undeniable that the basis and origin of these regulations are not the same, nor are they infinite in number. This being so, why did Gongja tell Jeungja, 'My Way has one thread running through it?'"

---

[161] The quoted line that provides the theme is from *Analects* 4.15.
[162] Traditionally said to be the relationships between parent and child, ruler and minister, husband and wife, elder and younger brother, and friend and friend.
[163] Reading 竅 as 竅 in the original.

I replied, "Have you not heard the theory that 'each possesses every-thing?'[164] Each receiving its proper nature as decreed by the changes and transformations of the Way of *Geon* is the myriad of different manifestations of the single source. Though we say each receives what is proper to it, they all find their source in a single Great Ultimate, and so the myriad of different manifestations have a single source. The single source is what 'everything' refers to; the myriad of different manifestations is what 'each possesses' refers to. If there were no myriad of different manifestations, the changes and transformations [of *Geon*] could not proceed; if there was not a single source, the changes and transformations would lack a place from which to originate. Only the nature of sages possesses an abundance of the heavenly. If you re-turn and explore it, you will find much more to learn from the teaching of 'one thread running through it.'"

[The questioner then] said, "Since I already have heard your instructions regarding how the Way of heaven has a single source, I asked about the Way of the sages, which has one thread running through it, but you replied by ap-pealing to the Way of heaven. Isn't this confused?"

I replied, "Please sit down and I will tell you. Earlier, didn't you talk about 'For everything born between heaven and earth, each has its particular na-ture?' What you refer to as the nature, how can it be sought for elsewhere? It is simply the Pattern-Principle of the Great Ultimate. The sages themselves also are the single Great Ultimate. Since the Pattern-Principle of the Great Ultimate already is said to be the myriad of different manifestations which have a single source, how could the Way of the sages differ from this? Oh! *Only the decree of heaven* freely operates and nurtures, giving birth to the myriad of different manifestations that are human beings and creatures. And yet, in itself, how *deep and unceasing.*[165] To be deep and unceasing, is this not to be one? Only the Way of the sages is able to extensively respond with the various proper standards and react appropriately to the myriad changes of things and affairs, but in itself it is perfectly unified and without flaw. To be perfectly unified and without flaw, is this not to be one? Now if you see the differences in its various manifestations but doubt that Pattern-Principle is

---

[164] This is the fundamental metaphysical belief of neo-Confucianism, that each and every thing possesses the Great Ultimate and a complete endowment of Pattern-Principle, the same original na-ture. The idea is closely related to the teaching "Pattern-Principle is one but its manifestations are many" (see note 46 in this chapter), meaning that there is an underlying unity beneath the phenom-enal diversity of the world.

[165] This and the earlier italicized line are from the "Sacrificial Odes of Zhou" (*Ju Song*; C. *Zhou Song* 周頌) section of the *Book of Poetry*, Mao #267. In both cases, the emphasis is added.

one, then how can you be ready to discuss the marvelous nature of the Way in itself? As for sages, their virtue is unified with heaven. And so, when I bring up the Way of heaven, the Way of the sages, which has one thread running through it, already is present therein. This is why I spoke in more detail about the Way of heaven and only more generally about the Way of the sages. You were not able to give me the other three corners [once I had provided you with the first][166] but instead replied that I am confused. Is this not strange?"

The person questioning me said, "Yes! Yes!" and retreated.

---

[166] Reference to *Analects* 7.8.

Admonitions (箴)

1. Admonition on the Heart-Mind

The first admonition is modeled on the "Four Admonitions" (Sa Jam; C. Si Zhen 四箴) of Jeong I, which concern four separate topics: looking (si; C. shi 視), listening (cheong; C. ting 聽), speaking (eon; C. yan 言), and acting (dong; C. dong 動). See the Collected Works for the Two Jeongs *9.8b. These four topics, in turn, are modeled on Analects 12.1, which begins "To overcome the self and return to rites is humaneness" and goes on to present four prohibitions (each in four-character lines): do not look, listen, speak, or act contrary to rites. Jeongildang's composition, like Jeong I's "Four Admonitions," is composed of sets of two interrelated four-character lines. We have tried to preserve this stylistic feature in the English translation.*

> The Heart-Mind originally is amorphous;[1]
> Spiritually mysterious, it is beyond comprehension.
> It goes forth and returns, following no fixed schedule;[2]
> It responds to things without leaving a trace behind.[3]
> If one holds fast to it, it is preserved;
> If one lets go of it, it is lost.[4]
> If one is not sincere, how can one preserve it?
> If one is not reverent, how can one nurture it?
> When the nature is manifested, it is subtle;
> When the physical form makes contact [with things], it is
>   precarious.[5]
> One must enlarge what is subtle;
> One must secure what is precarious.

[1] The first and fourth lines quote the opening lines of the first of the four admonitions by Jeong I.
[2] *Mencius* 6A8.
[3] The second line of Jeong I's "Admonition on Looking."
[4] See *Mencius* 6A8.
[5] The contrast between the "precarious" and "subtle" recalls two lines from "The Counsels of the Great U" chapter of the *Book of History*, which say, "The Human Heart-Mind is precarious. The Heart-Mind of the Way is subtle."

Korean Women Philosophers and the Ideal of a Female Sage. Philip J. Ivanhoe and Hwa Yeong Wang, Oxford University Press. © Oxford University Press 2023. DOI: 10.1093/oso/9780197508688.003.0006

Guard the subtle and examine the incipient and tenuous;

This is the standard for managing the Heart-Mind.

Remain constant whether it is hidden or manifest;

Do not let up even for a moment.

"[A fool] by thinking can become a sage;

[A sage] by not thinking can become a fool."[6]

[Consider the examples of] Emperor Sun and Robber Cheok;

The same Heart-Mind but as different as heaven and earth!

Some neither understand nor act [for the good];

With them, one still can talk.

Some understand but fail to act;

They throw themselves away.[7]

Do not say it is [too] lofty and remote;

If one acts one will get it.

[Apply yourself] from dawn to dusk;

Do not dare to be remiss.

"The Lord on High draws near to you;

Do not be of two Heart-Minds."[8]

Be thoughtful! Be reverent!

The Heart-Mind alone is a mirror.[9]

Heaven gave birth to the people;

And endowed them with a [moral] norm.[10]

Oh my soul!

Be as reverent and wise as you can be!

2. Admonition on Endurance

This admonition does not strictly follow the compositional model of sets of interrelated four-character lines, and so we have not tried to convey this in the translation.

---

[6] See the "Numerous Regions" (*Da Bang*; C. *Duo Fang* 多方) section of the "Book of Zhou" (*Ju Seo*; C. *Zhou Shu* 周書) chapter of the *Book of History*.

[7] See *Mencius* 4A10 for the notion of throwing oneself away.

[8] These lines are from the "Greater Hymns" chapter of the *Book of Poetry*.

[9] The thought being that only the Heart-Mind can accurately reflect and respond to things and events.

[10] Paraphrasing a line from the *Book of Poetry* that is cited by Maengja in *Mencius* 6A6. The poem is "The Multitude of People" (*Jeungmin*; C. *Zhengmin* 烝民) (Mao #260) and the line says, "Heaven gave birth to the multitude of people. And for each thing it established a norm."

My basic nature is to be impetuous. When I was young, if something did not feel right in my Heart-Mind, I was unable to tolerate it. When I grew older, I became aware of this affliction and made an effort to overcome and eliminate it, but the root of the affliction remains. At times, when this tendency is just subtly emerging; I find there is nothing I can do about it. This led me to think to myself, I have been decreed a most meager fate! Of the Four Deprivations, I suffer three.[11] When I gaze before me or look behind, there is no one to console me. From the past until the present, how many people have suffered a fate as meager as mine? Even with the strength of a man, one would barely be able to carry on. How much more difficult is it for a woman to endure? Nevertheless, those unable to endure [life's difficulties] would be fine if only they could find a way to avoid them. Since this is not possible, they should "preserve the Heart-Mind and nurture the nature in order to serve heaven."[12] Since heaven has endowed me with such a bitter [fate], must it not be to "move my Heart-Mind and temper my nature in order to improve and augment my deficiencies?"[13] If not, my crimes and sins must be severe and weighty in order to call for such extreme punishment! In that case, heaven must really just want me to end in this state, and I should simply obediently accept this as correct, without grumbling or assigning blame.[14] And so I wrote this admonition to alert myself to be on guard.

The lyric says:

> The petty person values life,
> The noble person values righteousness.
> If it is difficult to have both,
> Righteousness alone is the standard.[15]

---

[11] The Four Deprivations are to be a widower, widow, orphan, or childless. In the course of her life, Yunjidang suffered the last three.

[12] *Mencius* 7A1.

[13] *Mencius* 6B35.

[14] See *Mencius* 2B13, where we are told, "A noble person neither grumbles against heaven nor blames others."

[15] The themes here of a choice between life and righteousness, and what constitutes one's true destiny, echo and explore ideas raised in early Confucian texts. For example, *Analects* 12.5 says, "Life and death are matters of destiny; wealth and honor lie in Heaven." *Mencius* 6A10 explicitly presents the choice between preserving one's life and maintaining righteousness and insists that, if necessary, one must sacrifice the former in order to preserve the latter. *Mencius* 7B33 teaches that noble people pursue morality and leave their well-being concerning prudential goods, like longevity, wealth, and station, to heaven to decide. *Mencius* 7A1 urges us not to allow the desire to prolong our lives to affect our commitment to self-cultivation. *Mencius* 7A2 makes clear that one's proper destiny (*jeong myeong*; C. *zheng ming* 正命) requires one to dedicate oneself to morality. Overall, the idea is that one must pursue morality regardless of one's lot in life or how it affects one's prudential good. The former is within one's control; the latter often is not.

For those who meet many difficulties in life,
Death can prove to be a joy.
Long life and early death are matters of destiny,
Of what does our righteousness consist?
If something is said to be proper,
Look upon death as a returning home.[16]
If something is said to be improper,
Do not act contrary to [proper] destiny.
Simply cultivate yourself,
And always listen to heaven.
Do not dwell on your numerous concerns,
Maintain your role and rest secure in it.
How can one rest secure in it?
Endurance is the [requisite] virtue.
How does one endure difficulties?
One must be sincere in establishing a commitment.
Great indeed is having a commitment,
It leads one through a myriad of affairs.
The seven emotions follow their proper orbits,
The hundred parts of the body obey its commands.
If you are able to establish a commitment,
Through practice you shall form your nature.[17]

3. Admonition on Regular Practice

The title "regular practice" (si seup; C. shi xi 時習) is from the opening lines of the Analects: "Is it not a joy to learn and regularly practice [what one has learned]?" Like the first admonition, this one consists of four-character lines.

Heaven gave birth to the people;
And endowed us with the unvarying standard.[18]

---

[16] A common expression found in texts like the *Hanbija* (C. *Hanfeizi*) 韓非子 12.11b and the *Spring and Autumn Annals of Mr. Yeo* (*Yeo ssi Chunchu*; C. *Lü shi Chunqiu*) 呂氏春秋 2.6b.

[17] Quoting the "Tae Gab" chapter (*Tae Gab*; C. *Tai Jia* 太甲) (upper part) of the *Book of History*. For the same idea, see the third line from the end of the following admonition.

[18] See note 76, page 99. These lines also are quoted in *Mencius* 6A6.

We have received this [from heaven];
And so we should not lose it.
Few are those who perfect it;
Many are those who lose it.
What is the reason for this?
[The Heart-Mind] can become ensnared by *Gi-Material* and
    attacked by desires.
How can one return to its beginning?
Choose the good and hold on to it resolutely![19]
If one does not study, how can one attain clear understanding?
If one does not practice, how will one accumulate results?
[Attend to] each thought and every moment;
Focus upon this illustrious destiny.
Do not deviate by even a hair's breadth;
Or you will lose the unvarying standard.
Be wholehearted and diligent!
Renew yourself each and every day.[20]
Do not be lax, even for a moment;
This is the difference between becoming Emperor Sun or
    Robber Cheok.
When you sit, be upright (like the impersonator of the dead);
When you stand, assume a respectful and balanced stance.[21]
Let your eyes never look upon what is lewd.
Let your ears never listen to what is askance.
Do not speak recklessly.
Always act cautiously.[22]
To climb on high, one begins from what is low;
To travel afar, one starts from what is near.
This is regular practice;
Practice shall form your nature.
And so, I wrote this admonition;
Be on guard my soul!

---

[19] See chapter 22 of the *Doctrine of the Mean*.
[20] See chapter 6 of the *Great Learning*.
[21] See the "Summary of the Rules of Propriety" chapter (*Gongnye*; C. *Quli* 曲禮) (upper part) in the *Book of Rites*.
[22] These four lines reflect the four prohibitions described in *Analects* 12.1 and present a departure from the style of sets of two interrelated lines.

4. Admonition on Diligence in Learning: A Response to the Parting Poem of My Eldest Nephew

Since I was last separated from you,
Two years have passed by.
The sorrow and joy of parting and union,
Are constants [in human life] since ancient times.
Is this not more so in the case of a married woman,[23]
Who is far from her brothers and parents?
Those with understanding do not lament,
Those with knowledge harbor no remorse.
But you and I,
Are special in the feelings we cherish.
You lost the one upon whom you depended,[24]
And look upon me as a parent.
I have lost a son,
And look upon you as my child.
Now we are separated far from one another,
And I have no hope of meeting you again.
My heart falls into despair,
How can it not be scorched?
Nodding off, I see you before me,
Awakening, I beat my breast.[25]
Remembering past times when we were together,
Daydreaming of being with one another.
When all is quiet, I reflect on this,
Falling tears moisten my [face].
My Heart-Mind is exhausted and tired,
Unable to spread its wings and take flight.
I cannot flee from my destiny,
And reach your wide embrace!
And so what I hope for,
Is that you succeed in establishing yourself.[26]

[23] Yunjidang is referring to herself here.
[24] She is here referring to the loss of his mother.
[25] This line is from *the Book of Poetry*, Mao #26.
[26] *Analects* 2.4 says that a young man should take his stand or become established at age thirty.

You already are grown,

And it is hard to stop the flight of time.

The ancient sages did not waste a single minute,

You should not waste even a second.[27]

Hold close and revere your father's instructions,

"Be cautious and diligent all day long."[28]

"The burden is heavy and the way is long."[29]

Can a scholar take himself lightly?

He studies and improves himself,

He does not bring disgrace to his parents.[30]

Though I am not clever,

My words are logical and reasonable.

Do nothing careless or neglectful,

The refinement of your work lies in diligence.[31]

Be dedicated! Be assiduous!

Your achievement will be like gold and jade.

If your mother could know of this,

It would console her spirit.

In the past, sages issued a warning,

Which I will roughly summarize.

To love without instructing,

Is to offer the love of a bird or beast.[32]

I convey my feelings to you,

In response to the poem that you sent.

My love [alone] may be of no help to you,

[But] I hope you can infer how I feel.

---

[27] The text actually says he should cherish a period that would be six modern seconds (i.e., one-tenth of what is translated as a minute in the previous line).

[28] This is a very close paraphrase of a line found on the hexagram *Geon* in the *Book of Changes*.

[29] This is a very close paraphrase of a line found in *Analects* 8.7.

[30] This is a very close paraphrase of a line found in the "Minor Hymns" section of the *Book of Poetry*, Mao #196.

[31] Quoting a line from the Dang (C. Tang) 唐 (618–907 CE) dynasty Confucian Han Yu's (C. Han Yu) 韓愈 (768–824 CE) essay "Explaining How to Advance in Learning" (*Jinhak hae*; C. *Jinxue jie* 進學解). See the *Dongadang Commentaries on the "Collected Works of Changnyeo" (Dongadang changnyeo jip ju*; C. *Dongyatang Changli ji zhu* 東雅堂昌黎集註) 12.4b.

[32] Cf. *Analects* 14.7, "Can one love without laboring the object of one's love? Can one be loyal without instructing the object of one's loyalty?," and *Mencius* 7A37, "To love [a scholar] but not respect [him] is to keep him as a domestic animal." A similar sentiment is expressed by Sama Gwang during the Song dynasty. See *Precepts for Family Life* (*Ga Beom*; C. *Jia Fan* 家範) 3.5a.

Inscriptions (銘)

1. Inscription on [the Theme of] a Mirror

You are the full face of the moon,
The brilliant crystal of a sunny day.
The [icy] breath of a frosty morning,
The essence of autumn waters.[1]
Your Heart-Mind is unburdened by self-centeredness,
There is nothing your brightness does not discern.
The good is [revealed as] good; the bad as bad.
Even an *Imae* (C. *Jimei*) 魑魅[2] cannot hide from you.
You understand like a spirit,[3]
You are as straight as an arrow.
Polished, you become ever brighter,
Never allowing even a hair's breadth of distortion.
Oh! That human beings
Are not the equal of a thing!
Human beings are not your equal
When they are obstructed by things.
How can they remove these obstructions?
By clearing their Heart-Minds and overcoming themselves.
If for one day [they can] overcome themselves,[4]

---

[1] Autumn waters are thought to be especially pure and clear.

[2] The *Imae* is a demon that is said to dwell in the mountain forests. It has the face of a human beings, the body of a beast, and four legs. It has the ability to enchant and charm people, but a mirror will reveal its true form. The belief that mirrors have the power to reveal the true form of demons is found in both East and West.

[3] Section 10 of the "Great Appendix" (upper part) to the *Book of Changes* says that only the most spiritual thing in the world is such that "when stimulated it comprehends the principles of all things under Heaven."

[4] *Analects* 12.1 describes the task of attaining humaneness as "overcoming the self and returning to the rites" and says that "if one day one overcomes the self and returns to the rites, all under heaven will turn to humaneness."

Korean Women Philosophers and the Ideal of a Female Sage. Philip J. Ivanhoe and Hwa Yeong Wang,
Oxford University Press. © Oxford University Press 2023. DOI: 10.1093/oso/9780197508688.003.0007

Their bright virtue naturally appears.[5]

The purpose of this inscription,

Is to use a mirror to encourage vigilance.

2. Inscription on [the Theme of] a Short Sword

The nature of all human beings is good; why then are so many unable to become like Emperor Yo, Emperor Sun, the Duke of Ju, or Gongja? It is because their nature is injured by human desires. If one is able to control human desires, then the heavenly Pattern-Principle naturally shall be preserved, and one too can become like Emperor Yo, Emperor Sun, the Duke of Ju, or Gongja. And so Anja said, "What kind of person was Sun? What kind of person am I?"[6] Those who make an effort can also be like this. What does it mean to make an effort? It means that one clearly distinguishes and earnestly practices the distinction between heavenly Pattern-Principle and human desire. As soon as one understands that something is a human desire, one must decisively eliminate it, with the ferocity of a peal of thunder! As soon as one understands that something is a heavenly Pattern-Principle, one must resolutely practice it, like a mighty river bursting through its banks![7] Be like the keen edge of a sharp knife slicing something in half—do not allow the slightest hesitation to enter your thoughts! Now, the "keen edge of a sharp knife" refers to a short sword. The reason Anja could return [from an error] of no great extent and avoid transferring his anger [unto others][8] is because he had such a sword. The reason Duke Gwak[9] (C. Guo) 郭公 regarded the good as good but was unable to advance it and regarded the bad as bad but was unable to eliminate it is because he lacked such a sword. Lacking or having this sword depends only on whether one has or lacks courage; why is this?

---

[5] The opening chapter of the *Great Learning* begins, "The Way of the Great Learning is to make bright one's bright virtue."

[6] *Mencius* 3A1.

[7] Cf. *Mencius* 7A16.

[8] The first part of this sentence combines a line from the *Book of Changes* and one from the *Analects*. See the "Image Commentary" (*Sang Jeon*; C. *Xiang Zhuan* 象傳) on the hexagram *Bok* (C. *Fu*) 復 in the *Book of Changes* and *Analects* 6.3.

[9] Duke Gwak, whose name was Jang Bo (C. Zhang Fu) 長父, was minister to King Ryeo (C. Li) 厲 (r. 877–841 BCE or 857–842 BCE) of the Ju dynasty. King Ryeo brought disaster on his state and himself; while the details are unknown, Duke Gwak is blamed for failing to control the king's bad behavior and settle competition among his ministers.

What is called courage is really of two types.[10] There is physical courage,[11] which is something one must not have; there is moral courage, which is something one cannot do without. When physical courage retreats, moral courage advances. If one is able to nurture moral courage, then the short sword will naturally arise, and human desires will not dare to stand before it. If all of the operations and applications of one's Heart-Mind and every moment of movement and rest of every part of one's body are the flowing implementation of heavenly Pattern-Principle, then Emperor Yo, Emperor Sun, the Duke of Ju, and Gongja are here within me. Is it not amazing and spirit-like this short sword! This inscription is a warning to myself.

The lyric poem says:

> It shimmers like a cold frost,
> Its edge like the blazing sun.
> Its blade is insubstantial,[12]
> Yet its keenness cuts through iron.
> Wherever its sharp edge turns,
> Every malady is eliminated.
> The awesome extent of your power!
> The spiritual nature of your achievements!
> Onward! Short sword!
> Ignore that I am a woman.
> Urge on your keen blade,
> As if fresh from the whetstone.
> Destroy the swarm that opposes me,
> Cut down the thicket that blocks me.
> When the Four Evil Spirits[13] are eliminated,
> The sun of Emperor Sun shall appear in the heavens,
> Great peace will continue for ten thousand generations,
> And [one's] heavenly ruler will be calm.[14]

---

[10] The following analysis of courage owes much to *Mencius* 2A2.

[11] In the sense of something like macho courage.

[12] This invokes the story of a cook in the "Nourishing the Lord of Life" (*Yang Saeng Ju*; C. *Yang Sheng Zhu* 養生主) chapter of the *Jangja*, whose knife is said to be "without thickness" (*muhu*; C. *wuhou* 無厚) and so can easily move through the openings between the joints in the ox carcass he is carving.

[13] The demons of the four directions that Emperor Sun traditionally is said to have driven off. See the "Canon of Sun" (*Yo Jeon*; C. *Yao Dian* 舜典) chapter of *Book of History* and the *Chronicle of Jwa*, Eighteenth Year of Duke Mun (C. Wen) 文公.

[14] The last lines of Ju Hui's comment on *Mencius* 6A15 say, "The heavenly ruler will be calm, and every part of one's body will heed its commands." See *Collected Commentaries on the "Mencius"* (*Maengja jipju*; C. *Mengzi jizhu* 孟子集注). The "heavenly ruler" refers to the Heart-Mind.

3. Inscription on [the Theme of] a Ruler and a Scale

The August Lord on High,
Endowed even the [most] common people with a moral
    sense.[15]
What is this moral sense?
It is to be impartial and unbiased.
Collected together, as it is in itself,
This is the "balance and harmony" of the "virtuous nature."[16]
Manifested as function,
This is to follow the mean in speech and in action.
Only sages are able to rest peacefully in this,
The common people must make an effort to attain it.
As they make such effort, what [standard] should they follow?
[They should follow] the way you measure and weigh,
To determine light and heavy, long and short.
They should always follow the norm you provide.
"Be discriminating! Be unified!"[17]
Through a myriad of changes, respond in this way!
Emperor U and Anja practiced it easily,
This is called attaining the mean.[18]
A minute mistake [in the beginning] will lead to a monu-
    mental error [in the end],
[Then], if one does not become a follower of Yang Ju, one will
    become a follower of Muk[ja]![19]

---

[15] The first two lines are from the "Announcements of Tang" (*Tang Go*; C. *Tang Gao* 湯誥) chapter of the *Book of History*.

[16] For these terms, see chapters 1 and 28 of the *Doctrine of the Mean*, respectively.

[17] See the "Counsels of the Great U" chapter in the *Book of History*.

[18] In *Mencius* 7A26 we find Maengja insisting on the need to strike a balance and attain the mean, which he contrasts with *holding forcefully to a position in between extremes* (*jip jung*; C. *zhi zhong* 執中). This was the mistake of a thinker named Jamo (C. Zimo) 子莫, who held onto a position between the extreme egoism of Yang Ju (C. Yang Zhu) 楊朱 and the extreme altruism of Muk Jeok (C. Mo Di) 墨翟, an implication picked up in the final line.

[19] Cf. *Mencius* 3B9, where Maengja bemoans that the teachings of Yang and Muk fill the world and claims that if one does not follow the extreme view of the former, one will be led to adopt the equally extreme view of the latter. See the prior note as well.

Encomium (贊)

1. Encomium to Anja's Love of Learning

Our father is *Geon*; our mother is *Gon*,[1]
And we stand as the third power [in the universe].[2]
It is said we differ from birds and beasts,
It follows that we have the best of them.[3]
The foolish lose this,
While the wise secure it.
Losing it does not mean it then exists outside of us.
How could securing it add to what we already have?
What must be sought, already is within us,
We [must] return to what we originally possess.
I have heard there was one among the ancients,
Who heaven deigned to be born in spring.[4]
The foremost disciple at the gate of the sage,
How great to take him as your model![5]
But who is he who serves as this model?
For whom [learning] was like enjoying grass or grain-fed meat.[6]
Even when he wanted to stop, he could not.
[For him, the master's teachings] seemed ever more lofty,
      impenetrable, and evasive.[7]

---

[1] *Geon* and *Gon* are the first two hexagrams in the *Book of Changes* and represent heaven and earth.

[2] The trinity of heaven, earth, and human beings has been a long-standing theme of Confucian thought.

[3] Meaning that humans have received the best endowment from heaven and earth.

[4] This refers to Anja. See the *Extant Works of the Two Jeongs* 5.1a.

[5] See the *Book of Poetry*, Mao #195.

[6] A close paraphrase of *Mencius* 6A7, which says that the good pleases our Heart-Minds in the way fine food pleases our palates.

[7] The translation here is loose in an attempt to capture the meaning. This and the previous line are drawing from Anja's description of his study of the master's teachings in *Analects* 9.11, where he says, "When I gaze up at them, they seem more lofty; when I try to penetrate them, they seem more diffi-cult; when I look at them in front of me, suddenly they seem to be behind me . . . even when I want to stop [studying], I cannot."

Korean Women Philosophers and the Ideal of a Female Sage. Philip J. Ivanhoe and Hwa Yeong Wang, Oxford University Press. © Oxford University Press 2023. DOI: 10.1093/oso/9780197508688.003.0008

Had he been granted a few more years of life,

[His achievement would have been] equal to Gongja or the
 Duke of Ju.

[Gongja cried out,] "Heaven is destroying me!"[8]

He found [Anja's early death] very difficult to accept.

Among Gongja's three thousand disciples,

There was none who did not pursue learning.

But Anja's love of learning,

Distinguished him as something special.

Each day he overcame the self and returned to the rites,[9]

Following the two prescriptions and four admonitions.[10]

Great indeed was An, living in a [mean and narrow] lane![11]

He studied as if he would never attain his goal![12]

The master said, "Now there is none like him."[13]

Ja Gong (C. Zi Gong 子貢) asked, "[How] dare I compare
 myself [to An]?"[14]

Worthy of entering the realm of the sages,

A hundred generations shall look up to him as their teacher.

---

[8] When Anja died, Gongja cried out these words. See *Analects* 11.9.

[9] Referring to the ideal described in *Analects* 12.1.

[10] In *Analects* 6.3, we are told Anja never transferred his anger or repeated the same mistake. In *Analects* 12.1 he committed himself to not look, listen, speak, or act contrary to the rites.

[11] In *Analects* 6.11, Gongja expresses his admiration for Anja, who was happy despite his poverty, living in a mean and narrow lane.

[12] *Analects* 8.17.

[13] A close paraphrase of *Analects* 6.3. Gongja said this after Anja had passed away.

[14] A close paraphrase of *Analects* 5.9.

Funeral Orations (祭文)

1. Funeral Oration for My Eldest Brother, the Honorable Inspector[1]

On the first day of the sixth month in 1758, [your] younger sister, wife of Mr. Sin,[2] with simple yet carefully chosen words of grief spoken through bitter tears, presents an offering to the spirit of my eldest brother, the Honorable Inspector. Alas! Brother! Are you really gone? With your exceptional talent, incomparable wisdom, extraordinary ability, and command of worldly affairs, your courage stood out among all under heaven, and your aspirations were exalted in your time. You should have enjoyed a long life and served at court in [our] enlightened age, so that your achievements and reputation would be passed down in records made upon bamboo and silk and heard throughout later ages. How is it that you were abandoned as soon as you reached the court, and heaven did not allow you to remain behind[3] [here on earth] but snatched you away so abruptly? Is it because you so hated the turbidity [of this world] and wanted to return, pure and unblemished, or that the people suffer the bad fortune of having heaven deny its blessing to our Eastern [land] and brought you to this?

Alas! Across the vast range of human lives, each receives its (i.e., heaven's) mandate. The mandates thus received are not the same; some are thick and some thin, some receive nourishment and flourish, some are crooked and overthrown.[4] It is appropriate that those who are crooked are overthrown;

---

[1] The Honorable Inspector (*Jeongeongong* 正言公) refers to Im Myeongju 任命周 (1705–1757 CE), whose courtesy name was Baeksin 伯新; he passed the classics licentiate (*Saengwon* 生員) level of the civil service examination in the ninth year of King Yeongjo's (英祖, r. 1724–1776 CE) reign (1733 CE) and the higher literary examination (*Mungwa* 文科) in the twenty-third year of Yeongjo's reign (1747 CE). That same year he successively held the government posts of an Administrator for Seoul (*Hanseong Chamgun* 漢城 參軍) and Inspector in the Bureau of the Censor (Saganwon *Jeongeon* 司諫院 正言); later, he served as Inspector General (Saheonbu *Jipyeong* 司憲府 持平). Nevertheless, his time in public office was short-lived because of his involvement in political controversy. He died in the city of Jeonju 全州 at the age of fifty-three in the thirty-third year of King Yeongjo's reign (1757 CE).

[2] Indicating herself, Im Yunjidang.

[3] See the *Chronicle of Jwa*, Sixteenth Year of Duke Ae.

[4] See chapter 17 of the *Doctrine of the Mean*.

Korean Women Philosophers and the Ideal of a Female Sage. Philip J. Ivanhoe and Hwa Yeong Wang, Oxford University Press. © Oxford University Press 2023. DOI: 10.1093/oso/9780197508688.003.0009

yet, even so, there is something regrettable when this happens. How much more regrettable is it when those who are flourishing do not receive nourishment! [In such cases,] can one really fail to murmur against heaven?[5]

Alas! Had you not been endowed with talent, that would have been the end of it, but to be so endowed and not be able to apply it is perverse! Had you not been able to establish yourself at court, that would have been the end of it, but to have established yourself and not be utilized is an abomination! Someone might say that you just had a strange destiny, but then why would your life have started off so plentiful and thick and only later proven to be so impoverished and thin? Someone might say that our family just suffered a catastrophe, but the lingering influence of our father's abundant virtue must have exerted an influence upon his descendants. Thus, we, five brothers and two sisters, all survived our birth and grew into adults without suffering any infirmities in our youth, and people all said this was a consequence of our father's virtue.

Alas! How can I bear to talk about it anymore? In 1745, I mourned the passing of my third brother;[6] in 1756, I lost my younger, fourth brother.[7] Now, I also mourn the loss of my elder brother. Even the loss of one person hurts severely! When I had lost two people, I felt it was even worse, but now I have lost three! In the world there surely are those who flourish but are not nourished, but are there any families who have suffered as much as mine? Is there anyone who has suffered as much as my elder brother? Alas! That my gray-haired mother has encountered such boundless sorrow in regard to my siblings in successive years wounds me deeply. I have no words to describe it. Her spirit has melted away and she has suffered from a persistent affliction. Given your supreme filiality, if you, my brother, could know this, you would fill your grave with tears!

Alas! Our sins (i.e., all seven siblings) reached to the heavens! [And so,] in 1728, unexpectedly, we lost our father and thereafter served only our mother. But our family was poor, and our mother was old. Secretly, you were profoundly worried [about our situation]. In autumn of 1733, you, together with our second brother, passed the civil service examination.[8] In the end, you believed that since the customs of our age had declined, the only way

---

[5] *Analects* 14.35.

[6] Her third oldest brother Im Gyeongju 任敬周 (1718–1745 CE), courtesy name Jikjung 直中, pen name Cheongcheonja 青川子.

[7] Im Byeongju 任秉周 (1724–1756 CE), courtesy name Sukmun 叔文.

[8] More precisely, *Samasi* 司馬試 refers to the lower licentiate examination (*Sogwa* 小科).

for someone to advance himself was through passing the examinations. But success in the examinations was in the hands of human beings. Those with ability do not always receive the benefit they deserved. It is better to let the success of one's grasp of the classics lie within oneself.[9] [So] starting in the winter [of that year], you focused your Heart-Mind exclusively on mastering the classics, with the hope of establishing yourself and bringing glory to our family. Burning the midnight oil through until dawn, working relentlessly without rest, you showed that your sincere filial piety stood out among all under heaven and that your spirit far exceeded that of ordinary people. After working for more than ten years, you went up to take the classics examination[10] in spring of 1747. To the delight of our mother and the joyful congratulations of all the members of our clan, relatives, and friends, almost no one proved to be your equal.

At the time, the Way was in decline in the world and you became a censor. With great feeling you sighed and said,

> To serve as an official but not endeavor to carry out one's
> duties and instead only to enjoy one's salary is merely to
> occupy a position. What did the court have in mind when
> it established this position? When one is responsible
> for speaking,[11] if one should speak but does not, then
> this is what is called "[being one who says] of his lord that
> he is incapable [of becoming good] and thereby is a thief of
> one's lord."[12] This is something I simply cannot do!

And so, in the winter of that year, you presented a memorial concerning more than ten different current affairs,[13] which caused heaven (i.e., the king) to repeatedly shake with anger, to the point where he ordered an investigation. His anger was such that one did not know how far he would go. It would be difficult to describe the anxiousness and anxiety this caused our mother or the fear it provoked in our brothers and their wives and children. But you were calm and undeterred, saying simply, "I am prepared to die." Thanks to the protection of providence, the imperial anger subsided

---

[9] Cf. *Analects* 12.1.

[10] Refers to *Myeonggyeonggwa* 明經科, which is a type of higher examination (*Daegwa* 大科).

[11] See *Mencius* 2B14.

[12] *Mencius* 2A6.

[13] The details of his memorial and the king's response can be found in the *Veritable Records of King Yeongjo* 66.40b–43a [23(1747)/12/22/#01].

somewhat; you only were banished to the south and the catastrophe mitigated slightly. Although we said that this was remarkably fortunate, still, it required you to be separated far from us. How great was our sadness and grief! And this went on for four years! Fortunately, you received the king's favor; he pardoned you and you were able to return to us. From this point on, you again were able to serve the world, and we anticipated that your career would continue to develop; this was simply what one would expect as the normal course of events. Who would then have said that today everything would be turned in the opposite direction, so that not even the most slender fraction of your unparalleled talent and matchless aspiration could be applied in the world to serve as its pillars and beams, and you would not advance beyond your position as a censor? Silent and still, you have departed this world!

Alas! The pain! In the summer of 1755, you unexpectedly suffered a stroke. At the time, our second brother was serving as the governor of a city in the south. In order to see our aged mother and also to get medical treatment, you went in a carriage and stayed with them. I[14] and our elder sister also, in turn, returned there to visit.[15] All six of us—[four] brothers and [two] sisters[16]— were gathered together by [our mother's side]. Although we were in the midst of worry and misfortune, we felt profoundly gratified [to be together]. Each day, your symptoms gradually worsened, and then our fourth brother's[17] old ailment returned and his condition became critical. At this point, how anxious and afraid[18] our mother and all your siblings were! On top of your illness, you felt great anxiety that our fourth brother's ailment would further complicate the process of his convalescence. In spring of the following year, our fourth brother's illness reached the point where there was no further margin to spare; we could not but speak encouraging words and conceal the true state of affairs from you. Thereupon, on the tenth day of March, when we were on the way back to our natal home in Jigye 芝溪, how could we bear to think about whether he would remain with or leave us? [En route,] your illness worsened and you were not able to continue, so we stopped when we reached Wanju 完州.

---

[14] Here and below, Yunjidang refers to herself as "younger sister," but we translate this as the first-person pronoun for stylistic reasons.

[15] To be precise, *gwinyeong* (C. *guining* 歸寧) refers to a married woman's going back to her natal family for a visit. Cf. *Book of Poetry*, Mao #2.

[16] By this time, 1755, the third brother Im Gyeongju already had passed away.

[17] Refers to Im Byeongju, the fourth among five brothers, the sixth child of the seven siblings.

[18] Reading 惶 as 遑 in the original.

Alas! In the end, our fourth brother could not rise from his bed! We could not bear to report his death to you, and we all just said his condition was a bit improved. [At this news] you were beside yourself with joy and, [later,] in passing would ask if he continued to improve. At that time, [I felt that] "my heart is not a stone, it cannot simply be rolled about."[19] What grief and pain!

Our fourth brother's coffin first returned to our home in Jigye. Your elder sister and I were going to see it be put in the ground with the idea that we then would proceed toward Seoul.[20] So on the third day of April, we left the company of our relatives and paid our respects to you [along the way]. Your spirit and demeanor had not declined from earlier. You spoke continuously and without stop about how happy you were that our fourth brother's condition was a bit improved. Reflecting on this, your younger siblings' hearts were broken in two. We could not delay our return. Still, when we said goodbye, how could I think that the day we parted might be the last day we ever would bid farewell to one another? The pain! The pain!

In autumn of that year, I began my journey toward Seoul. You had left me a letter that said, "Younger sister, in autumn of next year, I will send a horse to bring you [home]; [that way] our next meeting won't be far off." After I arrived at Gyeonggi Province, I had to go down to Wonju[21] to make arrangements for an important mourning ritual.[22] Because of a continuous series of unforeseen difficulties,[23] I could not extricate myself from the situation and had to delay my departure until November.[24] Far off in the Southeast, we could not even exchange letters. Recalling our mother's face, my heart was burning with anxiety. And, when thinking about [you] my sibling, my tears would begin to flow without me even noticing. I had nightmares when I slept, which startled my soul and woke me. Day and night my stomach was in a knot and on fire;

---

[19] Reading 轉 instead of 朽. Cf. The verse "The Cypress Boat" (Baekju; C. Bozhou 柏舟) which seems to have inspired several ideas in this funeral oration. The verse expresses her distress at having to endure so many traumas and yet be unable to share them with her brother. She protests that her heart is not an insensitive and inanimate object that can just be rolled about, this way and that.

[20] Literally sanggyeong (C. shangjing 上京) means "going to the capital" or "the capital [area]." Their family home and lineage cemetery mountain were located in Jigye, Chungcheong Province. From Jeolla Province (Jeolla-do 全羅道), where they were staying, Jigye was nearer the capital. We translate this expression in various ways according to each context.

[21] Wonhyup 原峽 is another name of Wonju 原州 According to the Atlas of the Eastern Country (Haedong Jido 海東地圖), the Joseon court produced in the mid-eighteenth century, Wonju belonged to Gyeonggi Province.

[22] To be precise, the mourning ritual she had to manage was the Seungjungsang (C. Chengzhongsang 承重喪), which refers to a "double heir," a case in which a grandson mourns for his grandparents when his father, who should have been an heir, had died early.

[23] Among which were the loss of her aunt, wife of Mr. Song and in-laws; see Gim 2019, 143 and 291.

[24] Im Myeongju died in November 1757.

it almost destroyed me. I did not even know where I was. Subsequently, bad news arrived. Was it [the doing of] heaven? Was it [the doing of] spirits? What was this about? I called out to heaven and complained, but heaven paid no attention to me. I knocked my head on the earth and protested, but the earth did not respond.

Alas! The pain! If I could have come in autumn of that year, I could have looked upon your face again; I could have held your hand and said my farewell to you as you drew near to the end. But women are not free [to travel when they would like]. I only just now arrived. I did not get here before you had been interred, when I could have leaned against the side of your funeral carriage and wept at being separated from you. This eternal feeling of lingering regret is as boundless as heaven and earth!

Alas! You were profoundly humane and abundantly virtuous but were unable to hold a child in your arms in years gone by; in later life, at home you would often sadly say, "The most unfortunate are those who grow old without having children." This was something you wanted to resolve but never followed up on; only now have we formally designated the eldest son of our youngest brother as your heir. Alas! How regrettable! How can this be in accord with heavenly Pattern-Principle? Your sincere filial piety stood out among all under heaven. Whenever you entered the inner quarters, you always first checked our mother's face; if she was peaceful and happy [within], your joy would flow [and be manifested] outside. If, though, she was not feeling tranquil and calm, then a worried expression would take shape upon your face. One day, after you had been massaging and comforting our mother,[25] as you rubbed her legs you broke into tears and said, "My mother's legs have gotten to such a state!" That your earnest filial piety stood out among all under heaven can indeed be seen in this behavior!

The pain! The pain! Your younger sister [i.e., I], whose body still has not faded away, often hates that her fate is to somehow continue to live in a world that no longer holds any meaning for her. You were a particularly earnest friend to me; you once told me, "You, [my] younger sister, [wife of Mr.] Sin, are like my child and so you cannot travel far away and must always return home."[26] From this moment on, I will never again be able to receive the instructions of the highest brotherly love.

---

[25] See chapter "The Pattern of the Family" (*Nae Chik*; C. *Nei Ze* 內則) for the idea that children should check on their parents and parents-in-law, and if they are feeling any soreness or itching, the children should massage or scratch (*eokjo* 抑搔) wherever they are feeling discomfort.

[26] For the idea that a child should not travel far from her parents, see *Analects* 4.19.

Alas! The life of a human being is like fine dust settling in layers upon a weak blade of grass; in the case of one like me, who has experienced the extreme of sadness and suffered numerous grievances, who has been melted on the inside and burned on the outside—all that remains is a hollow husk. Now, moreover, I am afflicted with compound illnesses and have only a few days remaining before I die and am gone. I know that I will be following close behind you, and this is how I have begun to console myself.

This time, when I came to visit you, [I thought] I was going to see your dignified demeanor, but I could not see your joyful face; [I thought] I was going to listen to your [wise] words, but I could not hear your voice. It's so quiet and lonely;[27] you do not recognize me. Alas my brother, how can you bear to treat me like this?

Someone once said, "The highest emotions cannot be written about." In general, the idea is that writing cannot wholly convey such emotions. Even more so is this true of your younger sister now. My writing is clumsy and my heart confused. How could I describe even one ten-thousandth of my grief? Brother, are you conscious and aware? If you are, your tears must be falling in the darkness below. Alas! The pain! Please accept my offering!

2. Funeral Oration for My Second Eldest Brother Nokmun

On the sixth day of the third month in 1788, my second brother Nokmun 鹿門, the Honorable Seongcheon 成川公,[28] unfortunately had to abandon his later studies; on the second of the fifth month in that year, he was interred. I, his younger sister, widow of Mr. Sin, was far away in Wonhyeop 原峽; when I heard the news of your passing I burst into tears; this gave rise to feelings of grief and sorrow, which I expressed in wild and unrestrained language and sent to my grieving nieces and nephews. On the first day of this month, I prepared a meager offering of food and presented it before the altar.

Alas! The pain! You showed me the highest brotherly love. How can you now abandon me and precede me [into the realm of the dead]? Alas! You were ten years my senior, but your younger sister is frail and fraught with

---

[27] Reading 案 as 寥 in the original.
[28] To be precise, the Honorable District Magistrate (*Busa* 府使) of Seongcheon 成川, Pyeongan 平安 Province, the last official position he served.

illness. I am in decline and don't have much farther to go, but heaven granted you, brother, such exceptional talent! Your *Gi-Material* was clear and far-reaching, your character pure and substantial. Moreover, you nourished heavenly Pattern-Principle and protected heavenly Pattern-Principle. Heaven surely blessed you! It would have been proper for you to enjoy a long life. Your younger sister often secretly said to herself, "Surely I will die before my second elder brother. If I am able to get him to write an encomium of even a few lines for me, I will enjoy glory among both the living and the dead!" How could I have anticipated that the affairs of human beings could reverse so easily and end up like this!

Alas! Your younger sister's sins and offenses are deep and weighty. And so, last year, I lost my son, and today I have lost my second elder brother. Oh heaven! Oh spirits! How can you bear to see me like this? Alas, I stubbornly bear my fate. On both sides of my family [i.e., natal family and family-in-law], father and mother both are gone. Of our siblings, only you, youngest brother, and I remained. Moreover, we were scattered far and wide and it was difficult to bring us back together. And yet our hearts are bound to one another. In the spring of 1782, you came to live here in response to my waning condition. We relied upon one another continually and took great joy in life; what could be better than this? Our youngest brother was despondent that you were growing old and remained unsettled; he repeatedly asked you to return to our native home. In the spring of 1786, you subsequently led the family back to your old home in Nokdong 鹿洞.[29] After more than four years [together] without a break, suddenly we were separated, without hope of reunion. When the time came to part from you, how was my heart to feel?

The pain! The pain! After you had left us, in your letters you said how fortunate it would be if we have a chance to meet again before we die. And up to the second month of this year, when your illness had caused you to sink into and remain bedridden, still you managed to produce letters by dictation and remonstrated with me for allowing my grief to become excessive and injurious. You added, "If I am not able to see you again before I die then to what extremes might your grief reach?"[30] From when you wrote that until you abandoned this world has only been ten-odd days. This was your final piece of writing. From this point onward, though I yearn to hear such supremely

---

[29] To be precise, Nokmun-dong 鹿門洞, a village in Gongju 公州, which he moved to in 1758, and from which he took his pen name.

[30] *The Collected Writings of Nokmun* 10.29a.

loving instructions from you—how is this possible? When I think about this, my internal organs burst open; blood flows forth and covers my face.

Alas! Your younger sister is near death in her seventieth year, and moreover has suffered the pain of losing a child. My liver and gall bladder have turned to ash; my remaining days are few. I shall follow behind you in a matter of days. Perhaps this offers me a way to console myself. Since I was young, I received the highest brotherly love from you; you taught me the basis of proper conduct. That with my crude understanding I was able to cultivate myself and avoid falling into severe offense is only owing to your kindness. Though men and women are said to have different ways of conduct, nevertheless, they have always shared the same heavenly decreed nature. And so, whenever I had any questions or doubts about the meaning of the classics, you tirelessly provided me with great explanations, which enabled me to become enlightened in a way that put an end to my questions and doubts. After [you returned home] in the year 1786, the criticisms I was able to receive through the exchange of letters with you served as the basis for my enjoyment in my remaining days. Whenever I heard that you were not well, I became so anxious that I was unable to sleep. Though I am far away from you, my Heart-Mind often races to be by your bedside. From now on who will assiduously and attentively teach me? And about whom will I think so much that I am unable to sleep? Remote and eternal heaven above, how could you be so cruel to me! The pain! The pain!

The ancients had a saying, "Those with great virtue surely will receive position, salary, fame, and longevity."[31] The world considers [a life of] eighty years to constitute longevity; although you, my brother, were short of this by two years, one can still say you enjoyed a long life. A "position" is a way to refer to nobility; [among types of] nobility none is more honored than the nobility conferred by heaven.[32] You, my brother, had true knowledge and substantial achievement; humaneness and righteousness were filled out and piled high within you, and so, in terms of the honor of the nobility conferred by heaven, who is equal to you? Where nobility is preserved, there is sure to be salary; where substantial achievements are present, fame is sure to follow. These are the terms in which I often sing the praises of my brother! Nevertheless, I am not without some sense of dissatisfaction toward heaven. My second elder brother possessed exceptional ability, outstanding knowledge, and

---

[31] See chapter 17 of the *Doctrine of the Mean*.
[32] *Mencius* 6A16.

many years of accumulated study; he never paused in his labors while there was anything he had yet to grasp.[33] One by one, he thoroughly mastered the meanings of the classics and the theories of the rites, bringing these together in his Heart-Mind and expressing them in his writings. He took the lead in expounding many things that earlier people had yet to expound, and he never tired [of studying] nor grew weary [of instructing others].[34] He displayed unrelenting and complete commitment, and his integrity grew all the greater with age. In a letter from last year, you wrote to me, saying,

> I am close to eighty years old; my death is nothing to worry about. But it is extremely distressing to think that I will not be able to accomplish what I most want to do. I received the detailed hand-copied version of *Doubts about Ju Hui's Writings*[35] that the Governor of Gyeongsang Province (Gyeongsang Gamsa 慶尙監司)[36] sent to me. I did not expect him to produce such a great and wonderful work; it seems heaven must have assisted him in its composition. Nevertheless, in addition to [working through] this, there are many other things I want to do. My Heart-Mind cannot rest; the people around me ask, why bother? But this is what I enjoy, and I pay no mind to how tired it makes me. [The way I feel about it] is like what Master Han[37] said, "If even a little bit about me passes on [to future generations], though I die, I shall have no regrets."[38] These words are perfectly clear and true! I do not know how much work I will, at this point, be able to accomplish in the years or months I have left. My spirit feels as if I still can do it but my body is growing weak. I fear this wish will be difficult to pursue.

Alas! If heaven had granted you several more years so that you could have finished the work you had intended to complete in order to leave it to later students, you could not have shown a greater kindness nor made a more

---

[33] See chapter 22 of the *Doctrine of the Mean*.

[34] *Analects* 7.2.

[35] A work by Song Siyeol, the complete title of which is *Notes and Queries on the Complete Compendium of Master Ju's Works* (*Juja Daejeon chaui* 朱子大全箚疑); it is also known as *Jucha* 朱箚. Im Seongju took it as his mission to complete Song Siyeol's manuscript. His more than ten years' effort resulted in *Supplement to "Sketches of Doubts"* (*Chaui bo* 箚疑補). See the *Collected Writings of Nokmun*, Appendix 23b.

[36] Yeongbaek 嶺伯 refers to Governor of Gyeongsang Province.

[37] Refers to Han Yu.

[38] A close paraphrase of a line from *Ju Hui's Verified Edition of the Collected Works of Han Yu* (*Jumungong gyo Changryeo seonsaeng jip*; C. *Zhuwengong xiao changli xiansheng ji* 朱文公校昌黎先生集) 18.13b.

abundant achievement. But now, because of a single unexpected bout of ill-ness your work has come to an end here. How could heaven not have wanted to assist in the completion of this composition? This is something that leaves one dissatisfied with heaven. Moreover, had your exceptional learning and aspiration to surpass the ancients been allowed to develop and flourish, the work of Yi Yun and Bu Yeol[39] would have been upheld and carried forward. Heaven seemed to have a purpose in giving birth to you, but it relegated you to the provincial towns and left you to end your days in obscurity, without the chance to implement the Way throughout a benighted state, denying the people the opportunity of enjoying the benefits of your supremely good and fine governance and this generation the chance of again seeing the full flour-ishing of the Three Dynasties. Isn't this something really difficult to believe? This is another reason to be dissatisfied with heaven. In a deteriorating age, when the Way has declined, it is rare to find one who understands virtue; this has been true since ancient times. A noble person does not resent [not being known].[40] There is no need to mention this. In the past, a censor's slander caused you inestimable calamities. Your family and old friends all were ex-tremely anxious about this. Only you calmly said, "Our ruler above possesses sagely intelligence; slanderous accusations are unending, but this is nothing to worry about." It turned out just as you said it would; you often had told me, "Were it not for the virtue of our sagacious and supportive ruler, how could we have arrived at this day? There is no way for me to ever repay the state's infinite kindness, though I work to do so unto death." And so, although you remained hidden in the rustic hinterland, the sincerity of your love for our ruler and concern for our state was never forgotten for even one day. It is, though, a pity that your learning, which exemplified being inwardly a sage and outwardly a king,[41] in the end could not avoid being no more than empty words written upon a page.

Alas! The pain! Alas! The pain! I, your younger sister, did not have another chance to pay my respects in this life to you, my second eldest brother. When you passed away, I didn't have the chance to go and weep on the sacrificial offering mat [beside your grave]. Now, your mien is forever cut off from me

---

[39] Two worthy ministers of the Sang dynasty that Ju Hui singled out as among those who transmitted the Way in his preface (*seo*; C. *xu* 序) to the "*Doctrine of the Mean*" in *Sections and Sentences*.

[40] *Analects* 1.1.

[41] The phrase "being inwardly a sage and outwardly a king" is first seen in the "In the World" (*cheonha*; C. *tianxia* 天下) chapter of the *Jangja*, but it became a familiar and valued ideal among neo-Confucians.

in the [Yellow] Springs[42] below; my remaining grief and sorrow consumes my spirit and I am incapable of expressing even one ten-thousandth of my anguish. Holding my brush, my thoughts are blocked up; I don't know what I want to say. Alas! The pain! What manner of man were you?[43] Please accept my offering.

3. Funeral Oration for My Late Son [Sin] Jaejun

You have abandoned me and departed; a full year has gone by and still you have not returned! I was more than forty years old when you first became my child. Nevertheless, since you were born, I held you and nurtured you; you always regarded me as your own birth mother, and I always regarded you as a child I had borne. After you were weaned, you ate with me and you stayed with me; the toys you played with are all stored away in my place; you relaxed at ease in my room. As a widow, I relied on you for support. Once you had grown up you had a wife, a son, and daughter of your own; this comforted and pleased my Heart-Mind. And you sincerely served me with filial piety. You provided my everyday needs without me asking. This too comforted and pleased my Heart-Mind. Day and night, my sincerest wish, was that, before I died, I would see you attain success and progress in your studies, see you fill out and take shape physically, and see each of your sons and daughters grow up, so that your family flourishes. These were not excessive or exorbitant things [to wish for], but one morning you perished and my wishes crumbled to pieces, like a broken tile. With white hair, alone and distressed, with no one to rely upon—what a state to be in! How extremely obstinate I am! Loving you as profoundly as I did, when I lost you, I should have been immediately unable to go on. But now you are gone, and I have been completely alone in the world for all this time. Obstinate and befuddled, I eat when hungry and sleep when tired—the same as anyone else. Am I this way because my blood and *Gi-Material* are decayed and my spirit exhausted and I am unable to truly comprehend my grief and sorrow? Or am I this way because I have just accepted that there is nothing to be done about it and trust in heaven, seeing it simply as fate playing itself out? The pain! The pain! What crime could one with your humane and filial nature, your genial and

---

[42] The Yellow Springs (*Hwang Cheon*; C. *Huang Quan* 黃泉) refers to the underworld in Chinese mythology.
[43] Compare the verse from the "Minor Hymns" section of the *Book of Poetry*, Mao #199.

easygoing manner, comprehensive grasp of literature, and upright, pure disposition have committed against heaven? It must be because I obstinately clung to life—that I should have died but managed to live on— and thereby garnered resentment among the spirits high and low; so they snatched you from me so quickly and further impoverished me. A proverb says, "The years and months are a kind of medicine." But my present pain and suffering seem to grow more severe as time goes on. Only when I no longer live, will I not feel this grief. Enough!

Alas! The pain! "What manner of man were you?"[44] Human life really is [as fleeting as the sight of] a white colt running past, viewed through a crack in the wall![45] It is all the more so from the perspective of an old sickly woman like me on the verge of death. Moreover, last spring I lost my second elder brother and this winter I lost his younger son. The extreme pain I felt at the loss of each of these was difficult to bear; how much more so with three! I have melted on the inside and been burned on the outside. With each day I grow more and more forlorn and gloomy.[46] Though I am as stubborn as can be, still, I am not made of wood or stone—how can I go on? Nevertheless, each day seems like the passing of three autumns. I just want to return quickly and join you beneath the earth to continue the destiny we were unable to complete between mother and child here on earth. Alas! Almost three years have passed; your sacrificial mat and offering table are about to be moved to the ancestral temple.[47] From now onward, though I still want to weep for you so that the pain in my chest can be slightly diminished; the rites of the former kings put limits [on mourning]; so how is this possible?

Alas! Whenever I see the things you used to enjoy in the course of your everyday life, I feel a need to make offerings of food to you, because I believe you still are here. From now onward, I cannot continue to do this. The grief! The sorrow! What can I set my Heart-Mind upon to pass my remaining days? I want to avail myself of the time remaining before the move [to the ancestral temple] by weeping for you night and day in order to lessen slightly the pain and rancor in my heart. But my eyes have grown much darker; I am almost blind. And so I fear I might lose my vision and thereby violate the teachings

---

[44] See the previous note.

[45] A close paraphrase of a line from the "Knowledge Wandered North" (*Ji Bugyu*; C. *Zhi Beiyou* 知北遊) chapter of the *Jangja*.

[46] Reading 淹淹 as 奄奄 in the original.

[47] These accoutrements of ritual practice are moved to the ancestral temple at the end of the officially prescribed mourning period to show that formal mourning is complete.

of the sages.[48] Moreover, I fear that on some future day, I will not be able to recognize your face [when I meet you] in the world below. That I cannot do as I would like [i.e., weep for you day and night] is a further source of profound sadness. The pain! The pain! I cannot now get to see your face. Still, fortunately, I dream about your spirit and thereby can converse with you. Though this consoles my Heart-Mind, the feelings of grief remain intense. If you are able to continually appear in my dreams, it will ever so slightly relieve some fraction of your old mother's grief. Alas! The pain! Please accept my offering.

[48] In that this would violate the limits placed on mourning and also do harm to the body, which would violate the guidelines of filial piety.

Prologue (引)

1. Prologue Written on the Occasion of Sending a Hand-Copied Draft of My Manuscript to [Ji]gye[1]

Since I was young, I knew of the learning of human nature and Pattern-Principle. Once I had gotten a little older, I loved it all the more. It pleased me just as grass- and grain-fed meat pleases one's palate.[2] Even when I wanted to stop [learning] I could not.[3] Thereupon, I did not dare to limit my search; I concentrated my Heart-Mind and silently explored every book and document that recorded the remaining teachings of the sages and worthies. I followed this path for several decades and attained some degree of insight,[4] but still I did not wish to put it down in written form, so I kept it within and did not let it out. Once I had reached my waning years; I [realized that I might] die before too long. I feared that one morning, suddenly I would be rotting away along with the [fallen] grass and trees. And so, whenever I found a break from managing family affairs, I seized upon these moments and took up my brush. In this way, I completed one large scroll, a total of forty chapters. I wrote the part from the lead chapter "[Biography of] The Wife of Mr. Song" to the eighth chapter "Discourse on What Anja Took Joy In" while young. I wrote the part from the "Discourse on Jaro" onward in my middle and later years. Although the level of understanding is shallow and vulgar and the style of writing weak and clumsy and lacking in penetrating advice or marvelous explanations that can be passed down to later generations, nevertheless, if after I have passed away they become scrap paper used to cover jars, this still would be sad. And so, I have assembled these writings into a single volume in order to give it to

---

[1] Jigye 芝溪 is the name of the village in Gongju, Chungcheong Province, where her family home was located. At the time, her youngest brother was living there.

[2] *Mencius* 6A7.

[3] *Analects* 9.11.

[4] Reading 班 as 斑 in the original.

Korean Women Philosophers and the Ideal of a Female Sage. Philip J. Ivanhoe and Hwa Yeong Wang,
Oxford University Press. © Oxford University Press 2023. DOI: 10.1093/oso/9780197508688.003.0010

my son Jaejun. My youngest brother Chigong 穉共[5] said to Jaejun, "You cannot let my elder sister's writings sink into oblivion. Make a copy and send it to me." And so I asked my nephew, Jaeseung 在升, to make a small hand-copied volume and send it back to him.

Written in the year of 1785

---

[5] A courtesy name of Im Jeongju.

Works on the Meaning of the Classics
(*Gyeongui*; C. *Jingyi* 經義)

1. Six Items on the *Great Learning*

1. The first chapter of the classic says, "Things have their roots and branch tips" and "Affairs have their endings and beginnings." Whenever one talks about a determinate physical object (*jeongche*; C. *dingti* 定體), one calls it a "thing"; whenever one talks about a purposeful practice (*gongbu*; C. *gongfu* 功夫), one calls it an "affair." The text doesn't say [affairs having their] "beginnings and endings"[1] but instead says, "endings and beginnings." This is just fortuitous. If one attends to this matter too deeply, I fear one will lose the beauty of the expression.

2. Those who proceed from "knowing where to rest" and arrive at the point where "they are able to attain their end" can "follow whatever their Heart-Mind desires without overstepping the proper norm";[2] then they "rest in the highest good" of "making bright their virtue" and "renovating of the people."[3]

3. The third chapter quotes the poem "The Winding Course of the Gi (Gi Uk; C. Qi Yu 淇奧),"[4] and says, "*As one cuts and carves* concerns the learning of the Way and *as one files and polishes* concerns cultivating the self."[5] Juja explains this by saying, "This talks about how development follows a specific order and progressively reaches refinement."[6]

---

[1] One would expect "beginnings and endings" not only as the natural progression of start to finish but also in order to parallel "root" and "branch tip." Thus, the order in the text warrants comment.

[2] *Analects* 2.4. Gongja said he attained this state at the age of seventy, after fifty-five years of learning and practice.

[3] These three items are presented as constituting "the Way of the *Great Learning*" in the opening line of the text.

[4] A poem found in the *Book of Poetry*, Mao #55. The italicized lines to follow are from the poem, with the commentary being part of the *Great Learning*.

[5] The quoted lines are the commentary of Gongja on the text of the *Great Learning*. The italicized lines are from the *Book of Poetry*.

[6] See Juja's *The "Great Learning" in Sections and Sentences* (*Daehak janggu*; C. *Daxue zhangju* 大學章句). The original has the character 緒 instead of 序, but the meaning is the same.

Korean Women Philosophers and the Ideal of a Female Sage. Philip J. Ivanhoe and Hwa Yeong Wang,
Oxford University Press. © Oxford University Press 2023. DOI: 10.1093/oso/9780197508688.003.0011

At first, I thought that the way the classic put it was not as good as if it had said, "*As one cuts and files* concerns the learning of the Way and *as one carves and polishes* concerns cultivating the self*.*" I consulted my second brother[7] about this and he said, "In his *Questions on the "Great Learning"*, Juja says,[8] '[When one cuts and carves] bone or horn, one can follow the natural path of its inherent pattern, so one's carving will be easy; this is what is called 'the commencing of harmony.'[9] As jade and other gems are solid and firm, filing and polishing them is difficult; this is what is called 'the concluding phase of harmony.'"[10] When I thought it over carefully and in detail, I came to see that my prior view was mistaken.[11]

4. When chapter 7 says, "Then they will not attain what is correct," this refers to the emotions of ordinary people. Once any of the four [states mentioned] occurs[12] and is not carefully examined, it is easy to transgress the mean and lose its correct standard. The text does not say that people fail to reach the correct standard every time they experience these [emotions].

5. [Someone asked,] "The seventh and eighth chapters concern being unable to fully correct the Heart-Mind, but the account is divided into two principles in these chapters. Why is this?"
[I replied,] "When the Heart-Mind is correct, the self is cultivated and one's family can then be regulated; there is one thread running through and unifying it all.[13] And so the principles are similar. The four states that lead to being incorrect discussed in the prior chapter [i.e., chapter 7] are about being unsettled within. This concerns when the Heart-Mind is in contact with things and influences the self. The five forms of partiality[14] discussed in this chapter [i.e., chapter 8] are manifested toward things outside [oneself], when the self is in contact

---

[7] Her second brother was the famous scholar Im Seongju.

[8] *Questions and Answers on the "Four Books"* 2.8b.

[9] *Mencius* 5B10. The commencing of harmony is said to be "the work of wisdom."

[10] *Mencius* 5B10. The concluding of harmony is said to be "the work of sageness."

[11] The content of the letter between Yunjidang and her elder brother appears in the *Collected Works of Nokmun* 10.24b.

[12] The four states are being under the influence of excitement and passion, terror and fear, liking and joy, or sorrow and distress.

[13] The idea of "one thread running through and unifying it all" is from *Analects* 4.15. In this case the one thread connects the tasks of correcting oneself and regulating one's family; both require one to cultivate one's Heart-Mind.

[14] These are partiality arising from feelings of affection and love, despising and disliking, being in awe and reverence, sorrow and compassion, or arrogance and rudeness.

with things and affects the family. This is why although there is one Heart-Mind [the account] is divided into two principles."

6. [Someone asked,] "Chapter 10 discusses how noble people must be conscientious and trustworthy in order to possess the great Way and how they lose it through being arrogant and self-indulgent. What about this?"

[I replied,] "This is the way one cultivates the self in order to bring peace to all under heaven. Those who are conscientious and trustworthy are sincere. Those who are not sincere will have nothing. One's self will also not be cultivated, so how could one possibly govern others? And so only those who are conscientious and trustworthy can 'complete themselves and complete things'[15] and attain the highest good. Those who are arrogant and self-indulgent are the opposite of this and so lose it. Within this chapter, three ways of gaining and losing are mentioned,[16] but this is the root. And so [Juja's] The "Great Learning" in Sections and Sentences, says, 'This is the decisive issue concerning the preservation or loss of heavenly Pattern-Principle.'[17] Heavenly Pattern-Principle is the 'goodness' that appears in the second section when it says, 'through goodness one obtains it [the Way], and through want of goodness one loses it.'"[18]

2. Twenty-Seven Items on the *Doctrine of the Mean*

The numbering employed in our translation corresponds to the twenty-seven items of Yunjidang's work. These includes commentary on only selected "chapters" of the Doctrine of the Mean. *The first item is on the first chapter.*

1. [Someone asked,] "In Chapter 1, Jasa[19] opens the *Doctrine of the Mean* with the lines: '[What] heaven decrees is called the nature; [what] guides the nature is called the Way; [what] cultivates the Way is called teaching.' What about this?"

---

[15] See chapter 26 of the *Doctrine of the Mean*.

[16] These are failing in filial piety, failing in brotherly respect, and failing to be kind. These are directed to parents, elder brothers, and people respectively.

[17] See chapter 10 of Ju Hui's *The "Great Learning" in Sections and Sentences*.

[18] See chapter 10 of Ju Hui's *The "Great Learning" in Sections and Sentences*.

[19] Jasa (C. Zisi) 子思 (c. 481–402 BCE), the only grandson of Gongja, is traditionally regarded as author of the *Doctrine of the Mean*, which appears as chapter 31 of the *Book of Rites*.

I replied, "This makes clear that 'the great source of the Way comes forth from heaven.'[20] What is called cultivation is following what originally and inherently exists within this nature. According with what is proper to the Way, one adjusts one's norms; one does not forcibly impose one's self-centered knowledge as the model and rule and act in ways that interfere with [the Way]. As for heaven, does it ever speak?[21] And so, it gives birth to sages and entrusts them with the positions of ruler and teacher, leading them 'to continue [the work of] heaven and establish the ultimate [standard],'[22] teaching all under heaven for ten thousand generations. This is what is known as 'fashioning and completing the Way of heaven and earth.'[23] Jeongja said, 'From [the words] [*what*] *heaven decrees* until *teaching*, I would not add or delete a thing.'[24] These words simply should be trusted."

2. [Someone asked,] "Is 'what is not seen or heard' different from what is 'hidden and subtle?'"[25]

I replied, "What is being talked about is 'what is [inherently] one's own'; it refers to the state before thoughts have begun, the time before one has seen or heard [anything]. This belongs to the realm before [feelings] are manifested, the stillness of [the nature] in itself. As for the hidden and the subtle, since the text describes these in terms of [being watchful over oneself when] alone and [Ju Hui's] commentary[26] also talks about acting and knowing, [we know that] this refers to the point at which one's consciousness first begins to be active. When people can see and hear but have not yet seen or heard anything. This belongs to the realm after [feelings] are manifested, when the subtle springs of [the nature] are poised to function. If learners are able to be cautious and apprehensive about what they do not see or hear and are careful about things people do not understand in the midst of their seclusion and aloneness, then the 'great root' (*dae bon*;

---

[20] Paraphrasing a line by Dong Jungseo. See his biography in the *History of the Han Dynasty* (*Han Seo*; C. *Han Shu* 漢書) 56.38a.

[21] *Analects* 17.19.

[22] Part of Ju Hui's commentary to the opening sections of his *"Doctrine of the Mean" in Sections and Sentences* and *Collected Commentaries on the "Analects."*

[23] Quoting the "Image Commentary" on the hexagram *Tae* (C. *Tai*) 泰 in the *Book of Changes.*

[24] See the *Extant Works of the Two Jeongs* 1.17a. The original texts read "自天命以至於敎, 我無加損焉." Yunjidang omitted the character 以.

[25] Chapter 1 of the text includes the lines "The noble person is cautious about what he does not see and apprehensive about what he does not hear. There is nothing more visible than what is hidden, and nothing more manifest than what is subtle."

[26] See Ju Hui's remarks on chapter 1 in his *Collected Commentaries on the "Doctrine of the Mean."*

C. *da ben* 大本) will be established; the 'all-pervading Way' (*dal do*; C. *da dao* 達道) will be put into practice;[27] and one will begin to be able to avoid deviating from the Way. Nevertheless, if one's intelligence is insufficient to illuminate Pattern-Principle, one will be unable to differentiate between heavenly Pattern-Principle and human desires and [properly] apply [one's] effort. This is why it is necessary to begin the eight-step process of the *Great Learning* with the investigation [of things] and the extension [of knowledge]."

3. [Someone asked,] "What is '[the state] before happiness, anger, grief, and joy are manifested?'"

[I replied,] "It is the nature decreed by heaven, the Way in itself."

[Someone asked,] "What is '[the state] after they are manifested and all attain their proper measure?'"

[I replied,] "It is the Way of according with the nature, the functioning of the nature. If learners are able to constantly preserve an attitude of reverence and awe and quietly and attentively establish this impartial [state of the nature] in itself and respond to the myriad affairs simply as its functioning is manifested, so that everything is correct and appropriate and everything accords with Pattern-Principle and is without the errors of excess or deficiency, then they will have attained 'equilibrium and harmony' (*jung hwa*; C. *zhong he* 中和) and 'a happy order will prevail throughout heaven and earth' (*cheonji wi*; C. *tiandi wei* 天地位). If one attains this level in one's learning, one will be able to complete all affairs under heaven. Even a sage could add nothing more to this!"

4. [Someone asked,] "Chapters 6 through 10, all draw upon affairs involving wisdom, humaneness, and courage. What about this?"

I replied, "They do this in order to make clear that only after one possesses these three virtues can one enter the Way. Nevertheless, one must first clearly illuminate Pattern-Principle; only then can one 'get hold of' (*taek*; C. *ze* 擇) it and 'hold on to' (*su*; C. *shou* 守) it. And so knowledge takes the lead position and humaneness follows it. If one lacks courage, then one may not be able to avoid giving up only halfway along the path, and the supreme Way will not be able to take shape. And so courage takes the third position and is the completion of all-pervading virtue. If one abandons any one of these three virtues, one will not be able to complete the task, and yet once one has

---

[27] For the "great root" and the "all-pervading Way," see chapter 1 of the *Doctrine of the Mean*, etc.

completed the task, they all come down to humaneness. Humaneness is the virtue of the mean. Nevertheless, if one is not free of even the slightest trace of self-centered thoughts, one will not be able to achieve this humaneness; being able to know self-centeredness for what it is and being able to overcome and eliminate it is nothing other than wisdom and courage. This being the case, the reason the characters for wisdom and courage occur both prior to and following the character for humaneness is subtle. Readers should keep their eyes on this!"

5. [Someone asked,] "Chapter 11 includes two mentions of the term 'noble people.' In the first, it says, 'Noble people act in accordance with the Way but abandon it halfway along the path'; in the other, it says, 'Noble people rely upon the mean; even if they remain unknown and unrecognized by the world, they have no regrets.' Both of these are about noble people but differ in describing their strengths and weaknesses, eminence and lowliness. How are we to understand this?" I replied, "The term 'noble people' when used broadly is like the term 'good people.' When used more specifically it is a name for [those with] complete virtue. To 'act in accordance with the Way but abandon it halfway along the path' can only be used to refer to good people. How do we know this? If one 'acts in accordance with the Way,' one must have a settled intention to pursue the good and have the understanding needed to attain it. This is enough to call someone a good person. But 'abandoning it halfway along the path' shows that self-centered thoughts have inserted themselves [and interfere with the pursuit]; the behavior of such people will not be able to reach a certain level, and so they cannot be said to possess complete virtue. Those who 'rely upon the mean; even if they remain unknown and unrecognized by the world, they have no regrets' have complete virtue and have attained sagehood. How do we know this? Those who 'rely upon the mean' have 'complete understanding.'[28] Those who 'remain unknown and unrecognized by the world, [but still] have no regrets' have attained the height of humaneness; [they possess] the 'complete virtue of the mean, which does not require courage in order to flourish in abundance.'[29] And so, Gongja said, 'Only sages are able to attain this,'[30] and Ju Hui said, 'This is precisely my master's

---

[28] See Ju Hui's remarks on chapter 11 in his "Doctrine of the Mean" in Sections and Sentences.
[29] See Ju Hui's remarks on chapter 11 in his "Doctrine of the Mean" in Sections and Sentences.
[30] Gongja makes this remark in chapter 11 of the Doctrine of the Mean.

(i.e., Gongja's) affair.'[31] For the most part, this chapter continues to discuss Jaro's question about power, raised in the previous chapter. And so, in general, its main idea is similar. Because 'those who seek knowledge of hidden mysteries and practice extraordinary feats' value what is unusual and like what is lofty, they go too far in pursuit of such things. They are like those of the north, who will dive into boiling water or tread on sharp blades;[32] they possess an inappropriate type of power. This is why [Gongja] says, 'This is not something I do.'[33] Those who 'act in accordance with the Way but abandon it halfway along the path' are weak and cowering; they are not able to pursue the good through to the end. They are like those of the south [i.e., who possess the 'power of the south'], which can accept shame[34] and stick to the feminine,[35] who know to retreat but do not know to advance. And so, [Gongja] said, 'This is something I am incapable of doing.'[36] Only those who 'rely upon the mean, even if they remain unknown and unrecognized by the world, have no regrets' and those who 'take their stand upon the middle way without inclining to one side or another' [and] 'do not change their course even unto death' follow the proper Way of the noble person. And so, the previous chapter talks about the 'power of the noble person,' while this chapter talks about 'what only a sage is capable of doing.' In answering Jaro, Gongja offered three different sections in this chapter and presents his true intent in the final section in order to help learners get hold of it and put it into practice."

6. [Someone asked,] "In chapter 12, what does 'far and wide and yet hidden'[37] mean?"

I replied, "This is difficult to talk about. Though no one can fully fathom the marvelous nature of the Way in itself, one can talk about the aspects of its flowing operation that are manifested throughout all under heaven. If one talks about creatures, then there are such things as the flying of birds, the running of beasts, and their various periods of hibernation and awakening. If one talks about human

---

[31] See Ju Hui's remarks on chapter 11 in his *"Doctrine of the Mean" in Sections and Sentences*.

[32] That is, they have the strength or energy of the north, as discussed in the previous chapter, and are not deterred by the threat of death.

[33] Gongja makes this remark in chapter 11 of the *Doctrine of the Mean*.

[34] See the *Chronicle of Jwa*, Fifteenth Year of Duke Seon (C. Xuan) 宣公.

[35] See chapter 28 of *Dodeokgyeong* (C. Daodejing) 道德經.

[36] Gongja makes this remark in chapter 11 of the *Doctrine of the Mean*.

[37] Chapter 12 of the text begins by saying "The Way of the noble person extends far and wide and yet remains hidden."

beings, there are also such things as the knowing and acting of husbands and wives and what even sages do not know or are incapable of doing. Now hawks and fish[38] are insignificant creatures; why then did Jasa single them out to discuss? [Hawks] fly and ascend up to heaven; [fish] leap about in the deep—they all follow their natures. And so one can see that the Way in itself and its functioning are clearly manifested above and below and there is nowhere it is not present, and one also can understand why one cannot be separated from the Way; this is what is meant by 'far and wide.' Nevertheless, though 'the operations of heaven on high are without sound or scent,'[39] how could the so-called 'hidden' be sought for outside of these [various manifestations]? Ju Hui said, 'Far and wide means the function is broad and extensive; hidden means [the Way] in itself is subtle.'[40] This explanation is comprehensive and complete."

7. Among human relationships, that between husbands and wives is the greatest;[41] it is "the constant norm between heaven and earth"[42] and "the beginning of the human Way."[43] And so [the text says,] "Its beginning lies in [the relationship between] husbands and wives." If one understands the principle of its beginning and is not, in the slightest degree, remiss or complacent, then one's effort at being watchful over oneself when alone will be authentic and can be described as heavenly virtue.

8. From ancient times down to the present, the flowing operation of the Way has never ceased, and there is no place it does not exist: it is "far and wide." Nevertheless, one must preserve the thing in itself— that which makes it what it is—and only then will its marvelous functioning manifest itself and proceed. And so, [Ju Hui's "Doctrine of the Mean" in] Sections and Sentences, says, "the most hidden [thing] is preserved therein. Hidden means tranquil, still, and without sign. Far

---

[38] The chapter cites two lines from the Book of Poetry, Mao #239, which say, "Hawks fly up to heaven; fish leap about in the deep."

[39] See the Book of Poetry, Mao #235.

[40] See Ju Hui's remarks on chapter 12 in his "Doctrine of the Mean" in Sections and Sentences (italics added.)

[41] See chapter 20 of the Doctrine of the Mean and Mencius 5A2.

[42] This line appears in the "Biography of Dong Jungseo" in the History of the Han Dynasty 56.20b.

[43] This line appears in numerous places, such as the Imperial Readings of the Taepyeong Period (Taepyeong eoram; C. Taiping yulan 太平御覽) 102.16a and Ju Hui's Family Rituals 1a and General Exposition of the Book of Etiquette and Rites and Its Commentaries (Uirye Gyeongjeon Tonghae; C. Yili Jingzhuan Tongjie 儀禮經傳通解) 4.11a.

and wide means the myriad images are replete within."[44] These are the function and the thing in itself.

9. In chapter 13, Gongja says of himself, "[This is something I am] not yet capable of doing," which is what makes him a great sage. In general, the problem with people is that they are clear when it comes to holding others responsible but dull when it comes to holding themselves responsible; they often claim too much and fall short when it comes to action. And so they fail to cultivate themselves or advance their virtue. If learners can take the sage's Heart-Mind [as seen here] as their model and always keep in mind that the Way is inexhaustible while they themselves are deficient, then they may enter into virtue and discover that the Way provides more than they ever can use.

10. The main points of chapter 14 all concern doing what is proper for the station one occupies and having no affairs or concerns outside of this. What a noble person preserves is the Way. One simply occupies one's place and is perfectly content with it. No matter what failure or success, poverty or wealth, honor or disgrace, or gain or loss one might encounter under heaven, one "never finds oneself in a situation in which one is not contented." It is like it was when Sun was poor; he was just an ordinary man; he lived upon the irrigated fields; "he ate parched grains and herbs and felt no distress, as if he would end his life in this way. When he rose to become Son of Heaven and occupied the position of emperor, he wore embroidered robes and played the lute, but took no special delight in these, as if they had always belonged to him."[45] He followed along with whatever he encountered and did not decide things on his own. This is the way sages handle affairs; [they] rest secure [in their positions] and carry things out. As for learners, if they can start out able to be "poor but not engaging in flattery or rich but avoid becoming arrogant," if they can end up able to be "poor but full of joy or rich and loving the rites"[46]—this is "residing in ease and awaiting the decree." This is what is known as "noble people are satisfied and composed."[47] Petty people are the opposite of this. And so,

---

[44] This quotation first appears in the *Extant Works of the Two Jeongs* 15.16b. It is cited by Ju Hui in various works, though not in his *Collected Commentaries on the "Doctrine of the Mean."*

[45] The last several lines are quotations with brief elaborations of *Mencius* 7B6.

[46] See *Analects* 1.15.

[47] See *Analects* 7.37.

they "behave in dangerous ways" and are "always full of distress."[48] Is this not lamentable!

11. If noble people attain their aspiration and occupy a superior position, then they work to improve all under heaven and bestow benefits to the people below; how could they ever "show contempt for those below"? If they do not attain their aspiration and occupy an inferior position, then alone they improve themselves so that their names are handed down to later generations; how could they ever "curry favor with those above?" For this reason, noble people simply cultivate what is within themselves.

12. Someone asked, "Chapter 16 concerns 'the way the virtue of ghosts and spirits is manifested.' Some divide virtue and ghosts and spirits into the Way [on the one hand] and its implements [on the other],[49] taking ghosts and spirits to be *Gi-Material*. Some take the character 'virtue' to be more closely related to the characters for ghosts and spirits and take ghosts and spirits to be Pattern-Principle. I would like to hear a comprehensive and consistent account of this matter."

I replied, "In my humble view, the second explanation is probably correct. The first explanation appeals to Mr. Hu's (C. Hou) 侯[50] distinction between what is above and within form, but we already have Ju Hui's definitive account of this; so why is there any need for further debate? In general, ghosts and spirits are the spiritually bright aspects of the two primary *Gi-Material*s [yin and yang] and so are associated with[51] Pattern-Principle. This is rather broad[52] and imprecise and so there are those who exclusively categorize them (i.e., ghosts and spirits) as *Gi-Material*; the case of Baek Yu (C. Bo You) 伯有[53] becoming an evil

---

[48] The first phrase is part of the text; the second is from *Analects* 7.37.

[49] This idea distinguishes between a metaphysical Way, which is above physical form, and its various implements, which are the things of the phenomenal world. See the "Great Appendix" (upper part) to the *Book of Changes*, section 12: "What is above form is called the Way; what is within form is called implements."

[50] Hu Haenggwa (C. Hou Xingguo) 侯行果 (n.d.) was a well-respected scholar of the mid-Dang dynasty who wrote a commentary on the *Book of Changes*. His commentary is now lost, though parts of it survive in various other collected commentaries.

[51] Reading 一合 as 合一 in the original.

[52] Reading 點 as 占 in the original.

[53] Baek Yu is the pen name of Yang So (C. Liang Xiao) 良霄 (d. 543 BCE), a minister of the state of Jeong (C. Zheng) 鄭. He was killed as a result of a conflict with a member of powerful clan and was transformed into an evil apparition. See Duke So (C. Zhao) 昭公 Seventh Year of the *Chronicle of Jwa*. The example of Baek Yu was extensively discussed by neo-Confucians, including the Jeong brothers and Ju Hui, and in works such as the later Korean philosopher Yulgok Yi I's *Treatise on Life, Death, Ghosts, and Spirits* (*Sasaeng gwisin chaek* 死生鬼神策). For Ju Hui's views on ghosts and spirits, see note 57 below.

apparition offers an example.[54] There are also those who regard them as belonging to the same [category] as Pattern-Principle, the way ghosts and spirits are treated in this chapter offers an example.[55] How can we know that this is so? After the classic describes '[how abundantly the virtue of ghosts and spirits] is manifested,' it simply talks about how they 'are unseen and unheard' and yet 'enter into all things and no thing is without them' and 'how the outpouring of sincerity [in worshipping them] cannot be repressed.' In his remarks following his commentary on this chapter,[56] Ju Hui concludes his discussion simply by mentioning the two terms, 'far and wide' and the 'hidden' [seen in the previous chapter]; through his language we can understand how this chapter takes them as belonging to the same [category] as Pattern-Principle. Ju Hui also often discussed the principle of ghosts and spirits by saying, 'They are like Pattern-Principle in being subtle but leaving a trace behind; they are like *Gi-Material* in being spontaneous.'[57] Moreover, [the use of] the term 'subtle' in regard to spirits already places them, for the most part, on the side of Pattern-Principle; furthermore, the [sense of the] term 'spontaneity' is something the word *Gi-Material* cannot fully capture. In light of this, we can understand how ghosts and spirits are both *Gi-Material* and Pattern-Principle." Someone who was having difficulty with this said, "This is the same principle as seen in 'hawks flying and fish leaping.'[58] Hawks flying and fish leaping are *Gi-Material*; what allows them to fly and to leap is Pattern-Principle. But why did Jasa only talk about investigating what is above and within [the phenomenal world][59] and not about investigating what is above and within Pattern-Principle?"

[I replied,] "He wanted people to understand that the Way and its implements are not two separate things, and he wanted to avoid implying that hawks and fish are Pattern-Principle. This is just like the

---

[54] His case is thought to be an example of ghosts and spirits as *Gi-Material* since his evil apparition did not conform to the proper norms of Pattern-Principle.

[55] On Yunjidang's interpretation, this chapter highlights normative aspects of ghosts and spirits, and so is understood as an example of ghosts and spirits as Pattern-Principle.

[56] These are a retrospective summary of chapter 16 of the text; see Ju Hui's *"Doctrine of the Mean" in Sections and Sentences*.

[57] Ju Hui said, "If the Heart-Mind is compared to the nature, then it subtle but leaves traces behind; if it is compared to *Gi-Material*, then it is spontaneous and spiritual." See section 41 in the second of the chapters entitled "The Nature and Pattern-Principle" (*Seong ri*; C. *Xing li* 性理) in the *Classified Sayings of Master Ju* 5.9a.

[58] See note 38, page 156.

[59] Chapter 12 of the *Doctrine of the Mean*.

case of ghosts and spirits. Ghosts and spirits surely are *Gi-Material*, but he only said, 'They enter into all things and nothing is without them.' They are unseen and unheard, and yet the way they enter into all things [and so are 'far and wide'] and the way in which they are unseen and unheard [and so are 'hidden'] simply exists within them naturally [as Pattern-Principle]. This avoids explicitly claiming that ghosts and spirits are Pattern-Principle, as this language suggests. But only [Ju Hui's] *"Doctrine of the Mean" in Sections and Sentences* explicitly takes their 'entering into all things' as an illustration of being 'far and wide' and takes 'not being heard or seen' as an illustration of being 'hidden.' This shows that, in the end, ghosts and spirits cannot be separated from the notions of being 'far and wide' and being 'hidden.' Why is this? In general, the main point of this chapter, in the end, is very difficult to grasp and very difficult to express in words. Let us set aside the two irreconcilable aspects we have discussed for further consideration and await someone who understands the Way to address them."

13. [Someone asked,] "Chapter 17 says that 'those with abundant virtue are sure to receive the decree of heaven,' but Gongja did not receive an official position, nor was he particularly long-lived. Why is this? Was his virtue so greatly inferior to that of Yo or Sun?"

    I replied, "This is not the case. Gongja lived at a time when the turning of heaven had reached its absolute nadir and Pattern-Principle had lost its constancy. Or perhaps this is a case of what former Confucians referred to in saying, 'There are some things that heaven, earth, and the sages are unable to fathom.'"[60]

14. Chapter 20 takes the cultivation of the self as the root of heaven and earth. If the self is not cultivated, one will not be established, and so from where could the Way then come forth? And so, it is said, "The root of heaven and earth lie in the state; the root of the state lies in the family, and the root of the family lies in the self."[61] The root of the self also lies in heaven, but heaven is simply Pattern-Principle. To understand this Pattern-Principle and preserve it within the self is called cultivating the self. And so, the text says, "Those who think of cultivating the self cannot but understand heaven." This being the case, if one is not a sage who is "born with knowledge,"[62] one must

---

[60] Chapter 12 of the *Doctrine of the Mean*.
[61] *Mencius* 4A5.
[62] This idea is mentioned in the text, but see also *Analects* 7.20 and 16.9.

first study and only then can one understand. This is why nothing is greater than to "love learning."[63] If I wholeheartedly am able to love learning, understand that my nature "is the same as that of Yo or Sun,"[64] and "practice with an eye to advantage" and "practice through exerting great effort," after actually piling up effort over a long period of time, I can attain the level of a sage. And so it says, "Once the effort is complete, the achievement is the same."

15. To study, inquire, reflect, and discriminate[65] is the way one fully explores this Pattern-Principle and extends knowledge. To earnestly practice is how one preserves this Pattern-Principle and makes oneself sincere. But the Five Relationships[66] are the road from which all under heaven proceed. And so the text calls them the "all-pervading Way." The means by which one can carry out this all-pervading Way are the three all-pervading virtues of wisdom, humaneness, and courage. Wisdom is the way to understand this. Humaneness is the way one protects this. Courage is the way one enforces this.[67] And so the text says, "The ways in which one carries this out are three in number." Nevertheless, this is nothing but authentic Pattern-Principle. Those who are not sincere will have nothing. How can virtue establish itself on its own? And so the text also says, "The way in which one carries it out is singleness of purpose." Singleness of purpose is nothing more than sincerity.

16. "To love learning is to be close to wisdom."[68] If one understands that this virtue is originally bright and one desires to exert oneself in learning to make it brighter, though for the time being one has not attained wisdom, in the future one will attain it. This is why the text says, "[It is] close to wisdom." "To apply effort in carrying it out is close to humaneness." If one loves the good and applies effort in carrying it out with a desire to make oneself sincere, though for the time being one has not attained humaneness, in the future one will attain it. And so the text says, "[It is] close to humaneness." "To understand shame is close to courage." If one is ashamed of being inferior to others and

---

[63] This idea is mentioned in the text, but see also *Analects* 1.14, 5.15, 28, 17.3, etc.

[64] See *Mencius* 4B60; cf. 6A7.

[65] These four, along with earnest practice below, are discussed in chapter 22 of the text.

[66] Those between ruler and minister, father and son, husband and wife, between elder brother and younger, and between friends.

[67] See Ju Hui's remarks on chapter 20 in his *Collected Commentaries on the "Doctrine of the Mean."*

[68] See chapter 21 of the *Doctrine of the Mean*.

understands how to make oneself stronger, then in the future one will urge oneself forward and advance straightaway without worrying about "giving up only halfway along the path." And so the text says, "[It is] close to courage."

17. [Someone asked,] "What about the explanation about '[having it by] nature and [having to be] taught' in chapter 21?"

I replied, " 'Those who are born knowing' and those who 'practice with ease' refers to those who are understanding[69] by nature and illuminate all things. What moves them from sincerity to understanding is called the nature. 'Those who know through learning' and those who 'practice it for benefit' refers to those who choose the good and return to their nature as a result of being taught. What moves them from understanding to sincerity is called teaching. If one is sincere, one will understand; if one understands, one will be sincere. These [two possibilities] describe the difference between sages and worthies respectively. Though there is this difference between [having it by] nature and having to be taught, once they have completed the task, they are equal and one."

18. Sages are without any deficiencies by nature; they are like heaven, which achieves its ends through nonaction. And so it is called the "Way of heaven." Worthies attain sincerity by being taught; they follow the Way that is appropriate for human beings. And so it is called the "human Way."

19. Chapter 22 [describes how] the nature is the single source for all the myriad things. If one is able to fully develop one's nature, then one will be able to fully develop the nature of both human beings and creatures. Nevertheless, the *Gi-Material* of creatures is not as penetrating or correct as that of human beings. The *Gi-Material* of ordinary people is not as refined and pure as that of sages. This is the reason why there are differences between human beings and other creatures, and between sages and ordinary people. If not for the perfect sages under heaven, whose [goodness] cannot be further improved, who are able to discern what is original and essential to the nature, what actions are appropriate for different roles and obligations, and what are the norms and standards of good character, so that the lives of both humans and creatures can follow what is natural for each of their natures, then aside from those who are partial and blocked and become creatures—who of course are not worth discussing—how could those who are equally endowed with

---

[69] Literally, "those who are bright by nature."

correct and penetrating [*Gi-Material*] and who become human beings ever return to their nature and "form a trinity [along with heaven and earth]?"[70] And so, in my humble opinion, if sages are not born into the world, then ten thousand generations cannot avoid rushing into a long, [dark] night, where humanity is not much different from birds and beasts.[71] Oh, great indeed is the kind-heartedness of sages!

20. [Someone asked,] "What about the teaching about 'extending to the utmost the shoots of goodness within one' in chapter 23?"

[I replied,] "Although human nature is the same [in all], the endowment of *Gi-Material* is unequal. Ordinary people cannot compare to the complete perfection of sages. And so when the Four Sprouts are manifested, there are different degrees of dullness or brightness, frailty or flourishing. If learners are able to take up the good sprouts that get manifested and extend each and every one of them in an effort to reach their complete expression, they will be able to make what is dull bright and what is frail flourishing and have the means to unify the [complete] perfection [of sages] and purify the heavenly nature [with which they are endowed]. The absolute and unceasing sincerity of the sages can be attained through this means. And so it says, 'From [the shoots of goodness] one can attain sincerity.' When one is sincere, one's abundant virtue is manifest and naturally the six results listed [below] will follow.[72] Learners who attain this state are 'spirit-like.' Even ghosts and spirits will be unable to descry their limits."

21. [Someone asked,] "Chapter 25 says, 'Sincerity is how one completes oneself.' What does this mean?"

[I replied,] "Each of the myriad things receives its own authentic Pattern-Principle at birth. And so this line is saying that sincerity is how things complete themselves."

22. [Someone asked,] "It also says, 'The Way is how one leads oneself.' What does this mean?"

[I replied,] "To follow the nature is what is called the Way. And so this line is saying the Way is how things behave of their own accord. As for sincerity, this refers to being truly authentic and without deviance.

---

[70] Part of Ju Hui's commentary on *Mencius* 6A15. See his *Collected Commentaries on the "Mencius."*

[71] See *Mencius* 6A10.

[72] When one attains complete sincerity, the text says one's virtue will (1) become apparent, (2) become manifest, (3) become brilliant, (4) influence others, (5) change others, and (6) transform others.

In regard to heaven, it is called authentic Pattern-Principle. In regard to human beings, it is called the authentic Heart-Mind. In terms of Pattern-Principle, it is the ending and beginning of the myriad things; all of these are things accomplished by this Pattern-Principle. In terms of the Heart-Mind, it is the ending and beginning of the myriad affairs; all of these are things accomplished by this Heart-Mind. The sincerity spoken of here refers to the ending and beginning of things. In terms of heaven, 'What heaven decrees—how solemn and unceasing!'[73] And yet 'The four seasons proceed in order and the hundred things are born.'[74] All of these are cases of authentic Pattern-Principle. In terms of human beings, the Heart-Mind of the sage is 'absolutely pure and unceasing';[75] in 'responding to things it always hits the proper mark'[76] and 'replies appropriately to a myriad of changes.'[77] All of these are cases of the authentic Heart-Mind. If one has not attained the level of a sage, then the authenticity of one's original Heart-Mind cannot but suffer from interference and blockage, and when its functioning is manifested, it cannot be without deviance. When there is deviance, there is no sincerity; 'when there is no sincerity there is nothing.' This is why noble people value sincerity."

23. Though sincerity is how one completes oneself, there is no separation between things and oneself. Once one has completed oneself, one ought to extend this to complete things as well. "Completing oneself is humaneness." If one talks about establishing oneself, completing things pertains to knowing. If one talks about extending and reaching out [to things], completing the self pertains to completing things. Though there are distinctions between this and that in terms of Pattern-Principle, [fundamentally] they are one. And so the text says, "This is the Way to unite inner and outer." When one works at completing the self, cultivating the self is the root. When one works at completing things, extending oneself is the root. Completing the self and completing things each has its own guiding principle. And so the text says, "Whenever noble people employ them [i.e., these virtues], they will act properly."

---

[73] See the *Book of Poetry*, Mao #267. This line is quoted in chapter 27 of the *Doctrine of the Mean*.

[74] *Analects* 18.19. This is part of a passage in which Gongja defends his silence by saying, "Does heaven speak? And yet the four seasons proceed in order and the hundred things are born. Does heaven speak?"

[75] See chapter 27 of the *Doctrine of the Mean*, where this is used to describe the virtue of King Mun.

[76] Part of Ju Hui's commentary on *Analects* 4.15; see his *Collected Commentaries on the "Analects."*

[77] Part of Ju Hui's commentary on *Mencius* 6A11; see his *Collected Commentaries on the "Mencius."*

24. Chapter 27 effusively praises the Way of the sages; it also talks about how the Way will not accumulate unless one has the right kind of person <the character "accumulate" (*eung*; C. *ning* 凝) is particularly interesting here>, and the following section begins to describe in detail the method for entering into virtue. What does "method for entering into virtue" mean? It is nothing more than to preserve the Heart-Mind and extend knowledge. The text mentions "honoring the virtuous nature and pursuing the path of inquiry and learning." Honoring the virtuous nature is nurturing the original source. "To refrain from deviancy and preserve sincerity"[78] is how one preserves the Heart-Mind and reaches the greatness of the Way in itself. Pursuing the path of inquiry and learning is to read books and fully comprehend Pattern-Principle and to meticulously investigate and clearly discriminate; it is how one extends knowledge and fully understands the details of the Way itself. These two are the great beginning of cultivating virtue and accumulating the Way. [The work of] "extending it to its full breadth and greatness and reaching its full height and brilliance" as well as "reanimating the past and being earnest and generous" belongs to the category of preserving the Heart-Mind, which describes what is implied by the earlier line about "raising it up to the heights of heaven." To "fully understand the refined and subtle" and "treading the path of the mean" as well as "understanding the new" and "esteeming the rites" all belong to the category of extending knowledge, which describes what is implied by the earlier lines about the "three hundred [rites governing ceremony]" and the "three thousand [rites governing etiquette]." As for the Way of the sage, if we speak of what it is in itself, it is supremely great and extremely broad—vast and limitless! If we speak of its particular manifestations, they are exceedingly subtle and minute—brilliant but with an articulated order and pattern! Chapter 20 talks about "its greatness being such that nothing under heaven can encompass it" and talks about "its fineness being such that that nothing under heaven could further divide it." This is precisely what is referred to.

25. The Heart-Mind is the implement of the nature. To preserve the Heart-Mind is how one nourishes the virtuous nature. Knowledge

---

[78] Quoting the "Commentary on the Words" (*Muneon*; C. *Wenyan* 文言) commentary on the hexagram *Geon* in the *Book of Changes*.

is the intelligence of the Heart-Mind. To extend knowledge is how one makes bright one's virtuous nature. If one does not preserve the Heart-Mind, self-centered desires create confusion and chaos, the "great root" cannot be established, and one certainly lacks the means to extend knowledge. If one does not extend knowledge the Heart-Mind, as it inherently is in itself, remains obscured and benighted and the illumination of Pattern-Principle will not be bright. How, though, does one preserve the Heart-Mind? Preserving the Heart-Mind entails cultivating this great virtue and accumulating the greatness of the Way. Extending knowledge entails cultivating this lesser virtue and accumulating the minute aspects of the Way. This explanation of cultivating virtue and accumulating the Way is presented with urgency and vividly. It is connected with and unifies, in ways that mutually illuminate one another point by point, the discussion in the opening chapter above—about being careful and cautious and watchful over oneself when alone—with the discussion in chapter 30 below saying that "the smaller powers[79] are like river currents and the greater powers are like awesome transformations." [Ju Hui's "*Doctrine of the Mean*" in] *Sections and Sentences*, says the following about these five lines: "The great and the small mutually support one another; head and tail mutually respond to one another." Great and small refer to honoring the virtuous nature and pursuing the path of inquiry and learning. Head and tail refer to honoring the virtuous nature and pursuing the path of inquiry and learning in relation to the eight sentences that follow. If those who have "set their Heart-Minds on learning"[80] truly are able to apply their efforts to these tasks, then when they reach the state where "even though they want to stop they cannot,"[81] the Way can accumulate and they can learn to be sages. Oh! Those who make the effort should do so by asking, "What kind of person was Emperor Sun? What kind of person am I?"[82]

26. Chapters 29 through 32 all effusively praise the Way of the sages and the principle of "Heaven and earth flowing in a single stream."[83] But when we reach the final chapter, it raises the concern that learners will

---

[79] The character 德, here rendered "power," is throughout this translation more often translated as "virtue." See note 185, page 74.

[80] See *Analects* 2.4.

[81] See *Analects* 9.11.

[82] See *Mencius* 3A1.

[83] See *Mencius* 7A13.

be impetuous in pursuing what is "lofty, deep, marvelous, and far-off" and will therefore lack a foundation for advancing in virtue. And so it again presents the need for one to make oneself sincere so that learners understand how they must exert effort. When the text says, "Over her embroidered robe she puts a plain single garment,"[84] it is talking about cultivating what one has within oneself and not seeking to be known by others. When it says, "Though [fish] swim to the bottom, they are very clearly seen,"[85] and when it says, "Nothing is more evident than what is hidden, nothing is more manifest than what is subtle," it wants people to be cautious when they are isolated and alone. When it says, "Looked at in your room, free from shame in the light that shines in,"[86] it is saying that even in times of leisure when alone in one's room, prior to any budding thoughts or ideas, one must be careful, watchful, anxious, and afraid to ensure one is without the slightest trace of partiality or favoritism and without shame in the sunlight that shines into your room. This shows the Way for people to work on [cultivating] themselves in what can be described as a profound, appropriate, practical, and clear manner.

27. Someone asked, "The opening section of the text talked about being careful and afraid, but here [in the conclusion] it places being watchful over oneself when alone first. What about this?"

I replied, "Earlier, [the Way] in itself was placed first and its function later. And so being careful and afraid took precedence. Here, the concern is with moving from outside to inside <[i.e.,] from the myriad affairs to the single Pattern-Principle>. And so, being watchful over oneself when alone takes precedence. Putting the thing in itself first and its function later presents the Way in itself. Working from outside to inside presents purposeful practice. This surely is the main and guiding thought of this teaching, but in between its head and tail, in what comes first and what comes later, it preserves throughout the supreme Pattern-Principle. Readers should reflect upon it!"

---

[84] Quoting the *Book of Poetry*, Mao #57 and #88. Im's text has 衣錦尙褧 instead of the *Book of Poetry*'s 衣錦褧衣.

[85] Quoting the *Book of Poetry*, Mao #192.

[86] Quoting the *Book of Poetry*, Mao #256.

[The addendum begins here]

The *Doctrine of the Mean* is wholly dedicated to making clear the idea that one cannot depart from the Way, but it begins with an account of the great root of all under heaven <the state before [feelings] are manifested>. In its middle sections, it spreads out to explore the myriad affairs <from chapter 2 to chapter 32>. At its end, it unifies everything by bringing the discussion back to the great root. But the section on being watchful over oneself when alone is also the pivot of the middle sections on the myriad affairs and brings to a conclusion what is raised in the first section. <Being watchful over oneself when alone is an affair that penetrates sagely learning, from beginning to end. And so, in the opening chapter it talks about this right after discussing the state before feelings are manifested, to serve as an introduction to its account of the myriad affairs. In the concluding chapter [when it says], "[Noble people,] even when not moving, maintain an attitude of reverence," it again talks about this, to serve as a conclusion to its account of the myriad affairs.> Not only are the moral principles [of the text] refined and profound, the writing and presentation of ideas are extremely subtle and marvelous—indeed these are the words of a sage!

The Way of the Mean is nothing more than to be truly authentic and without deviation. And so the main and guiding point of this work from beginning to end is to focus on sincerity as the root and gradually extend this to earnestness and respect to achieve the flourishing of peace throughout all under heaven. This is none other than the natural and spontaneous response of the virtue of the sage's perfect sincerity and the ultimate extension of the transformative power of the sage's spirit. Since Jasa effusively praised the ultimate flourishing of the sage's virtue as "matching heaven," he had to conclude by saying, "The workings of high heaven are without sound or scent." There is nothing to add to his description of the marvelous nature of the sage's Way! Oh! Ju Hui said, "The virtue of perfect sincerity is something that only a perfect sage can understand!"[87] Does this not refer to Jasa!

When I was young and read the *Doctrine of the Mean* and the *Great Learning*, I wanted to write down my humble understanding of them but put it off and carried on as before, so that ultimately I never got around to completing anything. Now, I am seventy and feel some urgency about this; my feeble state of health is getting even worse. I know that my remaining days are numbered, and so in the winter of 1786 I made an outline of some

---

[87] Ju Hui says something very close to this as part of his commentary on chapter 32 of the *Doctrine of the Mean*: "Only a perfect sage can understand the Way of perfect virtue; only a perfect sage can enact the virtue of a perfect sage." See his *"Doctrine of the Mean" in Sections and Sentences.*

ideas that I had struggled to develop in the past. Since, within the women's quarters, I did not have the benefit of discussing and being questioned [about my ideas], I expended my spirit to the utmost [in an effort to improve them]. Most of the time what I wrote failed to express my intent; it was close to being like the case of the blind men feeling an elephant.[88] Nevertheless, I still proceeded in this way, because it enabled me, in some small measure, to realize my original aim and await someone who had the understanding to correct it.

What Jasa transmitted [the *Doctrine of the Mean*] is most difficult to read. Earlier I had made some notes [on it], [but] when I reconsidered them, I found that most of them lacked luster and really were worthy of an embarrassed sigh. Now when I assess those passages that I had skipped over in the past, in regard to this and my other comments on the meaning of the classics, I find myself, at times, peering at them with only vague comprehension. When I made an effort to revise them, they seemed to be better than what I had written before. But since the death of my son, everything seems like floating clouds to me; my Heart-Mind is like dead ashes. I lack any hope of further motivating myself. What can I do? In the past, I revised this piece, <these twenty-seven chapters> [on the *Doctrine of the Mean,*] and sent it [to you] via a messenger. When I reflect upon the ideas covered in this piece, I find them exceedingly subtle and marvelous. Prying into their meaning is very difficult; describing them [adequately] is even more difficult. They concern the most critical principles of the purposeful practice of the original source of the nature and this Heart-Mind. And so, from time to time, I collected and called upon my remaining energies and returned to revising my manuscript; still, I could not avoid sighing over its lack of luster. Truly, I found myself in the position of [a soldier] who "runs away fifty paces laughing at others who run a hundred paces."[89] Nevertheless, the revised version is still superior to the earlier one; so I would like to eliminate the earlier version and preserve this one. What do you think?

<Written as an addendum on the occasion of sending a revised version of the *Meaning of the "Doctrine of the Mean" in Twenty-Seven Chapters* to my youngest brother.>

---

[88] Reading the character 像 as 象. The idea is that blind men try to determine by their sense of touch what an elephant is but only guess on the basis of the part they are touching.

[89] *Mencius* 1A3. The point being that all of them deserted their post in the face of the enemy but some ran away less far.

THE EXTANT WRITINGS
OF JEONGILDANG

姜靜一堂

静一堂遺稿

Gang Jeongildang
1772–1832

The image above is a photolithic reproduction of the opening section of Gang's works, *The Extant Writings of Jeongildang* (*Jeongildang yugo* 靜一堂遺稿), from the 1836 edition held at Seoul National University, which begins with selections of her poetry.

Poems (詩)

1. Rhyme in Honor of My Mother-in-Law, Jiildang[1] <1797>

In elementary learning, the need is for sincere human relations,
Be kind to the young and give rest to the elderly.[2]
Driving straight ahead[3] following such behavior
Leads along the even and easy Way.[4]

<(Original Rhyme)[5]
Spring comes; flowers bloom in abundance,
Years go by; people gradually grow old.
I sigh, what good would it do?
I only want the one good Way.>

2. Beginning to Study <1798>

At thirty,[6] I begin my studies,
Not knowing which direction to turn.
From this day on, I must be diligent,
Aspiring to be like the ancients.

---

[1] Jiildang is a pen name of Jeongildang's mother-in-law, Lady Jeon. It was rare for a woman to have a pen name, which indicates her exceptional talent. It is said that she read the Confucian classics and historical texts extensively and grasped their overarching principles. See the *Collected Works of Gangjae* (*Gangjae jip* 剛齋集) 20.12b.

[2] Cf. *Analects* 5.26.

[3] The image and sentiment are similar to what is found in "Eulogy to the Steeds of No" (*No Song Gyeong*; C. *Lu Song Jiong* 魯頌駉) Mao #297, quoted in *Analects* 2.4, which praises the Marquis of Lu for driving his chariot without swerving from the path.

[4] This is a reference to a line under the hexagram "To Tread" (*ri*; C. *lu* 履) in the *Book of Changes*, that says, "treading the way that is even and easy" (*i do tan tan*; C. *lu dao tan tan* 履道坦坦).

[5] This poem provided the rhyme-scheme that served as the model for Jeongildang's poem.

[6] Since she was born in 1772, we should understand this as a poetic way of saying that she began her studies as she was approaching thirty years of age.

Korean Women Philosophers and the Ideal of a Female Sage. Philip J. Ivanhoe and Hwa Yeong Wang, Oxford University Press. © Oxford University Press 2023. DOI: 10.1093/oso/9780197508688.003.0012

3. Seeing a Boy Attendant at School Punished

If you are able to be cautious and careful,
How could you go wrong?
If now you have regrets,
Sincerely return to being solemn and serious!

4. Mountain Home

A noble person's home among the mountains.
You read books, facing the window's light.
A visitor arrives from afar,
An old dog barks outside the wicker door.[7]

5. Self-Encouragement

How fine and good it would be to enjoy life,
Wandering around carefree and unconstrained!
Take a lesson from those who failed to study,
Sinking into old age, sighing in their hovels.

6. Human Nature Is Good

Human nature originally is wholly good,
Developing it fully,[8] one becomes a sage.
To desire humaneness, humaneness lies therein,[9]
Make Pattern-Principle clear to make oneself sincere.

---

[7] The image of a wicker door implies a humble dwelling.

[8] Cf. *Mencius* 7A1, which discusses fully developing one's Heart-Mind and knowing one's nature.

[9] Cf. *Analects* 7.30: "The master said, 'Is humaneness far off? I desire humaneness, and behold, humaneness arrives.'"

7. For My Husband [1]

To my shame, I lack talent and virtue,
But I learned needlework as a child.
Authentic work requires exerting oneself;
Do not be concerned about clothes and food.[10]

8. Reverently Offered to My Husband as He Sets Off in His Carriage

In the clear dawn, shedding tears, I sent you off,
Traveling afar, among the lakes and mountains, you must not
    forget!
When you were about to depart, I had only one thing to say,
The affairs of this world turn in cycles, like the blue heavens above!

9. Moved to Chant on New Year's Eve

I have wasted precious time doing nothing,
Tomorrow, I shall be fifty-one years old!
What good to sigh with sadness halfway through the night?
Better to cultivate oneself throughout the remaining days.

10. After Illness <1822>

A dangerous illness, now fortunately has grown less severe,
A clear autumn day, the open door makes me feel refreshed.
How could my recovery be only the result of ginseng and herbs?
Now I truly understand the bright realm of sincerity.

[10] In this poem Jeongildang is urging her husband to focus on his studies and not worry about supporting the family, which she does through her needlework. This is a theme we also see in some of her personal missives. Nevertheless, it is her "authentic work" that enables his.

11. Impromptu Hymn [1]

I lack three-year-old mugwort,

Sunk in the throes of illness with no cure.

If by now I have not stored any away,

What is the use of regretting it another day?[11]

12. Reading the *Doctrine of the Mean*

A work transmitted by the sage Jasa[12]

Across the ages, inspiring so much achievement.

Substance stands upright, depending on nothing,

Function operates freely, without error or defect.[13]

If in the beginning one can be watchful and cautious,[14]

In the end one can achieve equilibrium and harmony.[15]

The Universal Way unites the Three Virtues,[16]

Sincere! What can be added to Pattern-Principle?

13. For the Wives of Geunjin,[17] Grandnephew <Lady Choe and Lady Gwon>

To be chaste and true are the top priorities;

To submit and obey are the primary tasks.

This is the Way of a wife,

Which you must endeavor to fulfill.

---

[11] Mugwort is a medicinal herb. This poem seems to be inspired by *Mencius* 4A9, which says, "Seek for three-year-old mugwort, to cure a disease that lasts seven years. If it has not been kept in storage, the patient may never get it."

[12] Jasa (C. Zisi) 子思 (c. 481–402 BCE), born Gong Geup (C. Kong Ji) 孔伋, was the only grandson of Gongja. He is credited with transmitting the Confucian Way to Maengja and writing four chapters of the *Book of Rites*, including the *Doctrine of the Mean*.

[13] This and the prior line juxtapose substance and function; see note 12, page 86.

[14] The opening chapter of the *Doctrine of the Mean* teaches that cultivated people are cautious from the very beginning and watchful over themselves when alone.

[15] The opening chapter of the text concludes with the lines "When the states of equilibrium and harmony exist in perfection, a happy order will prevail throughout heaven and earth, and all things will be nourished and flourish."

[16] Chapter 20 of the *Doctrine of the Mean* includes the lines "Ruler and minister, father and son, husband and wife, elder and younger brothers, the relationship between friends—these five are the Universal Way under Heaven. Wisdom, humaneness, and courage are the Universal Virtues under Heaven."

[17] An heir of the main line of a lineage (*jongson*; C. *zongsun* 宗孫) of Gang Jeongildang's husband; he was his grandnephew. Cf. note 42, page 206.

14. Sitting in the Night <1823>

Deep in the night, all movement ceases,
In the empty courtyard, the bright moon shines.
My Heart-Mind is pure, as if washed clean,
Suddenly, I see [the true form] of the nature and the feelings.[18]

15. Tanwon[19] 坦園 <1824>

Tanwon is secluded and still,
The abode of upright and cultivated people.
Independently searching through a thousand ancient texts,
Retired scholars reside in humble dwellings.

16. Thanking Haeseok 海石 Gim Sanggong[20] 金相公 <Jaechan 載瓚> for His Gift of a New Calendar <Written on Behalf of My Husband> <1826>

With the coming of spring, auspicious plants[21] kindly serve
    as neighbors,
Offering those living in the mountains a way to keep track of
    the seasons.

[18] The idea that after prolonged study one experiences a "sudden and unifying" (*hwaryeon*; C *huoran* 豁然) enlightenment is found in Ju Hui's commentary to chapter 5 of the *Great Learning*. The idea finds its origin in a famous four-line stanza attributed to Bodhidharma (Dumoulin 2005, 85). For the "nature and feelings" and their relationship to the Heart-Mind, see selection 30, "Governed by Reverence."

[19] *Tanwon* is the name of Jeongildang's family residence. Literally, it means "Tan's Garden." Tan is part of the pen name of her husband, Tanjae Yun Gwangyeon. But the word *tan* also means even, easy, and easy going (see note 4 above), and Jeongildang associated all of these meanings with the place. She discusses the name and the place in the "Commemoration of Tanwon," pages 226–227.

[20] Gim Jaechan was an official during the Joseon dynasty who attained the rank of Chief State Councilor (*Yeonguijeong* 領議政). Haeseok is his pen name and Jaechan his given name. *Sanggong* is an honorific title referring to the three chief councilors. In the parenthetical "written on behalf of my husband," we read 伐 as 代. The expression "written on behalf of my husband" (*dae buja jak*; C. *dai fuzi zuo* 代夫子作) appears numerous times throughout Gang Jeongildang's corpus. Though presented "on behalf of" her husband, these works primarily express her own thoughts and illustrate the degree to which she and her husband, Yun Gwangyeon, were partners in pursuit of Confucian sagehood. The literary device of writing on behalf of her husband gave Gang Jeongildang a voice that passed over (i.e., beyond) the walls of the inner quarters and afforded her a chance to participate in scholarly exchanges with male scholars of her time, even if only indirectly. For a detailed discussion of this issue, see Gim 2005, especially 54.

[21] *Myeonghyeop* (C. *Mingjia* 蓂荚) is a mythical plant that spouts a bud from the first to the fifteenth day of each month. From the sixteenth to the end of the month, it loses a bud each day. And so, it offers a kind of organic calendar.

Anxious only that time is passing on and on,
Reciting admonitions to be good, I hope for my daily renewal.[22]

17. Respectfully Offered to the Father of Cheonghanja[23] 青翰子 <Yi Gwanha 李觀夏> on the Occasion of His Sixtieth Birthday Banquet <Written on Behalf of My Husband>

Cultivating virtue at the foot of North Mountain,
Hiding your light increases the honor of your Way.
The purity of the crane's cry draws its children to respond,[24]
The green in the shadow of the bamboo gives birth to its
    grandchildren.
The arc of the arrow has returned to where it began,[25]
Guests and friends join in offering toasts.
Your good fortune has not yet run its course,
Elegant carriages wait before the gate of your home.

18. Presented to <Byeong-eun 秉殷> Bak Jungno 朴仲輅 <Written on Behalf of My Husband>

Though one esteems diligence in resolute action,
One must seek the correct gateway and path.
Over time, in the end, one will succeed,
Like building up a mountain or digging a well.[26]

---

[22] Chapter 6 of the *Great Learning* opens with the lines "The following words were engraved on the bathing tub of King Tang, 'If you can renew yourself one day, do so each day. Let there be daily renewal.'"

[23] Cheonghanja was an official of the late Joseon dynasty.

[24] See the "Image Commentary" on the hexagram "Moves Even" (*Jung Bu*; C. *Zhong Fu* 中孚) in the *Book of Changes*, which says, "[Like] the crane crying out in her hidden retirement, and her young ones responding to her. [It is as if it were said], 'I have a cup of good spirits,' [and the response were], 'I will partake of it with you.' Cf. Section 8 of the "Great Appendix" (upper part) of the *Book of Changes*.

[25] This image captures the idea that he has completed the full course of the sixty-year cycle described by the "Heavenly Stems and Earthly Branches" (*cheon-gan jiji*; C. *tiangan dizhi* 天干地支), which brings him back to the first stem.

[26] *Analects* 9.19 says, "In building up a mountain, if only one more basketful of earth is needed to complete the task and I stop, it is I who have stopped short." *Mencius* 7A29 says, "To dig a well to a depth of twenty-five meters but stop short of reaching the spring below is to throw away the well."

19. Shown to Various Friends My Same Age
\<Written on Behalf of My Husband\>

Even after fifty years, my recklessness and dullness remain;
I feel remorse and regret for being tough[27] as a mountain that
    none could inscribe.
From now on, let us all help and assist one another,
Relying upon shared kindness[28] to see us through our remaining
    years.

20. Three Stanzas Written in Tanwon
\<Written on Behalf of My Husband\>

Living in the forest, drinking in the valley,
Holding my books, enjoying myself.
Reflecting on my prior efforts at self-cultivation,
I come close to discerning something profound.
A knot of doubts obscures and blocks [the way],
To whom can I turn for help?
Following what is balanced and correct,
Easy and even is this Way.

The sun slants into the Dark Abyss,[29]
Ice and snow polish the mountains.
I fodder the horses and grease the axles,
On the road ahead, clouds stretch into the distance.
I am weak and find it difficult to drive on,
Pausing my ascent, I sigh.
Encountering these late years of life,
What can I do about my sadness and distress?

[27] See *Analects* 2.18, which says, "If in one's words one has few occasions for remorse and in one's conduct one has few occasions for regret, emolument will be found therein." This makes clear that Jeongildang's husband is concerned with regret and remorse about both what he has said and what he has done.

[28] See the "Image Commentary" on the hexagram "Lake" (*Tae*; C. *Dui* 兌) in the *Book of Changes*.

[29] The "Dark Abyss" roughly translates Uyeon (C. Yuyuan) 虞淵 (the "Yu Abyss"), a legendary, deep body of water into which the sun "sinks" at the end of each day. See the "Patterns of Heaven" (*Cheonmun*; C. *Tianwen* 天文) chapter of the *Hoenamja* (C. *Huainanzi*) 淮南子.

Birds cry out, seeking their flocks,
Fish dive deep, pursuing their schools.
The season unfurls the warmth of spring,
Their delight is free and easy.
Why do I live in isolation?
In the end, I rarely see old friends.
I wish to discuss the three beneficial things [with them],[30]
And have them diligently admonish my mistakes.

21. Verse Respectfully Matching the Rhyme of the *Guntan*[31] Poem of a Distinguished Elder Scholar <Written on Behalf of My Husband>

At the Royal Tomb,[32] I recalled weeping over Master Song,[33]
In the middle of the night, I mournfully chanted the poem
   written that day.[34]

[30] *Analects* 16.5 describes these as taking joy in the careful study of rites and music, speaking well of others, and having many worthy friends.

[31] The ancient Chinese kept track of time using the system of the Heavenly Stems and Earthly Branches, matching these to the movements of the heavens. One of the Earthly Branches is *sin* (C. *shen* 申), and years when the path of the pseudo-star Tae Se (C. Tai Sui) 太歲 across the ecliptic falls on a section of the heavens whose name contains this branch are known as *Guntan* (C. *Tuntan* 涒灘) years. Later Chinese thinkers came to believe that the start of a new Confucian golden age would begin in a *Guntan* year, and so writing a *Guntan* poem expressing one's desire for the start of this grand cultural renewal became a practice among them. Ju Hui wrote such a poem, expressing his regret that China was unable to repel the Jurchen-led Jin dynasty which had conquered and occupied Northern China and pushed the Chinese state to the south during the Southern Song dynasty (1127–1279 CE). His poem says, "Do we really know this Way is without end; Next year Tae Se will again be in *Guntan*" (極知此道無終否, 明年太歲又涒灘). See *the Collected Works of Hoeam* 9.20b. The "distinguished elder scholar" in the title probably refers to Ju Hui.

[32] Yeongneung 寧陵 is the royal tomb of King Hyojong 孝宗 (r. 1649–1659 CE), the seventeenth monarch of the Joseon dynasty, and Queen Inseon 仁宣 (1619–1674 CE), also known as Queen Dowager Hyosuk 孝肅. It is located in Yeoju City in Gyeonggi Province.

[33] Song Siyeol (see note 31, p. 12) was a royal tutor for King Hyojong and his political partner. While Song did not write a *Guntan* poem, he did develop an elaborate plan with the King for a northern expedition against the Manchus as revenge on behalf of the Cheong (C. Qing) dynasty for the collapse of Great Myeong dynasty, the symbol of Confucian civilization, based upon the righteous principles of the *Spring and Autumn Annals*. After the sudden death of the King Hyojong, Song Siyeol used to weep in memory of the king and their unrealized expedition. In his memorial of resignation to King Hyeonjong 顯宗 (r. 1659–1674 CE), the son of King Hyojong, Song Siyeol reminded the King that both the Song and Myeong dynasties were established in years with *sin*, citing Ju Hui's poem. See the *Veritable Records of King Hyeonjong* (*Hyeonjong sillok* 顯宗實錄) 13.23a–b [8(1667)/01/28/#3].

[34] This probably refers to the poem Ju Hui wrote, which Song Siyeol knew well and referenced. See the prior note.

Those in later generations solemnly recite the meaning of the
    Spring and Autumn Annals,
Moved, tears flowed uninterrupted, adding strands of dangling
    gray hair.

22. Encouraging the Youth

You must be diligent when reading books,
Do not squander the vitality of youth.
How can you be satisfied with just memorization and recitation?[35]
You should aspire to be a sage or worthy!

23. Written on the Occasion of the New Year's Eve

The ancient sages transmitted this Way,
Each and every person can act in accord with it.
The enlightened Heart-Mind is reflected in icy water,
Its radiant light shines for a thousand autumns.
Passing to one another the one word "reverence,"[36]
Who is able to unlock this bolt?
Flying wildly into the distance is only wasted labor,
If you want to make progress, you must seek what is near at hand.[37]
To the end of your life, continue to strengthen yourself,
If you aspire to attain the Way, can you dare to be tardy or lax?

[35] "Learning by memorization and recitation" (*gisong ji hak*; C. *jisong zhi xue* 記誦之學) was a common target of neo-Confucian criticism. It referred to a sterile type of learning and was opposed to "learning for oneself" (*wigi ji hak*; C. *weiji zhi xue* 爲己之學), which meant learning to improve oneself morally.

[36] Reverence was one of main virtues in Confucianism, but it attained a special status for Ju Hui as the guiding principle of the sages. See his *Classified Sayings of Master Ju* 5.9a. Korean Confucianism, especially the school of Toegye 退溪 Yi Hwang 李滉 (1501–1570 CE) emphasizes it as the core teaching of the sages—"the entrance to the Way and the foundation for accumulating virtue" (入道之門, 積德之基). See the chapter "Presentation Address of the *Ten Diagrams for Sagely Learning*" (*Jin Seonghak sipdo jam* 進聖學十圖箚) in his *Collected Works of Toegye* (*Toegye jip* 退溪集) 7.4b–35b.

[37] What is "near at hand" is one's own self or Heart-Mind. This is a common theme among Confucians. For its *locus classicus*, see *Analects* 6.30.

24. Presented to the Licentiate An Jungap 安駿甲 and Shown to Go Sinui 高信義 <[given name] Jeongsik> <Written on Behalf of My Husband>

> The Way of the sages is like a great road,
> People past and present have drawn upon it.
> There is nothing else to study or inquire about,
> You must seek and search ever higher.
> The art you need as your guide is in books,
> And clearly manifested in those who earlier cultivated it.
> Exert yourself! Drive on, keeping your reins straight!
> Wander at ease together in the realm of the Way!

25. For My Husband [2]

> Since the day you began to follow Ganjae 艮齋,[38]
> You have sought the Way and nothing else!
> Now it has been thirty years,
> How have you progressed in your studies?

26. Respectfully Offered to My Husband in the Early Morning of the New Year's Day <1830>

> If one has not heard the Way,
> Even if one does not die, there is nothing to celebrate.[39]
> We must uphold the master's teachings,
> And wholeheartedly strive to be sincere and reverential.

27. Removing Grass from the Courtyard

> The small hoe pulls thick weeds [from the soil],
> A welcome rain sprinkles the dusty ground.

---

[38] It is not clear who this is.
[39] This poem refers to *Analects* 4.8, which says, "If one hears the Way in the morning, one can die that evening contented."

Though worried what Old Yeom (C. Lian 濂)[40] would think,
I cleared an old path in front of the thatched mountain cottage.

28. Shown to My Nephew Seonggyu[41] 誠圭

Your teacher knows that you are filial,
So he had you carry on after his elder brother.
I hope that you will serve him [the teacher],
As you have served your father and mother.

29. [Untitled]

In the winter of 1822, my husband showed me a quatrain and encouraged me to aspire to advance my studies. I tried to compose a matching rhyme but could not do so [at the time]. Suddenly, in a dream last night, I recalled the rhyme scheme, and when I awoke still remembered it. So I wrote this down in order to preserve it. <1832> <Just three days before [her] death.>[42]

With only three days of life remaining,
I am ashamed of failing in my aspiration to be a sage or worthy.
Thinking admiringly of Jeungja,
It is time to correct the mat at the very end of life.[43]

30. Governed by Reverence
<From here onward, the year [of composition] is unclear.>[44]

The myriad Pattern-Principles are the origin of heaven and earth,
A single Heart-Mind unites the nature and the feelings.[45]

---

[40] This refers to the Song dynasty neo-Confucian Ju Doni by his posthumous name Yeomgye, who famously claimed that he could not bear to cut the grass in front of his window because he felt one with it. See chapter 3 of Ju Hui 1978.

[41] Seonggyu seems to have been her husband's nephew, who came to study under him.

[42] While she anticipated the day of her passing, the parenthetical remark was probably added by her husband.

[43] The story is from the "Dangung" chapter (upper part) of the *Book of Rites*. Jeungja was near death and someone noticed he was lying on a mat fit for a Great Officer. Jeungja insisted it be changed; when it was, before he could regain his composure, he passed away, fulfilling his wish to "die in the correct way."

[44] This is a note added by Jeongildang's husband.

[45] This idea first appears in Jang Jae's *Completed Writings of Master Jang* (*Jangja jeonseo*; C. *Zhangzai quanshu* 張子全書) 14.3b. Later, Ju Hui cites this idea in his commentary to *Mencius* 6A6. See Ju Hui, *Collected Commentaries on the "Mencius"* 5.36a.

If you are not governed by reverence,
How can you reach the distant goal?

31. Listening to Autumn Cicadas

Myriad trees welcome the crisp autumn air;
The sounds of cicadas raise havoc with the setting sun.
Deep in thought, I am moved by the nature of things;
Beneath the trees, alone, I pace back and forth.

32. Gazing up at Gongja

Great indeed is the master's virtue!
Like the azure sea, vast and boundless.
Oh! You who seek to measure [the ocean] with a ladle,[46]
How could you comprehend so many streams [of wisdom]?

33. A Guest Arrives

A distant traveler who admires my husband,
Says he came from the Northern Pass.[47]
Our family is poor, what is there to drink or eat?
All I can offer is three cups of wine.

---

[46] Trying to measure the ocean with a ladle made from a gourd is a trope for persons of limited capacity attempting something beyond their ability. The biography of Dong Bangsak (C. Dong Fangshuo) 東方朔 in the *History of the Han Dynasty* contains the line "To peer at the heavens through a tube, measure the ocean with a ladle, or sound a great bell with a twig." The earliest example of this kind of expression is the "Autumn Floods" (*Chu Su*; C. *Qiu Shui* 秋水) chapter of the *Jangja,* which has the line "peeping at the heavens through a tube, or measuring the earth with an awl."

[47] Referring to the Northern Pass implies that the visitor came from Hamgyeong Province 咸鏡道.

34. The Road in Front of Tanwon Passes through to a Broad and Open Thoroughfare

How sad!—this degenerate and fallen age,[48]
How many people pursue deluded paths!
Even and easy[49] (*tan tan* 坦坦) is the road [in front of] my home,
I want to say, "Hold the reins and drive straight ahead!"[50]

35. Hymn to Sincerity and Reverence

If not sincere, how can you have it?
If not reverent, how can you preserve it?
Only with both of these
Can you enter the gate of the Way.[51]

36. Rhyme in Solemn Reply to My Grandfather-in-Law's Warning about Smoking Tobacco

It is not proper to smoke the odious herb.[52]
In ancient times, one never heard of such a thing.
With the instructions handed down by my grandfather-in-law,
This becomes all the more evident and clear.

---

[48] See Gong Yeongdal's commentary to the *Chronicle of Jwa*, Twenty-Fourth Year of Duke Hui (C. Xi) 僖公. See *Zuo's Commentary on the "Spring and Autumn Annals" with Commentary and Subcommentary* (*Chunchu jwajeon jeongui*; C. *Chunqiu zuochuan zhengyi* 春秋左傳正義) 14.21b.

[49] See note 4 above.

[50] Cf. poems 1, 15, and 20 above.

[51] Cf. *Analects* 15.33.

[52] Tobacco was first introduced from the south (i.e., Japan) in 1615, and smoking tobacco was fashionable in Joseon society by 1621. At first, tobacco was recommended as a medicine and as a result came to be called the marvelous herb from the south (*Namnyeongcho* 南靈草). But soon its negative effects overwhelmed Joseon society; more and more fields were converted to cultivate tobacco and more and more children and women took up smoking, which was considered highly inappropriate. In addition, numerous fires were caused by smoking. Since the eighteenth century, smoking tobacco was considered harmful and as a result became known as the bewitching herb (*yocho* 妖草) and odious herb (*akcho* 惡草). See the *Veritable Records of King Injo* (*Injo sillok* 仁祖實錄) 37.13a–b [16(1638)/08/04#01]. Thanks to Hanna Kim for an earlier discussion of this poem.

37. Impromptu Hymn [2]

Resolute is the master's commitment,
Aspiring only to study the ancient sages.
When he knew, he always carried it forth in action,[53]
When he responded to things, he first corrected himself.

---

[53] All neo-Confucians aspired to the idea of the unity of knowing and acting: true or sincere knowledge motivates and guides proper action.

Letters (書)

1. Letter to [My Brother] Gang Chwiyeo \<Ilhoe\> \<Written on Behalf of My Husband\>

When your younger brother [Sihoe][1] came for a visit, he carried in his sleeve your kind letter. I opened and read it and came to know that you are well in the cool air of the early autumn. This news brought me comfort beyond compare. I heard that you have begun a period of mourning [for one of your relatives][2] and that you also have lost your child; how can I express my shock and astonishment [at this news]?

Given the situation, I wish I could offer some support [to you] even if only for a short time. But I am sick and my wife is ill. Over time, her condition has grown worse and persistent. I have no way to express how depressed this makes me feel. I heard the good news that your heir is growing up well. The progress that has been made in his early education will ensure that he will not stray from the proper path. At appropriate times, you must endeavor to instruct him so he can avoid the misfortune of becoming obstinate and rebellious. What do you think about involving his paternal cousins[3] \<the brothers Seonghoe 星會, who held the junior ninth rank,[4] and Unhoe 雲會\>[5] in his education? Fundamentally, their understanding of filial piety, friendship, integrity, and harmoniousness far surpasses that of ordinary people; their

---

[1] "Younger brother" (*Gyessi* 季氏) is an honorific expression for the listener's younger brother. Gang Chwiyeo 姜就如 is Yun Gwangyeong's brother-in-law. Gang Jeongildang had two elder brothers, Gang Ilhoe 姜日會 (courtesy name, Chwiyeo 就如) and Gang Sihoe 時會 (courtesy name, Seongchul 聖朮) (1794–?).

[2] Specifically, he had begun wearing the *gong* attire (*gongbok*; C. *gongfu* 功服), which is worn for nine months (*daegong*; C. *dagong* 大功) or five months (*sogong*; C. *xiaogong* 小功) depending on the situation. According to the *Master Ju's Family Ritual* (*Juja garye*; C. *Zhuxi jiali* 朱子家禮), *gong* mourning attire is worn for nine months for patrilateral first cousins and five months for patrilateral second cousins and maternal grandparents (see Deuchler 1992, 183). It is not clear for whom Gang Chwiyeo was mourning at the time of this letter.

[3] These were two paternal cousins through a common great-grandfather and so shared the same surname as Jeongildang.

[4] The Junior Ninth Rank (*Chambong* 參奉) is the lowest rank among court officials in the Joseon dynasty.

[5] The material within parentheses is an interlinear comment inserted by Gang.

character never strays beyond these moral principles. There is no need to search afar for a qualified teacher [for your heir]; just ensure that day and night he engages in proper learning and practice with them. [Then,] who could deny that this offers a convenient and practically efficacious way to proceed?

You've written that you intend to pass through here in the fall. I really look forward to it! I really look forward to it! Since my writing is of such poor quality, I have asked [my wife] for assistance in writing this letter. I know this is irregular.

Respectfully presented by [your] brother on the
nineteenth day of the seventh month, 1808

2. Letter to My Clansmen
\<Written on Behalf of My Husband\>

The frost and cold has tightened its grip; I humbly hope it will not affect the health of the members of our clan. Autumn has passed; I have yet to fully recover, and I have no way to express fully the melancholy I currently feel within me. I will simply report to you that for several years we have been working on a genealogical record of our branch that includes extremely de-tailed records of our ancestors' affairs and the names of their descendants. In 1804, a member of our clan by the name Yun Haeng 允行, who is said to live in Eunjin 恩津, came to see me several times. He told me that he wanted to take responsibility for composing the register [of the members of our lin-eage], and so I trusted him without entertaining any doubts. Soon afterward, he collected the preface for the register and the bulk of the individual lists and left. Several months later I heard that he privately had published this on his own, and so I did a careful study of this so-called published edition.

I found that the ordering of the ancestral tablets[6] was jumbled and chaotic, while legitimate and illegitimate children were intermixed and confused. There was no end to the other mistakes and errors that I found. This was nothing more than the work of some country bumpkin with no knowledge of what he was doing. With an overflowing reckless attitude, he produced this disastrous result. Now that we have taken over work on the genealogy, I fear that this person will come and want to join in and cause the project to suffer

---

[6] See the "Miscellaneous Records" (*Japgi*; C. *Zali* 雜禮) chapter (upper part) of the *Book of Rites*.

inaccuracies. Should this happen, I hope the members of our clan will sternly rebuke [this suggestion] and not accept his participation and moreover will reprimand him for his earlier misdeeds. I most reverently beseech you!

My thoughts about the matters presented above are things I dared not avoid; I regard it as my duty to inform you of them with this letter. This is all that I have to say. I humbly ask that you look into the matter.

Respectfully written by your clansman
(Yun Gwangyeon) on 15 September 1814

3. Letter to My Clansman Gwangju 光周
<Written on Behalf of My Husband>

The year is at an end and the snow is deep. I am really looking forward to visiting you; my only concern is whether you are at peace and resting well. I am living in isolation, groaning in agony from my illness. I am not getting any better, which is most depressing. I have just begun working on the essay regarding your esteemed ancestor,[7] but not only am I not the right person for this job but also my poor compositional style is unable to express his elegant and subtle glory. It is only because it was difficult to decline your generous offer that I undertook this awkward and clumsy effort. I cannot express how apprehensive and ashamed it makes me feel. Because of my lingering illness, I could not write this out properly; I hope you will understand.

Respectfully written by your clansman
(Yun Gwangyeon) on Hunting Day[8] 1815

4. Letter to My Clansman Gyeom 謙 in Busan
<Written on Behalf of My Husband>

I pass over the formalities of ritual propriety. Recently, we had a long and pleasant conversation, but now I write to offer my condolences. The funeral is already underway; how can you repress the pain of the filial thought that you will never see the deceased again? Not only have you been exhausted by

---

[7] The original text has the term *samse* (C. *sanshi*) 三世 here, which could refer to one or more unspecified ancestors.

[8] Hunting Day (Nabil 臘日) is the third *mi* day (未日) after the winter solstice.

your labors [organizing the funeral] but the weather has been exceptionally blustery recently as well. Your grief persists through all the work of making the sacrificial offerings, and so I cannot help worrying about your health. As for me, on top of my old illness, I also caught a cold, which has left me lying in bed moaning. How can I describe my melancholic suffering! As for the question about ritual that you posed to me, I consulted the explanation of Elder U (U Ong 尤翁),[9] which says, "If one receives notification of a death within the month in which the deceased passed away, just calculate from the month in which the deceased passed away and hold the annual commemoration ritual on the day on which the death occurred."[10] He also said, "The dates for wearing mourning garments should commence and be calculated beginning from the day on which one receives notification of a person's death. If one begins to wear mourning garments several months after one receives notification of a person's death, one cannot use the [earlier] date on which you received the notification to cut short [the proper period during which you must wear mourning garments]."[11] Since the explanation of this earlier worthy is so clear, one can follow it without harboring the slightest doubt. I must leave it at this, passing over the formalities of propriety.

Respectfully written by your clansman
(Yun Gwangyeon) on 25 February 1816

5. Letter to My Clansman *Taengnim* 澤霖 in *Pungcheon* <Written on Behalf of My Husband>

Half the year already has gone by and still I have received no news from you. How can I put an end to my disappointment and longing? At this point, the weather is gradually warming. Being far away, I cannot help worrying about whether, at rest or in activity, everything is good with you. As for me, my old illness afflicts me more frequently; I do not expect that I will get better, and I feel depressed and pitiful. Whenever I think of the mutual affection felt among all the members of our clan, I want to join them in endearing conversation and accompany them on outings to famous and inspiring places. My original plan was to set off for a visit this spring, but I was ill and my horse was not in good condition. In the end, I had to abandon this plan and move it back until sometime

---

[9] Elder U (U Ong 尤翁) is Song Siyeol (see note 31, p. 12).

[10] The *Great Compendium of Master Song* (*Songja daejeon* 宋子大全) 83:32a.

[11] The *Great Compendium of Master Song* 121:32a.

between autumn and winter. But if some young man among our relatives plans to come to Seoul during the imperial examinations scheduled for August, perhaps we can exchange letters and report what's happening with one another; what do you think? There is more to say, but the post office is closing soon, and so for now I must leave it at this. I hope you please will understand.

Respectfully written by your clansman
(Yun Gwangyeon) on 20 January 1824

6. Letter of Condolence to My Uncle <Jungsil 中實>
Gwon Ojae 權烏齋
<The date of composition is unclear but probably written in the late autumn of 1804>[12]

Couriers are few and the distance between us great. Receiving no word from you left me in an anxious mood. Last winter, [my brother] Chwiyeo 就如 returned with your reply [to my last letter]. It was only then that I heard the news that my aunt (your wife) was dwelling in the lands below. I was shocked and full of remorse; what can I possibly say? She had not reached old age and always showed such energy; anyone would have said she was very healthy. I personally thought and certainly expected her to join the ranks of those who attain truly venerable longevity. How could I ever have imagined what now has occurred? When I suddenly received this terrible news, I dared to think about you, uncle, trying to manage your crushing grief and pain; it must be so difficult to cope with and control. When I think of seeing before me the image of your child wailing in grief over the loss of his mother, I feel the tragic cruelty in an especially poignant way; I cannot stop thinking about it even while eating or resting. Though I want to dispatch a special messenger to offer my condolences to you and my nephew and thereby share my most intimate feelings with you, because I have recently become incapacitated by illness, I am afraid I will not be able to arrange this. I am constrained by circumstances from fulfilling my duties. If this makes me appear cold and indifferent,[13] I hold only myself to blame and so cannot overcome my sadness and grief.

---

[12] Note by Jeongildang's husband.
[13] Literally: "Like [the people of Jin 秦] looking at [the people] of Wol (C. Yue) 越." During the Spring and Autumn period (fifth century BCE) the state of Wol was in the extreme Southeast of China and the state of Jin was in the extreme Northwest. And so the two states became a trope for expressing extreme difference, distance, or in this case indifference.

At the start of summer, I heard through Chiheung 致興 that my second maternal cousin had passed away. How miserable; how miserable—that someone of such great strength and integrity will not be able to experience the caring and generous virtue of your profound humaneness—that so many cataclysms, truly beyond anything one could dream of, have piled up one after another in a short period of time! [Whether one will enjoy] long life is something that cannot be known; [this] is Pattern-Principle.[14] But, how could anyone suffer so many repeated disasters? In successive years, we have borne such upheavals. [Under such circumstances] even a well-to-do family wouldn't have everything they need; how much more so one that is struggling and poor? Over the entire course of carrying out and overseeing the ritual, there must have been times when [you] were hard-pressed for cash, and so there must have been some aspects of the funerary rite that you were unable to attend to properly. Moreover, you have suffered this unbearable experience repeatedly. Whenever I start thinking that all of this might lead you to not take proper care of yourself, my grief mounts and tears well up.

My illness has gradually become long and lingering. My husband has also been distressed for some time about his persistent malady. [As a consequence,] the other difficulties that life presents are simply growing worse over time. Last month I suffered the loss of my child, but as I am serving my parents-in-law, how could I express my emotions fully? All my emotions are piled up and go far beyond what I have said, but I cannot bear to write about all of them here. I wish you good health and great peace. This letter is incomplete, but please receive it.

7. Letter to My Husband
<Written in the Winter of 1830>

May I ask how your illness[15] was last night compared to the prior day? After your return from Hoedeok 懷德,[16] I had hoped to celebrate with you and pass

---

[14] Noble people do not concern themselves with longevity but with living morally upright lives. The span of their lives is simply a matter of destiny or fate and up to heaven. *Mencius* 7A1 teaches that those who seek to establish their true moral destiny must not be concerned with premature death or long life. To say that not knowing whether one will enjoy long life "is Pattern-Principle" is to say that this is what is proper. Jeongildang discusses this general issue in personal missive 54 in this volume.

[15] Reading 侯 as 候. *Sinhu* 愼侯 is a Korean-Chinese term referring to the illness of someone who is honored or esteemed.

[16] Hoedeok is a township located in Daejeon, South Chungcheong Province 忠清道, in which Yun's teacher Gangjae 剛齋 Song Chigyu 宋穉圭 (1759–1838 CE) resided. For Gangjae, see note 22, page 226.

along some recent news, but I experienced a recurrence of my dreaded illness, which left me unsettled and disoriented, I was worried that moving around too much at this time would make my condition worse. Moreover, throughout the day, our guests monopolized all of our attention, and so I have not been able to talk with you. This morning, however, my health was slightly improved and our guests have dispersed. Fortunately, there was some food and wine left over, so I thought I would wait, out of respect, until after the time for morning greetings and then would prepare and present these as an offering. By then it was already noontime, and I still had not received orders to prepare your wash basin. I dare to think that your health has lost its inner harmony and you have not yet fully recovered. I am very concerned about you.

I heard that when you were with your teacher, you received instruction concerning the lines about "not looking at, listening to, speaking, or acting in any way that is not in accord with the rites"[17] and want to carve these [onto a plaque] and display them above our library. I think this would be very auspicious and delightful! These four lines are Gongja's response to Anja [when he asked about the process leading to humaneness], and Anja took these as his guide until the end of his days, so that he could make progress toward the goal of becoming a sage. Moreover, your late grandfather often wrote these lines out in order to spur himself onward and teach those that followed. I dare to hope that you look up to this important lesson that Gongja handed down to Anja, keep in mind this supreme admonition and warning [bequeathed] by your ancestor, and carry on your teacher's thought to exert yourself earnestly—never lagging day or night and keeping it always before your eyes. The word "self" (*gi*; C. *ji* 己)[18] means that the desires of one's Heart-Mind are not fully in accord with the dictates of heavenly Pattern-Principle. The rites are the regulation and embellishment of Pattern-Principle.[19] One must first be clear about what is according to the rites and what is not; then, one must courageously cut off self-centeredness. When one completely accords with heavenly Pattern-Principle, one can attain the Way. I dare to urge you to look up to and exert yourself in this manner. I have more to say when we meet. [Please overlook the fact that] this letter is incomplete.

[17] *Analects* 12.1.

[18] Reading the character 未 as 夫. Members of the orthodox Jeong-Ju School of Neo-Confucianism tend to take "self" as indicating "self-centered desires." See, for example, Ju Hui's commentary on *Analects* 12.1, where he says, "'Self' refers to the self-centered desires of the physical self."

[19] This is a line that appears throughout Ju Hui's writings. For example, see his comments on *Analects* 1.12 and 12.1 in his *Collected Commentaries on the "Four Books" in Sections and Sentences* (*Saseo janggu jipju*; C. *Sishu zhangzhu jizhu* 四書章句集注).

Personal Missives[1] 尺牘

\<Offered to My Husband\>

1

This morning, an old woman arrived offering a peck of rice and a catty of meat. I asked her the reason and she replied, "When I was traveling outside the town, I was accosted by vagabonds. Your husband happened to be passing by and in tears I appealed[2] for his help [standing] at the foot of his horse. He harshly upbraided the vagabonds and, subsequently, I was able to avoid them. I was profoundly moved by his kindness, and so I offer this to show my sincerity."

When [the old woman came to our house,] I heard you entertaining visitors in the men's quarters and so did not dare to disturb you; on my own, I decided to return what she had offered. The old woman firmly and resolutely would not accept this, and so I told her, "Once, even after my husband had not eaten for seven days, he still declined a gift of one thousand gold coins. How can I possibly accept what you bring?" The old woman then sighed, picked up her rice and meat, and left.

Though she offered her gift with the sincere intention [of expressing her gratitude], had I accepted it, I would have been suspected of selling your favor, and so I handled it in this way. I don't know what you think about this.

2

Suddenly and unexpectedly, I thought I heard that on your way back from the city, you stopped by someone's house; this is true, isn't it? Although it was the house of a scholar, they now have started to sell wine there. It must have

---

[1] The original text contains a couple of places where it is not clear when or where a new missive begins. We have divided the text in ways that make the most sense in terms of content and style.
[2] Reading 訢 as 訴 in the original.

Korean Women Philosophers and the Ideal of a Female Sage. Philip J. Ivanhoe and Hwa Yeong Wang, Oxford University Press. © Oxford University Press 2023. DOI: 10.1093/oso/9780197508688.003.0014

been fortuitous that you and your guests visited there, but how can we be sure that some stranger will not say [that you went] to buy wine? The ancients had a poem, "The noble person prepares for what has yet to be and does not allow the possibility of suspicion."[3] Must we not be cautious and prudent?

3

Right now, I am sending some food along to you. I don't want you to think twice about it; just eat it all. Today, while there are many people at [our] home, there is enough food for everyone; please don't be concerned about this. Even if at times there isn't enough, a noble person should not be concerned [about things like] spoonfuls of rice.

4

Suddenly and unexpectedly, I heard you reprimand someone; your tone was overly harsh. This is not the middle way. If you seek to correct this person in this way—without first being correct yourself—how can this be regarded as acceptable? I hope that you will think about this further.

5

Yi Gyeongam's 李絅庵 <Jinyeon 晉淵>[4] eight-character line "preserve the Heart-Mind, never let go; follow Pattern-Principle without disobeying"[5] and Herald of the Crown Prince Hong's 洪 <Jikpil 直弼>[6] line, "carry out genuine affairs with a genuine mind," mutually complement one another, while Yi Yangwa's 李養窩 <Uiseung 義勝> four-line admonition to his sons—

> There is no greater good than correcting one's faults.
> There is no greater wrong than self-deception.

[3] *Categorical Medley of Literary Texts* (*Yemun yuchwi*; C. *Yiwen leiju* 藝文類聚) 41.23a.
[4] Yi Jinyeon 李晉淵 (b. 1770 CE), whose pen name is Gyeongam 絅庵.
[5] The original is eight Chinese characters long (存心不放 循理無違), though the translation only imperfectly reflects this.
[6] Hong Jikpil 洪直弼 (1776–1852 CE), pen name Maesan 梅山, attained the ninth rank, *Sema* 洗馬, in the Crown Prince's Guards (*Igwisa* 翊衛司).

There is no greater blessing than being broad-minded.
There is no faster route to calamity than anger.—

not only offers an admonition to his sons but is genuinely and substantially what a noble person should guard against and reflect upon. I hope that you will increase your efforts to admonish yourself.

6

Councilor (*Chamui* 參議)[7] Yu 俞 <Hanjun 漢雋, pen name Jeoam 著庵 (1732–1811 CE)> and First Secretary [of the Royal House Administration] (*Dojeong* 都正)[8] Yi 李 <Jeongin 廷仁, pen name Sasadang 四事堂 (fl. 1734 CE)>, both have reached their eighties, a venerable age, and yet frequently visit [this] far-off place. How could they do this simply as an expression of common courtesy? [It must be because they] care about your study and practice and look forward in anticipation to your success. I hope you will cultivate the substantial aspects of yourself and fulfill their expectations.

7

When dusk has fallen and you cannot travel, why don't you think about the words of Pak Gijae 朴其齋 <[given name] Jongjeon 宗傳>?

8

The *Book of Changes* says, "Be moderate in eating and drinking."[9] Wine is an important[10] part of eating and drinking. I hope you will be moderate in your drinking and careful in regard to your virtue.

---

[7] More precisely, *Chamui* 參議 refers to the rank of Third Minister of the Six Boards (Yukjo 六曹).
[8] More precisely, *Dojeong* 都正 refers to the rank of First Secretary of the Royal House Administration (Donnyeongbu 敦寧府).
[9] See the "Image Commentary" on the hexagram *I* (C. *Yi*) 頤 in the *Book of Changes*.
[10] Reading 犬 as 大.

9

Suddenly and unexpectedly, for some reason, you reprimanded someone harshly; might you have come close to overstepping the mean in your reprimand? Noble people must take special care to apply themselves in regard to their voice, expression, and speech. The *Book of Poetry* says, "The mild and respectful person. Such a one possesses the foundation of virtue."[11] I dare respectfully to counsel you that you were a bit lacking in mild and harmonious temperament when you reprimanded that person.

10

This morning our guest, <the Licentiate (*Sangsa* 上舍)[12] Yi Wonjung 李遠重>, departed; why did you not implore him to remain? It is not proper to treat even common people this way, how much less so a worthy! I think you must have done this because, with me being ill, you worried about how much work this would require [of me]. Nevertheless, there are still a few measures of rice in our storage jars, and my illness is slightly better than it was yesterday. How can you allow your concern for one woman's labor to come before the proper regulation of your family? The [importance of the] rites governing the reception of a guest comes right after that governing offerings to one's ancestors. This is a great affair for one's family; you must not be the slightest remiss in this regard.

11

[My younger brother], Ilhoe 日會, braved the cold this morning to come and visit us. [You must] have felt distressed over his being exhausted from this effort; is that why you instructed me to make him something to eat? It's been almost ten days since your uncle from Yesan 禮山, <[given name] Gwanghak 光學>, arrived to visit us, but [he] has been eating congee and even has missed several meals. Now, today, [if we] suddenly cook rice[13] for [my] younger brother Ilhoe, it is not simply that we were forced to do so; [people

[11] These lines are from the "Greater Hymns" chapter of the *Book of Poetry*, Mao #256.
[12] More precisely, *Sangsa* 上舍 indicates people who have passed the lower licentiate examination.
[13] The idea being that cooked rice is much more substantial and valuable than congee.

will say that] you show greater familial love to your wife's brother than to your own family, and [people will say that] I show favoritism to my own brother over the members of my husband's clan. Though this is a minor affair, still it would not be in accord with what is right. I am very sorry, but I do not dare to follow your instructions.

12

Ikjae 益齋, <pen name of Hwang Yunjong 黃潤鍾>, even in his youth never entered a wine shop; you always talk about how steadfast he is. And so, why is it that time and again you can be found sitting in [such places]? It seems you violate the idea of having one's words and one's deeds accord with one another. Please exert yourself more in this regard.

13

I have read what you wrote to me. It says that "I do not dare to say that I understand others;[14] I do not dare to say that I am a teacher of others.[15] But speaking of those who have come to study under me and work together with one another, each has some particular merit. For example, Gong Yunseok 孔胤錫 is a descendant of the ancient sage [i.e., Gongja] and has pure and substantial natural ability. Jo Inseok 趙仁錫 is a descendant of Songsan 松山[16] and has conduct that is filial and friendly. Pak Byeongeun 朴秉殷 is pure, solid, and sincere and loves the ancients. Bak Docheol 林道喆 is harmonious and happy and loves human relationships. Hwang Hosun 黃浩淳 continues the conscientiousness and filiality of Chupo 秋浦[17] and Jiso 芝所.[18] Yi Gyeonghyeon 李敬鉉 inherited the Dao learning of Gucheon 龜川[19]

---

[14] *Analects* 1.16 says, "It is a misfortune that I do not understand others."

[15] *Mencius* 4A23 says, "It is a misfortune that people so like to be the teachers of others."

[16] Probably Songsan Jo Gyeon 趙狷 (1351–1425 CE).

[17] Probably Chupo 秋浦 Hwang Sin 黃愼 (1560–1617 CE), who served during the Imjin 壬辰 war (1592–1598 CE).

[18] Probably Jiso 芝所 Hwang Ilho 黃一皓 (1588–1641 CE), an adopted son of Hwang Sin. He was an official during the Manchu War in 1636 (*Byeongja Horan* 丙子胡亂).

[19] Probably Gucheon 龜川 Yi Gu 李龜 (1469–1526 CE), who suffered from the two literati purges in Muo (1498 CE) and Gapja (1504 CE) years and then returned to the court after the Enthronement of King Jungjong (*Jungjong Banjeong* 中宗反正) in 1506. King Jungjong (r. 1506–1544 CE) was able to ascend the throne with the support of Confucian scholars from the school of Dao Learning (*Dohak*: C. *Daoxue* 道學).

and Jikjae 直齋.[20] Gwon Doin 權道仁 and Gang Giyeong 姜祈永 depend upon the good connections they enjoy through marriage. Im Dalyun 林達潤 and Gim Eungsu 金應洙 have the sincerity that enabled them, though weak, to overcome many difficulties and come from so far away, etc."

When I reflect upon you, I think sometimes you see one good act and immediately commend it; sometimes you see one bad act and are excessive in your reprimand. But how can you understand others through one good or one bad act? The *Book of History* says, "To understand others is wisdom; this is difficult even for the Lord [on High]."[21] How much more so for those who have not attained to the perception and insight of a sage? I hope that you will "look at the means that people employ, investigate the motivations behind their actions, and examine wherein they find ease."[22] If you follow the teachings of Gongja, you will investigate and confirm in a slow and deliberate manner—this is how to draw near to understanding [others]. Moreover, the way in which you seek to become a teacher of others is rash. If each day you renew yourself through the work of investigating [things], extending [knowledge], making sincere [your thoughts], and correcting [your Heart-Mind],[23] you naturally will affect others. You will not need to seek others; rather, young people will seek you; then what would be objectionable about liking to be the teacher of others? This is my humble opinion. I ask that you analyze my views and instruct me.

14

If I have real virtue, even if people do not know this, how does it harm [my virtue]? If I lack real virtue, even if people offer empty praise, how does this add to [my virtue]? If I have a piece of jade and people say it is just an ordinary stone, this does no harm to the jade. If I have a stone and people say it is a piece of jade, this does not add to the stone. I want you, my husband, to

---

[20] Probably Jikjae Yi Gihong 李箕洪 (1641–1708 CE). He was a student of Song Siyeol, who emphasized Dao Learning, especially the supreme principle expressed in the *Spring and Autumn Annals*.

[21] See the "Counsels of Goyo" (*Goyo Mo*; C. *Gaoyao Mo* 皋陶謨) section of the *Book of History*.

[22] See *Analects* 2.10.

[23] These are parts of the process of self-cultivation described in chapter 2 of the *Great Learning*.

work at real virtue. Do not be ashamed beneath heaven; do not be mortified upon the earth; do not be distressed whether people know or do not know.[24]

15

The way noble people manage the world's [affairs] is by inferring and investigating the principle of waxing and waning and the changes of things and affairs. Sancheonjae's 山天齋, <the pen name of Supervisor (*Gamyeok* 監役) Gim Sangak 金相岳>, study of the *Book of Changes*[25] and Pallyeondang's 八年堂, <the pen name of the retired scholar Sim Ryu 沈鎏>, discussions of numerology offer incisive principles and detailed explanations [concerning these endeavors]. If one studies these well, one can gain an understanding of what is essential. Duke Haksan's, <the pen name of the Royal Secretary Yun Jehong 尹濟弘>,[26] poetic rhymes are clear and well balanced. Cheonghanja's, <the pen name of Supervisor Yi Gwanha 李觀夏>, compositional style is rich and learned. The ability to cultivate the emotions and express feelings, communicate ideas and guide intentions are also things Confucian scholars cannot do without. I ask that whenever you have time in between exploring and contemplating the Six Classics,[27] you regularly work at these tasks.

16

The Gwon child, <Yongseok 用錫>, the older cousin of <[Gwon] Yongjik 用稷>, came to [study with] you. He received a careful and thorough education. You surely should not turn down anyone who comes [to study with you], how much more so one whose father and elder brother eagerly beseech you and who comes with a genuine Heart-Mind. Furthermore, you should teach him in light of the kind of person he is. For example, Hong Sameun 洪三隱, <[Sameun is] a pen name of [Hong] Uiseop 義燮>, and Jo Jaan 趙子安 <Inseok

---

[24] The idea that a person of genuine virtue is not concerned whether or not he is recognized is found in *Analects* 1.1. The metaphor of stone and jade recalls the well-known story of Mr. He's jade (*Hwassi byeok*; C. *Heshi bi* 和氏璧) in chapter 13 of the *Hanbija*.

[25] Gim Sangak 金相岳 (1724–1815 CE), the author of *Sancheon's Commentary on the "Book of Changes"* (*Sancheon yeokseol* 山天易說).

[26] Yun Jehong (1764–1840 CE) was also well known for his literati paintings (*muninhwa*; C. *wenrenhua* 文人畫).

[27] The Six Classics are the *Book of Poetry, Book of History, Book of Changes, Book of Rites, Spring and Autumn Annals,* and *Book of Music.*

仁錫> have sincerely filial Heart-Minds, and so it is easy to teach them the Way to serve their parents. Jang Jungsim 張仲深 <Yeon 淵> has a natural aptitude for humaneness and generosity, and so it is easy to move him to benefit others. From these two examples, you can infer what to do with the rest.

17

I have read the numerous careful and detailed instructions you have written to me. In general, a portrait is not the same as a spirit tablet. There is no need for the descent-line heir to preside over such; a son or grandson can maintain it. As long as they possess virtue and are admired by people, then even disciples and later students can lay a portrait in state or pay respects at the appropriate time. How much more so can a son or grandson! Gim Bupyeong 金富平, who truly has a natural aptitude for purity and filial piety, was adopted to become a descent-line heir to the direct descendant line; therefore, he was unable to preside over the sacrifices to his birth father. This pained him for all his days as he had no way to express his feelings. And so he placed a portrait of Duke Munchung[28] in an auxiliary building and each year performed the tea ceremony on the anniversary of his birth, as a way to express the sincere love of a child for his father. This truly is what is called giving rest to one's emotions; it in no way detracts from righteousness.

18

Song Mokcheon 宋木川 <Heumseong 欽成> is an heir of [Song] Gangjae 剛齋. The Licentiate Gim <Byeongun 炳雲> is the grandson of [Gim] Miho 渼湖.[29] They have called upon you repeatedly. Naturally, you were very interested in receiving them, but each time, because of our poverty and hardship, you were unable to do as you desired. How regrettable! I have heard that these two worthies are upright, honest, easygoing, and agreeable. I hope you will get together and have an earnest and urgent face-to-face discussion with them in order to encourage one another [to greater achievement]. What do you think?

---

[28] A posthumous name, meaning Duke of Literature and Loyalty (Munchunggong 文忠公).
[29] A pen name of Gim Wonhaeng 金元行 (1702–1772 CE).

19

The jealousy of a wife can reach extremes, even to the point where it destroys one's family and cuts off one's posterity. This is not only a failure to recognize what is moral but also a failure to understand what is beneficial and harmful [from a prudential point of view]. One's husband's children are one's children as well. If the family name flourishes, what greater blessing is there? Of the seven ritual prescriptions delineating the circumstances in which a woman can be turned out of a family,[30] jealousy should come first. Adultery, stealing, talking excessively, impoliteness, failing to bear a son, and contracting a hideous disease all come after it. And so, there is no offense greater than jealousy. I have heard that you want to write an admonition to give to the wives and daughters of your sons and grandsons. I ask that you devote one section to [the danger of] falling into jealousy to sharply warn those who read it and help them advance along the way of wifely virtue. What do you think? What do you think?

20

You offered some rich person three cups of wine [when he visited our home]; isn't this excessive? [On the other hand] Yeongwon 鈴原, <Second Minister (*Champan* 參判) Yun Haengjik 尹行直>,[31] who is an old man, was not even offered [a bowl of] soup or stew [when he visited]. Isn't that regrettable? Though it is a small thing, still, how can it not be taken into account?

21

Yi A's 李雅 <Siyeong 著英> preservation of his clan and protection of his family, his offerings of sacrifices to his ancestors, and his reception of

---

[30] According to the traditional rituals there are seven situations in which a husband can abandon his wife: being disobedient to the husband's parents, failing to produce children, adultery, jealousy, contracting a hideous disease, excessive talking, and stealing. See the "Basic Orders" (*Bon Myeong*; C. *Ben Ming* 本命) chapter of the *Book of Rites of the Elder Dae* (*Dae Dae Ryegi*; C. *Da Dai Liji* 大戴禮記).

[31] Yeongwon 鈴原 seems to be the fief title of Yun Haengjik 尹行直 (b. 1760 CE), who held the official rank of Second Minister. See the *Veritable Records of King Sunjo* (*Sunjo sillok* 純祖實錄) 23.30a [21(1821)/03/22#3].

guests—each of these is in its proper sequence and order, just as you have instructed. Please make greater effort to interact with him so that you will be able to perfect the beauty of the Way of friendship [with him].

22

Yi Myeongbu 李明夫 <Byeongdeok 炳悳> lives in a valley in the country-side. Although he has no teachers or friends living nearby, still, on his own, he earnestly pursues learning. Whenever I look at the letters he sends you, a sense of real learning permeates all that he has written, and I sigh in deep admiration. Please do your best to convey [these ideas][32] when you reply, so that he will increase his effort and achieve further advancement.

23

Father and son are one; a father should be kind [to his son] and a son should be filial [to his father]. I ask that you be more kind and loving to Heumgyu 欽圭.[33] A disciple should love his teacher as if he were a father. A teacher should regard his disciple as if he were his son. This is the Way of the ancients. I ask that, though you extend your love out broadly, you show greater love and sincerely teach those who make a wholehearted effort to improve themselves and see whether this proves successful.

24

While the long garment (simui; C. shenyi 深衣) can be worn on both auspicious and inauspicious occasions, during times of mourning, the ancients wore [special] mourning clothing. Today there is white-colored mourning attire, and one need not have dark hems or wear a colored belt [with it].[34]

---

[32] This line invokes a line from section 12 of the "Great Appendix" (upper part) of the *Book of Changes*, which describes how difficult it can be to fully express what one intends. It says, "Writing does not fully convey speech; speech does not fully convey ideas."

[33] Heumgyu was their adopted son.

[34] See "The Long Garment" (*Simui*; C. *Shenyi* 深衣) chapter of the *Book of Rites*. The belt could be embroidered or blue in color if one's parents or grandparents were alive.

And so, while Mr. [Song 宋] Gangjae has chosen to wear the long garment for mourning, I fear that this may not be an appropriate thing to teach.

25

While a head wrap (*bokgeon*; C. *fujin* 幅巾) is not prescribed by ancient [custom], Ju Hui advocated wearing one in his *Family Ritual*.[35] When one is preparing to conduct a sacrifice, a head wrap seems preferable to a hat of black silk.

26

The attire of a wife (*danui*; C. *tuanyi* 褖衣) is pure black in color. Wearing this [garment] on the day of the funeral sacrifice appears to be inappropriate. [Your] cousin[36] Noam 魯庵, <a pen name of Gijae>,[37] had prescribed this attire for a wife, but there is no way to confirm this. What do you think?

27

The "Hwa Cap" refers to a cap of the Chinese people (*Hwagwan*; C. *Huaguan* 華冠). It did not have this name in ancient times. After the great Myeong (C. Ming) 明 dynasty (1368–1644 CE) was overthrown, palace women who came east to avoid difficulties started wearing this cap. The people of the east began calling it by this name. However, when I look at commentaries on the hair-pinning ceremony, which girls undergo at the age of fifteen, it says that married women do not wear a cap; they hold their hair in place simply by using a hairpin.[38] I fear that the meaning of the character *gwan* (C. *guan*) 冠 is not well attested and ask that it be replaced by *gye* (C. *ji*) 筓 ("hairpin").[39]

---

[35] For a translation of this work, see Ebrey 1991a.

[36] More precisely, a cousin by one's father's sister.

[37] See personal missive 7 above.

[38] See the "Pattern of the Family" (*Nae chik*; C. *Nei ze* 內則) chapter of the *Book of Rites*. A very close paraphrase can be found in the *Collected Commentaries on the "Elementary Learning"* (*Sohak jipju*; C. *Xiaoxue jizhu* 小學集註).

[39] There had been debates on the exact meaning of the term *gwan* for women during the Joseon dynasty, and Gang Jeongildang seems to be aware of and engaging these.

28

Being cautious and fearful is the purposeful activity of the time before things are manifest, while being watchful [over oneself when alone] is [the purposeful activity of the time] after things are manifest. And yet, those occasions when others do not know and only oneself knows [about something] are the most pressing imperative. Recently, my degenerative illness has taken a turn for the worse; my spirit is increasingly spent. I am not able to apply myself to any other purposeful activity and just use my strength on this. It is not without some slight result, and I want you to wholeheartedly recognize and appreciate this too.

29

A year ago, when Yi Oheon 李梧軒, <Second Minister Ujae 愚在>, traveled to Bukgyeong (C. Beijing) 北京, he asked you to take care of his son. You resolutely declined and subsequently he humbly deferred [this honor] to Noho 老湖 <Tutor to the Crown Prince[40] Oh Huisang 吳熙常>. The day before, dozens of [students wearing] black linen caps[41] came from the countryside; hearing of your reputation, they led each other onward to pay their respects bearing gifts; moreover, the gifts they offered were great in number. You firmly declined to accept these. Overall, you handled the various situations discussed above well. Some gifts you could not rashly accept because you had done nothing for those who offered them; others you could not in good conscience accept because you honestly could not claim expertise in such matters. Although this seems to be in contradiction with what I said on the earlier occasion; the principles underlying these cases simply are very different. <The earlier reference to what I said refers to [the thirteenth personal missive, which begins] "I have read what you wrote to me.">

[40] More precisely, *Jinseon* 進善 refers to a fourth-grade minister in the Office of Tutor to the Crown Prince (*Seja Sigangwon* 世子侍講院).

[41] Wearing a black linen cap, *Jangbo* (C. *Zhangfu*) 章甫, indicates that these young men were Confucian scholars. See "The Conduct of a Scholar" chapter of the *Book of Rites* and *Analects* 11.26.

30

I humbly ask how your illness was last night. The wind-driven snow has been overpoweringly strong and the room is as cold as ice. I fear this will only add to your difficulties. Last month, Geunjin 謹鎭[42] gathered up the chestnuts in the courtyard; he selected more than a liter of the largest ones and along with several pieces of meat brought them as a gift, and so I stored them away. I just took them out to look at them and discovered that half the chestnuts had been eaten by rats and the meat had turned bad. I pared away the bad parts, washed what remained, and then roasted it over the fire. I still had a little money [that I had set aside] for buying paper and used it to purchase some wine, which I have warmed up and sent to you [along with this food]. Though it is a small thing, do not forget the difficulty [people had to undergo] to bring these to you. Once your hunger has abated a bit, turn back to your studies; do not waste any time. I pray for your success at all costs.

31

While Geunjin has superior basic substance, he falls short of the middle way. Nevertheless, this is still better than to be excessive in embellishment that destroys the basic substance. If this boy makes a promise, he always follows through on it. He can be relied upon to offer sacrifices to his ancestors and protect his family. In this respect, there is no one better than him in the clan. I hope you will guide and teach him and enable him to advance. Moreover, this boy lost his mother when he was young, and his grandmother is also quite strict by nature. He always thinks of you and me as his father and mother. He lives more than three miles out in the suburbs beyond the river and does not fear suffering the wind, rain, heat, and cold [in order to come to us]. He personally presents offerings of dried grain and morning and evening comes to serve. Time and again, whenever I think of him, my tears begin to fall. Should this boy commit even the slightest mistake, explain it to him thoroughly and don't neglect him. What do you think? What do you think?

---

[42] A grandnephew of Gang Jeongildang's husband. Cf. note 17, page 176.

32

As you have told me, Neungsan 菱山, <the pen name of Censor Hwang Gicheon 黃基天>,[43] is a master of literary composition; Giwon 綺園, <the pen name of Yu Hanji 俞漢芝 of Yeongchun 永春>,[44] is skillful and proficient in writing both seal and regular script calligraphy. But you are ill and old and have yet to assimilate and harmonize the learning of the classics and ritual—where do you have leisure to study such things [i.e., as composition and calligraphy]? I just hope you will earnestly exert yourself, search out the complex and accumulated mysteries of the Six Classics, and cross into the realm of the sages and worthies. Morning and evening be diligent and assiduous; do not forsake your earlier aspiration. By all means [do this]! By all means [do this]!

33

My younger brother Si <Sihoe 時會> was orphaned early in life and lost [the opportunity to] study. Nevertheless, he proved capable of applying himself to offering sacrifices to his ancestors and working harmoniously with the members of his clan. He loved his elder brother's children as if they were his own and with a genuine Heart-Mind (*silsim* 實心) educated and guided them. Unfortunately, he was not long-lived and had no children of his own. Now, it seems that Giyeong 祈永 intends to assign one of the male children of his clan to carry on sacrifices to him (i.e., Sihoe). This nephew (i.e., Giyeong) undertook this task with a sincere Heart-Mind and has been able to carry it out successfully. How remarkably fortunate! How remarkably fortunate! I would like you to send a letter to the elder brother of this clan <Changhoe 昌會> via Seo Ilsim 徐一心 <Hyeongbo 馨輔>, asking him to carefully attend to and instruct this boy as he did Giyeong, so that [this boy too] can preserve the family. This is incredibly fortunate indeed!

---

[43] Hwang Gicheon (1760–1821 CE) served as a fourth Censor (*Jeongeon* 正言); he was well known for his mastery of various styles of calligraphy.
[44] Yu Hanji 俞漢芝 (1760–1834 CE), whose pen name Willow Garden (Giwon 綺園), served as a county magistrate of Yeongchun, which is an old name of Danyang 丹陽 Country, Chungcheong Province. He was well known for his calligraphy, especially seal and ornamental script characters.

34

"The clothes of Munjungja (C. Wenzhongzi) 文中子 (583–616 CE)[45] were simple but clean."[46] Now your clothes are simple enough but not clean. To be simple is your virtue, my husband. If your clothes are dirty and filthy and are not washed clean or if they have rips and holes that are not patched, this is my fault. I am solemnly waiting with lye, needle, and thread for you to call upon me.

35

It is appropriate to plant flowers and other plants in our garden; it is not appropriate to plant them in our inner courtyard. It might be better to replant these somewhere between East Cliff and Moon Pond.[47] Garden balsams are used to dye one's fingernail tips. But I do not like doing this. What do you think of replanting all of these somewhere outside [our garden]?

36

I heard that one boy's family had not had firewood to burn for four days, while we had not lit a fire for three days. I could not accept the gift that he offered us, even more so because it was not his parent's idea to offer the gift but something he came up with on his own. Even had it been something as minor as a measure of rice, it would not have been in accord with righteousness. In cases like the gift the Gim 金 child offered, even if had been as much as a stone's[48] weight of rice, since it was given and received in friendship and his parents told him to offer it, it would have been inappropriate for me to refuse.

---

[45] Munjungja is a posthumous title of Wang Tong (C. Wang Tong) 王通 (583–616 CE) of the Su (C. Sui) 隋 dynasty (581–618 CE).

[46] See the *Collected Commentaries on the "Elementary Learning"* 6.39a.

[47] We take these to be places inside their family garden.

[48] A "stone" is a unit of dry measure for grain equal to 120 liters.

37

Righteousness is the source of good order; profit is the pivot of chaos. I have heard that lately some people come to the outer quarter and talk at length about profit. I fear that the students of our school will grow accustomed to hearing such talk and that it will slowly seep into them. Why didn't you keep such people at a distance early on? The way to keep them at a distance lies not in hating them but in being strict. Straighten your clothes and cap, respectfully fix your gaze upon them, and be completely devoid of any speech or action that is contrary to ritual; then they will distance themselves from you on their own.

38

People have humaneness and righteousness just as the four seasons have spring and fall. When one talks of humaneness, the rites are there within it; when one talks of righteousness, wisdom is there within it. There is no need for doubt.

39

Teachers are where the Way lies;[49] they are one with lords and fathers. Visiting one's teacher to inquire about his welfare is not different from going to ask about the welfare of one's parents. So how can you allow my current distress to stop you from going to see him [i.e., your teacher]? Though my illness is severe, it is not necessarily fatal. Like the master when he heard the Way, though I die I would be honored to do so.[50] I want you to drive on at full speed down this path!

---

[49] A close paraphrase of a line from the opening section of Han Yu's famous essay "A Treatise on Teachers" (Sa Seol; C. Shi Shuo 師說).

[50] Analects 4.8 says, "If one hears the Way in the morning, one may die that evening without regret."

40

To serve one's parents but be partial to one's wife is to be less than earnest in filial piety. To serve one's lord but be partial to one's wife is to be less than conscientious. To serve one's teacher but be partial to one's wife is to be less than sincere in one's learning. You can extend this to each and every affair. Though I am not clever, I do not want you to be partial to me. If you ever were to be partial and have it harm your virtuous achievements, though it would lead to me being rich, noble, peaceful, and at ease, I would rather die from poverty and hunger. Please make a greater effort in this regard! In all that I write and send to you, I am direct and blunt and thereby stray far from the proper Way for a wife to behave. Nevertheless, the elder Sim Guheon 沈思軒 <Sadong 師東> once said that you have some capacity for being open and receptive.[51] Moreover, I try to take up and follow the teaching of speaking directly in accordance with how things are. And so I dare not but say everything that is called for. If, when you have made a mistake, you show even a slight reluctance to emend your ways or you repeat your mistake after having corrected it earlier, then in the end you will have no way to advance in virtue. I ask you to put forth more effort, put forth more effort!

41

Poverty is the fate of scholars; simplicity is the root of things. To rest in fate, protect the root, and "pursue that which one loves"[52]—there is no greater joy than this![53] Whether it is the nobility of Three Ducal Ministers[54] or wealth from a vast salary, if it is not the way, I do not want your thoughts to linger upon it. Do we not have the teachings of Gongja, "Wealth and honor gained in ways contrary to righteousness are to me like floating clouds."[55]

---

[51] For the idea of "being open and receptive," see the "Image Commentary" on the hexagram *Ham* (C. *Xian*) 咸 in the *Book of Changes*.

[52] *Analects* 7.12.

[53] Cf. *Mencius* 7A4, where the same expression appears: "To examine oneself and find one is sincere, there is no greater joy than this!"

[54] The collective name of the three most eminent official positions in ancient China.

[55] *Analects* 7.16.

42

Yi Mo 李某 <Byeongdo 炳道> encouraged others to do what is wrong.[56] His wife warned and admonished him that this would cause him to lose the very essence of what it is to be a proper young scholar. This is extremely admirable and worthy of praise; how much more would it be so to do something even more than this![57]

43

I want you to be good but forget about the good, to be without transgressions but think about transgression, to see good as if it were your own, to see bad as if it were a pox upon you. A noble person cannot be without the courage to be moral and must not be angry. Now I heard that when you upbraided someone you were excessive in both expression and tone. If this is true, then it has done harm to your moral self-cultivation. Please be on guard against this.

44

It was the third morning I had not cooked anything when one of the boy attendants [from the school] came back with a rolled-up pumpkin vine. Looking through it, I found it concealed several fist-sized pieces of fruit. I cut them up and made soup but had no wine to serve with it. Since I only have this soup to offer, I cannot help sighing with anxiety. Virtue must be cultivated each and every day. Learning too must be discussed each and every day. In discussing learning, nothing comes before reading books. I have heard that you have just started reading the *Book of Changes* and that Yi Eunha's 李銀河 son <Manyeong 晚英> will come to spend

[56] Literally, [he teaches monkeys] to climb trees. For the original source, see the *Book of Poetry*, Mao #223.

[57] The implication being that it would be even better to teach him to do good in the world. This missive implies that a wife has a special ability and obligation to admonish and guide her husband to be better.

the winter. He is a Confucian who has studied the classics since he was a youth; it is great that the two of you will mutually be able to discuss and debate together. I hope that you will write down what you discuss each day on a piece of paper and show it to me. That would be most fortunate! That would be most fortunate!

45

The chilly weather has newly arrived in the suburbs; this is the season to draw close to the warmth of the lamp. I hope that aside from unavoidable tasks, like needing to receive guests and respond to affairs, you concentrate on reading. I too look forward to resting from my needlework and the preparation of meals, drawing the curtains in the middle of the night, [so that I can focus on] reading and coming to a deeper understanding of Pattern-Principle. My aim is to read all of the *Four Books*,[58] but I have yet to finish the last three chapters of the *Mencius*. Nevertheless, I should finish them soon. My plan is to begin this winter to follow your example and delve into the *Book of Changes*, but if our guests stay long, I won't be able to do this. I hope [you] soon will write to the Herald of the Crown Prince Gim 金, <[given name] Heon 鑛>, and ask him to please lend us his copy of the *Great Compendium on the "Book of Poetry" and "Book of History"* (*Si Seo daejeon*; C. *Shi Shu da quan* 詩書大全), so I can look it over.

The Herald of the Crown Prince Hong <[given name] Jikpil> once sent you a poem that read,

> I have not finished reading the *Cinnabar Classic*,[59]
> Yet my hair has turned white.
> For a hundred years,
> I have labored in vain as a man!

The point is to warn people to remain vigilant. I ask you to increase your effort to renew your virtue; make progress and never stop!

---

[58] The *Four Books* refers to the *Analects, Mencius, Great Learning,* and *Doctrine of the Mean.*

[59] The reference may be to the Daoist Inner Alchemy work the *Most Supreme Lord's Inner Alchemy Classic* (*Taesang Nogun naedan gyeong*; C. *Taishang Laojun neidan jing* 太上老君內丹經).

46

I am deeply distraught because it has been several days and you have not recovered from the disease afflicting your eyes. I would like you to close your eyes and sit up straight, relax and refrain from thought, ease your Heart-Mind and let your *Gi-Material* settle, preserve and nurture your Heart-Mind. This not only is a method to address your malady, but it will also assist in the work of honoring the virtuous nature.[60]

47

You have written saying that "doing good is the greatest of joys";[61] these words are extremely great. However, in the midst of handling things and affairs one must first inquire into the Pattern-Principle that makes things good and clearly understand the proper standard. Only then should one wholeheartedly devote oneself to the good and concretely practice it; then one can realize the greatest of joys.

48

Many cousins of the Licentiate Gim <[given name] Ro 鏴> often come to pay their respects. Moreover, there are many guests who arrive by carriage, coming to pay their respects from far away. This truly is quite moving. Nevertheless, it tests the limits of my ability to serve in my proper role as host. When I meet high officials, I must treat them with the rituals proper to high officials; when I meet young scholars, I must treat them with the rituals proper to young scholars. [My treatment of them] is not more or less serious in light of the power of their position, and so *this Heart-Mind*[62] remains constantly correct and does not incur any dishonor.

---

[60] "Honoring the virtuous nature" (*jondeokseong*; C. *cundexing* 尊德性) was the internal complement of "pursuing inquiry and study" (*domunhak*; C. *daowenxue* 道問學); together these comprised the orthodox neo-Confucian approach to self-cultivation.

[61] The precise phrase appears in the *Eastern Lodge Records of the Han* (*Donggwan Han gi*; C. *Dongguan Han ji* 東觀漢記) and *the History of the Later Han*.

[62] *This Heart-Mind* (*cha sim*; C. *ci xin* 此心) refers specifically to the innate moral Heart-Mind; the term can be traced back to the *Mencius* 1A7. Emphasis added.

The reasons guests come to visit is because you have the Way to improve oneself.[63] Seongdam 性潭, <the pen name of Associate Councilor Song Hwangi 宋煥箕 (1728–1807 CE)>,[64] said that reading books and fully comprehending Pattern-Principle is simply aimed at understanding the Way for oneself.[65] Chief Councilor Haeseok 海石[66] said that practicing conscientiousness and filial piety in order to develop virtue and the Way are all affairs concerned with what lies within oneself. These all discuss the tasks of investigating [things] and attaining [the highest good].[67] I hope you will assiduously and diligently exert yourself in these ways and commit yourself to realizing Master Ochon's 鰲村[68] teachings about sincerity and reverence so that in the end you achieve the highest good. Would that not be fine!

49

To act without ulterior motive is how noble people accord with the Pattern-Principle of heaven. To act for some ulterior motive is the way of petty people who have given in to human desires. If one can sincerely turn within oneself and look for it [i.e., the original Heart-Mind], clearly [understand] it, and act out of it, then calmly and easily, one will be in command and unopposed.

50

A proverb has it that "the Heart-Mind of a three-year-old is still present in an eighty-year-old." What this is saying is that it is difficult to transform the basic stuff of which we are made. For those whose basic stuff is superior in quality,

[63] This is a clear reference to "learning for oneself" (*wigi ji hak*; C. *weiji zhi xue* 為己之學), which refers to moral self-improvement, as opposed to "learning for others" (*wiin ji hak*; C. *weiren zhi xue* 為人之學), which means learning as a means to impress others and gain advantage. See *Analects* 14.24: "The master said, 'In ancient times, people learned with the aim of improving themselves. Today, people learn with the aim of winning the approval of others.'" Cf. the following missive.

[64] Song Hwangi, a fifth descendant of Song Siyeol, was widely respected for his scholarship and virtue by officials in the court and scholars in the outlying areas. His posthumous name is Mungyeong 文敬.

[65] There is no close paraphrase of this sentence in the *Collected Works of Seongdam* (*Seongdam jip* 性潭集).

[66] Probably Haeseok Gim Jaechan. See note 20, page 177.

[67] The tasks of rectifying the Heart-Mind and attaining the highest good are two of the steps in the path of moral and spiritual progress described in the first and second chapters of the *Great Learning*.

[68] Another pen name for Song Chigyu, the teacher of Yun Gwangyeon.

it is easy to become good. For those whose basic stuff is inferior in quality, it is difficult to enter onto the Way. Those who teach also should guide [each of their students] well, according to the superior or inferior [quality of their basic stuff].

Among my family members, only my younger brother, Ilhoe, ever since he was a young boy, would always think of saving or offering fruit to [his elders][69] and was diligent and assiduous in his studies. He didn't present anything to his elders that would cause them anxiety. When he grew up, he was filial, friendly, honest, and harmonious. No one had anything objectionable to say about him. He was exceptional in understanding and had begun to make real progress; unfortunately, he was destined to die young. My nephew on my father's side, Hunyeong 勳永, is calm and peaceful in manner; moreover, he loves to read books; he has exceptional potential. On my mother's side of the family, the Licentiate Jong 從 <[given name] Gugin 國仁> is weak and not fond of play.[70] [Nevertheless,] he is very earnest in his reading, and his compositions and behavior are worthy of praise. Uigyeong 誼卿 <Weoljeong 月正> has often shown what kind of man he is; he is upright, substantial, harmonious, and easygoing. He is serious on the outside and enlightened within; he is [artistically] talented but not flippant, wise but not contentious; he is sincere in his relationships and broadly steeped in culture. He maintains the instructions of his family and has a firm grip on established norms. He can be regarded as the best among those on my mother's side. Though I have not personally met Hwang Saeng 黃生 <Jonghoek 鍾濩>, I have never heard of him causing any commotion in the men's quarters. When he finishes eating or drinking, he leaves his setting orderly, not messy. He never wanders inside the orchard.[71] When he attends upon those seated listening to lectures, to the end of the day, he doesn't make a sound, as if there wasn't anyone there. His mind never strays, and he should prove to be successful. I would like you, my husband, to meet with him and introduce him to others; perhaps they can instruct and refine one another, so that they can, to some extent, improve themselves.

---

[69] This refers to stories about a legendary filial son and younger brother of the Eastern Han dynasty China. Yuk Jeok (C. Liu Ji) 陸績 of the Eastern Han saved fruits to offer his mother at the age of six. See the *Categorical Medley of Literary Texts* 86.23a–b. Gong Yung (C. Kong Rong) 孔融 (153–208 CE) was able to yield a bigger pear to his elder brother at the age of four. See the *Commentaries to the "Helpful Collection for First Education"* (*Monggu jipju*; C. *Mengqiu jizhu* 蒙求集註) 6b.

[70] See the *Chronicle of Jwa*, Ninth Year of Duke Hui 僖.

[71] That is to say, he doesn't enter into situations where he would be tempted to do wrong, for example, to take what is not his own.

51

You once said, "One should seek to marry someone similar to oneself; one should choose to befriend those who are better than oneself."[72] You also said, "The elder Gim Muju 金茂朱 <Jaewan 載琬> spoke broadly and at length about the faults and mistakes of others. When I turned and reflected upon this, [I came to see that] this describes a problem with him." When I heard this, I found it extremely revealing and enlightening. Now, someone [you know] married another who is unlike himself, and yet you did not dissuade him from doing so, and among your recent associates are many disadvantageous friends.[73] Moreover, at times, you discuss the faults and mistakes of others; this does not seem to comport well with what you yourself taught the day before. Why is this? I would like to hear the explanation.

52

In some cases, when the family of one of your students wants to offer a gift of some kind, I first report it to you and then decline the gift. In other cases, I don't seek your permission and decline it on my own. Recently there were two exceptional cases in which I did not seek your permission but still accepted the gift. The first was Gim Wonbaek's 金元伯 <Maengyeon 孟淵> offer of a pair of spectacles; the other was Hwang Uigyeong's 黃義卿 <Gyeongho 敬浩> offer of meat. In both cases, these are students who have studied with you since they were young. In Gim's case, you are truly despondent over your eyes growing dim; in Hwang's case I sincerely thought about the fact that we have no food. Since they were sent by their relatives, I regarded these as genuinely felt gifts. It seems that you, my husband, also would not reject them. And so, I accepted them without asking your permission. I don't know what you think of this.

---

[72] Cf. *Analects* 1.8 and 9.25, both of which teach that one should "have no friends who are not one's equal."

[73] See *Analects* 16.4, which describes three types of advantageous and three types of disadvantageous friends.

53

The way of the noble person is nothing more than to cultivate the self and bring good order to others;[74] one should be diligent and hardworking day and night and still worry that one will not reach one's goal. How can one spare the leisure for idle thoughts and ideas, idle words and speech, idle social communication and interaction, or idle comings and goings, whereby one injures one's commitment to take up the heavy burden and go the distance![75] I hope you will be cautious about this and exert yourself in this regard.

54

Whether human beings live long or die young, whether they succeed or fail—these are matters of fate.[76] But fathers and mothers [nowadays] listen to the common talk of the age and regard teaching their daughters to read as a great calamity; as a result, most women and girls don't know anything about morality. This is extremely laughable!

55

Im Yunjidang said, "Though I am a woman, still, the nature I originally received contained no distinction between male and female."[77] She also said, "Women who do not aspire to be a Tae Im and Tae Sa[78] all are 'throwing themselves away.'"[79] And so, though one is a woman, if one is able to apply oneself, then one can reach the level of a sage. I have not yet inquired about what you, my husband, think about this.

---

[74] A very similar idea is expressed in chapter 2 of the *Great Learning*.

[75] Paraphrasing *Analects* 8.7.

[76] Cf. *Mencius* 7A1.

[77] See Im Yunjidang's "Exposition on *Overcoming the Self and Returning to the Rites Is Humaneness*" in this volume.

[78] See note 7, p. 4.

[79] Quoting *Mencius* 4A10. See also "Extant Affairs" in *The Extant Writings of Yunjidang*, appendix 6a.

56

Im Yunjidang said, "Filial piety is the source of the hundred good acts.[80] Once one has lost the original source, though one exhausts the abilities of all the worthies in the world one still would be unable to attain the Way."[81] She also said, "There has never been anyone who failed to be filial to their parents and yet proved fully loyal to their lord."[82] This truly is a perfectly accurate account.

57

Yun Taekjin 尹宅鎭 and [Yun] Hakjin [尹]鶴鎭 have become associates of yours, and I have heard that they are pure and substantial in their basic substance, that they are good at arranging gifts for superiors, and that the sincerity of their thought is worthy of praise. It is appropriate that you teach them in accordance with what they are able to achieve. That way you will avoid the problem of them growing sick of the hardship and finding the practice too difficult.

58

One of Doam's[83] 陶庵 poems says that youthful years are easy to lose and difficult to regain. One must excel beyond the common run of person and become a sage.[84] Doam taught young people, as a warning, that it was easy to lose their youthful years. Moreover, those who have lost their youthful years—how can they not put forth a hundredfold effort! I hope you, my husband, will exert yourself in this regard.

---

[80] The hundred good acts are more detailed and specific norms for proper conduct referred to in various classical works such as the *Comprehensive Discussion of Virtue in the White Tiger Hall* (*Baekhotong deongnon*; C. *Baihutong delun* 白虎通德論), traditionally attributed to Ban Go (C. Ban Gu) 班固 (32–92 CE), which also claims that filial piety is the root of all such actions.

[81] See Im Yunjidang's "Discourse on On Gyo Tearing the Hem of His Garment" in the "Discourses" section of this volume.

[82] A very close paraphrase of Im's original line in "Discourse on On Gyo Tearing the Hem of His Garment."

[83] Probably Doam 陶菴 Yi Jae 李縡 (1680–1749 CE).

[84] Jeongildang seems to be referring to a verse that appears in the *Collected Works of Doam* (*Doam jip* 陶菴集) 2.12b, "I cannot retain my youthful years; / In poverty, it will be too late for regret. I still think of great men; / And resolutely hope to establish myself."

59

I am a housewife, sequestered in the inner quarters, not hearing or knowing about anything [outside]. Still, when I have a break from my needlework and cleaning, I study the classical writings, plumbing their moral principles and emulating the conduct they describe, longing to join those who have cultivated themselves in earlier times. As a man, you are free to establish a commitment and seek the Way,[85] follow teachers and choose friends, and diligently improve yourself. What is there that through study you are unable to do? What is there that through discussion you are not able to understand clearly? What is there that through implementation you cannot fully carry out? By acting out of humaneness and righteousness[86] you can establish what is balanced and correct.[87] Who can stop you from becoming a sage or a worthy? [You think to yourself] the sages and worthies were men; I too am a man—so what have I to fear! I entreat you myriad times to renew your virtue with each day[88] and to make becoming a sage or worthy your highest imperative!

---

[85] Compare *Analects* 2.4, which begins with Gongja declaring, "At fifteen, I set my heart on learning."

[86] See *Mencius* 4B19 for the idea of acting out of humaneness and righteousness.

[87] The idea of attaining what is "balanced and correct" (*jungjeong*; C. *zhongzheng* 中正) is found in works such as the *Record of Music* and *Doctrine of the Mean*, both chapters in the *Book of Rites*.

[88] Cf. chapter 6 of the *Great Learning*.

Additional Letters (附別紙)

1. Additional Letters Exchanged between Teacher and Students
\<Written on Behalf of My Husband\>

1. [Someone asked,][1] "If the long garment[2] can be worn on auspicious and inauspicious occasions, can one also wear it during periods of mourning?" <[The teacher] Gangjae responded, saying, "It appears that the issue of wearing the long garment during periods of mourning is not yet settled. I have not seen any clear evidence about this. How dare I decide the truth in this matter? Seongdam 性潭[3] replied, saying, "A long garment can be worn on auspicious and inauspicious occasions. Why would it be inappropriate [to wear it during periods of mourning]?" (1803)>

2. [Someone asked,] "In regard to [things about which one should remain] cautious and apprehensive,[4] Master Ju said one should 'always preserve an attitude of reverence and awe,'[5] which implies that one should [maintain these attitudes] during periods of activity or rest. But he also said one should 'cultivate through preservation and internal examination,'[6] which seems to imply that being cautious is something exclusively focused on the state of rest. What practice are we to follow [in this regard]?"[7] <Gangjae responded, saying, "Being cautious concerns times when one is 'watchful over oneself when alone'[8] and so it certainly belongs to the state of

---

[1] "Someone" probably refers to Tanjae Yun Gwangyeon.

[2] The chapter on the "long garment" (*Simui*; C. *Shenyi* 深衣) in the *Book of Rites* describes it as casual wear for all men at any rank. Later, neo-Confucian scholars tried to revive it, but their understanding of the ancient texts varied. Korean neo-Confucians continued this tradition, debating issues such as on which occasions it could be worn, based on Ju Hui's understanding and the new design he described in his *Family Rituals* and other writings.

[3] Seongdam is a pen name of Song Hwangi 宋煥箕 (1728–1807 CE), a descendant of Song Siyeol, who was respected for his knowledge and virtue.

[4] These lines are from the opening chapter of the *Doctrine of the Mean*.

[5] From Ju Hui's interlinear commentary on these lines in his commentary on the *"Doctrine of the Mean" in Sections and Sentences*.

[6] This is Ju Hui's summary comment on the opening chapter of the *Doctrine of the Mean*.

[7] Ju Hui's remarks concern the opening chapter of the *Doctrine of the Mean*. See chapter 1 of his commentary on the *"Doctrine of the Mean" in Sections and Sentences*.

[8] This phrase is from the opening chapter of the *Doctrine of the Mean*.

Korean Women Philosophers and the Ideal of a Female Sage. Philip J. Ivanhoe and Hwa Yeong Wang, Oxford University Press. © Oxford University Press 2023. DOI: 10.1093/oso/9780197508688.003.0015

being at rest. But in his '*Doctrine of the Mean*' in *Sections and Sentences* the two characters 'always maintain' surely are used as you say. And so Master Sagye 沙溪 taught that they apply to both periods of activity and rest. But my late father believed that within what must be separated, there is that which cannot be separated and that we must carefully and attentively experience this for ourselves and only then can we see this." (1808)>

3. [Someone asked,] "When writing the name of the deceased wife of a Gentleman for Transmitting Virtue on a spirit tablet, some suggest writing 'the Esteemed Lady' (*gongin*; C. *gongren* 恭人), while others suggest writing 'the Nurturing Lady' (*yuin*; C. *ruren* 孺人).[9] I am not sure which is correct."

<Gangjae responded, saying, "When writing the name of a deceased wife one should decide the issue based on the rank her husband actually held. Referring to the wife [of someone who merely claims] the rank of Gentleman as 'the Esteemed Lady' seems to be a quite common mistake."[10] (1809)>

4. [Someone asked,] "In regard to the offering of rice mixed with water,[11] I rely on the explanation of Doam 陶庵,[12] which says to carry this out in the course of the three-year mourning period. Some today, though, do this by adding one spoonful [of rice to the water], while others do it with three spoonfuls. Which way is correct? I dare to seek your instruction [in this matter]."

<Gangjae replied, "The *Book of Rites* does not talk about making offerings of rice mixed with water, and my family has never carried this out. How dare I decide the truth about whether one or three spoonfuls is correct?" (1809)>

5. [Someone asked,] "Sometimes, when I make an offering of congee, I include a spoon [with which to eat it]. What is the proper way to arrange this?"

---

[9] The terms we have here translated as "Esteemed Lady" and "Nurturing Lady" are rendered "Respectful Lady" and the "Child Nurturess," respectively, in standard English translations of Chinese Myeong dynasty official titles. See Zhang et al. 2017, 292.

[10] A "Gentleman for Transmitting Virtue" referred to an official of the fifth grade; therefore, "the Honorable" is the correct title for his wife. Still, Gangjae says this is wrong. It seems that he is referring to cases in which the title was given as an honorary position without portfolio or responsibilities. For instance, some chief clerks in local government offices, who had become notable in their areas, claimed this title for themselves. In the later Joseon period, increasing numbers of people wrote such self-proclaimed titles in their lineage and spirit tablets. Gang seems to be referring to and criticizing this practice.

[11] In Ju Hui's *Family Rituals*, "offering tea" 奉茶 was described as a part of the sacrificial rite. Since drinking tea was not a Korean custom and tea was expensive, Korean scholars suggested an alternative. They argued that since this was done to refresh one's mouth after a meal, it could be replaced with *suksu* 熟水, the Korean custom of drinking boiled water from a pot containing scorched rice (*sungnyung* 숭늉). See "Jeuicho (祭儀鈔)" in the *Complete Works of Yulgok* (*Yulgok Jeonseo* 栗谷全書) 27.30a. Doam suggests that the offering of tea can be replaced with the drinking of water in the *Easy Manual of the Four Rites* (*Sarye pyeollam* 四禮便覽) 8.25a. Later, Koreans replaced the offering of tea with *choban* (C. *chaofan*) 抄飯, offering a portion of rice mixed with water.

[12] Doam is the pen name of Yi Jae 李縡 (1680–1746 CE), who compiled the *Easy Manual of the Four Rites*.

<Gangjae replied, "When making an offering of congee, the spoon should be placed on the top of bowl with its handle toward the west; what harm could there be in doing so?" (1811)>

2. Reply to Gim Bupyeong 金富平 <Hoeng 鑅>, Additional Letters
<Written on Behalf of My Husband in 1827>

[For an adopted heir,] mourning for his birth parents is preceded by the [annual] commemorative sacrifice for his adoptive parents. He arranges for someone else to offer the libation; he simply enters to wail and then withdraws. Namgye 南溪[13] says that this is a well-attested practice.[14] In mourning for his birth parents, he should wear the attire appropriate for an adoptee when entering the ancestral shrine.[15] Suam says [the adoptee] should wear "a head covering and a long linen robe."[16] Doam says that "a rough hat of bamboo braid should be added to the head covering as well."[17] This should be complied with and carried out.

A woman should wear *Daegong* (C. *Dagong* 大功) attire[18] when mourning her husband's birth parents. Both ritual and law agree on this point. Moreover, this is [in keeping with] the final conclusions of Old Man Sa 沙翁 [on this topic].[19] In general, one ought to comply with this. Old Man U says that while a woman wears *Daegong* attire when mourning her husband's birth parents, in ordinary times (i.e., when at home) she can wear a jade-colored skirt and top.[20]

---

[13] This refers to Bak Sechae 朴世采 (1631–1695 CE), who compiled the *Namgye's Theories on Rites* (*Namgye yeseol* 南溪禮說).

[14] Cf. *Collected Writings of Master Namgye* (南溪先生文集), 12.26a–b.

[15] Once someone was adopted, his relationship toward his birth parents changed and this should be reflected in his mourning attire. For example, if he is adopted as the heir of his eldest paternal uncle, he should wear the funeral attire appropriate for a younger uncle when mourning for his birth parents.

[16] See the *Collected Writings of Hansujae* 6.4b–5a. Gang Jeongildang changed 布巾 into 孝巾; the two terms were used interchangeably.

[17] This is because "a head-covering is worn to hold a cap, but it is not a cap." See Yi Uijo's (李宜朝, 1727–1805 CE) *Extended Interpretations to the Family Rituals* (*Garye jeunghae* 家禮增解) 9.74a–b.

[18] *Daegong* (C. *Dagong* 大功) represents the third grade of attire in the system of mourning. The standard form for this grade of mourning is to wear mourning clothes made from greater processed cloth for a period of nine months.

[19] See the *Complete Works of Sagye* 24.36a.

[20] Jade-color clothing was worn as an alternative for the dark blue (黲色) clothing worn in China; this marked a Korean modification of Confucian ritual. Old Man U, Uam Song Siyeol, approved of wearing jade color during sacrifice as well as in ordinary times, i.e., at home. For the cited passage see the *Great Compendium of Master Song* (*Songja Daejeon* 宋子大全) 114.46a. Regarding the discussion of the mourning attire color for the birth parents, see the *Extended Interpretations to the Family Rituals* 7.57b–58a.

Commemorations (記)

1. Tomb Commemoration for My Ancestor the Honorable Yeongeun 永隱
\<Written on Behalf of My Husband\>

One of my ancestors, the Honorable Yeongeun, who was First Secretary in the Royal House Administration (Donnyeongbu 敦寧府) and [posthumously] granted the honorary title of Minister of Personnel (*Ijo panseo* 吏曹判書), along with a wife who was [posthumously] granted the honorary title of Chaste Woman (*Jeongbuin* 貞夫人)[1] Lady Gim and [another] wife who [also] was awarded the posthumous title of Chaste Woman Lady Gim, were all three buried in the same tomb, which is located with its back toward the west[2] on the east side of Powder Dirt Mountain (Buntosan 粉土山), about four kilometers east of Complete Scholar Valley (Hwansagok 丸士谷) in the Supporting Scholar (*Gasa* 加士) District of Anseong County 安城郡, Gyeonggi Province.

Geomancers call the shape of their tomb the Reclining Ox. Local residents refer to it as Yun's[3] Tomb, but the tradition of maintaining the site [as a tomb] already had been lost for some forty-four years. In 1798, during King Jeongjo's[4] reign (r. 1776–1800 CE), a descendant of the Honorable Yeongeun's second wife's family, Gim Ryeosun 金麗淳, reported this situation to Gwangyeon [me], saying, "Someone by the name of Gang Ilmun 姜一文

---

[1] *Jeongbuin* 貞夫人 is a title that refers to the second rank of *Oemyeongbu* 外命婦; it applies to women living outside the royal palace and was given to spouses of male officials.

[2] *Jwa* 坐 refers to the back portion of a tomb. *Sinjwa* means that the tomb has its back toward the direction *sin* 辛 on a traditional compass, which is divided into twenty-four orienting points. The translation provides only an approximate direction.

[3] The surname of her husband, Yun Gwangyeon.

[4] The King Jeongjo's original posthumous title was Jeongjong 正宗, but later King Gojong, the first emperor of the Empire of Great Han (Daehan Jeguk 大韓帝國), changed the posthumous titles of five immediate ancestral kings from *jong* 宗 to *jo* 祖. Generally, *jo* was given to kings who "laid the foundation of the lineage" and *jong* to kings who "succeeded and continued it." *Jo* was considered more honorable. Maengja says, "Noble people lay the foundation of the lineage, and hand down the beginning which they have made, doing what may be continued by their successors" (*Mencius* 2B21). For the changes of the posthumous titles, see the *Veritable Records of King Gojong* (*Gojong Sillok* 高宗實錄) 39.88b–89a [36(1899)/12/07#4]. For the differentiation between *jong* and *jo*, see the *Veritable Records of King Cheoljong* (*Cheoljong Sillok* 哲宗實錄) 9.13b [8(1857)/08/09#8].

Korean Women Philosophers and the Ideal of a Female Sage. Philip J. Ivanhoe and Hwa Yeong Wang,
Oxford University Press. © Oxford University Press 2023. DOI: 10.1093/oso/9780197508688.003.0016

has broken up the grave marker, buried the pieces, and made a report to the authorities, who repossessed the site as official colony land."[5] Gwangyeon [I] went out and excavated the site and found four or five pieces of the broken grave marker. When I put them together, I discovered there were no discrepancies in the official titles and names of our ancestor or his wives. When I put [the assembled pieces] onto the foundation [of the tombstone], they formed a complete whole. From that day forward, I began to replace and tend the grass over the tomb and offer sacrifices at the site. Moreover, there were three more burial mounds below this. I looked them up in our genealogy and found those of the Honorable Second Minister, <whose personal name was Buhaeng 傅行, who attained the post of Third Inspector (*Jangnyeong* 掌令)>;[6] the Honorable Literary Licentiate (*Jinsa* 進士),[7] <whose personal name was Geukhyeon 克賢, who held the posthumous title Director of the Royal Academy of Music>;[8] and the Honorable Royal Secretary (*Seungji* 承旨), <whose personal name was Jae Sin 在莘, who held the posthumous post of District Magistrate of Semaji 洗馬止>. I was told that these three generations of tombs were just as described above. I have no doubt that this is true, but since I have not yet been able to read the tomb tablet inscriptions myself, which I hope to do at a later date, I am not yet able to verify that this is so. <The annual sacrificial rite was fixed to be held during the first day of the tenth month each year.>

Solemnly written by the tenth-generation
descendant Gwangyeon.

2. Commemoration of Late to Awaken Studio <[Residence and] Pen Name of the Retired Scholar Hong Jongseon>[9] <Written on Behalf of My Husband>

In the learning of we Confucians, reverence is the guiding principle, but in order to be reverent it is essential that the Heart-Mind be awakened. One must constantly cleanse and uplift it, as if waking it from sleep or rousing it from

---

[5] Official colony land (*gwandunjeon* 官屯田) was controlled by the government; its revenue was used to support soldiers on the frontier or pay the expenses of magistrates' yamens.

[6] More precisely, *Jangnyeong* refers to Third Inspector in the Office of the Inspector General.

[7] More precisely, *Jinsa* refers to someone who has passed the lower licentiate examination.

[8] More precisely, the full name is *Jangagwon jeong* 掌樂院正.

[9] Hong Jongseon 洪宗善 (1768–1840 CE) seems to be the great-grandson of Hong Juhwa 洪冑華 (1660–1718 CE), pen name Maneun 晚隱, a student of Song Siyeol.

drunkenness. When water is still, the waves upon it grow still; when a mirror is clean, the dust upon it dissipates. Is this not simply the purposeful activity of taking oneness as one's guiding principle?[10] When human beings are born, there certainly are differences in the clarity and turbidity and the purity and impurity of their *Gi-Material*. It is easy for those who are clear and pure to become good; it is difficult for those who are turbid and impure to return to their nature. And so there are the most wise, whose brilliance penetrates throughout the universe, and the most stupid, whose ignorance and confusion remain until the end of their days.[11] This is why the sages and worthies of ancient times singled out the one word "reverence" as the key to the gate of virtue. The essential point is nothing more than to awaken the self and awaken others.

Now, Master Hong of Namyang 南陽[12] is peaceful and calm by nature and filial and friendly in his conduct; he proceeds through the [correct] gate and follows the [proper] path of learning and is earnest in pursuing self-cultivation. The studio in which he resides is called "Late to Awaken," and he asked me to write a commemoration of it. I am ignorant, benighted, and lost; how can I dare to analyze and explain the principle of awakening the Heart-Mind? I have, though, heard from my teachers and elders that reverence corrects a single thought and thereby conquers a hundred depravities, threads together activity and stillness and thereby penetrates both the beginning and the end. When it attains its highest form, one's spirit is clear and luminous and one's Heart-Mind is constantly awake. Next year, I will be fifty years old; when I think about how Baegok (C. Boyu) 伯玉[13] understood his faults, I know I have no hope of equaling him! Master Hong is of venerable age and outstanding in virtue; he can surely be called "one of heaven's people who is first to awaken"[14]—how could he possibly be said to be "late to awaken?" I found it difficult to turn down his earnest request, so as an

[10] "Taking oneness as one's guiding principle" (*ju il*; C. *zhu yi* 主一) is a signature teaching of the Jeong-Ju School. It was first brought to prominence by Jeong I, who linked it with the idea of maintaining an attitude of reverence. See, for example, chapters 15 and 24 of the *Extant Works of the Two Jeongs*, and it often was invoked by Ju Hui. See, for example, chapter 1 of the *Classified Sayings of Master Ju* or his commentary on *Analects* 1.5 in *Collected Commentaries on the "Analects."*

[11] *Analects* 17.3 says, "The master said, 'Only the most wise and the most stupid cannot be changed.'"

[12] Township in Gyeonggi Province, which is an ancestral home of the Hong Clan.

[13] Geo Baegok (C. Qu Boyu) 蘧伯玉 or Geo Won (C. Qu Yuan) 蘧瑗 was a worthy minister of the Spring and Autumn period renowned for reflecting on his own faults. The "On the Dao" (*Won Do*; C. *Yuan Dao* 原道) chapter of the *Hoenamja* says, "When he reached the age of fifty, he understood all that he had done wrong in the previous forty-nine years." He appears and is praised in several passages in the *Analects* (e.g., 14.25 and 15.7).

[14] See *Mencius* 5A7.

expedient, I drew upon an explanation of maintaining reverence. I offer this [as my commemoration] and will try to [use it to] improve myself.

3. Commemoration of Tanwon[15]

What is Tanwon? It is the garden (won; C. yuan 園) of Tanjae.[16] Why is it called Tanwon? The old name for the garden was Seowon 徐園, since the surname of the original owner was Seo 徐. It was also called Seowon 西園 since it is located in the western (seo; C. xi 西) part of Hansa 漢師.[17] Now, though, Master Tanjae resides there, so why should it not be called Tanwon? The Home of Venerable Jeong [Hyun] (Jeong Gong Hyang; C. Zheng Xuan Xiang 鄭公鄉),[18] the Village of Go Yang (Go Yang Li; C. Gao Yang Li 高陽里),[19] the Embankment of So [Sik] (So Je; C. Su Di 蘇堤),[20] the Pavilion of Gu[yang Su] (Gu Jeong; C. Ou Ting 歐亭),[21] all are [places] that were named after people, so is it not fitting to call [this] garden Tanwon, [the Garden of Tanjae]? Who gave [Yun Gwangyeon] the pen name Tan[jae]? Mr. Song Gangjae 宋剛齋[22] gave it to him. What does it mean to call one's residence Tan? [The Analects says,] "The noble person is easygoing (tan 坦) and composed."[23] If you were to look at Tanwon you would find its soil rocky and poor, its trees crooked and drooping, and its buildings narrow and cramped. Parts of it soar on high, such as Looking Down and Looking Up Terrace and Central Harmony

[15] For Tanwon, see note 19, page 177.

[16] Tanjae is a pen name of Yun Gwangyeon, Jeongildang's husband.

[17] Hansa 漢師 is another name of Hanyang 漢陽, an old name of Seoul. See the Veritable Records of King Sukjong (Sukjong sillok 肅宗實錄) 15A.3b [10(1684)/01/15#2].

[18] When Jeong Hyun came back to his hometown, Gomil (C. Gaomi) 高密, Bukhae (C. Beihai) 北海 Commandery (modern Weifang 濰坊, Shandong 山東), Gong Ryung (C. Kong Rong) 孔融 (153-208 CE), then the chancellor of Bukhae, established the village of Zheng gong xiang (The Venerable Zheng's Village) in Jeong Hyun's honor. See the History of the Later Han (Hu Han Seo; C. Hou Han Shu 後漢書) 65.16a-b. See also Knechtges and Chang 2010, 460.

[19] The village is named after Go Yang (C. Gao Yang) 高陽, one of five mythical rulers in ancient China. See the Book of the Later Han 92.2a.

[20] It is a mound of earth found on the shores of West Lake constructed by Dongpa (C. Dongpo) 東坡 So Sik (C. Su Shi) 蘇軾 (1036-1101 CE) when he was prefect of Hangju (C. Hangzhou) 杭州 out of mud dredged up from the lake. See the Unofficial History of the Scholars (Yurim oesa; C. Rulin waishi 儒林外史) 6.9a.

[21] It refers the Pavilion of Drunken Old Man (Chwiong Jeong; C. Zuiweng Ting 醉翁亭). Chwiong is a pen name of Guyang Su (C. Ouyang Xiu) 歐陽脩 (1017-1072 CE). He left the "Record of Drunken Old Man Pavilion" (Chwiong jeonggi; C. Zuiweng tingji 醉翁亭記). See A Later Collection on the True Treasure Great Compendium of Detailed Explanations of Ancient Writings.

[22] More precisely the reference is to Gangjae 剛齋 Song Chigyu 宋穉圭 (1759-1838 CE), the sixth descendant of Uam Song Siyeol. Gangjae is his pen name.

[23] Analects 7.37.

Altar;[24] others rise up precipitously, such as the Ascending Knoll and Culture Mound. Herb and Jade Path lies hidden and meanders away; Little Gon[25] Creek slants off and then makes a bend. One cannot really say that the garden is "easygoing" (*tan*). Nevertheless, its master has an easygoing Heart-Mind and follows an easygoing way.[26] [For him] "The wild stream in the valley no longer drops precipitously, the household living in the jade cave with a wicker door no longer is in distress."[27] Safeguard your treasure! Take the reins of the horses in your hands and drive straight to the realm of humaneness and righteousness. Look at the rocky and poor, the crooked and drooping, the narrow and cramped, the soaring on high and the rising up precipitously, the hidden and slanting off—wherever one turns, there is no even and easy path. [But] if one piles up [its] rocks, one can make a mountain; if one draws from [its] spring one can make a pond. One can plant flowers and cultivate fruits, grow vegetables, and raise medicinal herbs. One can support oneself in a leisurely way. While playing the lute, drinking, and reading books, one can spend days with friends from the mountains and guests from the wilds, wandering free and easy, doing as you please.[28] Make light of rank and salary in the company of high and mighty officials. This is the true joy of the master of Tanwon! "Those with fat [horses for their carriages] and [wearing] light furs,"[29] enjoying pleasant journeys along broad and even roads, will be knocked down and grow despondent when they encounter a reversal in fortune. How can this compare to wandering in a garden and always having an even and easy place? The *Book of Changes* refers to "[treading] the way that is even and easy."[30] It also mentions being "adorned by (the denizens of) hills and gardens."[31] This describes the master of Tanwon.

---

[24] The names Looking Up and Looking Down and Central Harmony come from the *Record of Music* chapter of the *Book of Rites*.

[25] The Gollyun (C. Kunlun) 崑崙 Mountains are one of the longest mountain ranges in Asia and form the northern edge of the Tibetan Plateau. "Little Gon" thus has the sense of a microcosm within the garden.

[26] See note 23 above.

[27] This is a rhymed couplet. "Living in the jade cave with a wicker door" indicates a household that is financially distressed. In this context it seems to refer to Yun Gwangyeon's household and indicates that the garden was a refuge for him and his wife.

[28] The language here is drawn from the *Jangja*—"Free and Easy Wandering" (*so yo yu*; C. *xiao yao you* 逍遙遊) is the name of the first chapter of this work—and implies spending leisure time with Buddhists, Daoists, and other recluses or refugees from normal society.

[29] *Analects* 6.4 talks about those with too much wealth having "fat horses for their carriages and wearing light furs."

[30] See note 4, page 173.

[31] We find this line under the hexagram "To Adorn" (*Bi*; C. *Bi* 賁) in the *Book of Changes*.

Forewords and Postscripts (題跋)

1. Postscript to Our Family Genealogy
<Written on Behalf of My Husband>

This is my family genealogy, listing the direct descendants of the Papyeong Yun clan; it begins from the first ancestor, the Honorable Grand Preceptor (*Taesa* 太師) and reaches down to unworthy descendants such as myself. In total, it spans twenty-eight generations. Collateral relatives as well as legitimate and illegitimate children all are recorded according to the orthodox method.

Last month, I was about to set off for Hoecheon 懷川 to present [the genealogy as] a gift to Master Song Gangjae, [seeking to become his student].[1] In order to make it easier for him to read, just before I left, I sought help from my paternal first cousin [Yun] Geoncheol [尹] 健喆 to print the pages of the manuscript. After I returned, I had them arranged into a book and asked the Honorable Yu Giwon 俞綺園[2] to embellish the volume with seal script style characters.

Eeee! Our ancestors established themselves as conscientious, filial, hard-working, and frugal. Their children and grandchildren declined into obstinance, rashness, perversity, and arrogance. If one desires to follow the model of those who established themselves [as virtuous] and be on guard to avoid declining [into vice], how can one abandon learning! I am now thirty-one years old; my native ability is below average, and I heard the Way very late in life. Morning and evening I am anxious and fearful. Wanting to reinforce[3] the warnings of our ancestors, I have sketched outlines [of their lives]

---

[1] Presenting a gift (*jipji*; C. *zhizhi* 執贄) is part of the rites associated with becoming someone's student. In *Analects* 7.7, Gongja said he never rejected a student who came with even a bundle of dried meat, i.e., a humble gift to show one's sincere commitment to learn from the teacher. In his commentary on this passage, Ju Hui said, "When people in the past met each other, presenting a gift was a necessary rite. A bundle of dried meat is the most meager of gifts." See Ju Hui, *Collected Commentaries on the "Analects"* 4.2b. In later periods, this rite was called *jipjirye* (C. *zhizhili*) 執贄禮.

[2] See note 44, page 207.

[3] Reading 忝 as 添.

Korean Women Philosophers and the Ideal of a Female Sage. Philip J. Ivanhoe and Hwa Yeong Wang, Oxford University Press. © Oxford University Press 2023. DOI: 10.1093/oso/9780197508688.003.0017

in this volume so that those who come after me can see this and severely re-proach me for my unworthiness.

> Solemnly written by this unworthy descendant on the
> nineteenth day of the ninth month, in the 181st year
> of Emperor Sungjeong (C. Chongzhen) 崇禎 (1808)[4]

2. Postscript to the Extant Affairs of My Deceased Maternal Grandparents
<Written on Behalf of My Husband>

What appears above is a brief account of the extant affairs of my deceased maternal grandparents. In the year 1809, my late mother was seventy-one years old. From the second month of that year, she was bedridden, and once summer had passed, her condition gradually worsened. She wrote a rough draft of this in Hangeul [vernacular Korean] and tasked me with producing a clear and accurate transcription [into literary Chinese]. In the ninth month of this year, she passed away. Alas! The pain!

In the two years 1810 and 1811, we moved graves [and carried out burial rites] spanning three generations, for my grandparents, parents, eldest brother, and eldest brother's wife, and then had to search out [accounts of] the extant affairs of all three generations. During the same period, I also [adopted and] established an heir for my eldest brother. Because there were numerous and assorted unforeseen things [that required my attention] I was unable to transcribe the text. The last day of last month, I was browsing through some writings and came upon my deceased mother's extant writings. Though it's been six years, her works looked as if they had just been written. [Looking at them] my tears flowed without end. It is profoundly unfilial of me to have delayed for so long and not carried out the work [of transcribing her writings]. So I cautiously have produced the faithful transcription that appears above.

> Written by her unworthy son, shedding tears of blood, on the
> twelfth day of the ninth month in the year 1814.

---

[4] Sungjeong was the reign name of the last emperor of the Myeong dynasty. Joseon kept using this name even after the fall of the Great Myeong as a symbolic gesture to remain loyal to this civilized culture, as a sole heir against the Cheong (C. Qing) 淸 dynasty, which they considered barbaric.

Epitaphs (墓誌銘)

1. Funeral Epitaph for Lady Gim 金
<Written on Behalf of My Husband>

At an earlier time, Old Man of the Woods (Imsu 林叟), the Honorable Gim 金, while away from his hometown, resided near South Great Gate (Namdaemun 南大門)[1] as my neighbor. He instructed his three children to come and learn how to read and write with me. In this way, I became familiar with his upright character and love of righteousness and [came to understand] how his wife was a model and exemplary woman.

The Honorable's spouse was surnamed Gim 金 and her natal home was Gimhae 金海.[2] In the early years of our [Joseon] dynasty, one of her ancestors, whose personal name was Siyeong 始榮, passed the military examination and served as Minister of Punishments (刑曹判書);[3] another, whose personal name was Yihaeng 履行, served as Provincial Naval Commander (*Susa* 水使).[4] These were her eleventh- and seventh-generation progenitors respectively. Her paternal great-great-grandfather, whose personal name was Byeongdo 秉道, was a military official [who served as] a District Magistrate (*Busa* 府使). Her great-grandfather was named Gye 啓, and her grandfather, named Eunghae 應海, served as an administrator of the Central Council.[5] Her late father, whose personal name was Gwangsi 光時, was [posthumously] granted the honorary title of Second Minister (*Champan* 參判). Her late mother was surnamed Yi 李, from the city of Jeonju 全州; she was a daughter of the [Confucian] student[6] Sihwi 時暉.

---

[1] Its official name is Revering Ritual Gate, *Sungnyemun* 崇禮門; it is the south gate of the capital of Joseon.

[2] Gyeongsang 慶尙 Province.

[3] More precisely, Minister of the Ministry of Punishment.

[4] An abbreviation of *Sugun jeoldosa* 水軍節度使.

[5] More precisely, *Cheomjungchu* 僉中樞 is an abbreviation of *Cheomji Jungchu busa* 僉知中樞府事, and refers to the supernumerary senior third-rank post of Fifth Minister of the Office of Ministers without Portfolio.

[6] *Haksaeng* 學生 is the title given to the student at Confucian schools. It was also given to the people who did not hold any official title.

Korean Women Philosophers and the Ideal of a Female Sage. Philip J. Ivanhoe and Hwa Yeong Wang,
Oxford University Press. © Oxford University Press 2023. DOI: 10.1093/oso/9780197508688.003.0018

On the twenty-fourth day of the twelfth month in 1754, the lady was born. As a youth she showed a virtuous nature. She was harmonious, kind, upright, and calm. She was filial to her mother-in-law and reverent to her husband and did not disobey. She was never in the slightest remiss when it came to preparing food for them, making its warmth and coolness [perfectly] appropriate. If any of them were not well, she would personally prepare the needed medicine and, though tired, would not change out of her clothes throughout the night. Her mother-in-law felt her sincerity and once said, "I wish my sons and grandsons all would behave like [this] new bride!" If her husband did something wrong, she would calmly analyze the situation and subsequently bring him back to the proper way. If he grew worried or distressed, she immediately would console him with a variety of well-reasoned analogies and examples. When her mother grew destitute and alone, she turned to and relied upon the lady. She supported her mother throughout her life, even providing for her funeral, leaving nothing in the slightest to regret. One of her younger brothers passed away when he was very young and left an orphan behind. She enabled the young man to establish himself so that he could offer sacrifices to his ancestors. She was clever and hard-working in support of her family, setting to work early and resting only when it grew late. She was skilled in needlework, economized on unnecessary expenses, and provided for the needs of those around her, begrudging them nothing. She would collect everything that could be used for carrying out sacrifices so that she had ample reserves in case she had to make an offering and would fast in advance to be sure she was pure.

She showed the utmost sincerity to her sisters-in-law. She managed the family in a straightforward manner and with sympathetic consideration. In her everyday life she was reticent and kind; one rarely saw her be quick in her speech or show alarm on her face. In one voice, all her family and neighbors sang her praises. In teaching children, she put filial piety first and foremost and was on guard to avoid pampering and spoiling children. When she became a widow, she would listen to her eldest son in regard to every aspect of family business and never did just as she pleased.[7] She passed away on the twenty-second day of the second month of the

---

[7] That is to say, she followed the womanly "way of three followings" (*samjong ji do*; C. *sancong zhi dao* 三從之道), which prescribes obedience to father, husband, and son. See the "*Bonmyeong* (C. *Benming* 本命)" chapter in the *Book of Rites by the Elder Dae* (*Dae Dae Ryegi*; C. *Da Dai Liji* 大戴禮記).

year 1813. Later, on the twenty-eighth day of the third month, her coffin was buried in a new cemetery on the plateau with its back toward the southeast, which is located on Exerting Virtue Hill (Deokga-hyeon 德加峴) in According with Ritual Village (Yedong-ri 禮同里), in the Outer North District (Oebuk-myeon 外北面) of Requiting Favor (Boeun 報恩) County.[8]

The Honorable Imsu's personal name was Myeongjo 命祖. His ancestral home was Gyeongju 慶州. His first wife was a Ms. Choi of Gangneung 江陵;[9] she gave birth to a daughter who married Yu Myeong 柳明. The lady was his second wife, and she gave birth to three boys. The eldest, Chiwon 致遠, married the daughter of a man named Gim Jingwang 金振光. The middle boy, Chido 致道, married the daughter of a man named Jin Ryang 陳亮. The third, Chidal 致達, married the daughter of a man named Son Seok 孫奭. Chiwon has three daughters, and Chido has one son, named Gyeong璟. They all are young.

Carrying his mother's short biography, Chidal came to me with an overwrought and bedraggled look and sought to entrust me with the task of composing his mother's funeral epitaph. I told him that I was not the right person to write such a thing, but through tears he continued to implore me to do it. I thought of the time when we were neighbors and how when my late mother had been sick, she was able to recover because of help from the lady. My late mother had admired her and praised her as a worthy. Could I now bear to not write something and simply remain silent? So I carefully wrote a summary outline [of the biography] and from it composed the following inscription:

Her harmonious [spirit] was sufficient to properly manage her household; her quiet [nature] was able to respond to a myriad of demands. These perfectly accorded with the correctness and firmness of her inner elegance[10] and the norms of the woman's quarters. I arrange these lines at her tomb. May they remain unmolested for a hundred generations!

---

[8] A place located in North Chungcheong Province 忠清北道.
[9] A place located in Gangwon Province 江原道.
[10] See the "Image" commentary on the hexagram Gon (C. Kun) 坤 in the *Book of Changes*.

2. Funeral Epitaph for My Deceased Daughter
\<Written on Behalf of My Husband\>

This was written on the occasion of the death of Gang Jeongildang's fourth daughter and ninth child, the last child she gave birth to.

Alas! This is the resting place of Papyeong Yun Gwangyeon's deceased daughter, who died in childhood. Her name was Gyesuk; her mother was Madam Gang.[11] Our child was born on the twenty-ninth day of the eighth month in 1814, in our residence Tanwon in Yakhyeon 藥峴.[12] On the outside, she was upright and correct; on the inside, she was bright and intelligent. At the age of three to four months, she was able to recognize her mother's and father's faces. Even when she was crying, she would immediately stop as soon as she saw her mother or father. When we drew close to her, she would smile; when we drew away from her, she would look after us. Isn't it as Ju Hui said, "Even a child lacking understanding will smile if it sees its father."[13] Earlier, five sons and three daughters had been born to us, all of whom passed away before they were able to speak. Their mother and father never heard any of these children call them "mother" or "father." This child was the last to be born. We had hoped she would grow up and we would love her as if she were a son. Unfortunately, from the moment she was born, her mother did not produce enough milk to feed her. When she was just seven days old, we wrapped her in a baby blanket and brought her to be nursed by others. She struggled to live on this weak trickle of milk, and so we paid no heed to the weather or distance and fed her rice gruel in between [such visits]. Outside she was assaulted by *Gi-Material*, so inside her stomach suffered damage; it was no surprise that she became ill. Her family was poor and it was a year of famine. Family and friends who knew of our situation wanted to help and provide for our needs, but it was difficult for them to continue supplying us. When she became ill, she suffered from severe diarrhea. Medicine fortunately enabled her to last out the month, but in the end, it could not save her. She died on the fourth day of the first month of 1815; her life did not last a full year.

Our family graveyard is located in Gwangneung 廣陵,[14] but my strength was not sufficient to travel all the way to it. And so we dug a shallow grave

---

[11] I.e., Gang Jeongildang.
[12] The current name of the place is Jungnim 中林 District in Seoul.
[13] Ju Hui's *Collected Works of Hoeam* 12.17b.
[14] Another name of Gwangju 廣州, Gyeonggi Province.

at the foot of the right-hand hill of Split Peak (Takbong 坼峯), south of our village, and, on the fourteenth day of the month, we laid her to rest there. Alas! All things with blood and *Gi-Material*, when they are given life, it must come to an end. "There is nothing that is not according to fate."[15] Those who do not get what is needed to nourish them and are not able to complete their nature—can't this too be regarded as fate? The short life of this child is surely the result of fate, but is it not also the fault of human failure? I cannot set aside my grief! And so I have written down a record of it. Is this not letting my emotions go too far? If only those in later times will forgive me and not plow over [her grave] and ruin it. Her father is Papyeong Yun Gwangyeon, [courtesy name] Myeongjik. Memorialized by her father.

3. Grave Epitaph for the Filial Son Mr. Yi <Written on Behalf of My Husband>

I have had a long and good relationship with the Honorable Deokrae 德來 of the Jeonui 全義[16] Yi 李 clan, the recluse of Venting Spring (Sicheon 始泉).[17] In the fifth month of 1822,[18] he visited my residence and in tears said to me, "My eldest son Wonbae 元培 died on the twenty-fifth day of the eighth month of last year. Since he was born on the fourth day of the tenth month of 1793, he was barely twenty-nine years old. He was temporarily interred in the New Temple District (Sinsa-dong 新寺洞) [near] Welcoming Dawn (Yeonseo 延曙) [Station][19] and we are about to move him to a plateau with its back toward the northeast, below the mountainside burial site of his mother in Four Tributaries (Sapa 四派) [Township], Yangju 楊州. Eeee! Wonbae was a filial son! None among his immediate or distant relatives says anything to the contrary. Moreover, had [he] gone [to study] with you, you too would commend him as filial. I would like to provide an inscription for his tomb that will attest to [his character] to future generations. If not you, to whom could I entrust this [task]? I dare to ask you [to write an epitaph for him]."

---

[15] *Mencius* 7A2.

[16] The name of a district in Yeongi 燕岐 Country, Chungcheong Province.

[17] The reference of this term is not wholly clear; it may have been his nickname, taking its meaning from the line "a spring first finding vent" in *Mencius* 2A6.

[18] The year *Imo* according to the ancient Chinese calendar system. *Hyeonik* (C. *Xuanyi*) 玄黓 is another name for *im* (C. *ren*) 壬, the Ninth Heavenly Stem, and *Donjang* (C. *Dunzang*) 敦牂 is another name for *O* (C. *Wu*) 午, the Seventh Earthly Branch.

[19] Its old name is Yeongseo Station 迎曙驛.

When I heard [this], I was sorely aggrieved. I gathered together some words and composed this epitaph.

> "Who is able wholly to fulfill,
> The unvarying standard[20] that heaven has endowed?"
> The son of Master Yi,
> [His courtesy name] was Baek-in 伯仁.
> Since he was but a child,
> He was fully filial and reverent.
> Providing warmth or coolness [to his parents] as appropriate,
> He accommodated their every need.
> Nourishing them in a hundred different ways,
> His Heart-Mind set on working to please them.
> Always prepared with wine and meat,
> Offering them savory flavors.
> When guests arrived, he happily received them,
> Offering endless cups of wine.
> If his parents went out on an excursion,
> He would always provide for their expenses.
> In the course of mourning for his mother,[21]
> He suffered grief and desolation.
> He consoled his widowed father in his pain,
> Morning and evening anxiously rushing about to serve him.
> He provided his father money for gambling,
> And storytellers to recite tales.
> He called together those hard-pressed in finances,
> Inviting them to share their worries and loneliness.
> Encouraging his brother to study under a teacher,
> He offered money for him to purchase food and clothing.
> In his relationship with others, he never spoke recklessly,
> His words always strengthened the moral ties between people.[22]
> His wife was known as Lady U,
> Matching him in virtue and humaneness.
> She cared for her ill parents-in-law,

[20] This refers to our innate moral sense. See the *Book of Poetry*, Mao #260. Cited, with minor textual variation, in *Mencius* 6A6.

[21] Observing the three-year mourning period prescribed by ritual.

[22] Cf. "Summary of the Rules of Propriety" (upper part) of the *Book of Rites*.

Her sincerity and respectfulness were known to all her
   neighbors.
Alas! That such a man
Was poor and penniless throughout his life.
He did not get to live out his years,
His two orphaned sons died young, one after the other.
He was not given what he deserved,
What can vast heaven above do about it?
I make a record with this inscription,
To inform those who come later.
May none plow [this ground],
And forever leave this grave in peace.

Short Biographies (行狀)

1. Family Biography of My Eldest Brother's Wife, the Late Madam Ryu
<Written on Behalf of My Husband>

The lady's surname was Ryu 柳; her descent group came from Munhwa 文化.[1] Her great-grandfather, whose personal name was Eungsu 應壽, served as an administrator of the Central Council;[2] her grandfather, whose personal name was Yeong 英 was a County Magistrate. Her father's personal name was Wondae 遠大. Her mother was from the Jo 趙 clan of Hanyang 漢陽,[3] and a daughter of Inbok 仁復, a Classics Licentiate (*Saengwon* 生員).[4] She was born in 1764. When she was eighteen years old, she married my eldest brother; this was in 1781. In the following year, 1782, my family had no permanent place to reside and [she went to] stay with her natal family. After another year had passed, we moved to a new location, but the lady still was not able to join us.[5] She often sighed and said, "A wife is supposed to follow her husband, a married woman should be with her husband's family, but I have not yet been able to do this, which I profoundly regret." By nature, she was sincere, diligent, gentle, and agreeable. Her father died when she was young, and [after that] she [continued to] serve her mother. She was thoroughly filial and helped to rear her younger brothers and sisters, displaying extreme kindness and love. Once she had married, she served her parents-in-law and her husband with complete sincerity and reverence. She interacted with her husband's younger brothers and sisters in amiable manner. If her parents-in-law, or husband were greatly displeased [with her], she would not dare to show even the slightest trace of anger in her countenance. In the end, she

---

[1] Munhwa is located in the Trustworthy Stream District (Sincheon-gun 信川郡), Hwanghae Province (Hwanghae-do) 黃海道, a place located in what is now North Korea.

[2] More precisely, *Cheomchu* 僉樞 is another abbreviation of *Cheomji Jungchu busa* 僉知中樞府事, which appears in note 5, page 230.

[3] The traditional name for Seoul.

[4] A *Saengwon* is a person who has passed the Classics Licentiate Examination (*Saengwonsi* 生員試), a lower level of the civil service examination.

[5] Her husband's family, being hard-pressed financially, could not support her during this period.

Korean Women Philosophers and the Ideal of a Female Sage. Philip J. Ivanhoe and Hwa Yeong Wang, Oxford University Press. © Oxford University Press 2023. DOI: 10.1093/oso/9780197508688.003.0019

would find a way to resolve the problem in a gentle and docile manner. Every day, she assiduously practiced her spinning and weaving. The members of the family rarely saw her extinguish the candles to rest. Her preparation of food, weaving, and sewing all displayed sophisticated standards and forms. On the sixteenth day of the ninth month of 1784, she passed away in her natal home of Cheongyang 青陽.[6] On an unknown day and month [of that year] she was buried on a plateau with its back toward the west of Causeway Village (Bangchuk-chon 防築村) in the South Top District (南上面 Namsang-myeon) of her natal province. On the twelfth day of the third month of 1811, she was reburied on a plateau with its back toward the northwest in Golden Valley (Geumgok 金谷) in the Retreat Borough (Duntoe-ri 遁退里), Prosperity District (Daewang-myeon 大旺面) of Gwangju 廣州 [in Gyeonggi Province], in the same tomb as her husband.

The lady had joined my family for less than four years; she was only twenty-one [when she died]. I surely cannot describe in detail her demeanor and conduct as a woman, but when I went and stayed with her in 1722, though her [family] suffered poverty and want, her filial, reverent, diligent, and clever attitude and character naturally were brilliantly manifested. At the time, I was only five years old and the lady nurtured me, often holding me in her arms and carrying me on her back. I cannot fully express my sincere feelings of gratitude [for this]. Even now, it seems as though I can clearly recall this. As for other behavior that is worthy of praise, when her late mother was still alive, whenever she said something untoward, the lady was able to overlook it. Eeeee! The lady always regretted that she could never join[7] her husband's family. In the end, she died young in her natal place. Hidden in a solitary grave, residing temporarily in Ho Province,[8] what inexhaustible feelings must she have had about her life and death? I am knotted up inside over this, and so have traveled a great distance to reverently transport her coffin for reburial, so that she can join my late brother in his tomb; thereby fulfilling the lady's own intention.

Written in the winter of 1811. Her husband's younger brother solemnly writes [this biography].

---

[6] A place located in South Chungcheong Province (Chungcheongnam-do) 忠淸南道.

[7] *Ugwi* (C. *yugui*) 于歸 originally refers to a woman's marriage; see the *Book of Poetry*, Mao #6. The Chinese Confucian marriage rite was adapted with modification in Korea. During the Joseon dynasty, uxorilocal marriage was not rare; husbands commonly brought their new brides home after three visits. But this "bride's entering the groom's house," the last act of the wedding ceremony, often was delayed, even for years, for many reasons, such as the economic situation of the newly related houses and the ages of the new bride and groom. For the details, see Deuchler 1992, 251–256.

[8] More precisely, Hohyang 湖鄕 refers to the area West of the Lake (Hoseo 湖西), in what is now Chungcheong Province. It is not clear which lake is referred to.

2. Biography of My Mother-in-Law, Lady Gwon of Andong
<Written on Behalf of My Husband>

My wife's mother was Lady Gwon 權; her ancestral home was Andong 安東. The founder of their lineage bore the personal name Haeng 幸; he assisted Taejo 太祖[9] (r. 918–943 CE) of the Goryeo 高麗 dynasty (918–1392 CE), serving him as Grand Preceptor. He had numerous prosperous sons and grandsons, who in succession received numerous ranks and titles. Among the brilliant and successful descendants is one whose personal name was Ham 瑊; he served both kings Yejong 睿宗 (r. 1468–1469 CE) and Seongjong 成宗 (r. 1469–1494 CE) of the Joseon dynasty as Merit Subjects (*Gongsin* 功臣),[10] was enfeoffed as [Lord] Hwacheon 花川, and given the posthumous name Yangpyeong 襄平. In the sixth generation, there was the Honorable Second Inspector (*Jibui* 執義), whose personal name was Gyeok 格 (1620–1671 CE), who was renowned for his uprightness and integrity. He had three sons. The eldest, Master Suam 遂庵, whose personal name was Sangha 尙夏 (1641–1721 CE), transmitted the moral tradition of Master Song[11] and became the head of the [orthodox] Confucian Community. His [Gyeok's] second son's personal name was Sangmyeong 尙明 (1652–1684 CE), who was resolute in aspiration and conduct but died young. He was given the [posthumous] title of Second Minister in the Ministry of Personnel (*Ijo Champan* 吏曹參判). The youngest son was Minister (*Panseo* 判書) [in the Ministry of Personnel] whose personal name was Sangyu 尙游 (1656–1724 CE); he was distinguished throughout later ages for his virtue and achievements. The Honorable Second Minister was the lady's great-great-grandfather. Her great-grandfather's personal name was Seop 燮 (1671–1759 CE) and his pen name was the Man of Jade Mountain (*Okso Sanin* 玉所山人). He was highly principled in his conduct and talented at writing compositions. [Initially] he concealed his virtue and did not serve [in the royal court], but he was given the [honorary] title of Fourth Minister of the Office of

---

[9] The founder of the Goryeo dynasty.

[10] This ancestor was rewarded with the title of Merit Subject under two kings for two different kinds of achievement. King Yejong awarded the title Ikdae Merit Subject (*Ikdae gongsin* 翊戴功臣) to thirty-nine people in 1468 for their "reverent support" in dealing with the traitor Nam I 南怡 (1441–1468 CE). King Seongjong awarded the title Jwari Merit Subject (*Jwari gongsin* 佐理功臣) to seventy-five people in 1471 for their "excellent contributions to good governance."

[11] Song Siyeol.

Ministers-without-Portfolio (Dongji jungchu *busa* 同知中樞府事) based upon his seniority.[12] Her grandfather's personal name was Choseong 初性; he served as a Gentleman for Transmitting Virtue (*Tongdeongnang* 通德郎). Her father's personal name was Seoeung 瑞應; he cultivated his purity and loved antiquity. Later people referred to him as the Reclusive Scholar of the Pure River (*Cheonggang Cheosa* 淸江處士). Her mother was a member of the Yi 李 clan of Yeonan 延安, who was the daughter of the [Confucian] Student Jecheol 齊哲.

On the tenth day of the fourth month of the year 1740, the lady was born in the family residence in the Yellow River Borough (Hwanggang-ri 黃江里) in Pure Wind (Cheongpung 淸風) [County, in Chungcheong Province]. By nature, she was dignified and chaste; in intelligence, she was superior to most. Ever since she was young, she was able to serve her parents with supreme sincerity. Each morning she inquired [about their health] and each evening adjusted [everything for their repose].[13] She delighted her parents, [serving] at their side with a "mild and compliant" [demeanor] and "gentle voice."[14] She was clever in her needlework and sophisticated in her preparation of meals. Her methods of spinning and weaving, tailoring, washing, and ironing and her ways of cooking and selecting and blending meals always brought comfort to her parents and pleased their palates. She had the ability to calculate even very large numbers accurately [with a technique] relying only on her fingers. Even those who excelled at the use of abacus could not keep up with her. When she read the *Biographies of Exemplary Women*,[15] *Instructions for Women* (*Buhun* 婦訓), *Lessons for Women* (*Yeogye*; C. *Nujie* 女誡),[16] and other such books, whenever she saw passages about ancient filial children and chaste women, she would wholeheartedly admire and emulate them. Toward her older and young sisters, she was sincerely kind and

---

[12] *Sujik* 壽職 or *Noinjik* 老人職 was a nominal post given to the elderly, over eighty years old, as an expression of filial piety at the state level.

[13] Cf. "Summary of the Rules of Propriety" (upper part) of *Book of Rites*.

[14] Cf. "The Meaning of Sacrifices" (*Jeui*; C. *Jiyi* 祭義) and "The Pattern of the Family" of the *Book of Rites*, respectively.

[15] The *Biographies of Exemplary Women* has been translated into English by Anne Behnke Kinney (2014).

[16] The reference of the *Instructions for Women* here is not clear. This title could be an abbreviation of *Mr. Han's Teachings for Women* (*Hanssi buhun* 韓氏婦訓) written by Han Wonjin 韓元震 (1682–1751 CE). But it might also refer to either the *Teachings for the Inner Quarters* (*Naehun*; C. *Neixun* 內訓) by Empress Inhyomun (C. *Renxiaowen*) 仁孝文 (1362–1407 CE) of the Myeong dynasty, China, or a work with the same title by Queen Sohye 昭惠 (1437–1504 CE) of Joseon. English translations of Empress Inhyomun's *Teachings for the Inner Quarters* and the *Lessons for Women* are published in Ann A. Pang-White (2018).

loving. If either of her parents was ill, she would remain with them deep into the night without even changing her clothes and would insist on personally heating medicine and cooking congee for them. Even as a child, her conduct was pure and her virtue beautiful. In general, this was because of the correctness of the education the Honorable Reclusive Scholar [her father] offered her, but it also reflected her natural inclinations; she did not need too much correction or encouragement.

When she was twenty, she joined the Gang family, which was a distinguished lineage. Her husband, whose personal name was Jaesu 在洙, possessed ample amounts of ambition and discipline. When the lady first married him, the family had declined[17] and their estate had withered. At the time, her grandmother-in-law, who was a succeeding wife, and mother-in-law were alive, but the family lacked the resources to provide for them [properly]. And so, the lady exerted all her mental and physical abilities to provide them with simple fare.[18] In the winter months, her hands and feet were chapped and chilblained, but she did not allow her suffering to show on her face. Her grandmother-in-law was stern by nature and difficult to serve, yet she provided what she needed even before the woman had thought of it herself. She remained ever respectful and cautious, and, in the end, her grandmother-in-law was moved, won over, and came to love her deeply. In serving her husband, she was reverent and did not disobey; in every affair, she never dared to insist on her own point of view. When her husband would grow distressed by their hardship, he would let out a worrisome sigh; she immediately would console him, with a variety of well-reasoned analogies and examples.

Every day, she woke up with the crowing of the cock and set about sorting out the family's business. When the night was halfway over, she [normally] would rest, though in some cases, she would work assiduously until dawn. She did not think that this was burdensome. She always took the lazy look and frivolous attitude of women as a warning [to herself]. At home, she would sit up straight and remain silent so even her female relatives would not dare to speak inappropriately or laugh uproariously when next to her. In these ways,

[17] Reading 桯 as 陧. Cf. "Speech of the Marquis of Jin" (*Jin Seo*; C. *Qin Shi* 秦誓) of the *Book of History*.

[18] The expression "simple fare" (lit. "bean soup and drinking water") alludes to the "Dangung" chapter (lower part) of the *Book of Rites*. There Gongja says that if one's parents are happy, offering them even bean soup and drinking water would be considered filial.

she restrained herself and inspired others to have confidence in her. She was profoundly reverent when making offerings to the ancestors. Whenever she came upon something that could be used to carry out the sacrifices, she would store it away for future use. She was well-versed in preparing for the sacrifices. Whenever anyone in the family had some issue [concerning sacrifice], they would consult the lady before carrying it out. An uncle of her husband's clan, [whose pen name was] Pavilion of the Mountains and Streams (Sansuheon 山水軒), [Gwon] Jineung[19] [權]震應 praised the sincerity of her filial piety and reverence and the quality of her womanly skills, saying, "Rarely have we had anyone comparable to her among the women of our clan." In teaching her children, she would often say [to them], "Mothers spoil and cover up the mistakes of their children and don't let their fathers know about them, but this only encourages bad behavior. I take this very seriously." Subsequently, her children never dared to do things contrary to what is right. Among the instructions she gave to my wife is one that says, "Women should obediently pursue their work, put chastity and honesty foremost, should speak in a soft and unhurried voice, and be constant in their actions." When my mother-in-law married off my wife, she warned her to "Be filial to your mother-in-law, revere your husband, and be harmonious with the wives of your brothers and sisters-in-law. This is what I wish you to do. If you are able to be like this, what greater way could there be to nurture a commitment to being filial? Wealth and poverty naturally are distributed [unevenly] as a matter of fate. If the wife of an impoverished scholar does not clearly understand this principle, she will always harbor thoughts of despising her poverty, but what good can this do!"

In 1772, the lady's grandmother-in-law passed away; five years later, she also mourned for her own mother-in-law. She carried out all these affairs according to what ritual prescribes; her grief and sadness exceeded the required norm. The Honorable Reclusive Scholar did not have any sons and so chose his nephew Jungsil 中實 to be his heir. Since the Honorable had lost his wife, Madam Yi, in 1773, he moved close to Jungsil to live in Je County (Jehyang 堤鄉).[20] The lady was given separate quarters next door so it would be easier for her to take care of him.[21] [In this way,] she showed him eight

---

[19] He was the great-grandson of Gwon Sangha; he attained the seventh-rank staff member, *Jaui* 諮議, in the Tutorial Office for the Crown Prince (*Seja Sigangwon* 世子侍講院).

[20] Jecheon 堤川.

[21] According to ritual, all children are to warm the bed for their parents in winter and to cool it in summer. See the "Summary of the Rules of Propriety" (upper part) in the *Book of Rites*.

full years of sincere filial piety. When the Honorable became seriously ill, for three months she brought him medicine and would not leave his side for even a moment. When he died, she expressed both grief and admiration. In the autumn of 1788, her husband was stricken with a sudden illness and became bed-ridden; by the time the funeral and internment had been completed, she swore that she did not want to continue living. But, when she thought about how young the orphaned heir was and how he had no one to rely upon, she made herself strong and continued to carry on, so that she could nurture and educate him. Once she became a widow, she never again saw the light of day.[22] Her accumulated wounds and pains developed into a chronic malady. In the end, several years after completing mourning [for her husband], she moved to Pure Wind [County].[23]

In 1794, she instructed her eldest son, Ilhoe, to go to Hansa or Yeon County (Yeonhyang 漣鄉)[24] in order to pursue his education. Ilhoe declined, because it would keep him away from his ill mother, but the lady encouraged him, saying, "Since you now have begun to grow up and my illness is no longer critical night and day, you must go to read books and cultivate yourself. Do not abandon the teachings left behind by those who preceded you and thereby compound my offenses." In winter of the following year, her illness became critical, and so he quickly packed his belongings and returned to his old home in Je County. Subsequently, on the thirteenth day of the eleventh month, she passed away, having enjoyed fifty-six years of life. On the fifteenth day of the second month of 1796, she was buried together, in the same tomb, with her husband, leaving behind her two sons, Ilhoe and Sihoe, and one son-in-law, [me,] Yun Gwangyeon. Ilhoe married the daughter of Gim Hwansam 金煥參 who gave birth to one son, Giyeong 祈永, and one daughter; both are young. Sihoe married the daughter of Yi Jaeman 李載萬, who gave birth to one daughter; she too is young.

Ah! The lady's conduct was upright and wholly sincere. Her ability and insight were outstanding and far-reaching. She lived in a remote and desolate county and tasted bitterness and poverty. All that she encountered would have been [too] difficult for most other people [to endure]. Nevertheless, the lady handled it all smoothly and with complete equanimity, calmly settling everything. She was able to sustain the family, working for those who came before and sheltering those who followed. In every respect, she can serve as a

[22] I.e., she never left her house.
[23] Cf. the earlier reference in this chapter.
[24] Yeoncheon (漣川), the county located next to Jecheon, where they were staying.

model for the women of the world. When I first married and met my mother-in-law, I was ignorant and mediocre. The lady asked me, "What books do you read?" and I responded by saying "the *Four Books* and *Elementary Learning*." The lady replied, "If you don't embody [their teachings], reading them is pointless." All I could say was, "I shall! I shall!" Thinking about this after she had passed, I began to understand the poignancy of her critique. Subsequently, I learned many lessons from her, [such as] the imperatives to serve parents and to be cautious in one's conduct or her method of cultivating the Heart-Mind and setting it on learning. She could rouse one to attend to such concerns with short and concise expressions that were simple and not in any way annoying. I particularly trusted the truths that her counsels contained; her understated excellence shined all-the-more brightly. Ilhoe had [laudable] aspirations but not a long life, and so the record of the family's affairs was lacking in detail. Sihoe feared that over time nothing would be passed on and so he entrusted this material to me. Since I had been so bold as to make a record of my father-in-law's words and actions, I also made a broad selection of the records my wife had made of the lady's extant affairs and those things that Sihoe had seen or heard. I combined all of these sources together and then compared and edited them, in order to prepare a work of representative selections for some later writer.

> Respectfully offered during the last ten days of the twelfth lunar month in 1815 by son-in-law Yun Gwangyeon of Papyeong.

3. Biography of the Esteemed Lady[25] Yi
<Written on Behalf of My Husband>

The Honorable Gim Myeongun 金命運, [whose pen name is] Gyeonghyeonwa 景賢窩, has been my friend for twenty years. He instructed his son Chwihwa 寂和 to come and study [under me] and this allowed me to gain a greater understanding of the source of his ancestors' virtue and the many ways his family could serve as a model to be passed down through the ages. Now, Chwihwa was instructed by his father to record many extant affairs of the Esteemed Lady. Bringing this [material] in his sleeve, he tearfully asked me to compose a biography. Recollecting the depth and breadth of my relationship with the Honorable Gim, how could I possibly refuse?

[25] See note 9, page 221.

To begin, the Esteemed Lady's family name was Yi 李, a Branch of Fine Jade (*Seonpa* 璿派).[26] Prince Gyeongmyeong 景明君 (1489–1526 CE),[27] who was a son of King Seongjong 成宗 (r. 1469–1494 CE)[28] and whose personal name was Chim 忱, was the progenitor of her line; his son was called Prince Annam 安南君, whose personal name was Suryeon 壽鍊. Annam gave birth to Prince Geumcheon 錦川君, whose personal name was Bo 俌. Geumcheon gave birth to Assistant Changwon (Changwon *Jeong* 昌原正),[29] [whose personal name was] Jehyeong 齊衡. These are the Esteemed Lady's ancestors in the sixth and fifth generation, respectively. Her great-great-grandfather's personal name was Saengin 生寅; he was a Literary Licentiate.[30] Her great-grandfather's personal name was Danseok 端錫; he was Second Minister in the Ministry of Personnel and [posthumously] was granted the honorary title of Minister. Her grandfather's personal name was Geukyeon 克淵; he served as a Gentleman for Transmitting Virtue.[31] Her father's personal name was Taesu 台秀; he was a Vice Assistant (*Cheomjeong* 僉正) of the Bureau of Military Training (*Hullyeonwon* 訓鍊院). Her mother was a Virtuous Woman (*Sukbuin* 淑夫人) of the Ryu 柳 clan of Jinju 晉州; she was the daughter of Dojang 道章, an officer of the fourth grade [in the Five Guards Directorate (Owi Dochongbu 五衛都摠府)].

On the sixth day of the sixth month in 1772, she gave birth to the Esteemed Lady. By nature, she [the Esteemed Lady] was warm, harmonious, kind, and magnanimous; her manner of speech was relaxed, unhurried, detailed, and clear. Ever since she was young, she was praised by the members of her clan for her filial piety toward her parents and love toward her siblings. When she married, she served her parents-in-law, extending them sincerity and reverence. Every morning she would wake up early and make sure they slept well; in the middle of the night, she would wait until they were settled before she

---

[26] A Branch of Fine Jade refers to branches of the royal Yi clan whose names appear in the *Book of Royal Genealogy* (*Seonwollok* 璿源錄).

[27] Prince Geongmyeong was born to one of the King Seongjong's concubines.

[28] King Seongjong was the ninth king of the Joseon dynasty.

[29] *Jeong* 正 is a title of the third grade, following Prince (*Gun* 君), a title of the second grade, for members of the royal clan. There is no standard English translation for *Jeong*. We translate it as "Assistant."

[30] Parts of Yun Gwangyeon's account do not match the record of the *Book of Royal Genealogy* held at Jangseogak Archive. For example, according to the *Book of Royal Genealogy* the personal name of Assistant Changwon is Seui 世義 and Jehyeong is the personal name of the Lady's great-great-grandfather. Saengin is the personal name of the fifth-generation ancestor. Also, Prince Annam and Prince Geumcheon are seventh- and eighth-generation ancestors, respectively. See Jangseogak Archives DB (http://royal.aks.ac.kr).

[31] Cf. the earlier reference in this chapter. See also note 10, page 221.

retired. She was scrupulously regular in her practices and for long periods of time would not be remiss [in serving her parents-in-law]. In cooking meals day and night, she would always offer well-flavored and delicious food. If [her mother or father-in-law] fell ill, she would prepare some tea, medicine, soup, or gruel and personally take charge of cooking and preparing these to ensure they were at the proper temperature before being offered. [When either of them was ill,] she would never loosen her clothes to go for a rest. Only once they had recovered would she stop [taking care of them]. In every affair she undertook, she would first think of how to comply; she would not insist on deciding even the smallest issue on her own. Her parents-in-law showered her with love; they often would stroke her back and say, "The worthy woman of our house!" She would often copy [passages from] *Lessons for Women*, the *Three Bonds* (*Samgang* 三綱),[32] and other books; she would transcribe [these] into vernacular Korean [Hangeul] and memorize and then admire and emulate them. If she saw anyone being unfilial toward their parents, she would sigh and say, "What kind of person is this? Their repayment [of their parents] is inferior to the repayment that birds offer [to their fathers and mothers]." When her mother and father had passed away and her father's concubine had no one to rely on, she asked her husband if she could bring her to live with them. For twenty years, her kind and righteous treatment of her father's concubine never changed.

She reverently served her husband and, in matters great and small, always followed his instructions. If her husband was angry, she would be anxious and not dare to utter a word. She once commented to someone saying, "When the head of our household becomes extremely angry, even though it is unwarranted, my way is only to modestly and obediently accept it. Even if he is seduced by another woman's beauty, it is fitting not to be jealous in order to follow the way of a wife." If she saw a woman from another family who, fierce with jealously, was unrestrained in her speech and drunk with wine, she would feel ashamed and profoundly guard against such behavior [in regard to herself]. Every morning she would wash and prepare herself and then sweep clean the house. Throughout the course of the day, she would work diligently, but the sound of her voice did not pass beyond the

---

[32] This seems to refer to *Exemplars of the Three Bonds* (*Samgang haengsil* 三綱行實). From the early period, the Joseon court published and distributed books like this to teach moral education about basic human relationships. For the Three Bonds, see note 111, page 58. There are a number of texts with this name, and it is not clear which version the author is referring to. We take this as a general name for this kind of book.

women's quarters; the tracks of her steps did not reach the outer residence.[33] In preparing food, she insisted it be delicate and pure; in tailoring clothes, she insisted the stitching be regular and straight. Her husband enjoyed the company of guests, and he had many acquaintances. The lady exerted her mind and strength in order to receive them. She always said, "When the men of my family go out, they are the guests of some other family; when the men of other families come, then they are the guests of my family. One should treat them with sincerity and cannot be negligent or slow. How much more so since the rituals concerning the reception of guests is second in importance only to those concerned with offerings to the ancestors. And yet often many of those who serve as hosts are not sincere. Women in the inner quarters are particularly negligent and inattentive. Servants are several times worse than this! Can one afford not to be attentive and make effort!" The lady never talked about other people's shortcomings, nor did she ever scold others or argue with them. She always said, "Even if someone praises me, if I am without merit, I am not pleased; even if someone disparages me, if I am without fault, I am not resentful."[34] When giving or receiving something, she made very clear the precise amount; when borrowing from someone else, she made a record of the month and day and made sure to repay what she owed by the date it was due. She enjoyed giving to others and took pity on the poor. If someone was cold, she would clothe them; if someone were hungry, she would feed them. [In these respects,] she left nothing to regret.

In teaching her only son, she followed clear rules and standards. She always said, "Who does not love their child! Those who are good at teaching are the ones who truly love [their] children. If you drown in sentimentality and don't understand how to teach them, then this is [to love them as] an animal loves its young.[35] Your way of loving them will simply harm them." When her son was young, he was lazy about doing his reading and so she repeatedly warned him saying, "What we esteem in a person is their conduct. Those who want to make bright their conduct must read books! I have heard that in the proper sequence of reading books, nothing comes before the *Elementary Learning*. You must read this and embody its teachings in your conduct!" Whenever her son did something wrong, she would invariably tell

---

[33] These are presented as examples of exemplary womanly conduct in "The Pattern of the Family" chapter of the *Book of Rites*.

[34] Cf. personal missive 14 in this volume.

[35] Cf. part of Ju Hui's commentary to 14.7 of his *Collected Commentaries on the "Analects."* The word here translated as "beast" is literally "calf."

her husband to reprimand him and to scold and cane him. She would say to her husband, "If you want to complete a vessel, you must seek for a good artisan! If people want to learn, they must seek a worthy teacher! I have heard that Master Yun is one who is worthy. In general, in order to encourage one's son to study, there are [the stories of] 'moving three times to learn'[36] and 'following a teacher for a thousand miles'[37] from the past; how much easier is it living in the same city [as a worthy teacher] and still fearing the difficulty of travel?" Her husband followed her advice and instructed Chwihwa to pursue his studies with me.

In the winter of the year 1805, because an ailment contracted after giving birth became serious in the course of the year, she said to the members of her family, "I know that in the end I cannot overcome this illness; the span of one's life is up to heaven. What is the use of resenting it? I only regret that I will not be able to see my son make progress, go on to marry, and inherit the wisdom of those who have gone before to efface the shortcomings of his parents."[38] On the full moon of the tenth month of 1806, her illness became critical, but she sent Chwihwa off to pursue his studies. Having walked only a hundred paces, suddenly his heart was alarmed and his body began to tremble; thereupon, he returned and looked after [his mother]. That evening the Esteemed Lady said to him, "Your father happens to be away [on business] and I fear my illness is beyond cure, which causes me great regret. After I am gone, do not waste the years and months; study well with your teacher in order to console me [below] in the Nine Springs."[39] She passed away on the very next day. On a certain day and month of that year she was buried on a plateau with its back toward a certain direction in a seat of Sparsely Wooded Borough (Mokhui-ri 木稀里), in the King's Tomb District (Wondang-myeon 元堂面) of Lofty and Bright (Goyang 高陽) [in Gyeonggi Province].

The Honorable Gim's courtesy name was Yeongji 永之; his grandfather's personal name was Heunggwang 興光; he was the third son of King Heongang 憲康 (r. 875–886 CE)[40] of the [Unified] Silla 新羅 dynasty

---

[36] A famous story from the biography of Maengja's mother, who as a widow moved three times in order to secure the right environment for her son's education. See "The Maternal Models" (Mo Ui; C. Mu Yi 母儀) chapter of the Biographies of Exemplary Women.

[37] A paraphrase of lines from chapter 2 of A Jade Forest of Youthful Learning (Yuhak gyeongnim; C. Youxue qionglin 幼學瓊林), which was originally called the Critical Lessons for Youthful Learning (Yuhak suji; C. Youxue xuzhi 幼學須知), an early primer written in the Myeong dynasty by Jeong Deunggil (C. Cheng Dengji) 程登吉.

[38] The final sentence contains a paraphrase of a line from hexagram Go (C. Gu) 蠱 in the Book of Changes.

[39] The Nine Springs or Yellow Springs refers to the underworld.

[40] King Heongang was the forty-ninth to rule the Silla kingdom.

(676–935 CE). Knowing that the nation was soon to descend into chaos, he fled to Gwangsan 光山 [in South Jeolla Province (Jeolla-do 全羅道)]. As a result, his sons and grandsons thought that this was their natal home. They flourished and prospered there and became one of the great families of the east.

In the current [Joseon] dynasty, one of them, whose personal name was Seongok 成玉, [passed] the highest civil service examination (*Mungwa* 文科) and [served] as Chancellor (*Daesaseong* 大司成) [of the National Confucian Academy (*Seonggyungwan* 成均館)]. Five generations [thereafter], another, whose personal name was Hyeop 浹, [passed] the highest civil service examination and [served] as Counselor (*Gyori* 校理).[41] Three generations [later], there was one whose personal name was Hyosin 孝信, who was the first person to pass the highest military examination (*Mujin* 武進).[42] He held offices up to First Secretary of the Bureau of Military Training and was awarded the title of Minor Merit Subject (*Wonjong Gongsin* 原從功臣). Subsequently, generation after generation passed the highest military service examination (*Mugwa* 武科) and served in a number of official positions. This [tradition] continued for four generations. There was also an ancestor who was Director of the Office of Transmission (*Seonjeon-gwan* 宣傳官) and was [posthumously] awarded the title Second Secretary (*Jwa Seungji* 左承旨), whose personal name was Hanmyeong 漢明. Another was Director of the Office of Transmission and was [posthumously] awarded the title Second Minister; his personal name was Seongpil 聖弼. A [third], whose personal name was Deukyeon 得衍, served as Fourth Minister of the Office of Ministers-without-Portfolio. These [the three above] were Honorable Gim's great-grandfather, grandfather, and father, respectively. His father originally married the daughter of [a man whose personal name was] Jaehu 載厚 of the Yeonan 延安 Gim 金 Clan, but since she did not bear any children, the Esteemed Lady became his second wife. She gave birth to a son, Chwihwa. In 1821, Chwihwa passed the highest-level military examination and married the daughter of Yi Sisang 李時祥, who was a military official (*Sagwa* 司果). Chwihwa had two daughters, both of whom are young.

The Honorable Gim was broad-minded, intelligent, trustworthy, and sincere. In the summer of 1800, I first met him face to face. As soon as he saw me, he spoke to me about taking care of his son's education; I did not dare to

---

[41] More precisely, a counsellor of the fifth grade.
[42] Military Presented Scholar (*Mujinsa* 武進士), one who has passed the highest military examination, the *Jeonsi* 殿試.

do so and so declined. For a number of years [five in total], I was very busy and did not have the leisure to pursue this further. After three more years had passed, in the tenth month of 1808, I was finally able to do as he had requested. Now, it already has been fifteen years [since I began to teach his son]. Considering how mean and lowly I am, how can I be regarded as qualified to serve as another's teacher? It is only because when I recall my affection for the Esteemed Lady and the many years of sincerity [she has shown me], I am led to sigh and be wholeheartedly committed [to undertake this responsibility]. How can I allow her death to interfere with [my teaching of her son]! Chwihwa has established a commitment and developed himself. In general, he understands where he is going; one can say he will live up to the moral education he was given. Though he continued the family's traditional occupation and studied archery and horsemanship [i.e., he followed the path of a military career], if one looks at his countenance and listens to his words, one knows for sure that he is a careful and proper Confucian scholar.

As for the Esteemed Lady's biography, I did not dare to refuse [the request to write it] and offer what you find here. Nevertheless, her outstanding virtue and good acts are things I could write about at greater length. Now I have only sketched out a general outline, respectfully awaiting a future person who can do her full justice.

> In the last ten days of the first month of summer in the Fourth Imo (C. Renwu) 壬午 year after the ascension of Emperor Sungjeong (1822),[43] I, Yun [Gwangyeon] of Pasan 坡山,[44] [write this down].

[43] See note 4, page 229.
[44] Another name for Papyeong.

Funeral Orations (祭文)

1. Funeral Oration for Old Man No-Mind, the Honorable Hong[1] 洪公 <Whose Personal Name Was Saho 絲浩> <Written on Behalf of My Husband>

In the Fourth Mujin (C. Wuchen) 戊辰 year after the ascension of the Emperor, on the twenty-ninth day of the eighth month of 1814, I, Yun [Gwangyeon] of Papyeong solemnly make this humble libation to the dead. Through tears, I announce to Old Man No-Mind, the Honorable Hong, Constitutional Asset Minister (*Jaheon daebu* 資憲大夫), an Administrator of the Second Grade of the Central Council (*Ji Jungchubu Sa* 知中樞府事) and Commander General (*Dochonggwan* 都摠管) of the Five Guards Directorate, this spirit feast, saying,

> Calm and incorruptible,
> Such was your constant virtue.
> Settled and pure,
> A model for your family.
> You administered the government of Ho township
> (Ho-eup) 湖邑,[2]
> Its people sang of your kindness and merit.
> You retired, [and lived like] Namgwak 南郭,[3]
> Enjoying your life at home.
> You were blessed with longevity,
> And granted high rank.

---

[1] Hong Saho (1720?–1813? CE). In his lineage, his name is recorded as Hong Sahan 洪絲漢. He was born circa 1720 and passed the highest military examination in 1740 at the age of twenty-one. See the *Veritable Records of King Jeongjo* (*Jeongjo sillok* 正祖實錄) 53.35a [24(1800)/02/13#2].

[2] More precisely, Cheongan 清安, now Goesan 槐山, in Chungcheong Province, which was referred to as Hohyang (湖鄉) or the West of the Lake (Hoseo 湖西).

[3] Namgwak Jagi (C. Nanguo ziqi) 南郭子綦 is a figure found in opening section of the "On the Equality of Things" (*Jemullon* 齊物論) chapter of the *Jangja*. He is described as having "lost" himself and become one with the Way.

Korean Women Philosophers and the Ideal of a Female Sage. Philip J. Ivanhoe and Hwa Yeong Wang, Oxford University Press. © Oxford University Press 2023. DOI: 10.1093/oso/9780197508688.003.0020

Heaven (i.e., the King) showered you with glory,

Repeatedly bestowing abundant favor.

Reaching the age of ninety, you became one of the Eight
　　Executives,[4]

Such a life is rarely enjoyed by a Protected Official![5]

Late in life we became neighbors,

Granting me the opportunity to assist you closely.

You never looked down upon the young,

But instead encouraged and guided them.

Rarely were you overly permissive,

But toward me you were so generous!

You encouraged me to develop my moral character,

Teaching me conscientiousness and filial piety.

You presented me large calligraphy of [these two] characters,

[Which should be] etched on the heart of every Confucian.

Suddenly, I found myself racked with sorrow,

The first anniversary of your death was near at hand!

Overcome with anxiety and worry,

I had yet to go and eulogize you.

[Recalling] my failure morning and evening,

[I felt] as if I was choking and gagging.

With poor wine and few words,

I now dare to convey my meaning.

Please accept my offering!

2. Funeral Oration for My Clansman Seonggwan 聖寬 <[Whose Personal Name Is] Gwangdeok 光德> <Written on Behalf of My Husband>

On the second day of the new moon[6] of the third month of 1814, I, your clansman [Yun Gwangyeon], solemnly make a libation of wine and fruit, delegating my disciple Han Honggi 韓洪基, tearfully to announce to clansman Seonggwan 聖寬 this spirit feast.

---

[4] This refers to eight of the most important posts in the central government.
[5] Protected Officials were those granted office on the basis of the status and achievements of their forefathers and without passing a civil examination.
[6] A funeral oration signifies the first day of the month when the sacrificial rite takes place.

Alas! This day is the end of the second year [of your mourning period].[7] The stars have passed and the frost has come and gone; your sacrificial mat and offering table are about to be moved to the ancestral temple. Two elderly parents wail in resentment. A solitary widow and orphan endure their suffering. Are you in the dark and unaware [of this], or have you gone off, not looking back? Alas! By nature and in conduct you were kind and humane; it would have been fitting that you enjoy great happiness, but instead you died young. The exquisite quality of your written works was able to rouse a house that is in decline, but it had yet to win you fame. How is this possible? The relationship among our people had been genuine and earnest for some time, but since your younger brother, <Gwanghak 光學>, was adopted as my uncle's heir, our feelings grew even more intimate and our love more sincere. My anticipation of sharing a long journey and a normal life [together] has now come to an end. Last year on my way to Ho,[8] I stopped by [your tomb] and mourned for you, but I have been unable to organize and write down the thoughts and feelings that block and clog my heart. Moreover, because vast mountains and streams separate us and my body is wrapped in illness, I am unable to personally offer a libation [to you]. Alas Seonggwan! Please understand my situation and enjoy the cup of wine I present to you. Please accept my offering!

3. Funeral Oration for Master Yuchwi 留取, the Honorable Gim Yunchu 金允秋 <Written on Behalf of My Husband>

In the Fourth Gyeongjin 庚辰 year after the ascension of the Sungjeong Emperor, the eighteenth day of the second month [of 1820], I, Yun Gwangyeon of Papyeong, heard that the coffin of Mr. Gim Yuchwi[9] was about to leave for Hwangnyeo 黃驪[10] [for burial]. Though ill, with great effort

---

[7] *Jongsang* 終祥 is the Korean Chinese expression for what in Chinese is called *Daesang* (C. *Daxiang*) 大祥.

[8] It is not clear whether this refers to Hohyang or Ho City. See note 8, page 238 and note 2 above.

[9] Yuchwi was his pen name and Yunchu his personal name.

[10] Another name for Yeoju in Gyonggi Province.

and haste, I came here. Solemnly, I make an offering of wine and fruit and through tears speak my parting words, saying,

> Alas!
> You set your heart upon the three moral excellences,[11]
> You were valiant, easygoing, and free.
> Wanting to study but unable to complete your inquiries,
> Late in life, you attained distinction.[12]
> In a gathering of old and distinguished seniors,
> The decline of this age stimulates reflection.
> Alas! The pain!
> Please accept my offering!

---

[11] *Samyeong* (C. *Sanying*) 三英 first appears in the *Book of Poetry*, Mao #80, meaning three ornaments. *The Commentary on the "Book of Poetry"* says that this refers to three virtues (*samdeok*; C. *sande* 三德), mentioned in the "Great Plan" (*Hongbeom*; C. *Hongfan* 洪範) chapter of the *Book of History*, which identifies these as correctness and straightforwardness (*jeongjik*; C. *zhengzhi* 正直), hard power (*ganggeuk*; C. *gangke* 剛克), and soft power (*yugeuk*; C. *rouke* 柔克).

[12] Literally the line refers to allowing the elderly to walk with a staff and to first enter a home before taking off their shoes.

Inscriptions (銘)

1. Inscription on [the Theme of] a Brush Holder

Made from scraps of Paulownia wood,
Stored away in my studio.
A gift from a good friend,
Whose integrity is not forgotten.

2. Inscription on [the Theme of] a Table

One's elbows never leave it,
One's work [upon it] calculated in years.
Like facing a stern teacher,
In reverent awe throughout the day.

3. Inscription on [the Theme of] an Inkstone Box

Squat in form,
The vault of secrets.
Please examine it carefully,
To ensure it is without corruption or flaw.

Korean Women Philosophers and the Ideal of a Female Sage. Philip J. Ivanhoe and Hwa Yeong Wang, Oxford University Press. © Oxford University Press 2023. DOI: 10.1093/oso/9780197508688.003.0021

4. Inscription on [the Theme of] a Fan

The moon[1] in one's hand,
The wind fills one's sleeves.

5. Inscription on [the Theme of] a Woodpecker

What bird is this,
In the corner of Tanwon?

---

[1] The shape of an open fan being like the shape of the moon.

Miscellaneous Writings (雜著)

1. A Record of Reflections on the Predilections [of My Ancestors]

1. In his youth, an eleventh-generation ancestor, the Honorable Uijeong 議政, once got drunk and fell asleep beneath a flowering tree.

2. A tenth-generation ancestor, the Honorable Minister [of Personnel],[1] built a studio at the foot of Flying Phoenix Mountain (Bibongsan 飛鳳山) and wrote a plaque naming it Eternally Hidden Hall (Yeongeundang 永隱堂). He also built a hall at the foot of Powder Dirt Mountain and wrote a plaque naming it Simple and Forthright Studio (*Baekjikjae* 白直齋).[2] Each day, he would discuss the classics and histories there with students or amuse himself by playing the zither and drinking wine.

3. An eighth-generation ancestor, the Honorable Forgetting Worldly [Concerns] Pavilion (Mangseheon 忘世軒) by nature enjoyed poetry and wine. He once said, "A poem does not have to be clever; if it expresses one's aspiration—that is enough. Wine should not make one disorderly;[3] once one feels harmonious and convivial—one should stop." <For the above, see *Old Stories of Generations of the Family* [*Gase gosa* 家世故事].>[4]

4. A sixth-generation ancestor, the Honorable Hidden by the Riverbank (Poeun 浦隱), was fond of reading books. He would stay up until midnight and only then go to bed; as soon as the cock crowed, he would rise. He was moderate in his drinking and eating and never ate

---

[1] This ancestor is also mentioned in the "Tomb Commemoration for My Ancestor the Honorable Yeongeun," page 223.

[2] The name is taken from a line from Ju Hui's commentary on the first chapter of the *Analects*. See *Ju Hui's Classified Sayings* 22.3b.

[3] Cf. *Analects* 10.8.

[4] It is not clear what work precisely this refers to; it seems to be something compiled by and for the family.

Korean Women Philosophers and the Ideal of a Female Sage. Philip J. Ivanhoe and Hwa Yeong Wang,
Oxford University Press. © Oxford University Press 2023. DOI: 10.1093/oso/9780197508688.003.0022

to excess. His wife, Madam Sim 沈, was endowed with great womanly virtue. She would regularly chant the *Analects* and *Elementary Learning* to cultivate and train herself. Every day, very late at night, she would pour wine into a small cup, add some honey or cinnamon powder,[5] bring it into [their room], and then discuss [with him] the meaning of the classics.

5. My great-great-grandfather-in-law, the Honorable Daeheon 大憲, by nature was fond of pine trees. His stool, cane, and utensils were all made of pine. He drank pine shoot wine[6] and took pine needle powder [as a supplement]. Everything about the pine's form, appearance, smell, and taste along with its integrity[7]—there was nothing he was not fond of. And so, people called him Old Man Pine (Song-ong 松翁). Though his death anniversary is in the winter months, <the ninth day of the tenth month>, [his son,] my great-grandfather-in-law would always have half-moon-shaped rice cake (*songpyeon* 松餅) [steamed on a bed of pine needles] and pine [shoot] wine, which he would offer in cups or plates made of pine. Even when great-grandfather-in-law was advanced in age, he did not abandon this practice. <I heard the above as part of my family's oral history.>

6. My great-grandfather, the Honorable Minister, enjoyed poetry and wine. He once said, "How can I dare to hope to reach [the level of] our ancestor, the Honorable Forgetting Worldly [Concerns] Pavilion's[8] virtuous conduct? Only in regard to these two things [poetry and wine] can I come close to him." Once, when he served as the magistrate of a city, there was a famine and a need to provide for the needy. He often would just take a sip of his congee and then offer it [to the needy]. By nature, he was extremely frugal. If his clothes or household utensils were the least bit extravagant, he would sternly remonstrate [with those who bought them]. Only in regard to the supply of wine and other liquor was it the case that even though more money was spent, he would offer no remonstrance. When friends arrived, he would offer

---

[5] This mixture seems to refer to Gyedangju 桂糖酒, which is spirit distilled from sorghum or maize with cinnamon powder and honey.

[6] That is wine made from the young shoots of pine trees, the shoots that are harvested right after the pine flowers have fallen out.

[7] Pine trees are symbols of integrity since they grow straight up and do not shed their needles even in the winter. Gongja expresses his admiration of them in *Analects* 9.28, "When the year grows cold, we then know the pine and cypress are last to shed their leaves."

[8] See item 3 above.

several rounds of wine. He would offer only some dried meat, fruit, and vegetables as accompaniment. Even if he drank a great deal, he would always be mild and self-controlled;[9] and would never get disorderly.[10] Once some relatives and friends addressed the Honorable, saying, "You have the character 克 as part of your pen name and although it comes from the word 'overcome' (*geuk*; C. *ke* 克) in the phrase 'overcome the self [and return to the rites]'[11] it also refers [in your case] to being mild (*on*; C. *wen* 溫) and self-controlled (*geuk*; C. *ke* 克)." The Honorable smiled and said, "Isn't being mild (*on*; C. *wen* 溫) and self-controlled (*geuk*; C. *ke* 克) the sprout of overcoming the self?"

7. Once, when my grandfather-in-law, the Honorable Deputy Director (*Jichu* 知樞),[12] was staying at an inn during *Jungchujeol* (仲秋節),[13] my late father-in-law asked what it was that he desired. The Honorable said, "I want nothing other than simply to make some wine and food out of newly husked rice and to have some well-marbled beef [to make raw] minced and roasted [meat]—that would be wonderful!" The Honorable's death anniversary is the ninth day of the eighth month. My father-in-law often said, "Although my sons and grandsons are poor, there are only four [things to prepare]. We should be able to manage through this time without too much difficulty. If we sincerely exert ourselves, we should be fine." <The above I heard from my husband.>

8. My grandmother-in-law, Chaste Woman Madam Yi, had a predilection for raw minced meat. Whenever it drew near to the time to offer a sacrifice, my mother-in-law always prepared it.

9. My father-in-law, the Honorable Self Abstention (*Jajae* 自齋), had a predilection for food firm in constitution. My late mother-in-law, [whose pen name was] Jiiljae 只一齋, only had a predilection for simple and plain food. She once said to me, "My late husband enjoyed eating dishes made with dried gourd, balloon-flower root, and bean sprouts. And so, on his birthday, <the twenty-fifth day of the sixth

---

[9] Cf. *Book of Poetry*, Mao #196.

[10] Cf. *Analects* 10.8.

[11] Cf. *Analects* 12.1.

[12] An abbreviation for Deputy Director of Office of Ministers-without-Portfolio (*Ji Jungchubu Sa* 知中樞府事).

[13] *Jungchujeol* (仲秋節) is another name for *Chuseok* 秋夕, which is roughly the Korean equivalent of Thanksgiving Day in the United States and is held on the fifteenth day of the eighth month.

month>, I always prepared these for him. My youngest son also shared this predilection, but his birthday was eight days after that of my late husband. And so I saved some leftover vegetables to feed him. After my husband passed away, on the anniversary of his death, I would also serve him these. I most enjoy polished white rice and dried yellow croaker, and my new daughter-in-law [you, Gang Jeongildang] shares the same taste. Father and son, mother and daughter-in-law have the same predilections. This is unusual!"

10. My late mother and father enjoyed dried fish and meat. Sometimes my late mother-in-law would tell us to send these [to them as gifts]. Recently, following my husband's instructions, we send [these as] small gifts in order to cultivate closer personal relationships. <The above are things I heard and saw.>

The ancients "served the living as they served the dead."[14] And so, on the day the ancients fasted [before making sacrifices to them] they reflected upon the ways their ancestors had lived, the ways they smiled and spoke, their aims and views, what delighted them, and what they had predilections for.[15] Nevertheless, when an impoverished family prepares to make a sacrifice, they must first plan ahead to make the arrangements. If they wait until the day of the sacrifice to think about such things, there will be many things they will not be able to do, which they will regret and sigh over. How much more is this true in the case of assisting with libations for the dead![16] This is a women's responsibility and is one that I have made particular effort to manage [correctly]. If I see one thing that can be used to make sacrificial offerings or anything that my ancestors had a predilection for or liked, with a sincere heart I store it away to have in reserve, so that I can use it when the time comes.[17] And so I made this record to guard against being negligent or forgetful and to lead the next generation to always pay attention to this so they will be able to requite and follow their ancestors[18] with complete sincerity.

---

[14] *Doctrine of the Mean*, chapter 19. This is the height of filial piety.

[15] "The Meaning of Sacrifices" chapter in the *Book of Rites*.

[16] "The Pattern of the Family" chapter in the *Book of Rites*.

[17] Cf. the similar line in the "Biography of My Mother-in-Law, Lady Gwon of Andong," in the "Short Biographies" section of this volume.

[18] Cf. "The Single Victim at the Border Sacrifices" (*Gyo teuk saeng*; C. *Jiao te sheng* 郊特牲) chapter in the *Book of Rites* and *Analects* 1.9.

2. Exposition on an Inkstone, Shown to the Child Yi Buleok 李弗億 <Childhood Name of Gyeonghyeon 敬鉉>

Inkstones have three virtues: the first is firmness, the second is stillness, and the third is weightiness. Because they are firm, they long endure. Because they are still, they are concentrated. Because they are weighty, they are un-yielding. This is why noble people value them. How much more should we value the overflowing kindness of the former king, which is preserved in the remaining kindly influences of our ancestors. I have heard that your grandfather, the Honorable Willow Garden (*Giwon* 杞園), when he served as a Counselor, was presented with an inkstone as a special reward by King Jeongjo,[19] who said to him, "You are the grandson of Upright Abstention (*Jikjae* 直齋), from a family of honest poverty. Make vigorous use of this [inkstone]! Make vigorous use of this [inkstone]!" The Honorable Willow Garden always treasured and made use of it. When he grew old, he handed it to you. Can you fail to revere it? It has been years since you began to study with the master. The master recently went on a trip to Hoecheon and will also tour the Gwanseo 關西 region.[20] [While away,] he entrusted your edu-cation to me.

You are young and your family is very poor. If you do not firmly establish a commitment [to learn and cultivate yourself], you will succumb and do violence to yourself or throw yourself away.[21] If that happens, not only will you disobey the intentions of your ancestors, but also you will turn your back on the command of the former king [to make vigorous use of it]. Always be fearful and apprehensive about this! Be diligent, both morning and eve-ning! You must take the three virtues [of inkstones] as the model for your axe handle.[22] Be resolutely constant [in your practice] as an inkstone is firm. Be exactly as disciplined as an inkstone is still. Be immovably self-restrained as an inkstone is weighty. Henceforth, be like this and advance without stop-ping. Then you will be close to working the field of the inkstone[23] and each day will harvest [good results].

---

[19] *Jeongmyo* 正廟 is a temple name (*Myoho* 廟號) of King Jeongjo.

[20] Now Pyeongan Province in North Korea.

[21] For making a commitment to learning, see *Analects* 2.4 For doing violence to oneself or throwing oneself away, see *Mencius* 4A10.

[22] This refers to a well-known line from the *Book of Poetry*, Mao #158 that is quoted in chapter 13 of the *Doctrine of the Mean*. In part, it goes, "In hewing an axe handle, in hewing an ax handle, the model is not far off. One grasps one ax handle to hew the other."

[23] The thought is that writing is like plowing a "field" with a brush.

Lost Works (拾遺)

Poems

This section contains one poem and twenty personal missives that were "lost" in the sense of not included in the original collection that served as the basis for The Extant Writings of Jeongildang.

1. Presented to My Clansman Dongbaek 東伯 <Seongdae 聲大>[1] <Written on Behalf of My Husband on the First Month of 1831>

> Through the meaning of words, the spirit of the elders is
> preserved,
> Widely proclaimed for upholding the king's commands in
> your governance of Dongdo 東道.[2]
>
> When you have nothing to do in the Provincial Office
> (*Dangheon* 棠軒), you chant poetry,
> The mountains, moon, streams, and clouds seem like a
> painting.

---

[1] The addressee of this poem may have been Yun Seongdae 尹聲大 (1776 CE–?).

[2] Now known as Gangwon Province. Yun Seongdae was appointed as Provincial Governor (*Gwanchalsa* 觀察使) of Gangwon Province in 1830. See the *Veritable Records of King Sunjo* (*Sunjo sillok* 純祖實錄) 31.25a [30(1830)/04/19#1].

Korean Women Philosophers and the Ideal of a Female Sage. Philip J. Ivanhoe and Hwa Yeong Wang, Oxford University Press. © Oxford University Press 2023. DOI: 10.1093/oso/9780197508688.003.0023

Lost Works (拾遺)

Personal Missives (尺牘)

This section contains twenty personal missives that were not included in the original collection that served as the basis for The Extant Writings of Jeongildang.

1

Your grandnephew's <Geunjin> daughter is now four years old. She is highly intelligent and has a very good mind. If she is patiently educated about her proper duties and guided to be sincere and correct, then it is likely that one day she will attain womanly virtue.

2

If one sleeps during the day, one's *Gi-Material* becomes muddled and one's commitment flags.[1] If one talks too much, this generates resentment and slander will arise. If one drinks wine to excess, this will damage one's nature and harm one's virtue. If one smokes a lot of tobacco, one will injure one's spirit and become obstreperous.[2] In all these cases, it is best to cease these behaviors.

3

Watering plants nourishes them, but watering rocks provides no nourishment to them. This is akin to teaching those who are most

---

[1] Cf. *Analects* 5.10.

[2] For Gang's views on smoking tobacco, see her poem, "Rhyme in Solemn Reply to My Grandfather-in-Law's Warning about Smoking Tobacco," poem #36 on page 185.

Korean Women Philosophers and the Ideal of a Female Sage. Philip J. Ivanhoe and Hwa Yeong Wang, Oxford University Press. © Oxford University Press 2023. DOI: 10.1093/oso/9780197508688.003.0024

stupid.[3] Nevertheless, if a sage were to meet them, who knows? He might draw upon a single sprout and transform them. I want [you] to not be distressed about whether [some students] are not nourished but instead be distressed over not being able to nourish them.

4

I have heard that Royal Transmitter (*Seungseon* 承宣) Yi's 李 <Jinyeon 晉淵> *Notes and Queries on the "Doctrine of the Mean" and the "Great Learning"* (*Yonghak chaui* 庸學箚疑) records his discussions and debates with Minister (*Sangseo* 尙書)[4] Hong 洪 <Seokju 奭周>, and that the ideas [discussed in these works] are comprehensive and meticulous. Moreover, [I have also heard that] works of his, such as the *Questions and Answers on Mountains and Fields* (*Sanya mundap* 山野問答) and *Erudite Summary of Investigations* (*Eombak jonghaek* 淹博綜覈)[5] will be of great benefit to the world. It would be wonderful if you could borrow these and show them to me.

5

The printing blocks for my ancestor, the Honorable Foolish Valley's[6] (Ugok 愚谷) book *Aphorisms for Children* (*Hunja gyeogeon* 訓子格言) have just been cut and are to be distributed to members of the family by [our clan's] elder brother[7] <Changhoe 昌會> (b. 1770 CE) in Crane Valley (Hakgok 鶴谷).[8] I think it would be auspicious to entrust one set of these to [our clan's] elder brother <Wonhoe 元會> (b. 1772 CE) in Three Islets (Samju 三洲)[9] to bring [to us]. What do you think?

---

[3] Cf. *Analects* 17.3.

[4] *Sangseo* is another name for the chief administrator of a ministry. Hong Seokju (1774–1842 CE) served as Minister of several ministries, such as Ministry of Military Affairs, Personnel, Rites, and Taxation.

[5] No extant versions or detailed descriptions of these two writings exist.

[6] Gang Deokhu 姜德後, the father of Gang Seokgyu 姜錫圭 (1628–1695 CE).

[7] Here, "brother" indicates a male with the same surname but who is not among the relatives who would wear mourning clothes.

[8] Probably a place in Chungcheong Province. There were several places with this name in the late Joseon period. It is not clear precisely which one is referred to here, though since the following place name is also in Chungcheong Province, this gives us some reason to believe this is the Crane Valley.

[9] A place in Chungju 忠州, Chungcheong Province.

6

You, my husband, once said that if someone shows you even a little kindness, it is appropriate to think of repaying it. Earlier you traveled with the Licentiate Choi 崔 <Hangi 漢綺> and were able to go to Pronouncement City (Seonseong 宣城),[10] the natal town that you miss so much. This certainly was not a small kindness; so why have you not thought about repaying him?

7

In our garden[11] is Smooth and Settled Terrace (Pyeongondae 平穩臺); Herald of the Crown Prince Yi 李 <Dojung 度中> named it. Its terrain is rugged and uneven and yet its name is Smooth and Settled. It would seem that, when the occasion permits, we should ask him why he choose this name. What do you think?

8

The ancients of the three dynasties did not abandon anyone who showed outstanding abilities. Now among the attendants in your school there is No Gwi 盧龜, who is meticulous and bright, Yi Am 李嚴, who is authentic and honest, and Yu Cheol 劉喆, who is filial and cautious. All of these can be taught. Please do not neglect them simply because they are lowly youths.

9

Our nephew on your side, Junyeong 濬永, treats his older male second cousin <Yunyeong 允永> as if he were no different from himself. Moreover, he is amiable to all his relatives. He is able to carry on the sincere conduct of our patriarch. Admirable indeed!

---

[10] An old name for Gyoha 交河 in Paju City, Gyeonggi Province.
[11] Tanwon, the name of their residence. See the "Commemoration of Tanwon," page 226.

10

The Honorable Dongju's 東洲—your uncle on your mother's side—calligraphy and painting were correct and upright. Uncle Munheon's 文軒 <Literary Licentiate Gwangui 光義, original personal name Gwangjae 光載> calligraphy was vigorous and agile. Now, in a chest, I only have a few examples of their work. Please divide these up and send them to your uncle in Rites Mountain (Yesan 禮山)[12] <Gwanhak 光學> and your nephew <Jahun 滋勳> and have them carefully maintain them and retain them as models.

11

It is a waste of time to pay attention to Sim Eunjin 沈恩津 <Munyeong 文永>; it makes one sigh. [But] the two worthies Im 任, <City Magistrate (*Moksa* 牧使) Ro 魯> (1755–1828 CE), and Yi 李, <County Magistrate (*Gunsu* 郡守) Hyeongsu 馨秀>, along with Licentiate Sim 沈, <Hongmo 弘模>, are coming to visit us one after the other. It would be great if you could report to me what books they teach and what problems they discuss.

12

You have instructed me concerning the teachings of elder Yi Yeongyang 李英陽 <Geonju 建胄>. In regard to a number of issues, [what he says] is right, and I sigh in admiration at the depth [of his learning] and [the breadth] of its application. However, in one section [he says that when] a husband offers sacrificial offerings to his wife, his son reads a prayer [board];[13] this does not agree in every detail with what former

---

[12] A place in Chungcheong Province.

[13] There was a long-standing debate among Confucians about how a wife should be mourned by her husband and son if her father-in-law was still alive. Korean neo-Confucian scholars continued this debate. In this passage, Gang reports that Yi Yeongyang suggests a son should read a prayer (board) during the ceremony, but this conflicts with the teaching of Sagye 沙溪 Gim Jangsaeng 金長生 (1548–1631 CE), the great master of Confucian ritual. And so she calls for further inquiry on the matter. For Sagye's saying, see Gim Gan's 金榦 (1646–1732 CE) *Collected Works of Hujae* (*Hujae jip* 厚齋集) 21.10a–b.

worthies have said. Why not ask the Erudite Hong 洪[14] <Jikpil 直弼> about this?

13

Minister Yun 允 <Gwangbo 光普> has shown me his verse on what is correct and incorrect.[15]

> When will right and wrong be settled?
> Who can settle right and wrong?
> If you say it's wrong to approve [of judgments of] right and wrong,
> Then right and wrong come down to the same thing.
> As soon as you say that there is right, there is wrong,
> And so, right and wrong always mutually oppose one another.
> Who can decide the case of right and wrong,
> And forever settle doubts about right and wrong?

This really is very moving. But in the poem, right and wrong are mixed together and it is not clear what they refer to. I fear that it is just a crude expression that cannot be harmonized. What do you think?

14

You showed me a verse:

> <I wish to study Gongja and Anja,
> You hope to become like [Tae] Im and [Tae] Sa.
> [We should] encourage one another in our aspirations and work,
> How much more so in the period of old age!>

I will chant this solemnly without end. Everyone knows that human nature is good. Everyone knows that the sages have fully developed the nature.

---

[14] Compare missive 20 below.
[15] Cf. chapter 2, "On the Equality of Things" in the *Jangja* and *Mencius* 2A6.

But if one does not know how human nature is good or how one can fully develop the nature, then what one knows surely is not real knowledge. Moreover, there are some who know and carry out this knowledge; nevertheless, they have not established a firm commitment. They start and stop and are not consistent. Day by day the years slip away and, in the end, they cannot avoid becoming reckless and impulsive. This is something I have feared. Now I continue to exert effort and urge [myself] on; can I dare not to keep this in mind?

15

Noble people do not talk about what is not in accord with the rites.[16] The Master (i.e., Gongja) did not talk about anomalies, feats of strength, disorders, or spiritual beings.[17] Recently, I have heard the young men in our school talking about profit and discussing anomalies. Unrestrained they pass the days—why have you not sternly remonstrated with them and make them read books with a proper posture and demeanor?

16

Among those you associate with, there are not many who, "from start to finish, have remained unchanged."[18] This is not something for which you can fault others; you must "turn and look for the reason within yourself."[19] If "one's words are not conscientious and trustworthy or one's conduct is not sincere and reverential"[20] or if one lacks substantial results in cultivating oneself, how can one find the leisure to examine others? The [classic] transmitted by Jeungja, says, "[One must] have it in oneself before one looks for it in others."[21] I dare to suggest that you exert yourself in this manner.

---

[16] *Analects* 12.1.
[17] *Analects* 7.21.
[18] See the biography of Yo Suk (C. Yao Shu) 姚璹 (632–705 CE) in the *History of the Former Dang Dynasty* (*Gu Dang Seo*; C *Jiu Tang Shu* 舊唐書) 89.26a.
[19] *Mencius* 2A7 and 4A4.
[20] *Analects* 15.6.
[21] See chapter 11 of the *Great Learning*.

17

Haeseok 海石 Gim Sanggong 金相公 once said to you, "I was in a pavilion in the mountain and throughout the day looked only toward Tanwon.[22] Seeing the smoke rising from [the chimneys of] the buildings there, I wondered whether you were cooking porridge. Seeing the students coming and going, I knew how many you were teaching." This surely was grounded in the mutual love between you two. Nevertheless, how do we know that it was not a warning to you to delight in the Way despite suffering from poverty[23] and to be diligent in your studies and instruct others?[24] Whenever I think of what he said, I feel the weight of profound responsibility.

18

The desire to have your late father's extant writings published and transmitted to posterity truly arose from a sense of filial piety, but to follow the example of his words and actions is even more important; one should exert oneself in this regard from morning till evening. Since the family is poor, to arrange for the publication of [his complete] written works, in the end, will be difficult. If, for the time being, you produced several handwritten sets [of his writings] and waited until our situation improved a bit [before producing printed editions], this would seem to in no way harm the expression of filial piety.

19

The publication of your father's manuscript is something you must want to complete and since Dongbaek 東伯, <Second Minister Seongdae 聲大>, and Seo Hajol 西河倅, <Grand Censor (*Daegan* 大諫)[25] Jehong 濟弘>, have kindly offered their assistance and family and old friends already have expended a great deal of effort as well, it is now fitting that you swiftly begin to bring this to a close. You cannot delay or procrastinate. If you end up

---

[22] The name of their residence. See the "Commemoration of Tanwon," page 226.
[23] Cf. *Analects* 1.15.
[24] Cf. *Analects* 7.2.
[25] An abbreviation of *Dae Sagan* 大司諫.

squandering people's support, [even if] you go quickly on your own, it will result in a bad outcome.

20

Herald of the Crown Prince Hong 洪 <Jikpil 直弼> says, "With a genuine Heart-Mind, carry out genuine affairs (*silsa* 實事)." Among your colleagues and friends, how many are there who are capable of this? If one has a genuine Heart-Mind and genuine affairs, then one will be consistent from start to finish[26] and inside and outside will accord with one another.[27] This is how you will know what kind of person they are.

---

[26] Compare missive 16 above.

[27] That is to say, one's feelings and one's appearance and actions will accord with one another.

Bibliography

Primary Sources

Analects (*Noneo*; C. *Lunyü* 論語).

Atlas of the Eastern Country (*Haedong Jido* 海東地圖).

Ban Go (C. Ban Gu) 班固. *Comprehensive Discussion of Virtue in the White Tiger Hall* (*Baekhotong deongnon*; C. *Baihutong delun* 白虎通德論).

Book of Changes (*Yeokgyeong*; C. *Yijing* 易經).

Book of Etiquette and Ritual (*Uirye*; C. *Yili* 儀禮).

Book of History (*Sangseo*; C. *Shangshu* 尚書).

Book of Ju (*Ju Seo*; C. *Zhou Shu* 周書).

Book of Poetry (*Sigyeong*; C. *Shijing* 詩經).

Book of Rites (*Yegi*; C. *Liji* 禮記).

Book of Rites of the Elder Dae (*Dae Dae Ryegi*; C. *Da Dai Liji* 大戴禮記).

Chinese Text Project. Ctext.org.

Chronicle of Jwa (*Jwa Jeon*; C. *Zou Zhuan* 左傳).

Collected Commentaries on the Helpful Collection for First Education (*Monggu jipju*; C. *Mengqiu jizhu* 蒙求集註).

Confucius's Family Teachings (*Gongja gaeo*; C. *Kongzi jiayü* 孔子家語).

The Daily Records of Royal Secretariat of the Joseon Dynasty (*Seungjeongwon ilgi* 承政院日記). http://sjw.history.go.kr/ and https://kyudb.snu.ac.kr.

Database of the Korean Classics (*Hanguk Gojeon Jonghap* 韓國古典綜合 DB). https://db.itkc.or.kr.

Desultory Records from the Studio of Corrigibility (*Neung gae jae mallok*; C. *Neng gai zhai manlu* 能改齋漫錄).

Doctrine of the Mean (*Jungyong*; C. *Zhongyong* 中庸).

Dong Jungseo (C. Dong Zhongshu) 董仲舒. *Luxuriant Dew of the Spring and Autumn Annals* (*Chunchu beollo*; C. *Chunqiu fanlu* 春秋繁露).

Eastern Lodge Records of the Han (*Donggwan Han gi*; C. *Dongguan Han ji* 東觀漢記).

Gang Jeongildang 姜静一堂. *The Extant Writings of Jeongildang* (*Jeongildang yugo* 静一堂遺稿).

Gim Gan 金榦. *Collected Works of Hujae* (*Hujae jip* 厚齋集).

Gim Sangak 金相岳. *Sancheon's Commentary on the "Book of Changes"* (*Sancheon yeokseol* 山天易說).

Gong Yeongdal (C. Kong Yingda) 孔穎達. *Commentaries and Explanations on the Mo Tradition of Poetry* (*Mosi juso*; C. *Maoshi zhushu* 毛詩注疏).

Gong Yeongdal. *Zuo's Commentary on the Spring and Autumn Annals with Commentary and Subcommentary* (*Chunchu jwajeon jeongui*; C. *Chunqiu zuochuan zhengyi* 春秋左傳正義).

Great Learning (*Daehak*; C. *Daxue* 大學).

Guyang Sun (C. Ouyang Xun) 歐陽詢. *Categorical Medley of Literary Texts* (*Yemun Yuchwi*; C. *Yiwen Leijü* 藝文類聚).

Gwon Sangha 權尚夏. *The Collected Works of Hansujae* (*Hansujae jip* 寒水齋集).

Han Bi (C. Han Fei) 韓非. *Hanbija* (C. *Hanfeizi*) 韓非子.

Han Yu (C. Han Yü) 韓愈. *Dongadang Commentaries on the "Collected Works of Changnyeo"* (*Dongadang changnyeo jip ju*; C. *Dongyatang Changli ji zhu* 東雅堂昌黎集註).

Han Yu. *Ju Hui's Verified Edition of the Collected Works of Han Yü* (*Jumungong gyo changnyeo seonsaeng jip*; C. *Zhuwengong xiao changli xiansheng ji* 朱文公校昌黎先生集).

History of the Former Dang Dynasty (*Gu Dang Seo*; C. *Jiu Tang Shu* 舊唐書).

History of the Former Han Dynasty (*Jeon Han Seo*; C. *Qian Han Shu* 前漢書).

History of the Han Dynasty (*Han Seo*; C. *Han Shu* 漢書).

History of the Later Han (*Hu Han Seo*; C. *Hou Han Shu* 後漢書).

History of the Song (*Song Sa*; C. *Song Shi* 宋史).

Ho Gwang (C. Hu Guang) 胡廣. *Great Compendium on Human Nature and Principle* (*Seongni daejeon seo*; C. *Xingli daquan shu* 性理大全書).

Hoenamja (C. *Huainanzi*) 淮南子.

Im Seongju 任聖周. *Collected Works of Nokmun* (*Nokmun jip* 鹿門集).

Im Yunjidang 任允摯堂. *The Extant Writings of Yunjidang* (*Yunjidang yugo* 允摯堂遺稿).

Imperial Readings of the Taepyeong Period (*Taepyeong eoram*; C. *Taiping yülan* 太平御覽).

A Jade Forest of Youthful Learning (*Yuhak gyeongnim*; C. *Youxue qionglin* 幼學瓊林).

Jang Jae (C. Zhang Zai) 張載. *Complete Works of Master Jang* (*Jangja jeonseo*; C. *Zhangzi quanshu* 張子全書).

Jangja (C. *Zhuangzi*) 莊子.

Jangseogak Archives DB. http://royal.aks.ac.kr.

Jeong Ho (C. Cheng Hao) 程顥 and Jeong I (C. Cheng Yi) 程頤. *Collected Works for the Two Jeongs* (*I Jeong munjip*; C. *Er Cheng wenji* 二程文集).

Jeong Ho and Jeong I. *Extant Works of the Two Jeongs* (*I Jeong yuseo*; C. *Er Cheng yishu* 二程遺書).

Ju Doni (C. Zhou Dunyi) 周敦頤. *Collected Works of Ju Doni* (*Juwongong jip*: C. *Zhouyuangong ji* 周元公集).

Ju Hui (C. Zhu Xi) 朱熹. *Classified Sayings of Master Ju* (*Juja eoryu*; C. *Zhuzi yülei* 朱子語類).

Ju Hui. *Collected Commentaries on the "Analects"* (*Noneo jipju*; C. *Lunyü jizhu* 論語集注).

Ju Hui. *Collected Commentaries on the "Elementary Learning"* (*Sohak jipju*; C. *Xiaoxue jizhu* 小學集註).

Ju Hui. *Collected Commentaries on the "Four Books" in Sections and Sentences* (*Saseo janggu jipju*; C. *Sishu zhangzhu jizhu* 四書章句集注).

Ju Hui. *Collected Commentaries on the "Mencius"* (*Maengja jipju*; C. *Mengzi jizhu* 孟子集注).

Ju Hui. *Collected Comments on the "Book of Poetry"* (*Sigyeong jipjeon*; C. *Shijing jizhuan* 詩經集傳).

Ju Hui. *Collected Works of Hoeam* (*Hoeam jip*; C. *Huian ji* 晦庵集).

Ju Hui. *"Doctrine of the Mean" in Sections and Sentences* (*Jungyong janggu*; C. *Zhongyong zhangjü* 中庸章句).

Ju Hui. *Extant Works of the Jeongs from Hanam* (*Hanam Jeongssi yuseo*; C. *Henan Cheng shi yi shu* 河南程氏遺書). Taibei Shi: Taiwan shang wu yin shu guan, 1978.

Ju Hui. *General Exposition of the "Book of Etiquette and Rites" and Its Commentaries* (*Uirye gyeongjeon tonghae*; C. *Yili jingzhuan tongjie* 儀禮經傳通解).

Ju Hui. *"Great Learning" in Sections and Sentences* (*Daehak janggu*; C. *Daxue zhangjü* 大學章句).

Ju Hui. *Outline and Detailed Account of the "Comprehensive Mirror on Government"* (*Jachi tonggam gangmok*; C. *Zizhi tongjian gangmu* 資治通鑑綱目).

Ju Hui. *Questions and Answers on the "Four Books"* (*Saseo hongmun*; C. *Sishu huowen* 四書或問).

Ju Hui and Yeo Jogyeom (C. Lü Zuqian) 呂祖謙. *Reflections on Things at Hand* (*Geunsarok*; C. *Jinsilu* 近思錄).

A Later Collection on the True Treasure Great Compendium of Detailed Explanations of Ancient Writings (*Sangseol Gomun Jinbo Daejeon Hujip*; C. *Xiangshuo Guwen Zhenbao Daquan Houji* 詳說古文眞寶大全後集). Version held at Korean National Library (Nl.go.kr).

Library of the Four Treasuries (*Sago Jeonseo*; C. *Siku quanshu* 四庫全書) Online. Wenyange edition. Hong Kong: Chinese University of Hong Kong & Digital Heritage Publishing.

Mencius (*Maengja*; C. *Mengzi* 孟子).

Most Supreme Lord's Inner Alchemy Classic (*Taesang Nogun naedan gyeong*; C. *Taishang Laojun neidan jing* 太上老君內丹經).

Noja (C. Laozi) 老子. *Dodeokgyeong* (C. *Daodejing*) 道德經.

O Gyeongjae (C. Wu Jingzi) 吳敬梓. *Unofficial History of the Scholars* (*Yurim oesa*; C. *Rulin waishi* 儒林外史).

Records of Surveying the Past (*Gyegorok*; C. *Jiguqi* 稽古錄).

Records of the Historian (*Sagi*; C. *Shiji* 史記).

Sama Gwang (C. Sima Guang) 司馬光. *Comprehensive Mirror on Government* (*Jachi tonggam*; C. *Zizhi tongjian* 資治通鑑).

Sama Gwang. *Precepts for Family Life* (*Ga Beom*; C. *Jia Fan* 家範).

Song Chigyu 宋穉圭. *Collected Works of Gangjae* (*Gangjae jip* 剛齋集).

Song Hwangi 宋煥箕. *Collected Works of Seongdam* (*Seongdam jip* 性潭集).

Song Siyeol 宋時烈. *Great Compendium of Master Song* (*Songja daejeon* 宋子大全).

Song Siyeol. *Notes and Queries on the Complete Compendium of Master Ju's Works* (*Juja Daejeon chaui* 朱子大全箚疑).

Songs of Cho (*Cho Sa*; C. *Chu Ci* 楚辭).

Spring and Autumn Annals (*Chun Chu*; C. *Chun Qiu* 春秋).

Veritable Records of King Cheoljong (*Cheoljong sillok* 哲宗實錄). In *Veritable Records of the Joseon Dynasty*.

Veritable Records of King Gojong (*Gojong sillok* 高宗實錄). In *Veritable Records of the Joseon Dynasty*.

Veritable Records of King Injo (*Injo sillok* 仁祖實錄). In *Veritable Records of the Joseon Dynasty*.

Veritable Records of the Joseon Dynasty (*Joseon Wangjo Sillok* 朝鮮王朝實錄). http://sillok.history.go.kr/main/main.do.

Veritable Records of King Hyeonjong (*Hyeonjong sillok* 顯宗實錄). In *Veritable Records of the Joseon Dynasty*.

Veritable Records of King Jeongjo (*Jeongjo sillok* 正祖實錄). In *Veritable Records of the Joseon Dynasty*.

Veritable Records of King Sukjong (*Sukjong sillok* 肅宗實錄). In *Veritable Records of the Joseon Dynasty*.

Veritable Records of King Sunjo (*Sunjo sillok* 純祖實錄). In *Veritable Records of the Joseon Dynasty*.

Yang Ung (C. Yang Xiong) 楊雄. 1965. *Exemplary Sayings* 法言. Taipei 臺北: Guangwen shuju 廣文書局.

Yeo Bulwi (C. Lü Buwei) 呂不韋. *Spring and Autumn Annals of Mr. Yeo* (*Yeo ssi Chun Chu*; C. *Lü shi Chun Qiu* 呂氏春秋).

Yeolja (C. *Liezi*) 列子.

Yi Bingheogak 李憑虛閣. *An Encyclopedia for the Inner Quarters* (*Gyuhap chongseo* 閨閣叢書).

Yi Hwang 李滉. *Collected Works of Toegye* (*Toegye jip* 退溪集).

Yi I 李珥. "Treatise on Life, Death, Ghosts, and Spirits" (*Sasaeng gwisin chaek* 死生鬼神策). In the *Lost Works of the "Complete Works of Master Yulgok"* (*Yulgok seonsaeng jeonseo seubyu* 栗谷先生全書拾遺), vol. 4.

Yi Jae 李縡. *Collected Works of Doam* (*Doam jip* 陶菴集).

Yu Hyang (C. Liu Xiang) 劉向. *The Biographies of Exemplary Women* (*Yeollyeojeon*; C. *Lienüzhuan* 列女傳).

Yu Hyang. *Garden of Persuasions* (*Seol Won*; C. *Shuo Yuan* 說苑).

Secondary Sources

Bak Hyeonsuk 박현숙. 2002. "Im Yunjidang gwa Gang Jeongildang ui munhak ui sasangjeok giban" 임윤지당과 강정일당 문학의 사상적 기반 [The Intellectual Basis of Im Yunjidang's and Gang Jeongildang's Writings]. *Han-Jung inmunhak yeon-gu* 한중인문학연구 9: 25–54.

Beasley, W. G., and Edwin G. Pulleyblank. 1961. *Historians of China and Japan*. London: Oxford University Press.

Choi, Suk Gabriel. 2019. "The Horak Debate concerning Human Nature and the Nature of All Other Beings." In *Dao Companion to Korean Confucian Philosophy*, edited by Young-Chan Ro, 233–251. Dordrecht: Springer.

Chung, Edward Y. J. 1995. *The Korean Neo-Confucianism of Yi T'oegye and Yi Yulgok: A Reappraisal of the "Four-Seven Thesis" and Its Practical Implications for Self-Cultivation*. Albany: State University of New York Press.

Deuchler, Martina. 1992. *The Confucian Transformation of Korea: A Study of Society and Ideology*. Cambridge, MA: Council on East Asian Studies, Harvard University; distributed by Harvard University Press.

Dumoulin, Heinrich. 2005. *Zen Buddhism: A History*. Vol. 1, *India and China*. Bloomington, IN: World Wisdom.

Ebrey, Patricia Buckley. 1991a. *Chu Hsi's Family Rituals: A Twelfth-Century Chinese Manual for the Performance of Cappings, Weddings, Funerals, and Ancestral Rites*. Princeton, NJ: Princeton University Press.

Ebrey, Patricia Buckley. 1991b. *Confucianism and Family Rituals in Imperial China: A Social History of Writing about Rites*. Princeton, NJ: Princeton University Press.

Gang Jeoingildang 姜静一堂. 2002. (*Gugyeok*) *Jeongildang yugo* 국역 정일당유고 [(Korean Translation of) The Extant Writings of Jeongildang]. Seongnam: Seongnam Munhwawon.

Gardner, Catherine Villanueva. 2018. *Women Philosophers: Genre and the Boundaries of Philosophy*. New York: Routledge.

Gilligan, Carol. 2016. *In a Different Voice*. Cambridge, MA: Harvard University Press.

Gim Gyeongmi 김경미. 2019. *Im Yunjidang pyeongjeon: gyubang ui salm eul beoseo deonjin Joseon choego ui yeoseong seongnihakja* 임윤지당 평전: 규방의 삶을 벗어 던진 조선 최고의 여성 성리학자 [Critical Biography of Im Yunjidang: The Best Female Philosopher of Joseon, Who Freed Herself from Life in Women's Quarters]. Seoul: Hankyoreh Press.

Gim Hyeon 김현. 2004. "Seongnihakjeok gachigwan ui hwaksan gwa yeoseong" 성리학적 가치관의 확산과 여성 [Extension of Neo-Confucian Values and Women in the Later Joseon Dynasty]. *Minjok munhwa yeon-gu* 民族文化研究 41: 455–488.

Haboush, JaHyun Kim, ed. 2009. *Epistolary Korea: Letters in the Communicative Space of the Chosŏn, 1392–1910*. New York: Columbia University Press.

Hochschild, Arlie, and Anne Machung. 2012. *The Second Shift*. New York: Penguin Books.

Hutton, Eric L., trans. 2016. *Xunzi: The Complete Text*. Princeton, NJ: Princeton University Press.

Ivanhoe, Philip J. 2015. "The Historical Significance and Contemporary Relevance of the Four-Seven Debate." *Philosophy East and West* 65, no. 2: 401–429.

Kalton, Michael C., Oaksook Chun Kim, et al. 1994. *The Four-Seven Debate*. Albany: State University of New York Press.

Kim, Hyoungchan. 2016. "The Li-Qi 理氣 Structure of the Four Beginnings and the Seven Emotions and the Aim of the Four-Seven Debate." In *Traditional Korean Philosophy: Problems and Debates*, edited by Youngsun Back and Philip J. Ivanhoe, 49–68. New York: Rowman & Littlefield.

Kim, Richard T. 2016. "Human Nature and Animal Nature: The Horak Debate and Its Philosophical Significance." In *Traditional Korean Philosophy: Problems and Debates*, edited by Youngsun Back and Philip J. Ivanhoe, 85–110. New York: Rowman & Littlefield.

Kim, Sungmoon. 2014. "From Wife to Moral Teacher: Kang Chŏngildang on Neo-Confucian Self-Cultivation." *Asian Philosophy* 24, no. 1: 28–47.

Kim, Sungmoon. 2017. "The Way to Become a Female Sage: Im Yunjidang's Confucian Feminism." In *Traditional Korean Philosophy: Problems and Debates*, edited by Youngsun Back and Philip J. Ivanhoe, 177–195. New York: Rowman & Littlefield.

Kim, Youngmin. 2005. "Hyeongyong mosun eul neomeoseo" 형용모순을 넘어서 [Beyond Oxymoron]. *Cheolhak* 83: 7–33.

Kim, Youngmin. 2011. "Neo-Confucianism as Free-Floating Resource: Im Yunjidang and Kang Chŏngildang as Two Female Neo-Confucian Philosophers in Late Chosŏn." In *Women and Confucianism in Chosŏn Korea*, edited by Youngmin Kim and Michael J. Pettid, 71–88. Albany: State University of New York Press.

Kinney, Anne Behnke, trans. 2014. *Exemplary Women of Early China: The Lienü zhuan of Liu Xiang*. New York: Columbia University Press.

Knechtges, David R., and Taiping Chang. 2010. *Ancient and Early Medieval Chinese Literature*. Vol. 1. Leiden: Brill.

Knechtges, David R., and Tong Xiao. 2014. *Wen Xuan or Selections of Refined Literature*. Vol. 1, *Rhapsodies on Metropolises and Capitals*. Princeton, NJ: Princeton University Press.

Ko, Dorothy, JaHyun Kim Haboush, and Joan R. Piggott, eds. 2003. *Women and Confucian Cultures in Premodern China, Korea, and Japan*. Berkeley: University of California Press.

Kohlberg, Lawrence. 1973. "The Claim to Moral Adequacy of a Highest Stage of Moral Judgment." *Journal of Philosophy* 70, no. 18: 630–646.

Lee, Pauline C. 2012. *Li Zhi, Confucianism, and the Virtue of Desire*. Albany: State University of New York Press.

Li, Chenyang, ed. 2000. *The Sage and the Second Sex: Confucianism, Ethics, and Gender*. Chicago: Open Court.

Makra, Mary Lelia. 1961. *The Hsiao Ching*. New York: St. John's University Press.

Noddings, Nel. 2003. *Caring*. Berkeley: University of California Press.

Pang-White, Ann A. 2018. *The Confucian Four Books for Women*. New York: Oxford University Press.

Pettid, Michael J., and Kil Cha. 2021. *The Encyclopedia of Daily Life: A Woman's Guide to Living in Late-Chosŏn Korea*. Hawaii: University of Hawaii Press.

Sartre, Jean-Paul. 1991. "Existentialism Is a Humanism." In *Existentialism from Dostoevsky to Sartre*, edited by Walter Kaufmann, 345–368. New York: Penguin Books.

Sih, Paul K. T., ed. 1961. *The Hsiao Ching*. New York: St. John's University Press.

Tillman, Hoyt Cleveland. 2004. "Zhu Xi's Prayers to the Spirit of Confucius and Claim to the Transmission of the Way." *Philosophy East and West* 54, no. 4: 489–513.

Tiwald, Justin, and Bryan W. Van Norden, eds. 2014. *Readings in Later Chinese Philosophy*. Indianapolis, IN: Hackett.

Yi Hyesun 이혜순. 2004. "Yeoseong damnon euroseoui Im Yunjidang ui igi simseong non- Joseon jo hugi yeoseong jiseongsa seosul eul wihan siron" 여성담론으로서의 임윤지당의 이기심성론-조선조 후기 여성 지성사 서술을 위한 시론 [Im Yunjidang's Philosophy Considered as a Discourse on Woman: Introduction to Women's Intellectual History in the Late Joseon]. *Gojeon munhak yeon-gu* 고전문학연구26: 321–353.

Yi Hyesun. 2007. *Joseonjo hugi yeoseong jiseongsa* 조선조 후기 여성 지성사 [Intellectual History of Women in the Late Joseon]. Seoul: Ewha Womans University Press.

Yi Hyesun and Hayeong Jeong 정하영. 2003. *Hanguk gojeon yeoseong munhak ui segye— sanmun pyeon* 한국 고전 여성 문학의 세계—산문편 [Korean Classical Women's Literature—Prose]. Seoul: Ewha Womans University Press.

Yi Yeongchun 이영춘. 2014. *Im Yunjidang ui saengae wa hangmun* 임윤지당의 생애와 학문 [The Life and Thought of Im Yunjidang]. Wonju-si: Wonju-si.

Yi Yeongchun. 1998. *Im Yunjidang: Gugyeok Yunjidang yugo* 임윤지당: 국역 윤지당유고 [The Extant Writings of Im Yunjidang–(Korean) translation Extant Writings of Yunjidang]. Seoul: Hyean.

Index